RETAIL MERCHANDISING

RETAIL MERCHANDISING PRINCIPLES AND APPLICATIONS

RALPH D. SHIPP, JR.
NASSAU COMMUNITY COLLEGE

HOUGHTON MIFFLIN COMPANY   BOSTON

ATLANTA   DALLAS   GENEVA, ILLINOIS   HOPEWELL, NEW JERSEY   PALO ALTO   LONDON

Copyright © 1976 by Houghton Mifflin Company. All rights reserved. No part of this work may be reproduced or transmitted in any form or by any means, electronic or mechanical, including photocopying and recording, or by any information storage or retrieval system, without permission in writing from the publisher.

Cover: Mimi Forsyth/Monkmeyer Press Photo Service.

Printed in the U.S.A.

Library of Congress Catalog Card Number: 75-31040

ISBN: 0-395-20271-X

CONTENTS

Preface / ix

1 What Is Merchandising? / 1
  Merchandising Defined / 2
  The Five Rights / 2
  The Merchandising Division / 4
  Branch Store Organization / 6
  The Merchandise Manager / 6
  The Buyer / 11
  Executive Compensation / 14
  Why Study Merchandising? / 18
  Your Future in Merchandising / 18

2 How to Find Profit / 23
  Nature of Profit / 24
  The Profit Mix / 25
  Manipulating Profit Variables / 27
  Planning Expenses / 30

3 How to Find Markup / 40
  The Nature of Markup / 41
  Markup Based on Retail / 42
  Markup Based on Cost / 46
  Buyer's Wheels / 48
  Cumulative Markup / 49
  Keystone Markup / 51

4 How to Average Markup / 56
  Reasons for Averaging / 57
  Average Markup on Total Purchases / 59
  Average Markup with One Cost and Two Retails / 62
  Average Markup with One Cost and Three or More Retails / 65
  Average Markup with Two Costs and One Retail / 67
  Average Markup with Three or More Costs and One Retail / 68

5 How to Plan Markup / 74
Initial Markup / 75
Maintained Markup / 77
Gross Margin / 81
Markup Relations Expressed in Percentages / 84

6 How to Plan Markdowns / 91
Markdown Defined / 92
Causes of Markdowns / 92
Markdown Policies / 94
The Markdown Request / 96
Control of Markdowns / 98
Markdowns Based on Original Retail / 102
Markdowns Based on Sales / 103

7 How to Use the Retail Method of Inventory / 108
Reasons for Taking Inventory / 109
Methods of Inventory Valuation / 110
FIFO and LIFO Methods of Inventory Valuation / 115
Book versus Physical Inventory / 116
The Profit-and-Loss Statement / 122

8 How to Price for Profit / 129
What Price to Charge? / 130
Pricing Techniques / 133
Analysis of Price Lines / 138

9 How to Calculate Stock Turn / 147
The Meaning of Stock Turn / 148
Calculating Stock Turn / 148
Advantages and Disadvantages of Rapid Stock Turn / 154
Capital Turn / 157
Stock-Sales Ratio / 159
Return on Merchandise Investment / 160

10 How to Plan Sales / 165
Importance of Sales Forecasting / 166
Factors to Consider / 169
Sales Planning for Branch Stores / 176
Sales Planning When Prices Are Stable / 176
Sales Planning With Fluctuating Prices / 182

11 How to Plan Stocks / 189
   Importance of Stock Planning / 190
   Factors to Consider / 192
   Stock Planning for Branch Stores / 193
   Stock-Planning Methods / 195
   Shortcomings of the Stock-Planning Methods / 202

12 How to Plan Purchases and Open-to-Buy / 208
   Planning Purchases / 209
   Open-to-Buy / 211
   The Model Stock Plan / 219
   How to Increase Open-to-Buy / 220

13 How to Plan and Control Fashion Merchandise / 230
   Understanding Fashion / 231
   Where to Buy Fashion Merchandise / 235
   The Nature of Fashion Buying / 241
   Elements of Fashion Merchandise / 246
   Control of Fashion Merchandise / 248
   Model Stocks / 251
   The Buying Plan / 252

14 How to Negotiate with the Vendor / 258
   The Need to Negotiate / 259
   Elements of Negotiation / 259
   The Buyer's Order / 271

15 Merchandising and the Computer / 279
   What the Computer Can Do / 280
   The Electronic Computer / 281
   Data Handling / 283
   Computerized Retail System / 288
   Tomorrow's Computer Technology / 295

Glossary of Merchandising Terms / 301

Appendix I Aliquot Parts / 305

Appendix II Markup Conversion Table / 306

Appendix III Mathematical Formulas for Merchandisers / 307

Bibliography / 309

Index / 311

PREFACE

This book is designed to provide the student of retail merchandising with an up-to-date, concise, and practical introduction to the field. Those functions usually handled by the controller's division in a store are given minimal treatment. It is expected that students planning careers in buying will benefit most from this book. The practices described have been written from the buyer's point of view and are similar to those actually encountered on the job.

Much merchandising theory is controversial, but nevertheless students must understand why they are applying a mathematical computation to a particular situation. Limited discussions of theory are included where they are needed. However, the accent is placed upon exercises that reflect real-life situations. This encourages the student to use a common-sense approach to a problem instead of performing a mechanical operation based upon rote learning.

The mathematics involved in this study of merchandising have been simplified as much as possible to enable the student to obtain a better grasp of the principles and not get bogged down in laborious computations. The illustrations and exercises often result in even answers thus reducing unneeded "busy work." In today's merchandising world, buyers and merchandise managers have access to business machines, buyer's wheels, calculators, and other devices to speed calculations. Furthermore, it is assumed that students of retail merchandising have mastered basic arithmetic skills.

With the advent of data processing, stores have been letting the computer do work that formerly took many people to accomplish. Aspiring merchandisers should be familiar with those processes that have become computerized. The roles of the buyer and the merchandise manager have changed greatly in recent years. This book will show how these machines have rendered some merchandising functions obsolete.

The importance of making a profit has been given emphasis throughout the book. Without a profit, no business institution can long survive. Retailers must be familiar enough with basic merchandising principles to insure that an eventual profit will be realized even though this is not always possible during the first or second year of operation. It must be remembered that buyers are judged largely on the profit they earn for their employers. Success in retailing is simply not possible without a margin of profit.

In creating practical exercises throughout the book, an attempt has been made to use today's lexicon to increase interest and make the material seem more alive. Review questions, problems and cases at the end of each chapter can be used to test knowledge and stimulate thinking. An Instructor's Manual is also provided. This manual contains the answers for all questions, problems, and cases. Also included in the manual are examination questions and problems.

BEHAVIORAL OBJECTIVES

Retail Merchandising is an action-oriented book. It provides the background and knowledge necessary to buy merchandise profitably. With mastery of its contents, the student will be able to:
1. Understand the role of the buyer in relation to other store personnel.
2. Plan and figure markup and control expenses so a profit can be made.
3. Use the retail method of inventory.
4. Develop a sales and merchandise plan so enough stock will be purchased to satisfy customer demand.
5. Compute open-to-buy.
6. Perceive the differences in buying fashion and staple merchandise.
7. Appreciate the importance of vendor relations.
8. Grasp the increasing importance of the computer in merchandising activities.

ACKNOWLEDGMENTS

This book would not have been possible without the generous help and encouragement of many academic colleagues and retail executives. I am greatly indebted to my consultant Herbert Brown, merchandising representative at Associated Merchandising Corporation, for his advice and cheerful cooperation. I would also like to express special thanks to Professor Lawrence Orilia of Nassau Community College for his assistance in preparing Chapter 15 and to Professor Carol Stewart of Nassau Community College who helped develop the Instructor's Manual and checked the accuracy of the problems. Other colleagues at Nassau Community College to whom I am deeply grateful are my chairman, Professor Jay Diamond, Professor Fred Terry, and Helen Tuzinkiewicz, who typed the manuscript.

    I am especially grateful to Dr. Mary Ellen Oliverio, formerly of Teachers College, Columbia University, who was largely responsible for my entry into the teaching field and who gave me support and encouragement for this project.

    I would also like to thank the following colleagues who read the manuscript at different stages in its development and provided many helpful comments and suggestions: Professor Clifford L. Butt, Suffolk County Community College, Selden, New York; Professor Robert H. Thomas, University of Maine at Machias; Professor John W. Lloyd, Monroe Community College, Rochester, New York; John Bruning, Owens Technical College,

Perrysburg, Ohio; David Kelmar, Santa Monica College; Thomas Hopkins, Spokane Falls Community College; and Elizabeth Helseth, City College of San Francisco.

Retail executives who made significant contributions are too numerous to list, but I would like to acknowledge in particular, John Shepardson, Lord and Taylor; Elsie Harnett, Alexanders; Richard Liebelt, Shillitos; and Lynn Eller, formerly of Burlington Hosiery Company.

Ralph D. Shipp, Jr.

RETAIL MERCHANDISING

1

WHAT IS MERCHANDISING?

KEY POINTS

1. Merchandising deals with the buying and selling of merchandise at a profit. More specifically, it involves internal planning to insure that the right merchandise is available at the right place, at the right time, in the right quantity, and at the right price.

2. The person in charge of the merchandising division is the general merchandise manager, whose job it is to interpret and execute the merchandising policies of the store.

3. The buyer is a key merchandising executive, because it is his or her responsibility to see that the store is supplied with merchandise.

4. Although merchandising executives are usually paid a straight salary, they are often given added compensation based on overall performance.

5. Merchandising offers particularly attractive opportunities to young people of either sex who are talented and possess a strong will to succeed.

MERCHANDISING DEFINED

Merchandising has been defined in many different ways. It is generally thought of as all those activities involved in the buying and selling of merchandise. But more specifically, it is the *internal planning* that takes place within a retail organization in order to present merchandise to the customer so that a profit will be realized. Merchandising is only one part of the retailing process. It does not include such activities as the actual buying of merchandise, the promotion and selling of the merchandise, and the management of the store itself. Instead, it involves making sure there are adequate amounts of merchandise on hand to be sold at prices that customers are willing to pay to insure a profitable operation. However, when buyers go to the market, they must certainly employ a variety of merchandising techniques, many of which will be discussed in this text. Indeed, merchandising skills affect almost all facets of store operation.

THE FIVE RIGHTS

Perhaps the role of the merchandiser will become clearer if the famous "five rights" are explained. To be successful, a merchandiser should have the (1) *right merchandise* at the (2) *right place* at the (3) *right time* in the (4) *right quantity* and at the (5) *right price*.

Right Merchandise

Retailers must fill their shelves with the merchandise that customers want. Many items are basic necessities and enjoy a continuing demand. Boys' denim dungarees are an example of merchandise that can be called a staple or "never out" item because they should always be in stock in a full range of sizes. Greater skill is required for stocking fad or fashion merchandise. A fad, like the famous hula hoop, is an item that experiences quick popularity for a short period of time. A fashion has more lasting power and is accepted by a larger number of customers. But the merchandising of both these kinds of items involves considerable risk. Some seasons ago many retailers were left with huge inventories of unsold midi-length coats and dresses. In spite of the dictates of French designers, American women refused to wear the "longuette," as the length was referred to by the prestigious trade paper *Women's Wear Daily*. The merchandise was simply not wanted.

Right Place

The location of merchandise within the store is of prime importance. Main-floor locations are usually reserved for those departments stocking items high in demand with quick turnovers (rates at which stocks are depleted and replenished). Upper floors are often assigned merchandise with higher unit values and slower turnovers, for example furniture. Customers do not mind seeking out the furniture department where they are free to browse in a less hectic atmosphere. It is considered wise to place men's departments near a separate entrance on the street floor, since many men do not consider themselves "shoppers" and prefer to do their buying quickly and easily. One famous New York store has express elevators to speed customers to upper floors reserved entirely for men's wear. Departments usually found on the street floor where customer traffic is the heaviest include women's accessories, stationery, and notions.

Right Time

Much merchandise is seasonal in nature and must be on hand when it is most needed. A merchandiser would be foolish indeed to try to sell Valentine's Day candy during any time other than early February. Similarly, it would be poor merchandising policy to stock ski sweaters and other items of winter apparel during the spring and early summer months. Many merchandisers have added a "fifth season" to the traditional spring, summer, fall, and winter seasons. This season, which usually begins after Christmas and runs well into January, has become the time to sell cruisewear to those Americans affluent enough to escape to the sunny climates. It is also the ideal time to promote white sales and clearance sales of winter apparel.

Right Quantity

Providing the amount of inventory necessary to meet customer demand can present a formidable challenge to the merchandiser. If not enough merchandise is on hand to satisfy customer wants, the store's reputation suffers and many sales may be lost. Conversely, too much merchandise will result in costly markdowns. A profitable balance between volume of sales and amount of inventory is the desired goal. Sometimes this balance seems next to impossible to achieve, especially when special sales items are featured. Specially priced merchandise often sells out in a matter of hours, with customer dissatisfaction an unwelcome side effect. With a really fast seller, stores sometimes reserve the right to limit quantities purchased by individual customers.

Right Price

Setting the right retail price presents yet another challenge. The merchandiser must arrive at a price high enough to give the store some hope of profit and yet low enough to meet competition. Many stores advertise "loss leaders," which are items sold at near or below cost to stimulate customer traffic.

THE MERCHANDISING DIVISION

There are wide variations in store organization today. Many stores have been patterned after the four-functional plan devised by Paul M. Mazur in 1927. Under this plan, the merchandising division is one of four main divisions in the store, along with sales promotion, control, and management. At the head of the merchandising division is the general merchan-

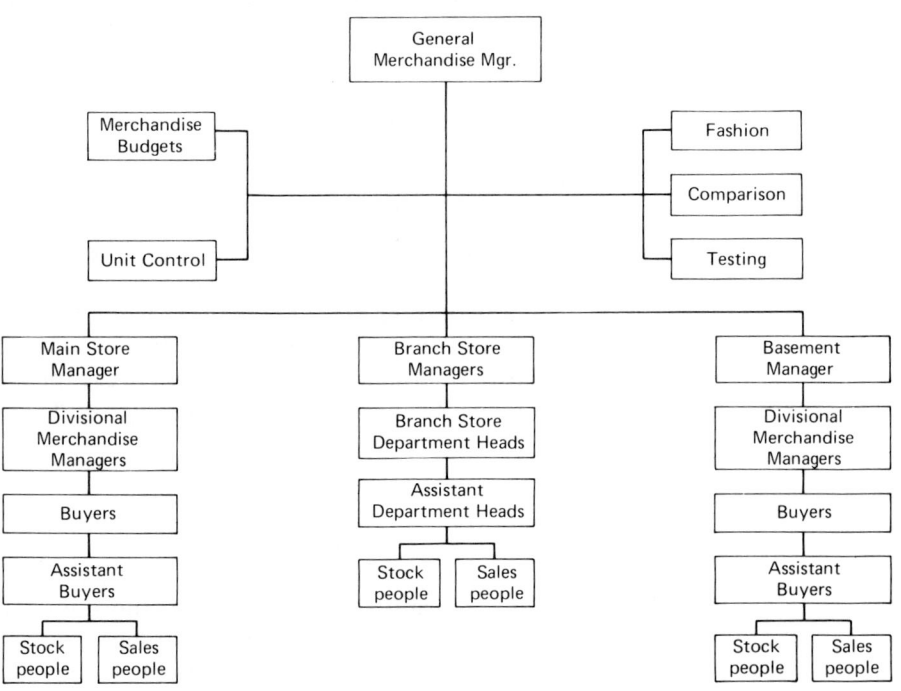

Figure 1.1
ORGANIZATION OF THE MERCHANDISING DIVISION

dise manager whose job is to interpret and execute the merchandising policies of the store. Often a general merchandise manager is also instrumental in setting merchandising policies after consultation with other members of top management. The general merchandise manager is responsible for merchandising activities not only in the parent store but in the branch stores and buying offices as well. The organization of a typical merchandising division is shown in Figure 1.1.

The general merchandise manager is assisted by divisional merchandise managers. Although the number of divisions may vary from store to store, many large retailers have set up seven divisions of merchandise as follows: main floor, ladies' apparel, ladies' accessories, men's and boys' wear, home furnishings, children's wear, and the basement operation. Each division has its own merchandising manager who directs his or her staff of buyers. Figure 1.2 gives a closer look at the way a merchandising division might be organized.

Note that both line and staff authority are involved in an organization such as this. There is a direct chain of responsibility (sometimes referred to as the *chain of command*) leading from the general merchandise manager all the way down to the salespeople. At each level in the chain orders are received from those directly above. This is the *line organization* and can operate smoothly only if the chain of command is not broken. Ignoring the chain of command will lead to disharmony and ruffled feelings.

Those employees who assist and give advice to line personnel are called the *staff* members of the organization. Typical staff bureaus are pictured in Figure 1.1. The buyer's clerical and stock help shown in Figure 1.2 are also staff people because their function is to assist the buyer, his assistant, and the head of stock. Staff personnel tend to be specialists. For example, the comparison shoppers shown in Figure 1.1 are experts trained to visit competing stores to find out what kinds of merchandise are being offered, how they are priced and displayed, and other useful information about the store's competitors. The information they obtain is passed along to the merchandise managers and the buyers, but comparison shoppers are not in a position to command or direct merchandising personnel. Of course, there

Figure 1.2
LINE AND STAFF AUTHORITY IN A MERCHANDISING DIVISION

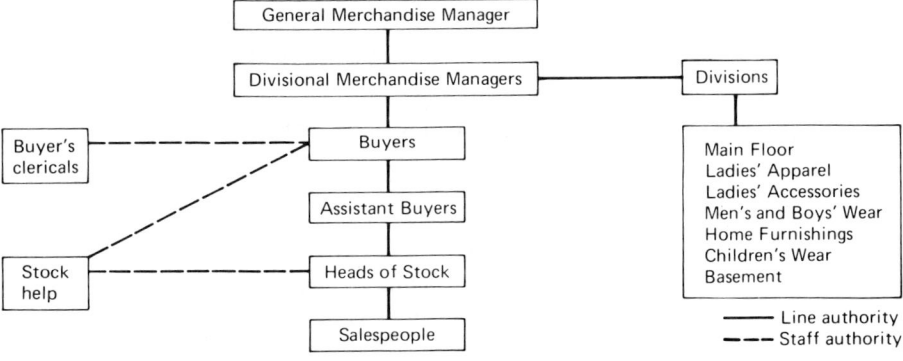

may be a line organization within a staff bureau. The head of the fashion bureau is often called the fashion coordinator and will direct the activities of assistants, models, and others reporting to him or her.

BRANCH STORE ORGANIZATION

In the late 1960s sales in suburban department and discount stores began to equal the sales in parent stores downtown. By 1972, 68.5 percent of total department store sales and 68.3 percent of specialty store sales came from suburbia.[1] There are now some 15,000 suburban shopping centers doing a retail business of $153 billion.[2] Many more suburban stores than urban stores are being built, and the trend is expected to continue for some time to come.

Store organization charts have come to reflect the increasing importance of branch stores. In Figure 1.1 branch store managers report directly to the general merchandise manager in the downtown store for merchandise needs and guidance. Although not shown, in such an organization branch managers would also report directly to heads of other main divisions of the store; the branch store is thought of as merely an extension of the parent store in this case.

Because branch stores have become so numerous and large, many firms have altered their organizations. The manager of a branch store may report to a single executive in charge of all suburban stores, as illustrated in Figure 1.3 This executive has a direct line to the president, passing only through the executive vice president in charge of all stores and operations. In essence, the branch store manager now has only one boss instead of four or five. All buying is still done in the parent store, but branches may be responsible for many of their own functions outside of buying, such as personnel management, control, and merchandise handling.

THE MERCHANDISE MANAGER

The merchandise manager is one of the most important executives in a store and one of the best paid. It is not uncommon for a divisional merchandise manager to earn between $25,000 and $50,000 and a general merchandise manager to earn between $50,000 and $100,000 annually in a large store. Most merchandise managers have been promoted through the ranks after having served as buyers or managers of key operations.

Duties of the Merchandise Manager

Since the most important duty of the merchandise manager is to execute the merchandising policies of the store, most of his or her time is spent in supervising the activities of the buyers. The merchandise manager must act

[1]*Financial and Operating Results of Department and Speciality Stores,* National Retail Merchants Association, Controllers Congress, New York, 1972.
[2]"Shopping Centers," *New York Times,* February 2, 1975, p. 8.

Figure 1.3a ORGANIZATION FOR SUBURBAN STORES

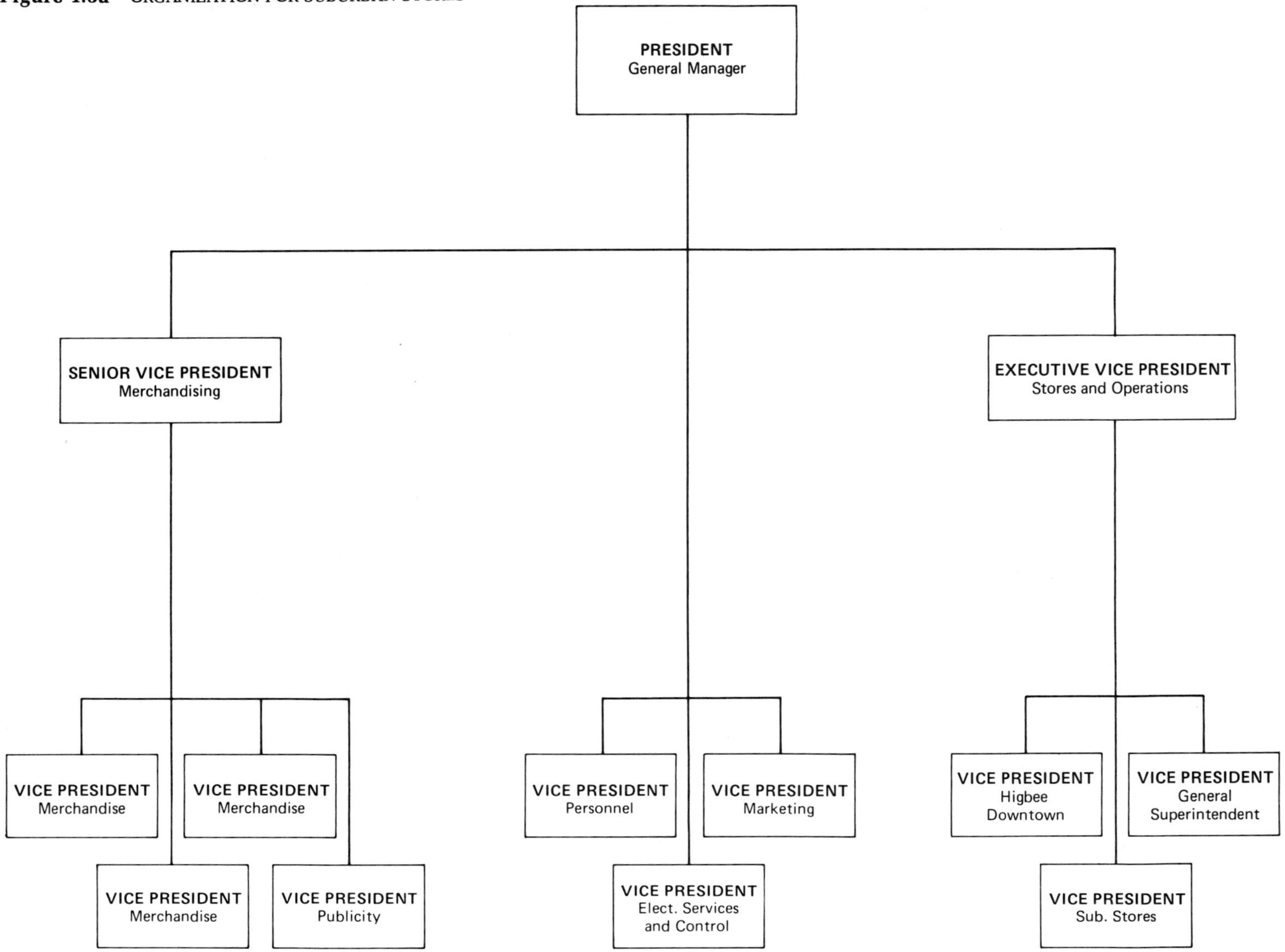

```
                                    PRESIDENT
                                  General Manager
                                        |
        ┌───────────────────────────────┼───────────────────────────────┐
        |                               |                               |
SENIOR VICE PRESIDENT                   |                     EXECUTIVE VICE PRESIDENT
    Merchandising                       |                       Stores and Operations
        |                               |                               |
  ┌─────┼─────┐                   ┌─────┴─────┐                   ┌─────┴─────┐
  |     |     |                   |           |                   |           |
VICE  VICE  VICE               VICE         VICE              VICE          VICE
PRES. PRES. PRES.              PRES.        PRES.             PRES.         PRES.
Merch. Merch. Merch.          Personnel   Marketing        Higbee         General
                                                           Downtown      Superintendent
        |                           |           |                           |
      VICE                        VICE                                    VICE
      PRES.                       PRES.                                   PRES.
    Publicity                 Elect. Services                           Sub. Stores
                               and Control
```

SOURCE: The Higbee Company, Cleveland, Ohio

THE MERCHANDISE MANAGER   7

Figure 1.3b ORGANIZATION FOR SUBURBAN STORES

```
                                    VICE PRESIDENT
                                      Sub. Stores
    ┌──────────┬──────────┬──────────┼──────────┬──────────┬──────────┐
Youngstown  Severance  Westgate    Parma    Great Lakes  Midway   Belden Village
VICE PRES.  General Mgr General Mgr General   General     General    General
General Mgr VICE PRES.  VICE PRES.  Manager   Manager     Manager    Manager
            Operations  Operations
    │          │          │          │          │          │          │
General    Operations Operations Operations Operations Operations Operations
Merchandising Manager   Manager    Manager    Manager    Manager    Manager
Coordinator
    │          │          │          │          │          │          │
Division A Division A Division A Division A Division A Division A Division A
Merchandise Merchandise Merchandise Merchandise Merchandise Merchandise Merchandise
Coordinator Coordinator Coordinator Coordinator Coordinator Coordinator Coordinator
    │          │          │          │          │          │          │
Division B Division B Division B Division B Division B Division B Division B
Merchandise Merchandise Merchandise Merchandise Merchandise Merchandise Merchandise
Coordinator Coordinator Coordinator Coordinator Coordinator Coordinator Coordinator
               │          │                     │
           Division C  Division C            Division C
           Merchandise Merchandise           Merchandise
           Coordinator Coordinator           Coordinator
```

SOURCE: The Higbee Company, Cleveland, Ohio

8 WHAT IS MERCHANDISING?

as a "watchdog" over each buyer's *open-to-buy* (the amount of money the buyer has to spend after all of the merchandise on order has been subtracted from planned purchases) to make sure that the buyers stay within their budgets. These budgets reflect the collective best thinking of the buyers, the merchandise manager, and the controller before the season begins. The merchandise manager must continually examine sales and stock positions in each department as the season progresses to determine whether the budgets have been planned too high or too low. If additional open-to-buy is indicated, the merchandise manager must make sure the buyer gets it. If sales slip below the plan, he or she must recommend that the buyer's open-to-buy be reduced. The merchandise manager must also review each buyer's buying plan before the controller gives final approval.

Promotional activities are also part of a merchandise manager's job. Having had extensive previous experience, the merchandise manager is able to give the buyers valuable advice on how to promote sales. It is also a merchandise manager's job to be in constant touch with developing fashion trends so as to be able to steer buyers in the right direction, thus minimizing serious buying mistakes.

Although visits to the market are a regular part of the buyer's job, merchandise managers sometimes travel as well. While in New York they might be asked to help develop a private brand through the store's resident

Buyer talking with divisional merchandise manager
SOURCE: Sybil Shelton/Monkmeyer Press Photo Service

buying office or engage in other activities that will benefit the store. When in a market city, whether it be New York, Chicago, Dallas, Atlanta, or some other merchandising center, merchandise managers may help their buyers select merchandise, although the actual buying is always the buyers' responsibility. Occasionally a merchandise manager may take a trip to Europe or the Far East but again in an advisory capacity; most buyers would resent a purchase made by their merchandise manager, especially if they had not been advised beforehand.

Most stores are associated with a resident buying office, which is nearly always in New York. This office acts in an advisory capacity to assist stores with their buying problems. There are several different types of resident buying offices. The *fee* office is completely independent of subscribing stores and charges a rate based on the store's sales volume for its services. Kirby Block and Company and Independent Retailers Syndicate are examples of fee offices. An *associated* office is owned and managed by the stores it serves; these stores are usually not connected in any other way than through their mutual affiliation with the resident buying office. The country's largest associated offices include Associated Merchandising Corporation, Frederick Atkins, and Specialty Stores Association. A *syndicate* office is owned by a chain of department stores and serves all member stores of the corporation. Macy's, Gimbels, and the May Department Stores all maintain syndicate offices. A fourth type, the *private* office, is almost extinct, but Neiman-Marcus is still represented by its own New York resident buying office.

Merchandise managers are intimately involved in the hiring and firing of executives within their division. Since they work so closely with their buyers, a harmonious relationship must be maintained. Progressive merchandise managers are also keenly interested in the assistant buyers in each department and watch closely for promising young people in junior-executive training programs. Wise merchandise managers realize only too well that the success of their departments depends on the skill and dedication of those second and third in command.

Qualifications of the Merchandise Manager

Although merchandise managers generally come up through the ranks as buyers, not all buyers would make effective merchandise managers. Merchandise managers must, above all, be leaders. Hundreds of people in a large store look to the merchandise manager for direction, and he or she should possess tact, be able to instill confidence, and make sound judgments. Being a high-level executive, the merchandise manager must also exercise much initiative and be able to motivate those under him or her. A merchandise manager must further be adept at analyzing merchandising figures and be able to spot trouble areas and initiate correctives quickly. Cost-consciousness is almost built into the job, and profit must of course always be uppermost in the merchandise manager's mind.

THE BUYER

The duties of the buyer differ markedly from those of the merchandise manager, but the buyer must also be a skilled merchandiser. Whereas the merchandise manager is interested in the profit picture for the entire division, the buyer's concern is primarily with the profit of his or her own department or departments. The key to effective buying is a buyer's sales and merchandise plan, which will be discussed in detail in a later chapter.

Duties of the Buyer

The buyer's chief responsibility is to buy merchandise that will sell quickly and be profitable for the department. A buyer must visit the market as often as is necessary to procure merchandise. The center of most market operations in the United States is still New York City, although buyers now also travel to Florida, Texas, California, and other places. Stores also send buyers to foreign countries in ever-increasing numbers. Buyers from smaller stores often visit regional trade marts, such as those in Chicago, Dallas, Atlanta, Los Angeles, and Denver. These trade marts, or merchandise marts as they are often called, rent spaces to manufacturers for permanent display of their products. The showrooms, all under one roof, are open only to buyers and wholesalers. They are staffed by manufacturers' representatives who show and sell the merchandise. It is common to refer to these sellers as vendors or resources. In fact, whenever a buyer wants to purchase merchandise, he or she must deal with the seller or vendor.

One of the largest merchandise marts is located in Chicago and serves as

Chicago Merchandising Mart
SOURCE: Chicago Merchandise Mart

the merchandising center for much of the Midwest. Many top manufacturers maintain displays there.

Manufacturers' sales representatives still travel extensively to show buyers their lines, but it is not always possible to carry the complete lines of merchandise with them. It is also difficult for a sales representative to visit every account, large and small, on a regular basis, particularly if he or she has a large territory. For this reason, small stores often order merchandise from catalogs over the telephone or by telegram. But no matter what buying procedure is used, buyers must constantly seek out the unusual and the most wanted merchandise.

Once merchandise has been bought, the buyer also has a responsibility to see that it is sold. Buyers must be promotion minded and look for new and better ways to push the sale of merchandise. The most successful buyers create interesting counter displays, fight for window display space, and assist in the preparation of various forms of advertising; this necessitates a close working relationship between the buyer and the sales promotion division. Many buyers try to spend part of each day they are in the store on the selling floor. They also visit their branch operations as often as time permits. By talking with customers and actually selling the merchandise, they are able to gauge customer demand and learn why some items sell well and others do not. Wise buyers hold departmental meetings at least once a week. During these meetings they review promotional plans, show new merchandise, conduct training sessions, and discuss departmental problems.

Having to work extensively with figures, a buyer must pay close attention to details. Purchase orders must be written, markdowns taken, invoices checked, items priced, and basic-stock books kept up to date. These and many other clerical activities produce a large amount of paperwork. A buyer is often able to delegate much of the "pencil-pushing" to assistants and clerks. But accuracy and prompt attention to paperwork is essential, since the final responsibility for departmental operations rests with the buyer. Many financial and operating reports flow across a buyer's desk. It is important that the buyer be able to understand these reports. Knowledge of the mathematics needed to describe how the department is doing is a necessity.

Buyers have a great deal to say about who works in their department. Departmental personnel needs are usually filled by the personnel office in the case of salespeople and stock and clerical help. However, most buyers prefer to interview and select their own assistant buyers and heads of stock. If someone is to be discharged or transferred, buyers like to give the final approval. The buyer, then, must be a supervisor of people, and in large stores and departments this can be a major responsibility.

Qualifications of the Buyer

Buyers must be *merchandise specialists.* They should be able to recognize quality and judge workmanship, and they must have adequate merchandise knowledge regarding materials, color, and design. Although buyers should be able to appreciate the aesthetic appeal of merchandise, they must be prudent enough to buy what they think will sell rather than what might be in good taste in their opinion. Fledgling buyers often make the mistake of buying what they like personally instead of considering the possible likes and dislikes of their customers. It is usually not necessary to know all the technical aspects of how a product is made. More important is a "sixth sense" about whether an item will sell well. Experience plus a natural talent will aid buyers here.

Buyers must learn how to be *traders*. The profit margin of their departments will be bigger if they can negotiate low purchasing prices and take advantage of vendor helps as well. Discounts, preticketing, advertising and promotional allowances, and prepaid freight should be eagerly sought. Through experience buyers learn to arrive at purchasing prices that will benefit both parties and make a continued business relationship possible.

Buyers should be *good managers*. At the end of a day they seldom feel their work is done. Therefore, they must know how to manage not only the people who report to them but also their valuable time. Too often buyers get bogged down in paperwork or become too involved in the details of running their department. The ability to delegate authority and discern priorities should be developed early in their careers. Otherwise, they will soon find themselves on a treadmill leading nowhere.

Another important qualification is closely allied with a buyer's personality and physical makeup. A successful buyer must exhibit an uncommon amount of *drive* and *a will to succeed*. Buying is a highly competitive and

Vendor showing items to buyer at San Francisco Merchandise Mart
SOURCE: Clinton S. Bond/B.B.M. Associates

exhausting job. Although the rewards are many, some persons cannot take the daily strain of meeting people, bargaining with vendors, placating customers, and pleasing superiors. Buyers are more subject to "ups and downs" than are persons in many other lines of endeavor. Buyers must be firm and decisive because quick decisions are part of their everyday lives. In order to cope with these tensions, buyers should enjoy conflict. People who are not aggressive and whose feelings are easily hurt will probably find that buying and merchandising are not for them.

Finally, buyers should possess *personal integrity*. Because they sign purchase orders amounting to hundreds of thousands of dollars, buyers are under great temptations to make "deals" with vendors. Stores expect their buyers to be incorruptible, and no buyers can do the best job possible for their stores unless they are incorruptible. Buyers caught accepting kickbacks or engaging in some shady practice are subject to immediate dismissal. Word quickly spreads if a buyer is on the "take," and professional reputations are easily ruined. High personal and business ethics cannot be measured in dollars and cents.

EXECUTIVE COMPENSATION

Merchandising executives are highly motivated and talented individuals, and they should be compensated according to their ability and contribution to the store. It is common for buyers and department managers to be paid a straight salary plus added compensation based upon overall performance. Their performance should be reviewed frequently to let them know how they are progressing and to form a basis for a salary increase. An example of how a merchandising executive might be rated is shown in Figure 1.4. This thorough performance review consists of six pages. It

Figure 1.4
MERCHANDISE EXECUTIVE RATING SHEET

```
                              (1)
              SHILLITO'S EXECUTIVE PERFORMANCE REVIEW

    For _____
    Position _____
    Prepared by above executive and _____


    I.  BUSINESS RESULTS AND OBJECTIVES
        A.  Results from previously set business objectives.

                              (2)          Name _____

        B.  Key business objectives for coming twelve months and ways by which they can
            be achieved.
```

PERSONAL EVALUATION FOR MERCHANDISING EXECUTIVES. (3)

Name _____

A. Please indicate degree of proficiency under one of the choices on each characteristic. Brief comments required to either substantiate rating or specify improvement needed.

		Low			High	Comments
		1	2	3	4	5
1.	Knowledge of market						
2.	Vendor relationship						
3.	Knowledge of merchandise						
4.	Ability to spot trends and take action						
5.	Knowledge of and reaction to competition						
6.	Ability to use statistical data						
7.	Ability to: (a) plan assortments						
	(b) make projections						
	(c) make buying plans						
	(d) develop EOM plans						
8.	Ability to maintain proper stock content						
9.	Ability to communicate: (a) write						
	(b) talk						
	(c) listen						
10.	Ability to work with selling organization						
11.	Leadership, ability to: (a) train, delegate and follow up						
	(b) instill interest and enthusiasm						
12.	Ability to set and meet deadlines						
13.	Ability to carry out agreed upon directions						
14.	Creative ideas and accomplishments in developing business						
15.	Administrative conduct of inventory control procedures						

(4)   Name _____

B. Personal Aspirations

(To be filled out by the executive being reviewed only.)

If you wish to record your aspirations regarding development of your career, please comment below. If you feel you need certain experiences (in-store or out-of-store) to aid in your development, please note in your comments.

(5)   Name _____

<u>THIS PAGE TO BE COMPLETED BY THE IMMEDIATE SUPERVISOR ONLY</u>

C. Personal Growth

1. Your comment on how realistic preceding self-expressed aspirations are:

2. Your evaluation of growth potential (complete either a or b or c). These comments are primarily for the record and should not be discussed with the executive by the immediate supervisor without prior approval of management member. If such discussion did occur, please give brief synopsis at bottom of this page.

   a. Has potential for future growth.
      (1) Recommend next move to _____
                                    (job title or area)
      (2) When ready for above _____
      (3) Long-range potential _____

or b. Is at limit in present position.
      (1) But very valuable _____
   or (2) But good in job _____

or c. Below standard, recommend following action:
      (1) Close monitoring for _____
                                 (specific time period)
   or (2) Transfer to _____
   or (3) Demotion to _____
   or (4) Warning action _____

ANNIVERSARY				(6)			Name	

NOT FOR DISCUSSION BETWEEN EXECUTIVE AND IMMEDIATE SUPERVISOR.
FOR MANAGEMENT USE ONLY.

Birth Date	Ent. Date	In job since	Date last increase	Amt. last increase	Present salary	Proposed salary	Job Classification	
							#	Salary range

III. SALARY ADJUSTMENT RECOMMENDATION

Immediate Supervisor:

DATE SUBMITTED TO INTERMEDIATE SUPERVISOR: _____

Intermediate Supervisor:

DATE SUBMITTED TO MEMBER OF MANAGEMENT _____

Management Member:

SOURCE: Shillito's Division, Federated Department Stores, Inc.

shows the executive's ability to meet past business objectives together with a statement of future goals and how they will be attained. Fifteen merchandise executive characteristics are listed, and the immediate supervisor checks the number from 1 (lowest) to 5 (highest) that best reflects the executive's ability. Space is provided for comments that back up the rating given. The immediate supervisor also evaluates the executive's potential for future growth.

Some stores provide added incentive to the buyers and department managers by letting them participate in profit sharing. Most profit-sharing plans are based on a buyer's "controllable profit." There are some expenses, such as rent, heat, and lights, over which a buyer has no control. On the other hand, he or she can exercise considerable control over such expenses as advertising and payroll. A small percentage of this controllable profit is sometimes given to the buyer or manager at the end of a fiscal year as a bonus. A variation of this kind of profit-sharing plan is the quota-bonus plan. Here the executive is given a percentage of controllable profits above a minimum profit quota. For example, the quota assigned to a particular department may be $150,000 in controllable profits, and the buyer may receive as much as 10 percent of the controllable profits over his or her quota in the form of a bonus on top of his or her base salary.

Although profit-sharing and quota-bonus plans add important incentives, there are inherent dangers in their use. The plans have a tendency to destroy teamwork. Thus department heads may be driven to get what they can for themselves, and the store as a whole may suffer. Short-range views may dominate over the all-important long-range views. An increase in the sales volume of one department is not healthy if it is accomplished at the expense of another department in the same store.

Merchandise managers are usually paid a straight salary plus a bonus based on the profits from the various departments in their division. Although they are necessarily very anxious to have their own departments succeed, they should nevertheless let the best interests of the entire store take precedence over the interests of individual buyers and department managers.

WHY STUDY MERCHANDISING?

It has often been said that retailing is a field where experience is the best teacher. There are still a few "self-made" men and women in stores today who have reached the pinnacle of success with little or no formal education. But if one aspires to an executive career in merchandising today, college training is almost always considered a necessity. On the other hand, many stores will admit college graduates to their executive-training programs with little regard to the types of degrees they hold. These stores maintain that they prefer to train their future executives on the job once they have found individuals who possess enthusiasm and initiative and are willing to work hard.

Why, then, study merchandising at all? The answer is three-fold: (1) to build an "awareness" of the problems that face retailers, (2) to build a firm foundation of merchandising theory as a basis for sound practice, and (3) to facilitate the planning of careers. Students who have grasped the rudiments of merchandising while in school often progress more rapidly in a retailing organization, all else being equal. Many schools offering retailing programs place students in stores as part of "field training" programs. Students are thus able to apply what they have learned in the classroom to actual work situations. After completing the retailing program combining both classroom theory and actual store experience, students are better able to decide whether the field is really for them. In this way they may be able to avoid the months or even years of subsequent experimentation.

Merchandising is an exciting and purposeful vocation with never-ending variety. It is extremely satisfying because the end results (sales and profit) are tangible and easily measured. The human element is also ever-present. Merchandisers work closely with vendors, store personnel, and are in constant contact with customers. Because of this unique exposure to both merchandise and people, many find that merchandising is the right career for them.

YOUR FUTURE IN MERCHANDISING

For those interested in a merchandising career, the prospects have never been brighter. Although the nation's birth rate has slowed in recent years, total population continues to rise, bringing an ever-increasing demand for goods and services. Established department stores keep expanding by opening new branches. Independent and franchised retailers of all types are increasing in number and variety. Each time a new store is opened, more management positions are created. In a field where there is one executive for every seven nonexecutives, opportunities abound for the college-trained merchandiser.

The accent on youth is very evident in retailing today. Young merchandisers are promoted quickly if they show they can produce, and stores are filled with buyers for major departments who are still in their twenties. Moreover, many of these success stories involve women. Women comprise at least half of most buying staffs, and in fashion-oriented stores the figure may run as high as 70 percent.

Starting salaries in retailing are low, but executive trainees should not be discouraged. Stores pay their buyers very well. It is common for beginning buyers to earn between $14,000 and $18,000, and experienced buyers for large departments may earn as much as $40,000 annually. Fringe benefits are attractive: for example, the employee discount on store purchases, which may be as high as 25 percent.

Of course, merchandising is not for everyone. Some people find the hours too long and the pressures too great. If an aspiring buyer has not made the grade within three to five years after junior executive training, he or she would be wise in most cases to seek other means of employment. But for those with the necessary knowledge and stamina, the future in merchandising appears very favorable.

CHAPTER SUMMARY

In a broad sense, merchandising is the buying and selling of goods at a profit. More narrowly defined, it is the planning within the store to make sure that the famous five rights of merchandising are accomplished. Without the right merchandise at the right place, at the right time, in the right quantity, and at the right price, a retailer cannot enjoy maximum success.

The merchandising division is certainly one of the most important, if not the most important, in a store. Merchandising executives are responsible for the procurement of merchandise, and without merchandise the store would have no reason to exist. Many stores have patterned their organizations after the four-functional Mazur plan, according to which a store is organized around four divisions: merchandising, sales promotion, control, and management. As stores have grown larger, many with multi-unit operations, wide variations of the Mazur plan have appeared.

The chief executive of a merchandising division is usually called the general merchandise manager. Merchandisers responsible for whole divisions are called divisional merchandise managers; they report directly to the general merchandise manager. Each divisional merchandise manager is assisted by a corps of buyers. The number of buyers in each division usually runs between seven to ten, but this can vary considerably.

Merchandise managers execute the merchandising policies of the store and supervise the buyers in their respective divisions. Most of them have come up through the ranks as buyers and are therefore well versed in merchandising strategies. They seldom do any buying themselves. Their task is to advise and aid their buyers in matters of promotion of goods, fashion trends, merchandise development, and fiscal accountability.

The buyer holds the key to the success or failure of a department. It is the buyer who selects the merchandise to be sold. A buyer must be a specialist who knows how best to satisfy customers with the merchandise they want. He or she must know how to negotiate with the vendor for low prices and advantageous terms, and be able to manage both people and time. To do all this, a buyer needs stamina, enthusiasm, creativity, and a strong desire to succeed without sacrificing his or her personal and business ethical standards.

The retailing business is expected to continue expanding and should offer many new merchandising openings each year. The future has never seemed more promising for qualified individuals in search of challenge and reward. Although beginning salaries are often lower than the average in other businesses, merchandisers have a great earning potential in five to ten years. Well-trained college graduates, many of whom took merchandising courses, find advancement to responsible positions very rapid. The opportunities for women are especially bright. Stores have promoted many young people to important buying positions while they are still in their twenties.

QUESTIONS FOR REVIEW

1. Name the so-called "five rights" of merchandising and explain why each is important.
2. Why do stores pay increasing attention to the "fifth" season? What are some items sold during this season?
3. Explain how the Mazur plan operates. Why have many stores found it necessary to modify it?
4. Explain the differences between line and staff authority.
5. Are there any differences between the ideal qualifications of a merchandise manager and a buyer? Explain your answer.
6. What is the chief function of the resident buying office? Name and describe the principal types of resident buying offices.
7. Who is a vendor? What are some synonyms for the word *vendor*?
8. Explain how a buyer might be compensated for his efforts. How much can a buyer expect to earn today? a merchandise manager?
9. Why is it so important for buyers to possess a keen sense of personal integrity?
10. What are some advantages and disadvantages of making merchandising your career?

DISCUSSION QUESTION

It is said that buyers should buy what their customers want even if the merchandise is not in "good taste." Is there such a thing as "good taste"? Defend your answer with examples.

CASE PROBLEMS

THANKS, BUT NO THANKS

Alice Murphy, a twenty-seven-year-old children's wear buyer for a leading store on the West Coast, was wrapping up a whirlwind trip to the New York market to pick up some needed holiday items for the Christmas season just ahead. Ms. Murphy had been promoted to her present position just over a year ago after only two years as an assistant buyer. Her first Christmas season and the months that followed had established her as one of the bright, young merchandising talents in the store. She was typical of the new breed that had replaced the stereotyped middle-aged buyer with a big hat, too much makeup, and a theatrical manner.

Ms. Murphy had spent two hours during her last afternoon looking at a line of holiday sweaters at one of her major suppliers. She had placed a sizable order and was about ready to leave the showroom when George Pierson, the salesman who had always showed the line, stopped her and said, "Wait a minute, Alice, I have something here for you." Mr. Pierson handed her a white envelope and asked if she would tuck it away in her brief case and open it later. Ms. Murphy stared at the envelope and said, "What is this?" "It's nothing," Mr. Pierson said, "just a small token of our appreciation for all the business you have given us this past year. Please don't open it now—wait until you get back to your hotel room."

Suddenly Ms. Murphy became suspicious. "George, I think I should open it right now." Inside the envelope were two crisp $100 bills. Ms. Murphy quickly handed the envelope back to Mr. Pierson. "George, you know I can't take this." "Why not?" a reddened Mr. Pierson said. "You know very well why not" came the answer. "If you want to do something nice for me, pick me up tomorrow morning at the hotel and drive me to the airport."

1. Did Ms. Murphy do the right thing in returning the money? Why or why not?
2. Do you think Ms. Murphy sacrificed her position by suggesting a ride to the airport?
3. Why do stores take such a firm stand in not allowing buyers to accept gifts?

A TOUGH DECISION

"I just don't know what to do!" wailed Sue Wasserman as she sat facing Professor Gilchrist in his office one day in early June. "I've had two great job offers, but I like school and wonder if I shouldn't go on for a four-year degree."

Sue had been one of Professor Gilchrist's best students. She had just received her two-year retailing degree from Gotham Community College. During her last semester she had fulfilled her field training assignment by working eight weeks in the ladies' better sportswear department of a leading New York City department store. The store had given her high marks for her work. Sue was personable, conscientious, bright, and a hard worker. She had graduated from Gotham with honors.

Professor Gilchrist had recognized long ago that this young lady possessed unusual potential for a merchandising career, and he was anxious to help her as much as he could. "Tell me more about your job offers, Sue, and let's see if we can talk this thing out."

Sue related that she had had a very successful interview at a resident buying office. They had offered her an assistant buyership in children's wear at a starting salary of $140 per week with a salary review every six months. She would be expected to handle much of the clerical work in the office, but would also accompany the buyer to the market nearly every day. The job sounded interesting and Sue liked the idea of so much New York market exposure.

The other job was in the store where she had done her field training. The better sportswear buyer had liked her work so much that she was invited to stay on as head of stock in the same department. The store would start her at $135 per week with frequent reviews, and there was a strong possibility she would be given a crack at the junior executive training program if her performance remained at a high level. The store also agreed to pay half of her tuition cost if she decided to take evening courses at a local university to pursue a four-year degree.

Sue continued that as attractive as these offers were, she wondered if she might benefit more in the long run from a four-year degree. Her parents had offered to send her to any local college she might choose. She had wanted to be a fashion buyer for as long as she could remember. She just wasn't sure whether two more years in college would be as valuable as two years spent in the field.

When Sue had finished, Professor Gilchrist thought for a long moment. He didn't want to make the decision—Sue must do that. He could, however, point out the advantages and disadvantages of starting a job now or continuing with her education.

1. Enumerate the advantages and disadvantages of each job described.
2. What are the advantages and disadvantages of pursuing a four-year degree in Sue's case?
3. If you were Sue, what would you do?

2

HOW
TO
FIND
PROFIT

KEY POINTS

1. Profit is the money left over at the end of the year after all the expenses have been deducted and taxes paid.

2. Many stores that are ultimately successful fail to earn a profit during their first years of operation.

3. Showing profits as a percentage of net sales is a more meaningful gauge of operating efficiency than reporting actual dollar earnings.

4. The four profit variables should be manipulated until the most profitable mix is found.

5. Expense planning and control are essential to a store's profitable operation.

NATURE OF PROFIT

We invest money at a risk in the hope of making money. The money that is returned in excess of original investment is the profit. Profit is the catalyst that energizes our whole economic system. From a retailer's standpoint, profit is the *money gained* from the buying and selling of merchandise. In a sense, it is the *reward* a merchant gets in the form of taking in more money than he or she puts out.

It used to be that store owners had only a haphazard notion of how much actual profit was being made. If at the end of a year they had more money than when the year began, they assumed their operation was profitable. In 1913 the federal income tax law changed all that. Retailers were now required to submit annual income tax returns, and in order to do that, they had to keep accurate books. Their determination of profit became much more sophisticated. This, of course, was to their advantage since they became better able to see how business was progressing and to locate weak spots that needed improvement.

When they first start out, many businesses do not make a profit. Sometimes it takes several years before profits begin to show on the books. Patience, faith, and fortitude are a new merchant's needed virtues. But if the location is right, the merchandise is wanted, and expenses are not too high, a success is bound to come eventually.

Profit is usually given in terms of dollars or as a *percentage of net sales*. The latter is a more meaningful measure of profit than dollar figures and can vary a great deal. It is not at all unusual for a large supermarket chain to report yearly earnings of less than 1 percent. In fact, the net profit as a percentage of sales reached the lowest levels for supermarkets in 1972 since the 1930s. The after-tax net was only 0.49 percent among major supermarket chains.[1] The profits of independent grocers were slightly

---

[1]*Progressive Grocer*, Forty-First Annual Report, April 1974, p. 108.

higher. Specialty and department stores usually report better profit performances. According to some recent statistics, the after-tax earnings of specialty stores doing a yearly business of over $1 million were 2.4 percent; those of department stores with the same volume were 3.4 percent.[2]

THE PROFIT MIX

Four profit variables make up what is popularly known as the *profit mix*. Profit results from the proper adjustment of these four factors. The factors are:

1. price
2. sales volume
3. cost of goods sold
4. operating expenses

The relations among these variables can be seen clearly when a highly simplified profit and loss statement is examined. Assume that an appliance dealer stocks a 21-inch color television set that retails for $500. If he sells 100 sets during the year, the operating profit on this particular model of television will look something like this:

Sales (100 sets × $500)	$50,000
Less cost of goods sold (100 sets × $300)	30,000
Gross margin or gross profit	20,000
Less operating expenses	15,000
Operating profit	$ 5,000

In this example, the operating profit will be a healthy 10 percent ($5,000/$50,000). However, the dealer is bound to sell other types of television sets and many other items as well, so that constructing a profit and loss statement for one item in a store is not very practical. It is done here for illustrative purposes only.

As we can see in this example, the *gross margin* or *gross profit* must be larger than the operating expenses if a profit is to be made. "Gross margin" is considered a better term than "gross profit," because profit is such a small part of the figure.

The operating profit is usually increased by the addition of other income. A store may derive monies from sources other than the actual sale of merchandise. It may receive interest and dividends from investments, earn money in the form of carrying charges on installment purchases, and often charge interest on the unpaid balance of customer charge accounts. After other income is added, we have what is called *net profit before income taxes*. This amount less the income tax is the *net profit after income taxes*. With these additions and subtractions, the statement above then looks like the one shown on the following page:

[2]*Financial and Operating Results of Department and Specialty Stores*, National Retail Merchants Association, Controllers Congress, New York, 1972.

Sales		$50,000
Less cost of goods sold		30,000
Gross margin		20,000
Less operating expenses		15,000
Operating profit		5,000
Other income		1,000
Net profit before income taxes		6,000
Less income tax		1,400
Net profit after income taxes		$ 4,600

ILLUSTRATIVE PROBLEM A sporting goods store realized net sales of $80,000 during the past year. The merchandise sold had cost the store $50,000. Expenses were $22,000 and other income amounted to $2,000. Find (a) the gross margin, (b) the operating profit, and (c) the net profit in dollars and in percentage of sales.

SOLUTION (a) Find the gross margin:

Net sales	$80,000
Less cost of goods sold	50,000
Gross margin	$30,000

Gross margin in percentage of sales = $\dfrac{\$30,000}{\$80,000}$ = ⅜ or 37½%[3]

(b) Find the operating profit:

Gross margin	$30,000
Less expenses	22,000
Operating profit	$ 8,000

Operating profit in percentage of sales = $\dfrac{\$ 8,000}{\$80,000}$ = 1/10 or 10%

(c) Find the net profit:

Operating profit	$ 8,000
Plus other income	2,000
Net profit	$10,000

Net profit in percentage of sales = $\dfrac{\$10,000}{\$80,000}$ = ⅛ or 12½%

EXERCISES

1. The sales in a one-man frame shop were $30,000 for the year. Although the cost of goods sold was only $10,000, expenses were $18,000 due to high labor costs. What was the (a) gross margin and (b) net profit in dollars and percentage?
2. A china department reported net sales of $565,000 for the fall season. The cost of goods sold was $300,000, and expenses for the department totaled $250,000. Determine the departmental (a) gross margin and (b) net profit in dollars and percentage.
3. A hardware store registered sales of $150,000 for the year. The cost of

---

[3] It would be helpful at this point to review aliquot parts, because many problems may be solved more quickly if their fractional equivalents are known. The commonly used aliquot parts are given in Appendix 1. If an aliquot part cannot be used, it is suggested that all percentages be rounded off to the nearest tenth of a percent.

merchandise sold was $90,000, expenses were $50,000, other income amounted to $3,000, and taxes were $2,000. Find the net profit after taxes in dollars and percentage.

MANIPULATING PROFIT VARIABLES

It is interesting to note how the variables that make up the profit mix can be adjusted to increase or reduce profits.[4] The effects of these variables on profit can be examined by manipulating them up and down. In the interest of continuity, the example of the appliance dealer mentioned earlier in the chapter will be used again.

Change in Price

Let us assume that the appliance dealer is worried about his competition. He feels he should lower his price to compete more effectively with the discount houses and department stores in his area. So he reduces the retail price of the television set from $500 to $475.

Sales (100 sets × $475)	$47,500
Less cost of goods sold (100 sets × $300)	30,000
Gross margin	17,500
Less operating expenses	15,000
Operating profit	$ 2,500

Note what a drastic effect this reduction in price will have on profits. Although the retail price is reduced by only 5 percent, there will be a 50 percent drop in dollar profits. (Here, as elsewhere, the percentage of increase or decrease is given in terms of the previous figure as the base.)

Change in Sales Volume

The dealer wonders how many more sets he will be able to sell if he lowers his retail price by 10 percent and undersells some of his competitors. (It is assumed here that he is not bound by fair-trade laws.) He discovers that he is able to sell 125 sets, yielding the following figures:

Sales (125 sets × $450)	$56,250
Less cost of goods sold (125 sets × $300)	37,500
Gross margin	18,750
Less operating expenses	15,000
Operating profit	$ 3,750

It is evident that although a further reduction in the retail price has improved profits somewhat, the dealer was still better off when he sold the sets at $500 each. However, in order to sell the set at this higher price, he will have to provide better and more personalized service. Otherwise, customers will tend to buy the television sets where the price is lowest.

[4]For another discussion of the impact of variables on profit, consult William R. Davidson and Alton F. Doody, *Retailing Management*, Ronald Press, New York, 1966, pp. 51 - 53.

Change in Cost of Goods Sold

The dealer hears about a Japanese firm that manufactures television sets of reputable quality. He discovers that he can buy these sets for only $285 each, instead of $300. Assuming that other factors remain unchanged, he will have these figures:

Sales (100 sets × $500)	$50,000
Less cost of goods sold (100 sets × $285)	28,500
Gross margin	21,500
Less operating expenses	15,000
Operating profit	$ 6,500

With the acquisition of this less expensive line, the profit percentage will increase from 10 percent to 13 percent. It is possible that advertising costs will go up in order to promote a new line; however, it is doubtful that they will go up enough to prevent the Japanese line from being more profitable.

Change in Operating Expenses

The dealer decides not to replace two retiring employees but to put more emphasis on self-service. By thus reducing expenses, he hopes to achieve a higher profit:

Sales (100 sets × $500)	$50,000
Less cost of goods sold (100 sets × $300)	30,000
Gross margin	20,000
Less operating expenses	10,000
Operating profit	$10,000

When expenses are reduced by one-third, dollar profits will rise by a whopping 100 percent! Perhaps this example illustrates the reason that merchants are so "expense conscious" and try to cut corners wherever possible.

Some tentative conclusions can be reached by studying the above examples. All else being equal, if prices and volume are increased, profits will increase. If prices and volume are reduced, profits will decrease. If there is a decrease in the cost of goods sold and in operating expenses, profits will rise. Conversely, if the cost of goods sold and the operating expenses go up, profits will decrease. In actual practice, however, these relations do not always hold true. Volume may increase, but there may be such an increase in expenses due to increased selling costs, that any gain in profit from increased volume may be completely offset. A price increase may reduce volume to such an extent that the contemplated profit gain may be entirely wiped out. Expenses may be reduced to such a degree that sales volume suffers. Thus retailers must continually experiment with the profit variables in order to find the most profitable "mix."

ILLUSTRATIVE PROBLEM Last year the organ department in a music store sold 50 organs at a retail price of $2,000 each. The organs had cost the store $1,000 each. Operating expenses amounting to $45,000 were allocated to the department. This

Wrapping and packaging meats—one of the operating expenses of food stores
SOURCE: Elizabeth Hamlin/Stock, Boston

year another brand of organ costing only $950 each will be stocked. If the volume, retail price, and expenses remain constant, by what percentage will dollar operating profit be increased?

SOLUTION (a) Find the operating profit for last year:

Sales (50 units × $2,000)	$100,000
Less cost of goods sold (50 units × $1,000)	50,000
Gross margin	50,000
Less operating expenses	45,000
Operating profit	$ 5,000

(b) Find the operating profit for this year:

Sales (50 units × $2,000)	$100,000
Less cost of goods sold (50 units × $950)	47,500
Gross margin	52,500
Less operating expenses	45,000
Operating profit	$ 7,500

(c) Find the percentage increase in operating profit (note that the previous year's profit is used as the base):

Operating profit this year	$7,500
Operating profit last year	5,000
Difference in dollars	$2,500

Percentage increase = $\dfrac{\$2,500}{\$5,000}$ = ½ or 50%

EXERCISES

1. Sales of $32,000 were recorded last season for men's pajamas. The cost of the goods sold was $20,000. Expenses amounted to $10,000. The plan for this season is to reduce expenses by 10 percent. If this is accomplished, how much increase, in percentage, will there be in dollar operating profit?
2. A luggage department sold 80 footlockers at $30 each during the past year. The lockers had cost $18 each. This year the department will reduce the retail price to $25 in order to sell twice as many. If the projected sales figure is correct, what will be the increase in gross margin in dollars and in percentage?
3. Last year a fur salon sold 70 mink stoles at $800 each. The stoles had cost the store $350 each. Expenses were $25,500. This year the store feels it can sell 10 percent more stoles if they are advertised more heavily. The increased advertising expenditure will increase expenses by 5 percent. Would you recommend this course of action to the store? Defend your answer with figures.

PLANNING EXPENSES

Nature of Expense

The expenses of doing business can be more worrisome to retailers than any other facet of their operations. All the "five rights" of merchandising can be handled expertly, but unless expenses are kept in line, a profit will not be made. For this reason, retailers watch their expenses very carefully and continually seek ways to trim them without hurting business. One famous New York store was concerned over increased customer delivery costs. Signs that read "Be an angel—carry your small packages with you" were posted throughout the store. Customers cooperated, and delivery expenses were reduced.

Payroll has traditionally been one of the major expenses in the retail business. With increases in the minimum wage, aggressive union activities, and competitive pressure from other industries, retailers have been faced with skyrocketing labor costs. It has become imperative to find ways to make each employee more productive. Consolidating small departments, using more part-time help especially during peak selling hours, and stressing customer self-service have been effective payroll savers. But stores must always be careful not to eliminate too many people from the sales force, since sales may be lost for lack of service and security problems can easily get out of hand.

Expenses are often planned a season or a year in advance, just as other merchandising figures. After sales projections have been made, it is common to forecast the gross margin. A dollar profit goal is then set up, and estimated expenses make up the difference between the gross margin and the profit. Expenses should not be planned rigidly. As a season progresses, heavy promotion may be called for to stimulate sales. An unexpected rate increase may boost light and power costs. The planned expense figure, then, should act as a guide and not as a figure to be met by every possible means.

Classification of Expenses

There are many ways to classify expenses. The Controller's Congress of the National Retail Merchants Association has listed eighteen natural divisions, as shown in Figure 2.1.

Figure 2.1
NATURAL DIVISIONS OF EXPENSE

1. *Payroll:* wages, salaries, commissions, and bonuses paid to all employees of the store.
2. *Advertising:* costs for all forms of advertising media, such as newspapers, radio, television, handbills, billboards, and direct mail.
3. *Taxes:* all taxes paid to federal, state, city, and county agencies to cover unemployment, social security, real estate, and occupancy assessments. Does not cover income taxes as these are deducted from profit.
4. *Supplies:* costs incurred in supplying store with wrapping paper, twine, sales books, stationery, pencils, and other materials necessary to running a merchandising operation. Also includes housekeeping and repair materials.
5. *Services purchased:* protection, light, heat, power, delivery service, cleaning service.
6. *Unclassified:* cash shortages, subscriptions to periodicals, memberships in organizations.
7. *Travel:* domestic and foreign buying trips, trips to branch stores, attendance at meetings.
8. *Communications:* postage, telephone, telegrams, cablegrams.
9. *Pensions:* payments to retirement plans.
10. *Insurance:* premium payments for all types of insurance purchased to run the store.
11. *Depreciation:* allowances for losses in value due to wear, tear, and obsolescence on building, furniture, fixtures, and equipment.
12. *Professional services:* covers fees paid to outside specialists such as accountants, lawyers, appraisers.
13. *Donations:* contributions to welfare, charitable, and educational institutions.
14. *Bad Debts:* uncollectible checks, notes, and accounts receivable.
15. *Equipment rental costs:* cash registers, computers, delivery trucks, etc.
16. *Real property rentals:* outlays for rented or leased property.
17. *Expense transfers*
18. *Outside revenue and other credits:* includes payments which must be made on borrowed money and the interest on the owner's capital invested in the business.

SOURCE: *Financial and Operating Results of Department and Speciality Stores,* National Retail Merchants Association, Controllers Congress, New York, 1972.

Another way to classify expenses is to divide them into three groups depending on their relationship to sales volume. Those expenses bearing little or no relationship to sales volume are called *fixed* expenses. Examples of fixed expenses are rent, lights, heat, air conditioning, and the depreciation on fixtures. Expenses that contain fixed elements but may also vary with sales volume to some extent are called *semivariables,* Payroll and traveling costs are examples. Expenses that are closely related to sales volume are known as *variable* expenses. Variable expenses usually include such items as wrapping supplies, receiving and marking room costs, and expenses incurred in the adjustment department where customer complaints are heard and settled.

From the buyer's viewpoint a practical way to classify expenses is to think of them as either *controllable* (direct) or *fixed* (indirect). Since the buyers are responsible for the profitability of their respective departments, they are anxious to control expenses when they have the power to do so. Although they have little control over the fixed expenses mentioned above, they are in a position to influence the amount of money spent on advertising, the size of their payroll, and the quantities of wrapping materials used in their departments. It is easy enough to allocate expenses to the various departments if they are direct. It is more difficult to allocate those expenses incurred by the store as a whole. Some stores do not try to prorate the indirect expenses for each selling department. Instead, they subtract the direct expenses over which a buyer has some control from the departmental gross margin to arrive at a *controllable margin*. The indirect expenses are then deducted in total from the margin for the store as a whole. Other

A self-service store—one way to cut payroll expenses
SOURCE: David A. Krathwohl

stores take each and every indirect expense and allocate them to individual departments. Different criteria are used for allocating different expenses. For example, mail and phone order expenses are assigned on the basis of the number of transactions handled. Real estate costs would be allocated according to the square footage of departmental floor space. Although it is costly to divide indirect expenses, it does make buyers more conscious of expense control. It can also help in the evaluation of buyers. Those who take expense control seriously usually run more profitable departments and should be compensated accordingly.

ILLUSTRATIVE PROBLEM

Last year a store achieved sales of $100,000. The gross margin was 34 percent, and operating expenses were 28 percent. One-half of the expenses were fixed, one-fourth varied directly with sales (variable), and one-fourth varied by half the sales variation (semivariable). This year the store plans a 10 percent increase in sales and gross margin. Given that expenses are planned at the same proportion, find the (a) planned fixed, semivariable, and variable expenses in dollars, (b) planned expenses in percentage of sales, (c) planned dollar profit, and (d) planned profit percentage.

SOLUTION

(a) Find the planned fixed, semivariable, and variable expenses:

	LAST YEAR	THIS YEAR
Sales	$100,000	$110,000 (up 10%)
Gross margin (34%)	34,000	37,400 (up 10%)
Operating expenses (28%)		
Fixed (14%) $14,000		14,000 (no change)
Semivariable (7%) 7,000		7,350 (up 5%)
Variable (7%) 7,000		7,700 (up 10%)
Total expenses	$28,000	$29,050

(b) Find the planned expense percentage:

$$\text{Planned expense percentage} = \frac{\text{Expenses}}{\text{Sales}}$$

$$= \frac{\$29,050}{\$110,000}$$

$$= 26.4\%$$

(c) Find the planned dollar profit:

Planned dollar profit = gross margin − expenses
= $37,400 − $29,050
= $8,350

(d) Find the planned profit percentage:

$$\text{Planned profit percentage} = \frac{\text{Profit}}{\text{Sales}}$$

$$= \frac{\$8,350}{\$110,000}$$

$$= 7.6\%$$

EXERCISES

1. Last year the ABC Company had sales of $200,000. This year sales are projected to increase 20 percent. The gross percentage margin last year was 32 percent, and expenses ran at 29 percent. One-half of the expenses were fixed, and the rest were variable. If the gross percentage margin remains the same, what will be the (a) dollar expenses and (b) dollar operating profit for this year?

2. Ivey's Department store is located in a deteriorating neighborhood. Sales last year totaled $3,200,000, but a 10 percent decline in sales is forecast for the coming year. Gross margin was a respectable 35 percent, but operating expenses were running at 30 percent. Sixty percent of the expenses were fixed and 40 percent were variable. If the gross margin remains the same, what is this year's estimated (a) expense percentage and (b) operating profit percentage?

3. Upon analysis, a store's expenses last year turned out to be one-third fixed, one-third variable, and one-third semivariable (they fluctuated by one-half of the sales variation). Total expenses were 27 percent of sales. If the store expects a 10 percent increase in sales volume from last year's $200,000, what will be the dollar breakdown by classification of the expenses for this year?

ILLUSTRATIVE PROBLEM

Cheatum's ladies specialty shop is divided into two sections: ready to wear and accessories. Each section has its own buyer. The accessories buyer has been under pressure to improve the profitability of her section; she is trying to improve her controllable margin as one means of doing this. Her figures for the season just ended are as follows:

Sales	$200,000
Gross margin	34%
Expenses	
Payroll	10%
Advertising	2%
Rent	4%
Heat, lights, power	2%
Wrapping supplies	1%
Selling supplies	1%
Depreciation on fixtures	1%
Marking and receiving	1%
Delivery	3%
Unclassified	10%

(a) Find this buyer's controllable margin in dollars and as a percentage of sales.
(b) What is her operating profit in dollars and as a percentage of sales?

SOLUTION

(a) Find the controllable margin in dollars and as a percentage of sales: In order to find the buyer's controllable margin, it is necessary to separate those expenses over which she has some control from those that she cannot control. The direct or controllable expenses can be listed as follows:

Gross margin	34%
Direct expenses:	
Payroll	10%
Advertising	2%
Wrapping supplies	1%
Selling supplies	1%
Total	14%

Controllable margin = 14% of $200,000
= $28,000

(b) Find the operating profit in dollars and as a percentage of sales:
The operating profit cannot be found until the indirect expenses have been added to the direct expenses. Total expenses are 14% + 21% or 35% of sales. The operating profit (in this case loss) is therefore:

Gross margin	34%
Less operating expenses	35%
Operating loss	1% or $2,000

Note: The poor profitability performance in this case may not be entirely the buyer's fault. The store should take a close look at those expenses over which the buyer has no control. In this case, nearly two-thirds of the expenses are indirect, whereas the buyer's responsibility theoretically ends with her controllable margin.

CHAPTER SUMMARY

Retail profit is the money gained from the buying and selling of merchandise. It can be an elusive reward particularly for new merchants. Time and skill are needed to build up a loyal clientele, and enough capital must be held in reserve to cover anticipated losses during a shakedown period sometimes lasting several years or more.

Profit is usually reported as a percentage of net sales. This figure often seems surprisingly low to the layman, but the actual profit in dollars may be great. For example, a department store with a 3-percent net profit on sales of $50 million actually realizes dollar profits of $1,500,000. On the other hand, because dollar profits can vary so widely as a result of differences in sales volume, profit percentage gives a truer picture of operating efficiency.

The profit mix is made up of four variables: price, sales volume, cost of goods sold, and operating expenses. The interaction of these variables produces a profit or a loss. Through experience the merchandiser can learn how to manipulate the variables to achieve maximum profit. Generally profits will rise if the price and sales volume increase and the cost of goods sold and expenses are reduced. However, the relations are seldom so straightforward. For example, a price increase may produce a drop in sales volume and result in overall reduction in profit.

Expenses can have such a devastating effect on profit that merchants search constantly for better ways to plan and control them. When faced with mounting operating costs and dwindling profits, stores naturally look first at the payroll, the largest single expense factor. Personnel cuts may save money, but too much reduction in customer service may lead to loss of sales.

Since the buyers are responsible for the profit performance of their respective departments, they are usually eager to reduce expenses whenever they can. Buyers and department managers are apt to become even more aware of expense control when part of their compensation is based on controllable profits. Some expenses, such as heat, rent, air conditioning, and lights, are fixed and not controllable by individual buyers. Other expenses, such as advertising, payroll, supplies, and travel, are direct and can be controlled wholly or in part by frontline merchandise executives. These direct expenses are deducted from the department's gross margin when calculating a buyer's controllable margin or profit.

QUESTIONS FOR REVIEW

1. In addition to observing the law, why has it been advantageous for retailers to have to file income taxes?
2. If someone steals a $3.00 steak from a typical supermarket, how much merchandise will the store have to sell to make up for the loss?
3. Why is "gross margin" a more accurate term than "gross profit"?
4. What are some of the ways in which a store can increase operating profit to gain a higher net profit?
5. What are the four profit variables that make up the "profit mix"? Give some examples of how they can be related to one another to affect the operating profit.
6. Other things being the same, an increase in which two profit variables will bring about an increase in profit? Explain why an increase in price may not result in increased overall profit.
7. Why is it wise to hire part-time sales help instead of staffing a store with full-time sales people only? Can you think of any problems that might develop if only part-timers were employed?
8. Explain the differences among fixed, variable, and semivariable expenses.
9. What is a buyer's controllable margin?
10. When calculating an increase over or decrease under last year's sales, which figure is always used as the base?

DISCUSSION QUESTION

How would you classify the expenses involved in sending buyers to the market? Explain your answer.

PROBLEMS FOR REVIEW

1. A store achieved net sales of $1,000,000 during its first year of operation. The cost of the goods sold was $600,000, and operating expenses were $350,000. There was no other income. Find the (a) gross margin and (b) net profit before taxes in dollars and percentage.
2. Last year a suit buyer sold 150 designer suits at $500 each. The suits had cost $250. This year the buyer plans to sell an equal number of similar suits at a unit retail price of $550, with the cost remaining the same. By what percentage will the buyer's gross margin be increased?

3. A ladies' sportswear buyer sold 200 leather coats last year at $90 each. They had cost her $45 each. This year the buyer has decided to reduce the retail price by 10 percent, hoping thereby to sell twice as many coats. If the projected sales are realized, how will her gross margin be affected?
4. A luggage department reported net sales of $400,000 last year. Sixty percent of the luggage sold belonged to the Samsonite line. The cost of these items had been $90,000. This year Samsonite will increase the wholesale price by 5 percent across the board. Expenses in the luggage department last year were $200,000. If the expenses due to selling the Samsonite line are calculated according to sales volume, and if the sales of this line of luggage remain the same, by what percentage will the operating profit in dollars on the Samsonites be reduced?
5. A book department is planning a 20 percent increase in sales for this year due to a relocation on the street floor. However, because of increased floor space, expenses are expected to rise by 10 percent over the 30 percent of the previous year. The planned gross margin is again 35 percent. What will be the percentage change in operating profit?
6. Last year a new store showed a loss of 3 percent on a sales volume of $1,500,000. Gross margin was 32%. If sales this year increase by 5 percent and the gross margin percentage and the dollar expenses stay the same, will the store show a profit? Defend your answer with figures.
7. A notions department reported a sales volume of $300,000 last year. An analysis of the expenses, which amounted to 30 percent of sales, revealed that one-third were fixed, one-third were variable, and one-third were semivariable. Sales are expected to increase by 10 percent this year. If these expense ratios stay the same, and if sales do increase as planned, what will be this year's expense in percentage of sales?
8. A fabrics store called The Linen Closet had sales last year of $400,000. The cost of goods sold was $250,000. Expenses were 32 percent of sales, half of which were fixed and the rest variable. This year a sales increase of 20 percent is planned, but it is expected that the cost of goods sold will increase by only 10 percent. If the expense percentage and the proportion of fixed to variable expenses stay the same, what will be the store's profit in dollars and percentage?
9. An umbrella department with net sales of $250,000 had a gross margin of 35 percent. Expenses charged to the department included salaries, 7 percent; advertising, 3 percent; rent, 1 percent; heat and lights, 0.5 percent; supplies, 0.5 percent; and miscellaneous indirect expenses, 11 percent. What was the controllable margin in percentage of sales?
10. A ladies' better-shoe department reported a gross margin of 36 percent on net sales of $600,000. Expenses charged to the department were heat, lights, and power, 1 percent; payroll, 8 percent; depreciation on fixtures and furniture, 1 percent; rent, 2 percent; delivery costs, 1 percent; wrapping and selling supplies, 2 percent; insurance, 1 percent; advertising, 4 percent; and other fixed expenses, 12 percent.

What was the controllable margin in dollars and as a percentage of sales?

CASE PROBLEMS

THE EMPTY TREASURE CHEST

Mr. and Mrs. Paul Simon have operated a very successful gift shop in Cleveland, Ohio, for twenty years. The shop is called The Treasure Chest and features fine-quality leather goods, crystal, ceramics, jewelry, linens, and other items.

The Simons, who are in their midforties, close their shop every August so they can take a well-deserved vacation. They usually spend the month in the Colorado Rockies and have grown to love the city of Denver and the surrounding area. Several years ago they decided to retire in Denver, but they did not want to wait another twenty years before doing so. They persuaded their older son to take over the management of the Cleveland store if they could find a suitable location in Denver to open a Colorado branch of The Treasure Chest.

Last August the Simons negotiated a lease for the new store on the ground floor of a just completed skyscraper in lower downtown Denver. The area had once been a slum, but with federal and municipal aid, it was being transformed by the gleaming new office buildings and apartment houses. Although the established department stores, specialty shops, theaters, and hotels were located farther uptown, the Simons felt that the lower downtown section had a promising future due to the extensive reconstruction in progress. At a considerable investment they began stocking their new store with the same high-quality merchandise that their Cleveland customers had appreciated. Expensive fixtures and carpeting were installed to add to the aura of quality.

The Simons held their grand opening on October 1. They were somewhat alarmed when fewer than a hundred people appeared on opening day. They had placed quarter-page advertisements announcing the opening in both of Denver's daily newspapers, and a great response was expected. However, they reminded themselves that the building was only 20 percent rented, and they thought that the empty store space around them would surely be leased in the near future.

The Simons were dismayed that six months later business remained disappointing. There seemed to be practically no "drop-in" customer traffic from the street. A few office workers from the building came in during lunch hours, but it was not unusual for an hour to pass without a single customer entering the store. Fortunately it had been possible to hold expenses to a minimum. There was no payroll to meet, and advertising costs had consisted of only the opening-day advertisements and a listing in the Yellow Pages. Rent was high, but heat and light bills were nominal. Other expenses, such as insurance and depreciation on fixtures, were not great.

Operating losses during the first half year had been much higher than expected, but the Simons were able to draw upon profits from their Cleveland store to pay current expenses. They felt that if customer traffic could be built up, the store would begin to turn a profit. However, they did not feel they could operate the store at a loss indefinitely and decided to give themselves five years to make their Denver Treasure Chest a going concern.

1. What actions could the owners take to build up sales volume?
2. Are the chances for the store's eventual success good or poor? Explain your answer.
3. Is location one of the prime factors to consider when starting a new business? Why?

FROM A ROSY VISION INTO THE RED

S. Parcor, Incorporated owns and operates a chain of ten discount houses in and around a large city in the southwestern part of the United States. The first store was opened in 1955 in center city as a discount appliance store. It became so successful that other types of durable goods were added, and later soft goods were brought in as well. Today all ten stores stock a large assortment of general merchandise.

All the Parcor stores are located in suburban areas with the exception of the flagship store downtown. It has been customary to open a new store about every two years. Parcor's competition has come mainly from department store branches and units of national mail order chains. The firm's buyers are located in the downtown store, but they visit the suburban operations as often as they can.

Like other discount houses, Parcor's is noted for its low prices and wide selections. The stores maintain a supermarket atmosphere. The accent is on self-service, and customers are encouraged to use shopping baskets. There are few customer services: no charge accounts, no free delivery, and no gift wrap. Parcor's has, however, instituted installment credit plans for major appliances.

In the past few years Parcor's rosy outlook for continued growth and high earnings has turned sour. More and more customers complain of poor quality, low in-stock positions, and bad service. Store theft has risen at an alarming rate. As a result of declining sales volume, profits have plummeted, with several stores now operating in the red. It appears that for the first time in its history the entire chain may show an operating loss for the year just ending.

Members of the top management have been called together to discuss possible means of saving the chain. An effective survival kit is clearly needed.

1. What steps might be taken to improve the merchandising results of the chain?
2. Based on your own observation, do you believe discount chains will continue to hold their share of the market?

3

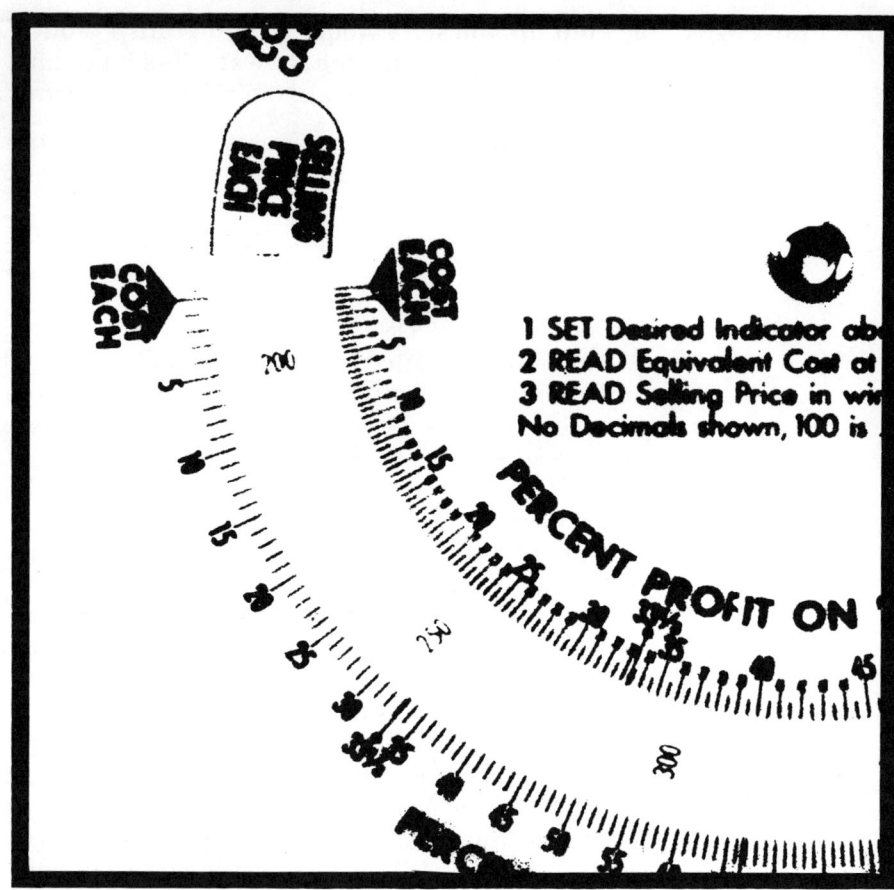

HOW TO FIND MARKUP

KEY POINTS

1. Dollar markup is the difference between the cost and the selling price of an article of merchandise.

2. Most stores today use a retail rather than cost base in calculating markup percentages.

3. A "keystone markup" is applied to certain items of merchandise by simply doubling the cost to arrive at the selling price.

4. Instead of calculating markup by hand, most buyers let the buyer's wheel do the work.

5. Buyers are more interested in the cumulative markup for their entire department than the markup on individual items.

NATURE OF MARKUP

The purpose of opening a retail establishment is to make a profit. As was mentioned in Chapter 2, this expected profit may not be realized during the first few years of operation, but it must come if the store is to remain in business. Thousands of firms close their doors each year because they are not profitable. To be more specific, Dun and Bradstreet reported that 9,566 businesses of all kinds failed in 1972, and almost half of these failures, 4,398, were in the retail field.[1] Managerial inexperience or ineptitude was the underlying cause of more than nine out of ten retail failures. The immediate causes were inadequate sales, competitive weakness, poor location, heavy operating expenses, and inventory difficulties. Of all the many kinds of retailers, men's wear stores had the highest failure rate: 97 per 10,000 operating concerns. Sound merchandising techniques might have prevented many of these failures.

In a retail business there can be profit only if, on the average, the selling price of an article is substantially higher than its cost. The difference between the cost and the selling price is called the *markup*. If only one item is involved, we have an *individual markup*. If more are involved, we say there is *cumulative markup*. The markup must be an amount large enough to cover not only the expected profit but other factors as well, such as expenses incurred in doing business and resulting from merchandise shortages.

Markup is defined by the simple formula:

$$Cost + Markup = Retail$$

The formula is sometimes written $C + MU = R$, which can be transposed as follows:

---

[1] *The Business Failure Record 1972*, Business Economic Department, Dun and Bradstreet, New York, 1973, p. 8.

$$MU = R - C$$
$$\text{or} \quad C = R - MU$$

When this formula has been mastered all markup problems can be solved easily.

ILLUSTRATIVE PROBLEMS

1. A store is selling a man's shirt for $10. The shirt cost the store $6. What is the markup?

SOLUTION

$$\begin{aligned} \text{Markup} &= \text{Retail} - \text{Cost} \\ &= \$10 - \$6 \\ &= \$4 \end{aligned}$$

2. A radio retails in a store for $20. The markup is $8. What is its original cost?

SOLUTION

$$\begin{aligned} \text{Cost} &= \text{Retail} - \text{Markup} \\ &= \$20 - \$8 \\ &= \$12 \end{aligned}$$

3. A store buys a television set for $300 and decides to put a markup of $200 on it. What will the store sell it for?

SOLUTION

$$\begin{aligned} \text{Retail} &= \text{Cost} + \text{Markup} \\ &= \$300 + \$200 \\ &= \$500 \end{aligned}$$

EXERCISES

1. A long-sleeved turtleneck in sizes 4 - 6X sold for $6.00. It cost the store $42.00 a dozen. What was the markup?
2. A parka jacket retailed for $20.00. The markup was $8.00. What was the original cost?
3. A buyer made a selection from a line of ladies' shoes that cost $16.00 a pair. If the markup is $11.00 per pair, what will the shoes retail for?

MARKUP BASED ON RETAIL

Markup may be calculated as a percentage of the cost or of the retail price. Most stores today prefer to use the retail base, for the following reasons:

1. The goal of every store is to make a profit. Profits, however, cannot be realized until goods have been sold. Therefore, merchandisers tend to "think retail" when planning their stocks and shaping their prices. It follows that the convenient thing is to base their markups on the retail or selling prices.
2. Most merchandising statistics are expressed in terms of percentage of net sales. For example, the National Retail Merchants Association (NRMA) issues many interesting statistics comparing store operations, and in these data retail sales are usually used as the base. (See *Merchan-*

dising and Operating Results and *Financial and Operating Results*, published annually.) In keeping with this practice, it is desirable to express markups in terms of percentages of retail prices.

3. A markup based on retail price is always a smaller percentage figure than one based on cost. The former can never be higher than 100 percent, whereas the latter can be much higher than 100 percent. Consumers naturally hope for lower markups, so for psychological reasons stores would rather quote a percentage markup based on retail price than on cost. For example, an item that costs $5.00 and retails for $10.00 has a markup of $5.00. The markup percentage based on cost is 100 percent:

$$\frac{\text{Markup}}{\text{Cost}} = \frac{\$5.00}{\$5.00} = 100\%$$

But based on the retail price, it is only 50 percent:

$$\frac{\text{Markup}}{\text{Retail}} = \frac{\$5.00}{\$10.00} = 50\%$$

Stores using different bases (cost and retail) often compare markup percentages. For this purpose the markup conversion table in Appendix 2 is very useful. The table shows that markups based on retail prices are always lower than those based on costs.

4. Most stores today use the "retail method of inventory." Items are listed according to their retail values, which can be readily obtained from the price tickets. If a cost price is wanted, a cost code may be used, or the planned markup may be subtracted from the retail price.

Since the retail base is more commonly used in practice, we shall assume in this book that all markups are based on the selling price unless stated otherwise. For the sake of comparison, however, it will be shown in this chapter how markups based on both cost and retail price can be determined.

Although it is important to know what the markups are in dollars and cents, stores are more anxious to know the markup percentages. Buyers are often asked to maintain a certain markup percentage for their departments. When vast amounts of merchandise are involved dollar figures are not very meaningful. Markup percentage, on the other hand, can let a merchant know whether he is on the right track in meeting profit goals.

When retail price is used as the percentage base, the same retail price is obviously 100 percent of itself. Similarly, when cost is used as the percentage base, that cost is 100 percent of itself.

Finding markup percentage when cost and retail prices are given. Since markup is the difference between cost and retail, the markup percentage is found by dividing the markup by either the cost price or the retail price, depending on which base is used.

ILLUSTRATIVE PROBLEM A necklace is being sold in a jewelry store for $60. The necklace cost the store $30. What is the markup percentage?

SOLUTION

Cost + Markup = Retail
Markup = Retail − Cost
= $60 − $30
= $30

To express the markup as a percentage of retail price, put the markup in dollars over the retail price in dollars as follows:

$$\text{Markup \%} = \frac{\$ \text{ Markup}}{\$ \text{ Retail}}$$

$$= \frac{\$30}{\$60} \text{ or } 1/2$$

$$= 50\%$$

ILLUSTRATIVE PROBLEM
A housewife purchased a vacuum cleaner for $40. The store had bought it from the manufacturer for $25. What was the markup percentage?

SOLUTION

$$\text{Markup \%} = \frac{\$ \text{ Markup}}{\$ \text{ Retail}}$$

$$= \frac{\$15}{\$40} \text{ or } 3/8$$

$$= 37\ 1/2\%$$

EXERCISES

1. A boutique owner bought a dress in Italy for $30 and retailed it for $75. What was the markup percentage?
2. An oil painting was found in England by an antique dealer, who paid $200 for it. It was put on sale in his shop in New York with a price tag of $600. What was the percentage of markup?
3. What was the percentage of markup on a pen that retailed for $3 and cost the store $24 per dozen?

Finding the cost price when the retail price and markup percentage are given. A buyer often buys merchandise with definite retail price lines in mind. It is important to know how much an item will cost using a certain markup percentage.

ILLUSTRATIVE PROBLEM
A lamp retails for $50 with a markup of 40%. What was the cost?

SOLUTION

Cost + Markup = Retail

STEP 1
Construct a box with the given information filled in as follows:

	$	%
C	X	60
+MU		40
R	50	100

44 HOW TO FIND MARKUP

Let X be the unknown quantity (cost). We recall that the retail price must be 100 percent of itself. Then since the markup is 40 percent and $C + MU = R$, the cost must be 60 percent of the retail price.

STEP 2

Set up a proportional equation that says X is to 60 (top line of box) as 50 is to 100 (bottom line of box):

$$\frac{X}{60} = \frac{50}{100}$$

Cross-multiplying, we have

$$100X = 3000$$
$$X = \$30 \text{ (cost)}$$

Note: the proportion may also be written as follows:

$$X : 60 = 50 : 100$$

The two extremes are multiplied together (X times 100) and the two means are also multiplied (60 times 50) to give:

$$100X = 3000$$
$$X = \$30 \text{ (cost)}$$

ALTERNATE SOLUTION

$$C = R \times (100\% - MU\%)$$
$$= 50 \times 60\% \text{ or } 50 \times 0.60$$
$$= \$30$$

EXERCISES

1. A coat with a markup of 50 percent retails for $80. What was the cost?
2. What was the cost of a used Persian rug that retailed at $85 and was marked up 70 percent?
3. A bedspread retailed for $20 with a 35 percent markup. What was the cost?

Finding the retail price when the cost price and the markup percentage are given. When a buyer finalizes a cost price for an item or an assortment of goods, the desired markup percentage is applied to determine the retail price.

ILLUSTRATIVE PROBLEM

A buyer was shopping for boys' shirts and selected a group priced at $36 per dozen. He decided to place a 40 percent markup on them. What would the retail price be?

SOLUTION

$$C + MU = R$$

Again, construct a box filled in with the given information (it is necessary to divide the cost per dozen by 12 in order to obtain the unit cost):

	$	%
C	3	60
+MU		40
R	X	100

MARKUP BASED ON RETAIL 45

Added vertically, with X as the unknown quantity (in this case, the retail price), the retail price is still 100 percent of itself. Setting up the proportion and cross-multiplying, we obtain:

$$\frac{X}{100} = \frac{3}{60}$$
$$60X = 300$$
$$X = \$5 \text{ (retail price)}$$

ALTERNATE SOLUTION

$$R = \frac{C}{100\% - MU\%}$$
$$= \frac{3}{60\%} \text{ or } \frac{3}{0.60}$$
$$= \$5$$

EXERCISES
1. A piece of costume jewelry that cost a store $10 was given a 60 percent markup. What was the retail price?
2. A high-fashion store bought a dress from a famous designer for a special customer for $200 and placed an 80 percent markup on it. How much did the customer pay for the dress?
3. A German camera was imported by a camera store with gross costs amounting to $38. It was decided to mark up the camera 62 percent. What was its retail price?

MARKUP BASED ON COST

Some stores, especially small ones, still use the cost base. Using the retail base is a newer procedure, but sometimes merchants are reluctant to change their old habits. Fruit markets often use the cost base, because their goods are perishable and retails may vary from day to day. Some hardware stores also use the cost base because of the multiplicity of items and complexity of the stock.

The same formula (Cost + Markup = Retail) applies, but instead of using the retail price as the base and letting it equal 100 percent, the cost base is now equal 100 percent.

Finding markup percentage when cost and retail are given. As explained above, there are stores that find the cost base easier to use and more stable. Remember, any markup percentage of 100 percent or higher is the result of using a cost base instead of a retail base.

ILLUSTRATIVE PROBLEM
A lawnmower cost $20 and retails for $30. What is the markup as a percentage of cost?

SOLUTION
The difference between the cost and the retail price is the markup. In order to find the markup percentage based on cost, we must put the dollar markup over the cost:

$$\text{Markup \%} = \frac{\$ \text{ Markup}}{\$ \text{ Cost}}$$

Then we have

$$\text{Markup \%} = \frac{\$10}{\$20}$$
$$= 1/2 \text{ or } 50\%$$

EXERCISES

1. A hand-painted vase carried a selling price of $180. It cost the store $100. What was the markup percentage based on cost?
2. A pen sold in a stationery store for 19 cents. Its cost to the store was $12.96 per gross. What was the percentage of markup based on cost?
3. What is the markup percentage based on cost of a blouse retailing at $22 whose cost to the store was $11?

Finding the cost price when the retail price and the markup percentage are given. If a buyer uses a cost base and tries to maintain a certain retail price line using a planned markup percentage, he or she will need to know how much the item should cost.

ILLUSTRATIVE PROBLEM

A leather coat that retails for $240 was given a markup of 60 percent of cost. What was its cost?

SOLUTION

$$C + MU = R$$

Once again, construct the familiar box. But this time we let cost equal 100 percent:

	$	%
C	X	100
+MU		60
R	240	160

The proportional equation now looks like this:

$$\frac{X}{100} = \frac{240}{160}$$

Cross-multiplying as before, we obtain

$$160X = 24{,}000$$
$$X = \$150 \text{ (cost)}$$

ALTERNATE SOLUTION

$$C = \frac{R}{100\% + MU\%}$$
$$= \frac{\$240}{160\%} \text{ or } \frac{\$240}{1.60}$$
$$= \$150$$

EXERCISES
1. A pair of shoes that retails for $54 has an 80 percent markup on cost. What was its cost?
2. A jeweled flower pin retailing at $525 carries a markup of 150 percent on cost. What was the cost?
3. What was the cost of a leather gaucho bag marked up 70 percent on cost and sold for $17 in the store?

Finding the retail price when the cost price and the markup percentage are given. It is easier for a merchant to figure the retail price if a cost base is used because the result of the cost price times the markup percentage is simply added to the cost price.

ILLUSTRATIVE PROBLEM
An electronic calculator cost $200 and was marked up 75 percent on cost. What was the retail price?

SOLUTION

C + MU = R

	$	%
C	200	100
+MU		75
R	X	175

Then

$$\frac{200}{100} = \frac{X}{175}$$

$$100\,X = 35{,}000$$

$$X = \$350 \text{ (retail)}$$

ALTERNATE SOLUTION

R = C × (100% + MU%)
  = $200 × 175%
  = $200 × 1.75
  = $350

EXERCISES
1. A set of stainless steel was bought by a store for $15. If it is marked up 40 percent on cost, what will the retail price be?
2. If a lucite ice bucket costs $8 and is marked up 45 percent on cost, what should the retail price be?
3. Pantyhose that cost the store $18 per dozen were marked up 60 percent on cost. What is the retail price?

BUYER'S WHEELS

When shopping for merchandise, buyers often make use of *buyer's wheels*, sometimes referred to as markup or profit calculators. When the cost arrow is correctly set, the retail, markup, or markup percentage based on either cost or retail price may be found at a glance. This invaluable device can save buyers from time-consuming mathematical computations relating to individual markups.

Figure 3.1 shows a typical profit calculator. Note that cost prices are shown per case of 24, per gross (144), and per dozen in addition to an individual cost. After setting the appropriate cost arrow, the profit percentage based on either cost or retail can be determined quickly by reading the numbers at the bottom of the wheel.

Because the buyer's wheel can save so much time, it has become almost indispensable to the average buyer. Recently, the pocket calculator has arrived on the scene, giving the buyer still another useful aid in making all sorts of mathematical computations. The calculator is easy to handle and is more accurate than the buyer's wheel.

As valuable as these tools are, the merchandiser should be able to determine markups and markup percentages without them. Most important, the theory behind all computations should be clearly understood and appreciated.

CUMULATIVE MARKUP

Buyers or merchants are not as concerned with the markup of an individual item as much as with the markups of all of the merchandise in their areas of responsibility. After all, it is the profitability of their entire operations that

Figure 3.1
PROFIT CALCULATOR

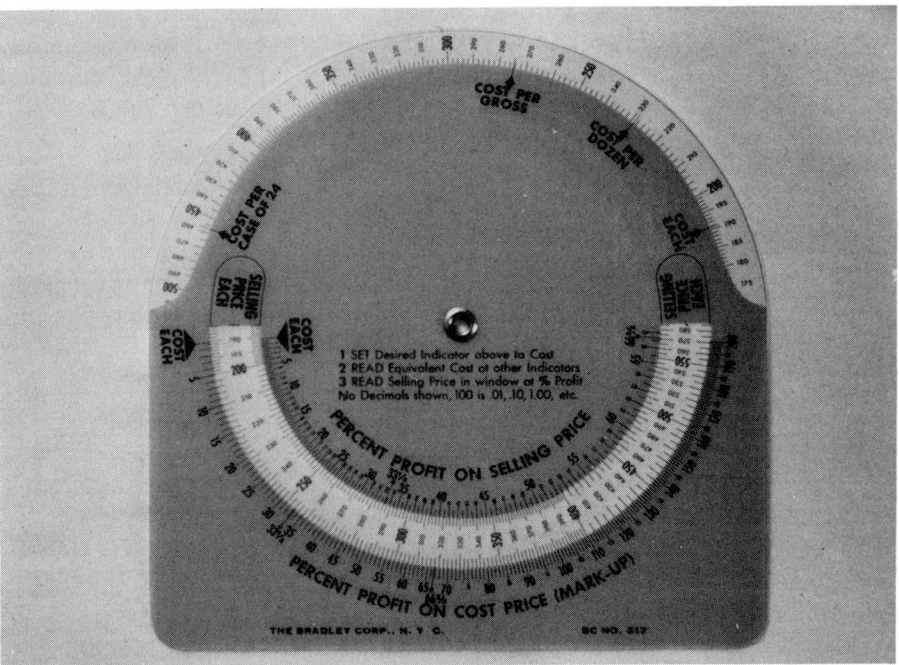

SOURCE: Bradley Corporation, Bayside, New York

matter. The sum of all the individual markups make up what is called the *cumulative markup*.

ILLUSTRATIVE PROBLEM Gladys Smith, the buyer of ladies' gloves at the Greenwillow Department Store, is planning her purchases for the coming month. Her inventory at the beginning of the month is valued at $80,000 retail. The cost was $50,000. She plans to buy an additional quantity of merchandise at a cost of $15,000 to be sold for $25,000. What will be the cumulative markup percentage?

SOLUTION

	COST	RETAIL
Beginning inventory	$50,000	$80,000
Planned purchases	15,000	25,000
Total merchandise handled	$65,000	$105,000

Then,

$$\begin{aligned} \text{Markup \%} &= \frac{\$ \text{ Markup}}{\$ \text{ Retail}} \\ &= \frac{\$105,000 - \$65,000}{\$105,000} \\ &= \frac{\$ 40,000}{\$105,000} \\ &= 38.1\% \end{aligned}$$

ILLUSTRATIVE PROBLEM Kevin Steele is a buyer of men's furnishings for Gladstone Department Store. He has been told by his merchandise manager that he should aim for a 45 percent markup in his department. According to his merchandising plan, he can spend $150,000 at retail for new merchandise during the next six months. He is expected to carry over merchandise with a total retail value of $80,000, which cost the store $47,500.

(a) What will the new purchases cost?
(b) What will be the resulting cumulative markup percentage?

SOLUTION (a) Assume the buyer is successful in applying a 45 percent markup on the new purchases. The cost of the merchandise is determined by the basic formula C + MU = R. Using the same procedure as before, we write:

	$	%
C	X	55
+MU		45
$	150,000	100

Thus we have:

$$\frac{X}{55} = \frac{150,000}{100}$$
$$100X = 8,250,000$$
$$X = \$82,500 \text{ (cost)}$$

50 HOW TO FIND MARKUP

(b) To find the markup percentage, we write:

	COST	RETAIL
Beginning inventory	$ 47,500	$ 80,000
Purchases	82,500	150,000
Total merchandise handled	$130,000	$230,000

Then

$$\text{Markup \%} = \frac{\$ \text{ Markup}}{\$ \text{ Retail}}$$
$$= \frac{\$230,000 - \$130,000}{\$230,000}$$
$$= \frac{\$100,000}{\$230,000}$$
$$= 43.5\%$$

EXERCISES

1. At the beginning of the month a buyer finds that he has an inventory with a retail value of $65,000. The merchandise had cost $40,000. During the month he plans to purchase additional merchandise retailing at $15,000 and costing $10,000. What will be the cumulative markup percentage?

2. Ms. Smith, buyer of junior dresses, has been requested by her merchandise manager to increase her cumulative markup percentage to help improve the slipping profitability of her department. At the beginning of March her department shows an inventory of $80,000 at cost and $130,000 at retail. During the month of March she makes new purchases amounting to $6,000 to which she applies a 40 percent markup.

    (a) What is her cumulative markup percentage?
    (b) Has this percentage increased with the addition of the new merchandise? If so, by how much?

3. Mr. Greene is the owner of a small boutique called The Leatherstocking. From past experience he knows that he needs a markup of at least 48 percent on new purchases to realize a satisfactory profit. He takes a trip to the Chicago Merchandise Mart to buy new merchandise to be sold at $60,000 retail. His present inventory is valued at $20,000 at cost and $40,000 at retail. What will be the cumulative markup percentage after the addition of the new merchandise?

KEYSTONE MARKUP

It is becoming more common simply to double the cost of an item to arrive at a selling price. This procedure is popularly known as *keystoning* the markup and is prevalent among apparel, cosmetics, fashion accessories, and shoe departments as well as some others. For example, if a pair of

Ticketing merchandise—a high expense factor
SOURCE: Sybil Shelton/Monkmeyer Press Photo Service

women's shoes cost the buyer $18.75, the practice is to sell the shoes at twice the cost or $37.50. Using the keystone markup on every item in a department will insure a cumulative markup of 50 percent, because the keystone markup is an increase of 50 percent on the selling price.

Not so long ago the keystone markup would have been considered exorbitant in most departments. Today it is readily accepted among retail stores, not only because it is easy to apply, but also because it acts as a hedge against spiraling costs of doing business. Some of the costs that stores have found increasingly difficult to control are payroll expenditures, energy costs (heat, lights, air conditioning), shipping and receiving expenses, packaging and delivery costs, and insurance (property, fire, and liability). Stores also have a continuing need to update fixtures and remodel existing structures to attract customers. Bigger markups such as the keystone become imperative if a store is to maintain a gross margin larger than the expenses it incurs. Otherwise, obviously there can be no profit.

CHAPTER SUMMARY Markup is the difference between the cost of an item and its retail or selling price. It may be expressed in dollars and cents or as a percentage. The markup on a single piece of merchandise is called the individual markup. That on more than one item is called the cumulative markup.

Most retailers today use the retail base, not the cost base, for calculating markup percentages. Stores often compare their operating results with those of other similar stores, and these comparative statistics are nearly always reported with a retail base. Stores also take stock of their inventories on the basis of retail price. When markup percentages are computed using retail price as the base, the retail price itself always equals 100 percent. Similarly, when percentages of cost are being considered, cost always equals 100 percent.

The basic markup formula (Cost + Markup = Retail) is relatively simple to apply, but most buyers prefer to use buyer's wheels or profit calculators for speedy and accurate calculations. These devices enable the buyer to determine at a glance markups in dollars and cents or in percentages. Although they are time-savers and are considered almost indispensable, it is important that every merchandiser understand the markup theory and be able to calculate markups without their assistance.

When a buyer purchases an article of merchandise, it is given an individual markup. However, usually a multitude of items are bought every season, and a buyer must be aware of the total or cumulative markup percentage for his or her area of responsibility. A markup percentage goal is often planned for each department, but some items are usually given higher markups and others lower markups. The departmental goal applies to the cumulative markup.

Due to spiraling operating costs, stores have been forced to increase markups. The keystone markup is currently in favor in many departments. The cost of an item is doubled to arrive at the retail price, which is the same as applying a 50 percent markup on retail. Buyers find the keystone markup easy and convenient to apply, and it certainly helps to insure that the department will be profitable as well.

QUESTIONS FOR REVIEW

1. What was the underlying cause of most retailing failures in 1972?
2. What is markup?
3. Explain the difference between an individual markup and a cumulative markup.
4. Why do most stores today prefer to use a retail base for calculating markup?
5. When you hear that the markup on an item is over 100 percent, what can you say about the base of this markup? Is the markup cost or retail based?
6. Why are markup percentages more meaningful to merchandisers than the dollars-and-cents figures of markups?
7. What does NRMA stand for?
8. Why would a bakery probably prefer to use the cost base for computing markups?
9. Why is the buyer's wheel such a valuable tool for a buyer?
10. What is keystone markup?

DISCUSSION QUESTION

Is it easier for most people to find the markup percentage when it is based on cost? Explain.

PROBLEMS FOR REVIEW

1. A man's suit retails in a store for $95. It carries a markup of $20. What did the suit cost the store?

2. What is the markup percentage on a leather reclining chair that cost $100 and retails for $180?
3. What was the cost of a watch that retails for $120 with a markup of 60 percent?
4. A coat that cost $38.88 is marked up 46 percent. What is the retail price?
5. A scatter rug that cost a store $8 is retailed for $15. What is the percentage of markup on cost?
6. What is the retail price of a pair of boy's jeans that cost $24.00 per dozen and has been marked up 70 percent on cost?
7. A markup of 150 percent on cost is given to a diamond pin that retails for $250. What was the cost?
8. The inventory of a bookstore at the beginning of the month has a value of $80,000 at cost and $150,000 at retail. During the month additional books are purchased at a cost of $15,000 to be retailed at $30,000. What is the resultant cumulative markup percentage?
9. The men's shoe department of Sandage Department Store showed an inventory of $75,000 at cost and $130,000 at retail at the beginning of February. The departmental markup is 45 percent, and new shoes that cost the store $15,950 have been added to the stock during the month.

    (a) What is the retail value of the new stock?
    (b) What is the cumulative markup percentage?

10. A buyer in the market is offered a special promotional deal of 100 dozen of a particular product at $19.80 a dozen. He wants a higher-than-average markup, for example 56 percent, on this promotional purchase. Calculate the retail dollars that will secure this markup.

CASE PROBLEMS

A CLOSE-OUT WITH A CATCH

Ed Tolliver is the new buyer of boys' wear for the Red Brick Department Store. The previous buyer, Gene Cox, was fired because of his inability to show a profit in the department for several years. According to rumors, the department had suffered from severe inventory shortages and Cox had not been able to maintain a cumulative markup of 48 percent, which was considered necessary to insure a profit.

Mr. Tolliver is now in the New York market on his first buying trip. His resident buyer has told him of an outstanding close-out of boys' name-brand hip-length winter jackets, so the two of them are visiting the manufacturer's warehouse in New Jersey to look at the merchandise. The jackets feature sturdy dacron/cotton shells and are lined with heavy nylon pile. Each has a detachable hood and comes with knit collar and cuffs. However, instead of the traditional zippered front, the jackets are equipped with Velcro fasteners made of tiny nylon threads which close securely when pressed together. The jackets are all preticketed, showing a suggested manufacturer's unit retail price of $24.95. The lot, in assorted colors and sizes from eight to twenty, is available at a closeout cost of $10 per jacket if the entire lot of 1,000 is taken.

After a quick calculation Mr. Tolliver figures that the jackets can be retailed in his store at $16.95 each, yielding a 41 percent markup. The size breakdown of the lot, however, is somewhat uneven, and not all colors are represented in every size. He checks his buying plan and notes that his department usually sells about 2,000 jackets of this type and size range during the fall and winter season.

1. Why should Mr. Tolliver buy the jackets?
2. Why should Mr. Tolliver think twice before making the purchase?
3. What would you do if you were Mr. Tolliver?

NO CATALOGS FOR THE READING ROOM

The Reading Room is a small specialty shop featuring bath accessories in a remote resort town in the mountains of northern Georgia. It is owned and operated by a widow, Karen Hitchcock, who opened the shop soon after her husband's death. For the past two years the Reading Room has provided Mrs. Hitchcock with an adequate income and has kept her busy and happy.

When the Reading Room first opened, Mrs. Hitchcock was visited regularly by vendors representing some of the leading manufacturers of bath accessories. She stocked several nationally advertised brands, and her customers often complimented her on the wide assortments and unique merchandise found in the shop. Although business during the winter months was slow, her summer business boomed and by the middle of September her stocks were depleted.

Mrs. Hitchcock counted on sales representatives to stop by to look at her carry-over inventory and to offer suggestions on how she should replenish her stock. It has now been some months since she last saw a vendor. Letters to several companies asking why a sales representative had not come by were answered with the polite, "If you need something, please look through our catalog and send your order in." These replies angered Mrs. Hitchcock. She needed items that were unusual and eye-catching. She wanted the same personalized service she had enjoyed when placing the large opening orders. Selecting merchandise from a catalog just was not good enough for Mrs. Hitchcock.

1. Why have vendors stopped making calls at the Reading Room?
2. Besides relying on the services of sales representatives or consulting catalogs, how can Mrs. Hitchcock best buy new and exciting merchandise for her shop?

4

HOW TO AVERAGE MARKUP

KEY POINTS

1. For a variety of reasons it is not possible for a buyer to apply the same markup percentage to every item purchased.

2. Fashion merchandise and expensive items such as fine jewelry demand higher markups than staple merchandise.

3. Sale merchandise is often given a lower markup to draw customers into the store.

4. One indication of a buyer's skill is his or her ability to average out high and low markups to meet the planned markup goal.

5. When a job lot is purchased, it is often possible to use several retail prices depending on the quality of the goods.

REASONS FOR AVERAGING

The buyer's job would be greatly simplified if he or she could apply the same markup percentage to all the items bought. This, however, can seldom be done for a variety of reasons. A category of merchandise, say men's dress shirts, may be bought from several manufacturers at slightly varying costs. It would not make sense to apply the same markup percentage to all these shirts and sell them, say, for $12.67, $12.73, $12.89, $12.98, $13.03, $13.22, and $13.25. One retail price of $12.95 would eliminate much confusion for the store and customers alike. The setting up of this one retail price is achieved by means of *markup averaging*.

Some items must carry higher markups than others because it costs more to stock them. For example, fine jewelry is usually marked up much higher than costume jewelry because there is a greater risk of theft. Also expensive jewelry must be displayed and sold differently. Fashion merchandise is usually given a higher markup than staple merchandise. The salability of fashion goods is subject to rapid change depending on the whims of the public, and today's winner can easily become next season's markdown. Staple goods usually rate lower markups because their salability is known; often they are nationally branded and, due to competitive pressure, sold at the manufacturers' suggested retail prices everywhere. The markups assigned to fashion and staple merchandise are averaged out to attain a final markup goal.

Brand-new items are often given large markups because of high promotional costs. Their acceptance is an unknown factor, and stores prefer to "play it safe." For example, when electric blankets first made their appearance, markups were high. Later, after the blankets had proved to be good sellers, the markups and retail prices were lowered. Markup averaging had to be done in the blanket department to allow for the introduction of this new product. Recently retail prices of pocket calculators have been lowered substantially on account of wide customer acceptance and heavy competition among manufacturers.

Specially priced merchandise to draw customers into the department
SOURCE: Cary Wolinsky/Grafia

Sale or promotional merchandise is often given a lower-than-average markup to draw customers into a store. The hope is that customers looking for bargains will also buy merchandise carrying higher markups. Again the buyer must mix high-markup merchandise with low-markup merchandise to achieve the overall markup goal.

When merchandise is priced at or below cost, we have what is called *leader pricing*. Since there is no markup at all on leader items, the term *loss leader* was coined. Actually, however, loss leader is a misnomer; the expression *profit leader* would be more descriptive of the leader's function, which is to attract more customers and thereby generate net increases in total volume and profits.[1]

It is evident, then, that the buyer must assign higher markups to some merchandise due to higher costs of storage, handling, and promotion, and greater risk. Lower markups can be applied to merchandise with lower handling costs and little likelihood of fashion obsolescence, as well as to sale merchandise for purposes of building up store traffic. The overall markup should average out to the level of the markup goal for the department.

Buyers, however, often find that as a season progresses, they are not meeting their markup goals on purchases to date. Manufacturers may raise wholesale prices in the middle of the season, and buyers may find it

---

[1] William J. Stanton, *Fundamentals of Marketing*, McGraw-Hill, New York, 1971, p. 473.

difficult to raise retail prices for competitive reasons. Alternatively, buyers may find it necessary to lower some of their planned retail prices to compete with other stores. When these things happen, they must take longer markups on merchandise procured for the balance of the season wherever possible in order to meet the final markup goals.

AVERAGE MARKUP ON TOTAL PURCHASES

When remaining purchases are planned at retail prices for a given period. If the buyer finds that his markup on purchases to date is slipping below the departmental goal, an effort should be made to take larger markups on purchases later in the season. Buyers have ready access to records showing the cumulative markup on completed purchases. Remedial action may be necessary, but the buyer needs to know exactly how big future markups need to be to realize a satisfactory average markup for the season. One way to find this out is to plan remaining purchases at retail prices using the planned markup goal.

ILLUSTRATIVE PROBLEM

According to a buyer's records, the inventory of his department on February 1 consists of merchandise worth $30,000 at cost and $45,000 at retail. Orders have been placed for delivery from February through May amounting to $100,000 at cost and $180,000 at retail. He has $40,000 left to spend at retail during the last two months of the season. If he wants an average markup of 44 percent, what should be the markup on his remaining purchases?

SOLUTION STEP 1

Find the total retail value of the merchandise to be handled:

	COST	RETAIL	MARKUP
Beginning inventory	$ 30,000	$ 45,000	
Purchases already made	100,000	180,000	
Remaining planned purchases	B ?	40,000	C ?
Total merchandise handled	A ?	$265,000	44%

STEP 2

To find the total cost of the total merchandise handled, apply the wanted average markup of 44 percent to the total retail value of the goods as follows:

	$	%
C	X	56
+MU		44
R	$265,000	100

Then:

$$\frac{X}{56} = \frac{265,000}{100}$$

$$100X = 14,840,000$$

$$X = 148,400 \text{ (cost of total merchandise handled, or } A)$$

The problem now looks like this:

	COST	RETAIL	MARKUP
Beginning inventory	$ 30,000	$ 45,000	
Purchases already made	100,000	180,000	
Remaining planned purchases	B ?	40,000	C ?
Total merchandise handled	$148,400	$265,000	44%

STEP 3

Now we can calculate the cost and markup of the remaining purchases. The cost of these purchases can be found easily by subtracting $130,000 from $148,400; it is $18,400, which is B. The markup needed on the remaining purchases to give an average markup of 44 percent may be found by using the basic formula:

$$\text{Markup \%} = \frac{\$ \text{ Markup}}{\$ \text{ Retail}}$$
$$= \frac{\$21,600}{\$40,000}$$
$$= 54\% \text{ (on remaining purchases, or } C\text{)}$$

EXERCISES

1. Ms. Baxter is a buyer of children's wear for the March Company. She is planning her forthcoming market trip to New York for her new-season purchases. Although she needs an overall markup of 42 percent to achieve a satisfactory profit for her department, she has been having difficulty in reaching that goal. The carry-over inventory from her previous season, which cost $84,000, has a retail value of $130,000. She has $200,000 to spend at retail value and has already placed new orders amounting to $25,000 at cost and $45,000 at retail. What markup percentage must she have on her remaining purchases to achieve the average markup goal of 42 percent?

2. The manager of a leased better-jewelry department in a department store in the Southeast is on a market trip to buy new merchandise. He has to spend at retail $175,000 and is trying for a markup of 60 percent so he can show a respectable profit. His present inventory is valued at $50,000 at cost and $120,000 at retail. After two weeks his purchase orders have a total value of $30,000 at cost and $70,000 at retail. What should the average markup be on his remaining purchases for him to achieve the average markup goal of 60 percent?

3. A hardware store owner is getting ready to visit the hardware show in Chicago, where he plans to buy new merchandise worth $150,000 at retail. He wants to maintain an average markup of 38 percent. At present he has an inventory of $45,000 at cost and $75,000 at retail. What percentage markup must he apply to his new purchases?

When remaining purchases are planned at cost for a given period. Instead of planning remaining purchases at retail, the buyer may decide how much he would like to spend at cost. If costs can be brought down with quantity discounts or by placing the entire season's requirements early in the season with a blanket order, a longer markup will be possible, assuming retail prices stay the same. Cost-cutting may also be achieved through buying goods out of season or purchasing close-outs and irregulars. These lower costs will help provide the extra markup necessary to meet the desired average markup goal for the period.

ILLUSTRATIVE PROBLEM A toy buyer has $80,000 at cost to spend for the current season. Her departmental markup is 40 percent. So far she has spent $62,000 with a markup of 38 percent. What must be the markup on her remaining purchases in order to achieve her desired average markup?

SOLUTION STEP 1
Find the unknown retail values:

	COST	RETAIL	MARKUP
Purchases already made	$62,000	A ?	38%
Remaining planned purchases	18,000	C ?	D
Total merchandise handled	$80,000	B ?	40%

Given the two markup percentages corresponding to the cost amounts of $62,000 and $80,000, we find the unknown retail values A and B as follows:

(a) Let X be the retail value of the purchases already made:

	$	%
C	62,000	62
+MU		38
R	X	100

Then

$$\frac{\$62,000}{62} = \frac{X}{100}$$

$$62X = \$6,200,000$$

$$X = \$100,000, \text{ which is } A$$

(b) Now let X be the retail value of the total merchandise handled:

	$	%
C	80,000	60
+MU		40
R	X	100

Then

$$\frac{\$80,000}{60} = \frac{X}{100}$$

$$60X = \$8,000,000$$

$$X = \$133,333, \text{ which is } B$$

(c) The retail value of the remaining planned purchases can be found easily by subtracting $100,000 from $133,000; it is $33,333, which is C.
The problem now looks like this:

	COST	RETAIL	MARKUP
Purchases already made	$62,000	$100,000	38%
Remaining planned purchases	18,000	33,333	D?
Total merchandise handled	$80,000	$133,333	40%

STEP 2

Find the markup on the remaining purchases by using the basic formula as before:

$$\begin{aligned}\text{Markup \%} &= \frac{\$ \text{ Markup}}{\$ \text{ Retail}} \\ &= \frac{\$15,333}{\$33,333} \\ &= 46\% \text{ on remaining purchases, } D\end{aligned}$$

EXERCISES

1. A book buyer has $5,500 to spend at cost for the current month. Her markup goal is 45 percent. To date her purchases have amounted to $4,480 at cost with a markup of 44 percent. What must the markup on her remaining purchases be in order for her to achieve the markup goal?
2. A merchandise manager is concerned about the average markup being obtained by her better-dress buyer. The buyer has $70,000 to spend at cost for the month of February, and has already purchased merchandise costing $52,000, for which an average markup of 48 percent has been achieved. The departmental goal, however, is an average markup of 50 percent. What must the markup on the remaining purchases be in order to attain the goal?
3. A buyer's records show that during February he purchased goods amounting to $30,000 at cost with a retail value of $50,000. He has permission to spend $125,000 at cost for the rest of the season, of which $77,000 has already been committed with an expected average markup of 45 percent. How much must the markup be on his remaining purchases to yield an average markup of 45 percent?

AVERAGE MARKUP WITH ONE COST AND TWO RETAILS

Sometimes a buyer finds it desirable to set two or more retail prices for similar merchandise even though it was purchased at only one cost. For example, if a buyer finds a profitable job lot, that is an assortment of merchandise of top quality but only in scattered sizes and/or less desirable colors and patterns, he or she may wish to work the merchandise into the regular stock at several established price lines. As another example, inflation may require a price increase in a line of merchandise, but the buyer may want to maintain a generally accepted price line and set up a new price line for that part of the merchandise that is of better quality. Naturally, the buyer wants to realize the average markup goal, so he or she must know the proportion of the merchandise to be stocked for each retail price.

Buyer purchasing a job lot of assorted colors and sizes
SOURCE: Cary Wolinsky/Grafia

ILLUSTRATIVE PROBLEM		A swimsuit buyer for a mail-order firm has placed large orders with a California manufacturer for several years. She pays $60 a dozen for each season's collection, and the suits have enjoyed excellent customer acceptance at the retail price of $8.00 each. Now the vendor wires from California that, because of increased labor and material costs, the new collection will cost $66.00 a dozen.

The buyer decides to keep the successful $8.00 retail price in deference to her loyal customers. However, she must maintain an average markup of 37½ percent, so she picks out some of the better-quality suits in the collection and prices them at $10.00 each. In what proportions must she divide the suits according to retail prices to realize her desired average markup percentage?

SOLUTION STEP 1
Find the required average retail price given the new cost:

	$	%
C	$5.50	62½
+MU		37½
R	X	100

Then:

$$\frac{5.50}{62½} = \frac{X}{100}$$

$$62.5X = 550$$

$$X = \$8.80 \text{ (average retail price)}$$

STEP 2

Now find the ratio of $8.00 suits to $10.00 suits to determine how the new purchases should be retailed:

```
Established retail prices              $8.00         $10.00
Average retail price with 37½% MU       8.80           8.80
Difference                             −0.80          +1.20
Reduced to lowest terms                −0.2           +0.3
```

The ratio is 3:2. For every five suits purchased, three should be retailed at $8.00 and two at $10.00 in order to achieve an average markup of 37½ percent.

CHECK YOUR ANSWER

Let us assume that the buyer buys 100 dozen of the swimsuits. Her cost is 100 × $66.00 or $6,600. The retail value of these suits is:

$$\begin{aligned}
3/5 \text{ of } 1{,}200 &= 720 \times \$\,8.00 = \$\,5{,}760 \\
2/5 \text{ of } 1{,}200 &= 480 \times \$10.00 = \underline{4{,}800} \\
\text{Total retail} & \$10{,}560
\end{aligned}$$

The markup percentage is:

$$\begin{aligned}
\text{Markup \%} &= \frac{\$\text{ Markup}}{\$\text{ Retail}} \\
&= \frac{\$\,3{,}960}{\$10{,}560} \\
&= 37\tfrac{1}{2}\% \text{ (average markup)}
\end{aligned}$$

EXERCISES

1. A buyer purchased a special selection of boys' corduroy sport coats for $12.00 each. She decides to retail some of them at her established retail price of $18.00 each but also to set up a new price of $25.00 for some of the more attractive coats. In what proportion must she retail the coats in order to achieve an average markup of 40 percent?

2. A buyer of men's slacks was given the opportunity to buy a selection of double-knits at the low cost of $9.90 a pair. He knew that he could work most of them into his regular $20.00 price line, but wanted to retail some of them at the lower price of $15.00 a pair to attract customers into the store. In what proportion must he sell the slacks to maintain an average markup of 45 percent?

3. A close-out sale of last season's cashmere sweaters was offered to a ladies' sportswear buyer at a cost of $16.00 each. The buyer planned to advertise some of them to sell for only $25.00 but decided to retail those in the more fashionable colors at her regular price of $40.00. If her average markup was planned at 50 percent, in what proportion must she sell the sweaters?

AVERAGE MARKUP WITH ONE COST AND THREE OR MORE RETAIL PRICES

Buyers frequently find merchandise offered at one flat cost that they will wish to sell at more than two retail prices. For example, a job lot may be made up of items of quite different qualities, and the buyer must make a decision as to how best to work them into the existing stock.

ILLUSTRATIVE PROBLEM A basement buyer of infants' wear is offered a job lot of 500 toddler dresses in sizes 3 to 6X by one of her key vendors. The desired average markup is 40 percent, and the dresses are offered to her at an across-the-board cost of $2.00 each. She inspects the dresses carefully and finds that she can work 150 of them into her low-end price line of $1.95 and 100 of them into her better price line of $4.95. In what proportion should she retail the remaining 250 dresses in the lot at her established retail prices of $2.95 and $3.95 in order to achieve the average markup goal of 40 percent?

SOLUTION STEP 1

Find the average retail price for the remainder of the lot.

(a) Let X be the total retail necessary to achieve a 40 percent markup:

	$	%
C	1,000	60
+MU		40
R	X	100

Then

$$\frac{\$1,000}{60} = \frac{X}{100}$$

$$60X = \$100,000$$

$$X = \$\;1,667$$

(b) The dresses already priced will gross:

$$150 \times \$1.95 = \$292.50$$
$$100 \times \$4.95 = \;\;495.00$$
$$\text{Total} \quad\quad\quad\;\; \$787.50$$

(c) The balance of retail needed is:

Total retail at 40% markup	$1,667.00
Less retail of merchandise already priced	787.50
Balance	$ 879.50

(d) Therefore, the average retail price required is:

$$\frac{\$879.50}{250} = \$3.52$$

STEP 2

Now find the ratio of $2.95 dresses to $3.95 dresses:

Established retail prices	$2.95	$3.95
Average retail price	3.52	3.52
Difference	−0.57	+0.43

Thus of every 100 dresses, 57 should be retailed at $3.95 and 43 at $2.95; or 57 percent should be retailed at $3.95 and 43 percent at $2.95.

The dresses will now be retailed as follows:

150 at $1.95	=	$ 390.00
108 at $2.95 (43% of 250)	=	295.00
142 at $3.95 (57% of 250)	=	395.00
100 at $4.95	=	495.00
Total retail		$1,575.00

Note: Experienced buyers will often look at a job lot, decide exactly how the merchandise will fit into their price lines, and then make a decision as to whether the lot should be bought or rejected on the basis of the resulting average markup. Take, for example, the preceding problem. The buyer may well decide after inspecting the dresses that they will fit into her price lines as follows:

200 at $1.95	=	$ 390.00
100 at 2.95	=	295.00
100 at 3.95	=	395.00
100 at 4.95	=	495.00
Total retail		$1,575.00

The resulting markup percentage would be figured as follows:

Retail	=	$1,575.00
Less cost	=	1,000.00
Markup	=	$ 575.00
Markup %	=	$ 575.00
		$1,575.00 = 36.5%

In this case the buyer would probably not buy the job lot, because the average markup that would be obtained is far below her goal of 40 percent. Of course, if the buyer is running well ahead of her markup plan, then she may consider taking the lot.

EXERCISES

1. Ms. Carr, a buyer for the Mayberry Company, has found a selection of 900 girls' jackets at the low cost of $4.00 each. She thinks that half of them should not be sold for more than $5.00 each but that the remaining 450 could be worked into her regular $8.00 and $10.00 price lines. How many should she sell at $8.00 and how many at $10.00 in order to average out with a markup of 40 percent?

2. A shoe buyer is shown a close-out of 500 pairs of bedroom slippers. The cost is $3.00 a pair. He wants an average markup of 42 percent and decides that he can retail 200 pairs of the lot for $3.00 a pair. These will be his loss leaders. He will work the other 300 pairs into his regular $6.00 and $8.00 price lines. How many must he retail at each of these prices?

3. A skirt buyer has located an end-of-season job lot of 2,000 wool skirts at a cost of $10.00 each. She feels she can still sell the skirts at her regular retail prices as follows: 500 at $14.50; 1,000 at $16.00; and 500 at $18.00. Should she buy the job lot if her average markup is planned at 40 percent?

AVERAGE MARKUP WITH TWO COSTS AND ONE RETAIL

As mentioned earlier in this chapter, buyers often find it unwise to carry as many retail prices as there are wholesale prices. Too many retail prices are confusing to customers and therefore make it more difficult to sell the merchandise. They make it necessary to carry a wider assortment of stocks to provide depth in every price line. Inventory-taking also becomes more complicated and burdensome.

Therefore, buyers often try to set one retail price for items which vary slightly in cost. It is important to know how to average markups so that buyers can decide on the proper distribution of merchandise according to varying costs in order to arrive at their desired markup percentages.

ILLUSTRATIVE PROBLEM
A buyer for the bath shop in a department store has had notable success in selling bathroom rugs at $8.00 each. He uses two key vendors and purchases rugs from one at a cost of $4.75 each and from the other at $5.00 each. If his average markup should be 40 percent, in what proportion will he buy the rugs from the two vendors?

SOLUTION

STEP 1
Find the average cost that will yield a 40 percent markup at the retail price of $8.00:

	$	%
C	X	60
+MU		40
R	$8	100

Then:

$$\frac{X}{60} = \frac{\$8}{100}$$

$$100X = \$480$$

$$X = \$4.80 \text{ (average cost)}$$

STEP 2
Now find the required ratio:

Actual costs	$4.75	$5.00
Average cost	4.80	4.80
Difference	−0.05	+0.20
Reduced to lowest terms	−0.01	+0.04

The ratio is 4:1. For every five rugs purchased, four should be bought at $4.75 and one at $5.00.

CHECK YOUR ANSWER
Assume that the buyer has bought 600 rugs. His total cost is $2,280 ($4.75 × 480) plus $600 ($5.00 × 120) or $2,880. Then:

$$\text{Markup \%} = \frac{\$ \text{ Markup}}{\$ \text{ Retail}}$$

$$= \frac{\$1{,}920}{\$4{,}800}$$

$$= 40\% \text{ (average markup)}$$

EXERCISES

1. A buyer of better handbags has a $80 price line. She buys her bags from one manufacturer for $38 each and another for $45 each. If she wants an average markup of 50 percent, what ratio must she use?
2. A buyer of men's sport coats relies on two famous brands. The coats are retailed at $75 each. One manufacturer sells the coats for $40 each and the other for $42 each. How many coats will be purchased from each manufacturer if the total commitment is for 200 coats and an average markup of 45 percent is wanted?
3. A housewares buyer stocks candles costing $.46 and $.50, selling at the same retail price of $.80. If an average markup of 40 percent is desired, in what proportion must she buy the candles?

AVERAGE MARKUP WITH THREE OR MORE COSTS AND ONE RETAIL

Buyers seldom limit themselves to only two vendors when buying goods. They usually visit many showrooms before making final selections. When deciding what to buy for one particular price line of merchandise, they may need to consider a number of costs from different manufacturers.

ILLUSTRATIVE PROBLEM

The owner of a small boutique in Dallas stocks a line of $20 dresses. She estimates that she needs one hundred additional dresses in that price line to last out the current season, so she visits the Dallas Merchandise Mart to see what she can find. She selects some attractive dresses from three different houses costing $10.78, $12.28, and $14.00 each, all of which she wants to work into her $20 price line. Her average markup is 40 percent, so she decides she can buy only 10 percent of the dresses from the $14 house. How many dresses from each of the other two houses should she buy?

SOLUTION

STEP 1
Find the average cost of the dresses, given the retail price and the markup percentage:

	$	%
C	X	60
+MU		40
R	$20	100

Then:

$$\frac{X}{60} = \frac{\$20}{100}$$

$$100X = \$1{,}200$$

$$X = \$12 \text{ (average cost)}$$

STEP 2
Next find the desired ratio to determine how the dresses should be bought:

Cost of 100 dresses	$1,200
Less cost of 10 dresses at $14 each	140
Cost of remaining 90 dresses at $10.78 and $12.28	1,060
Average cost of 90 dresses ($1,060 ÷ 90)	$11.78

Actual costs	$10.78	$12.28
Average cost	11.78	11.78
Difference	− 1.00	+ .50

The ratio is 2:1. Of every three dresses bought, two should be bought at $12.28 and one at $10.78.

STEP 3
Determine the quantity to be bought at each cost:

30 at $10.78 =	$323.40
60 at $12.28 =	736.80
10 at $14.00 =	140.00
Total cost	$1,200.20

CHECK YOUR ANSWER

We have:

$$\text{Cost} + \text{Markup} = \text{Retail}$$

$$\text{Markup \%} = \frac{\$ \text{ Markup}}{\$ \text{ Retail}}$$

$$= \frac{\$ 800}{\$2,000}$$

$$= 40\% \text{ (average markup)}$$

EXERCISES

1. A drugstore buyer decides to buy 200 additional electric razors for the Christmas season. His established competitive retail price is $25, and he wants a 50 percent average markup. The three vendors he has been doing business with charge him $10, $13, and $15 for each electric razor. If 20 percent of the razors are purchased at $15 each, in what proportion should the remaining purchases be distributed?

2. A candy buyer wants four varieties of Valentine's Day boxed chocolates to sell at $2.00 per box. Her average markup is to be 40 percent. The chocolates cost $1.15, $1.20, $1.25, and $1.35 per box. If she plans to buy 20 percent of her chocolates at $1.25 a box and 10 percent at $1.35 a box, in what proportion should she distribute her purchases of the $1.15 and $1.20 varieties to maintain the desired average markup?

3. When his basic stock of white shirts began to run low, a basement men's buyer decided that he needed 100 dozen for immediate delivery. He had been buying three well-known brands at costs of $34.50, $36.00, and $37.00 per dozen. His standard retail price was $4.80 a shirt, and his average markup should be 37½ percent. He decided to order 20 percent of his needs from the manufacturer asking $37.00 per dozen. How many shirts should he order from each of the other two manufacturers?

CHAPTER SUMMARY

When a buyer puts a retail price on merchandise bought, he or she always has a markup percentage goal in mind. For a variety of reasons some markup percentages may exceed the goal, and others may fall short of it. The buyer invariably hopes that by the end of the season, the overall markup percentages will average out very close to the planned figure.

It is advisable to take long markups on some categories of merchandise. Expensive items, such as fine jewelry and furs, need special handling to guard against theft. Fashion merchandise requires above-average markups because of the tendency toward fashion obsolescence. New products are usually given high markups to offset promotional costs. After the products have been accepted and can be mass produced, lower markups become possible.

Staple merchandise can be assigned an average markup, but promotional merchandise is usually given a lower-than-average markup. This is especially true with so-called loss leaders, for example, where there may be no markup or almost no markup at all. To permit loss leaders and special sale merchandise to be sold, however, enough long markups must be taken to insure that the final average markup percentage for the season will be on target.

Buyers often find that job lots afford a means to lift sagging markups. The better-quality items in a lot can be absorbed into regular stock, thus yielding high markups because a job lot is purchased at low cost. The remaining items in the lot may be treated as sale merchandise with average or below-average markups.

It is a good policy to give similar items with only slightly varying costs one retail price. Too many retail prices will confuse both the customers and the sales people. Again, however, the end result, after averaging, should be a markup percentage close to the planned goal.

QUESTIONS FOR REVIEW

1. Explain what is meant by *averaging markups*. Give some reasons why this concept is important.
2. Why is it important to take a longer markup on fashion merchandise than on staple merchandise?
3. Why is it that a box of chocolates may need a higher markup than a box of boys' cotton T-shirts?
4. What is a *loss leader*?
5. Is markup averaging more important in a department using many resources for one category of merchandise? Explain.
6. What are some products that over the years have had their markups lowered because of increased customer acceptance and mass production?
7. If a buyer finds that his or her markup goal is slipping as the season progresses, what is one course of action he or she might take?
8. What kinds of merchandise are very often assigned lower-than-average markups?
9. What is a *job lot*?

10. Why is it not practical to carry as many retail prices as there are wholesale prices?

DISCUSSION QUESTION	How can a buyer purchase job lots in order to improve his average markup position? What are some of the risks involved?
PROBLEMS FOR REVIEW	1. A merchandise manager indicates her dissatisfaction with a department's markup, which is now running at 41 percent while planned at 42 percent. Assuming a total available inventory of $100,000 at cost and $169,500 at retail, what is the markup that the buyer must put on his current purchases of $25,000 at cost in order to achieve a total markup of 42 percent? 2. A fabrics buyer has an inventory at the beginning of the month worth $30,000 at cost and $45,000 at retail. Her new purchases during the month amount to $20,000 at cost and $35,000 at retail. If she intends to buy more merchandise worth $15,000 at retail before the month is over, what must she pay for it to insure an average markup of 38 percent? 3. The owner of a small stationery store decides to increase her stock by $25,000 in retail value for the back-to-school season. She already has merchandise on hand amounting to $14,000 at cost and $23,000 at retail prices. What must the markup be on the new merchandise to result in an average markup of 36 percent? 4. A women's sportswear buyer purchased merchandise costing $30,000, which represented her open-to-buy for the month. She marked up the merchandise 52 percent and then found an outstanding job lot that would cost her an additional $8,000. What markup would she need on this lot to yield an average markup of 50 percent? 5. An attractive job lot of boys' dress shirts was offered to a buyer for $28.80 per dozen. The buyer thought he could retail them at $3.95 and $4.25 each. In what proportion must he divide the lot into these retail prices to arrive at an average markup of 40 percent? 6. A pillow buyer can buy both velvet and corduroy pillows at the same price of $4.95 each. She decides to retail the velvet pillows at $9.25 each and the corduroy ones at $8.50 each. In what proportion must she distribute her purchases of the two kinds of pillows to give her an average markup of 45 percent? 7. A special close-out of 300 designer dresses are offered to a discount house for a cost of $48.14 each. The buyer decides that she can retail 150 of them for $95 each. How many should she retail at $70 and $80 to achieve her desired average markup goal of 42 percent? 8. A buyer of sporting goods has his basketballs priced at $20 each. He can buy some balls from one manufacturer for $10 and the rest from another manufacturer for $10.50 each. In what proportion should he distribute his purchases of basketballs to realize an average markup of 48 percent? 9. An assistant glove buyer is looking for merchandise for the annual

Assistant Buyer's Day sale. She needs 1,000 pairs of leather gloves, which she wants to retail at $10 a pair with an average markup of 38 percent. She finds some excellent gloves in one showroom for $6 a pair and another fine selection in another showroom for $6.50 a pair. How many gloves should she purchase from each vendor?

10. A buyer of men's furnishings wants to retail all of his support stockings at $5.00 a pair and maintain a 40 percent average markup. He stocks three top brands at costs of $38.40, $36.60, and $35.16 per dozen. If he wants 20 percent of his stock made up of the most expensive brand, in what proportion should he stock the other two brands?

CASE PROBLEMS

A CASE FOR UNISEX

Jane Bixby and Bill Baxter are both young buyers for a large-volume department store in the Northeast. Ms. Bixby buys girls' wear in sizes 7 through 14, and Mr. Baxter is responsible for boys' wear sizes 8 through 20. Contrary to the way most large stores are organized, the infants' wear and all the boys' and girls' wear departments are grouped together in one division. The merchandise manager for this division is Anne Fielding, a veteran retailer with nearly forty years of experience. Both Ms. Bixby and Mr. Baxter joined the store only five years ago and were enrolled in the same junior executive training program. Now in their third year as buyers, they have just returned from their first buying trip abroad.

One of their major commitments while in Europe was a large order of Danish toggle coats. They had attended a trade show together in Copenhagen and had become acquainted with a friendly Danish vendor who subsequently offered them an excellent buy. The all-wool coat, which came with bone buttons and a hood, seemed far superior in workmanship and quality to similar car or stadium coats manufactured in the United States. Even with the addition of all the extra costs for shipping and import duties, the total cost would be so reasonable that a markup of 65 percent seemed logical. Both buyers were delighted with this long markup, since it would help to bring up the average markups in their respective departments.

Six months later, the receiving-room manager calls Mr. Baxter to tell him the coats have arrived. Mr. Baxter immediately contacts Ms. Bixby and Ms. Fielding and asks them to join him in the receiving room to inspect the shipment. He crosses his fingers that the coats will appear as attractive as they did in Copenhagen.

He arrives in the receiving room first, and begins examining the boys' coats and finds them to be made exactly according to specifications. They are indeed beautiful. Then he walks over to where the girls' coats are hanging. At first glance they appear to be just as beautiful. Suddenly, however, he realizes that something is very wrong. The boys' and girls' coats are all alike! While in Copenhagen, the two buyers thought they had made it very clear to the Danish vendor that in the United States boys' coats button on the right-hand side and girls' coats on the left-hand side. The Dane spoke English well, and it did not seem necessary to include this specification on the purchase orders.

Now the two women arrive. Ms. Bixby realizes almost immediately with dismay that hers are boys' coats, not girls' coats. It is already late August. She has 2,000 coats she cannot use, and Copenhagen seems far, far away. Ms. Fielding is furious. She says, "Jane, come to my office. We are going to call that Dane collect and tell him what he's done to your coats. Then we'll decide what to do."

1. What courses of action are open to Ms. Bixby?
2. In your opinion, were the two buyers negligent when they placed the orders?
3. If you were Ms. Bixby, would you do business with the Danish vendor again?

A HARD BARGAIN

"I'll buy your line with one condition: give me an exclusive agency and get rid of all those little stores in the suburbs!"

The young sales representative was stunned. He has been trying to sell women's shoes to this store, the largest in Birmingham, ever since he took over the territory just a year ago. He has called on Martha every time he has been in town, and they have become friendly enough to have enjoyed several bowling dates together. Bowling is Martha's favorite sport, and a night at the lanes is her idea of a perfect evening *if* business isn't discussed. Now after all his hard work, victory was at hand, or almost.

"Martha, would you give that to me again?" the sales representative asked. "Look, friend, I like your line of shoes. It's nationally advertised, has a reputation for fine quality, and I can use the long markup I'll get. You've told me about your promotion plans, and the store can certainly benefit from the cooperative advertising money you've offered. I've heard you deliver on time. Your shoes will add some prestige to my department, and since the store is 'trading up' right now, my merchandise manager will be pleased. But I want to be able to advertise 'Ours Alone in Birmingham.' Get the point?"

"Martha, do you really mean you won't buy from me unless I stop selling to the smaller stores? I've got my shoes in six specialty stores in the area. Some of these buyers have been giving our company business for twenty years! I can't just tell them the party's over. Surely, you don't expect me to do that!"

"Suit yourself. I've told you how I'll buy your line. If you're interested, I'll sit down with you next week and we'll map out our fall program."

1. If you were the sales representative, how would you deal with this proposal?
2. How could an exclusive-agency arrangement benefit both the buyer and the seller?

5

HOW
TO
PLAN
MARKUP

KEY POINTS

1. The first markup applied to merchandise is called the initial markup. It must be high enough to cover retail reductions, operating expenses, and expected profits.

2. Retail reductions take away from the original selling price. They include markdowns, discounts to employees and customers, and shortages.

3. Maintained markup is the actual markup achieved at the end of the season after the retail reductions have been subtracted from the initial markup.

4. Gross margin is found by subtracting total merchandise costs from net sales. It is the same as maintained markup unless cash discounts and alteration expenses are involved.

5. Cash discounts earned can turn an unprofitable operation into a profitable one.

INITIAL MARKUP

In our discussions so far we have referred to markup in a very general way, that is, as the difference between the cost of an article and its selling price. We have also discussed *individual, cumulative,* and *average* markups, and explained how the markup on one piece of merchandise or on large numbers of merchandise can be calculated. We have also discussed how buyers strive to meet a markup goal and how important it is to average markups to meet the goals.

It is now necessary to make a further distinction in our concept of markup. A markup on an item usually does not stay constant during the course of a selling season. Some merchandise does not sell well, so it is reduced in price. Some merchandise is stolen, some is broken or damaged, and some is sold at discounts to employees and customers. It is rare, indeed, that when a buyer buys $6,000 worth of goods and marks them up by $4,000, the full $10,000 will be obtained in sales.

The *first* markup put on merchandise is called the *initial markup.* It is the margin between cost and original retail price and should be high enough to cover retail reductions, operating expenses, and the expected profit. Expenses and profit have already been discussed in Chapter 2. It is now time to examine the nature of retail reductions.

Retail reductions take away from the original selling price of an item. They include markdowns, discounts to employees and customers, and shortages. A *markdown* lowers the selling price to promote the quick sale of an item. Markdowns will be discussed at greater length in the next chapter. *Discounts* are regularly given to employees as a fringe benefit and as an incentive to increase sales volume. The amount of employee discount allowed varies from store to store. Many stores permit discounts between 10 and 20 percent on all items purchased, but some often allow a much higher discount on clothing to be worn during working hours. Customer discounts may be given on merchandise that has been soiled or damaged or to meet competition when it appears that customer goodwill may be in jeopardy.

Shortages are the difference between book inventory and physical inventory, that is, between the amount of merchandise that should be on hand and the amount actually on hand. Shortages may occur for a variety of reasons: merchandise may be lost, stolen, or broken; there may have been improper handling of cash or charge transactions, errors in counting merchandise, or mistakes made by the bookkeeping department. But it is the shortage caused by pilferage by both customers and employees that has been of particular concern to retailers in recent years. Across the nation, store theft has increased by about 174 percent just in the last decade. The loss amounted to $3.5 billion in 1972 alone, according to the National Retail Merchants Association. Generally stores lose between 2 and 5 per-

Retailers have had to take severe measures to combat pilferage of merchandise.
SOURCE: Cary Wolinsky/Grafia

cent of sales each year due to theft. One might think that as people become more affluent, store theft would decrease. However, this does not seem to be the case. Authorities offer two reasons for the enormous increase in shoplifting. They say that today's moral values permit it and that the method of merchandising, with its emphasis on eye appeal and easy availability of goods, encourages it.[1]

Pilferage has become such a major problem that stores have had to adopt extreme measures to help combat it. In addition to the usual corps of store detectives, many stores have installed an electromagnetic tag system for use in apparel departments. When an article of clothing is purchased, a tag is deactivated by a special machine; if the tag is not deactivated, a buzzer will sound. Some stores use television cameras and screens to monitor selling floors, and others have two-way mirrors or observation vents in women's and men's dressing rooms. As an additional security measure some even use trained dogs to patrol the stores after business hours.

In spite of these antishoplifting programs, however, store theft continues to increase. The consumers are the ultimate victims, because stores must raise prices to cover their losses.

MAINTAINED MARKUP

The markup that the buyer actually realizes on his goods is called *maintained markup*; it is what is achieved after retail reductions have been subtracted from the initial markup. It is a more realistic measure of profitability than the initial markup, because it indicates the actual amount of money obtained after the merchandise has been sold. To put it in another way, the initial markup is the "hoped for" markup, and the maintained markup is the "achieved" markup. The season must be completed before buyers can see how well their planning has paid off. Naturally buyers strive for as high a maintained markup as possible, since it has an important bearing on how much net profit is finally realized.

ILLUSTRATIVE PROBLEM The owner of a small boutique, My Flair Lady, plans purchases of merchandise worth $6,000 for her upcoming spring season. She plans to retail the merchandise at $10,000. She knows that some of the merchandise will not sell at the original retail price, so she has included in her plans markdowns totaling $1,000. (a) What is her initial markup percentage? (b) What will be her maintained markup percentage?

SOLUTION The initial markup percentage measures what the manager hopes to retail her goods for, and maintained markup percentage measures what actually happens. In this case, the hoped for retail of $10,000 will be reduced in value to $9,000 after the planned markdowns of $1,000 have been taken. The cost remains the same.

[1]Irene Backalenick, "Spreading suburban menace: shoplifting, mainly among young," *New York Times*, October 17, 1972, p. 46.

(a) Find the initial markup percentage:

Cost + Initial markup = Original retail

Then

Initial markup = Original retail − Cost
= $10,000 − $6,000
= $4,000

And

$$\text{Initial markup \%} = \frac{\$ \text{ Initial markup}}{\$ \text{ Original retail}}$$
$$= \frac{\$ 4{,}000}{\$10{,}000} \text{ or } 4/10$$
$$= 40\%$$

(b) Find the maintained markup percentage (remember that the retail and sales figures are the same because sales are made at retail):

Cost + Maintained Markup = Retail (net sales)

Then

Maintained markup = Net sales − Cost
= $9,000 − $6,000
= $3,000

And

$$\text{Maintained markup \%} = \frac{\$ \text{ Maintained markup}}{\$ \text{ Sales}}$$
$$= \frac{\$3{,}000}{\$9{,}000} \text{ or } 1/3$$
$$= 33\ 1/3\%$$

ILLUSTRATIVE PROBLEM A luggage buyer bought 100 briefcases at a cost of $15.00 each. He decided to retail them at $25.00 each. Some of the briefcases, however, did not sell during the season, so he marked them down by a total of $400. Also several coworkers had bought them at a total employee discount of $100. (a) What was the buyer's initial markup percentage? (b) What was his maintained markup percentage?

SOLUTION (a) Find the initial markup percentage:

Cost + Initial markup = Original retail

Initial markup = Original retail − Cost
= $2,500 − $1,500
= $1,000

Then

Initial markup % = $\dfrac{\$ \text{ Initial markup}}{\$ \text{ Original retail}}$

$= \dfrac{\$1{,}000}{\$2{,}500}$

$= 40\%$

(b) Find the maintained markup percentage:

Cost + Maintained markup = Net sales

Maintained markup = Net sales − Cost
 = $2,000 − $1,500
 = $500

Also

Maintained markup % = $\dfrac{\$ \text{ Maintained markup}}{\$ \text{ Net sales}}$

$= \dfrac{\$500}{\$2{,}000}$

$= 25\%$

EXERCISES

1. A buyer of men's furnishings bought 100 dozen ties at $36 a dozen. He retailed them for $5.00 a tie. During the season, 600 of the ties didn't sell and were marked down to $4.00 each. (a) What was the initial markup percentage? (b) What was the maintained markup percentage?
2. A men's store bought 100 sport coats at $30 each and retailed them for $60 each. All but 20 of the coats sold at the regular price, and the remaining 20 were marked down to $40 for quick clearance. Compute (a) the initial markup percentage and (b) the maintained markup percentage after all the coats were sold.
3. A toy buyer was concerned with the effect of pilferage on the profit performance of her department. During the season she had bought merchandise for $50,000, which she had retailed for $80,000. Total markdowns had amounted to $4,000, and discounts to employees and customers had totaled $500. Yet the inventory results showed a whopping $1,500 in shortages. What was the maintained markup percentage at the end of the season?

ILLUSTRATIVE PROBLEM

At the end of the season the owner of a small stationery store found that she had realized net sales of $80,000. During the six-month period, she had taken markdowns of $1,200, given discounts of $600 to employees, and had shortages amounting to $1,200. The merchandise had cost $50,000. (a) What was the maintained markup percentage? (b) How should the initial markup percentage have been planned?

SOLUTION When the net sales figure is given instead of the original retail, the retail reductions must be *added* to the sales figure to obtain the original retail. It is impossible to subtract retail reductions as before because the net sales figure already reflects what has transpired during the season; i.e., markdowns were taken, discounts given, and shortages recorded. The original retail figure is almost always higher than the net sales figure, and the initial markup percentage is greater than the maintained markup percentage.

(a) Find the maintained markup percentage:

Cost + Maintained markup = Retail (Net sales)

$$\begin{aligned}\text{Maintained markup} &= \text{Net sales} - \text{Cost} \\ &= \$80{,}000 - \$50{,}000 \\ &= \$30{,}000\end{aligned}$$

Then

$$\begin{aligned}\text{Maintained markup \%} &= \frac{\$30{,}000}{\$80{,}000} \\ &= 37.5\%\end{aligned}$$

(b) Find the initial markup percentage:

Cost + Initial markup = Original retail

$$\begin{aligned}\text{Initial markup} &= \text{Original retail} - \text{Cost} \\ &= (\$80{,}000 + \$1{,}200 + \$600 + \$1{,}200) \\ &\quad - \$50{,}000 \\ &= \$83{,}000 - \$50{,}000 \\ &= \$33{,}000\end{aligned}$$

Therefore,

$$\begin{aligned}\text{Initial markup \%} &= \frac{\$33{,}000}{\$83{,}000} \\ &= 39.8\%\end{aligned}$$

EXERCISES

1. A buyer plans to purchase some merchandise costing $10,000. His planned net sales are $20,000, including planned markdowns of $1,000. What should be his initial markup percentage?
2. It is expected that jewelry costing $30,000 will finally sell for $65,000. Planned markdowns total $5,000 and shortages are estimated at $3,000. Determine (a) the initial markup percentage and (b) the maintained markup percentage.
3. A buyer of women's dresses had invested heavily in midi-length styles and was forced to plan heavy markdowns amounting to $15,000 in order to move the merchandise. Discounts amounting to $3,000 and shortages totaling $2,000 were also planned. Net sales of $90,000 were forecast. What should the initial markup percentage be if the merchandise had cost $50,000?

GROSS MARGIN

It has been said that maintained markup is the markup achieved after retail reductions have been subtracted from the initial markup. Therefore, maintained markup is actually the difference between the net sales and the gross cost of the merchandise. The merchandising term for the difference between the net sales and the *total* merchandising costs is *gross margin*.

The two factors that change gross cost to total cost, thereby changing maintained markup to gross margin, are (1) cash discounts and (2) alteration expenses. If neither of these are present, which is unlikely, the maintained markup and the gross margin are exactly the same.

Cash Discounts

Cash discounts are often given to a store by a manufacturer if payments for merchandise are made on or before the due date. For example, an invoice for $600 worth of merchandise may contain the purchase term "2/10, net 30," meaning that the store will be allowed a 2 percent cash discount if the invoice is paid no later than ten days after the date on which the invoice was issued and the full amount must be paid within thirty days. Cash discounts reduce the cost of the merchandise and are subtracted from the gross cost to give a net cost.[2] Buyers are under considerable pressure to obtain high cash discounts, but it is the controller's office that is responsible for paying the invoices ahead of time.

The reason cash discounts are so important to a store is that they act as a *profit cushion*.[3] The retailer sets his selling price according to the gross cost of the merchandise. If a cash discount is granted by the manufacturer, it acts as a contribution to profit. Since cash discounts earned often amount to over 2 percent of net sales, a store showing a loss of 1 percent can become a profitable operation by paying all its bills promptly.

When manufacturers for some reason do not want to allow cash discounts, they are often asked to *load the invoice*, that is, raise the gross cost of the merchandise to permit a cash discount that will yield the original net cost. In this way, the retailer can nevertheless add a discount as a profit cushion. Loading the invoice and cash discounts will be considered in greater detail in Chapter 14.

Alteration Expense

Most stores find it necessary at times to make alterations on their merchandise to satisfy particular customer needs. Sometimes customers are charged for these alterations, and sometimes they are not. Alterations are

---

[2]Some stores treat cash discounts earned as "other income" and show it as an addition to the operating profit.

[3]Jerome M. Ney, *The Buyer's Manual,* National Retail Merchants Association, New York, 1965, p. 90.

Alterations expenses must often be assumed, at least in part, by retailers.
SOURCE: Cary Wolinsky/Grafia

usually associated with the sale of clothing, but they also occur when carpeting, draperies, silver, furniture, and other items are sold. Stores that are customer-service oriented frequently perform alterations with little or no charge. However, with labor costs skyrocketing, more and more stores are finding it necessary to pass along some or all alteration costs to their customers. Even when charges are made, however, stores find that the receipts are usually not sufficient to cover actual alterations costs, so they constitute an extra expense in doing business. This expense is added to the net cost of the merchandise sold to yield the *total* merchandise cost.

The following figures illustrate how cash discounts and alteration expenses can affect gross margin:

Net sales		$100,000
Gross cost of merchandise sold	$77,000	
Less cash discounts earned	3,000	
Net cost of merchandise sold	$74,000	
Add alteration expenses	1,000	
Total merchandise cost		75,000
Gross margin		$ 25,000

Using the same figures, we can show the relation between maintained markup and gross margin as follows:

Net sales	$100,000
Gross cost of merchandise sold	77,000
Maintained markup	23,000
Add cash discounts earned	3,000
	$ 26,000
Less alteration expenses	1,000
Gross margin	$ 25,000

Still another way of showing this relationship is:

Gross margin = Maintained markup + Cash discounts earned − Alteration expenses

Maintained markup = Gross margin − Cash discounts earned + Alteration expenses

It is interesting to note that gross margin is usually higher than maintained markup, because cash discounts earned are often larger than alteration expenses.

ILLUSTRATIVE PROBLEM The net sales in a silver department for the month were $53,000. The gross cost of the merchandise was $30,000. There was a total markdown of $2,000. Cash discounts were $1,500, and engraving expenses amounted to $500. What were the department's (a) maintained markup and (b) gross margin?

SOLUTION The markdown figure of $2,000 is not needed in this problem, because it is already included in the net sales figure. Engraving, on the other hand, is one type of alteration.

(a) Find the maintained markup:

Maintained markup = Net sales − Gross cost of merchandise
  = $53,000 − $30,000
  = $23,000

(b) Find the gross margin:

Gross margin = Maintained markup + Cash discounts − Alteration expenses
  = $23,000 + $1,500 − $500
  = $24,000

ILLUSTRATIVE PROBLEM A boys' clothing department had a gross margin of $83,000. Alteration expenses were $2,000, and cash discounts earned were $3,100. What was the department's maintained markup?

SOLUTION Maintained markup = Gross margin − Cash discounts + Alteration expenses
  = $83,000 − $3,100 + $2,000
  = $81,900

EXERCISES
1. What was the gross margin of a department that had a maintained markup of $30,000, markdowns of $3,000, alteration expenses of $1,500, and cash discounts of $2,000?
2. The net sales of a tobacco shop for the month of February were $10,000. The gross cost of the merchandise was $5,000. Cash discounts earned totaled $250. What were (a) the maintained markup and (b) the gross margin?
3. Determine the maintained markup of a health food store that had a gross margin of $60,000 and cash discounts earned of $3,000.

MARKUP RELATIONS EXPRESSED IN PERCENTAGES

So far we have explained the concepts of initial markup, maintained markup, and gross margin with dollar figures instead of percentage figures because students usually find dollar concepts easier to grasp. However, in planning business expenses, profit, retail reductions, and alteration costs, percentage figures are often used instead of dollar amounts. With the exception of initial markups, which are calculated on the basis of the original retail price, planned figures are usually expressed as percentages of net sales. Percentage figures lend themselves to meaningful comparison with the operations of other stores; comparisons of dollar figures alone, on the other hand, mean very little. For example, a store with a yearly sales volume of $200,000 and an expense percentage of 30 percent has expenses amounting to $60,000; another store with a sales volume of $150,000 and an expense percentage of 31 percent has expenses totaling $46,500. The percentage figures show that the two stores compare favorably with each other in terms of business efficiency. The dollar figures, on the other hand, are very misleading unless the sales volumes are also known.

Initial Markup as a Percentage

Earlier in the chapter it was stated that the initial markup must be large enough to cover expenses, profit, and retail reductions. Later it was shown that cash discounts earned can help reduce the amount of initial markup needed for a certain profit goal. Alteration expenses, however, are additional expenses in doing business.

The following formula should be used when finding the initial markup as a percentage:

$$\text{Initial markup \%} = \frac{\text{Expense \% + Operating profit \% + Reduction \% - Cash discounts earned \% + Alteration expenses \%}}{\text{Net Sales \% + Reduction \%}}$$

It is important to remember that the net sales alone cannot be used as the base. Retail reductions must be added to the net sales (which is always considered 100 percent) to obtain the correct original retail percentage.

If there are no cash discounts or alteration expenses, it was said that gross margin and maintained markup are the same. Expenses plus profits equal gross margin or maintained markup, so the formula may be simplified as follows:

$$\text{Initial markup \%} = \frac{\text{Gross margin (or Maintained markup) \% + Reduction \%}}{\text{Net sales \% + Reduction \%}}$$

ILLUSTRATIVE PROBLEM

What should the initial markup percentage be in a department having the following planned figures:

Operating profit	4%	Operating expenses	34%
Shortages	2%	Alteration expenses	1%
Employee discounts	3%	Cash discounts	2%
Markdowns	6%		

SOLUTION

Using the formula above, we have:

$$\text{Initial markup \%} = \frac{34\% + 4\% + 11\% - 2\% + 1\%}{100\% + 11\%}$$

$$= \frac{48\%}{111\%}$$

$$= 43.2\%$$

EXERCISES

1. A store has a gross margin of 37 percent, markdowns of 6 percent, and discounts to employees of 2 percent. What is the initial markup percentage?
2. The expenses of a department are 30 percent, the operating profit is 5 percent, and reductions total 6 percent. Find (a) the maintained markup percentage and (b) the initial markup percentage.
3. Determine the initial markup percentage of a department with the following planned figures:

Operating expenses	33%
Operating profit	3%
Markdowns	5%
Discount to employees	1%
Cash discount earned	3%
Shortages	2%

Maintained Markup as a Percentage

Maintained markup is the markup actually realized on sales. In dollar figures it is easy to subtract reductions from the original retail to get a sales figure.

When working with percentages, however, we cannot just subtract the reduction percentage from the initial markup percentage to obtain the maintained markup percentage, since the initial markup percentage is based on the original retail, whereas the reduction percentage is based on net sales. Moreover, when the original retail is reduced in value through reductions, there is also a reduction in cost. The reductions, then, represent the depreciation in both the cost and the retail value of the goods. To take into account the cost portion of the reduction, we may use the following formula when the percentages are known:

Maintained markup % = Initial markup % − Reduction %
× (100% − Initial markup %)

ILLUSTRATIVE PROBLEM The initial markup of a department is 50 percent. The markdowns total 8 percent, and the shortages are 2 percent. What is the maintained markup percentage?

SOLUTION Maintained markup % = Initial markup % − Reduction %
× (100% − Initial markup %)
= 0.50 − 0.10 × 0.50
= 0.50 − 0.05
= 0.45 or 45%

CHECK YOUR ANSWER Now, substitute dollar figures for percentages. Suppose that the cost of the goods in the above problem is $5,500 and the original retail is $11,000. Reductions amount to $1,000. We have:

Cost + Initial markup = Original retail
Initial markup = Original retail − Cost
= $11,000 − $5,500
= $5,500

Initial markup % = $\frac{\$5,500}{\$11,000}$
= 50%

And

Cost + Maintained markup = Net sales
Maintained markup = Net sales − Cost
= $10,000 − $5,500
= $4,500

Maintained markup % = $\frac{\$4,500}{\$10,000}$
= 45%

Gross Margin as a Percentage

We recall that maintained markup and gross margin are the same unless there are cash discounts and alteration costs. Once we have the maintained markup, it is easy enough to find the gross margin by adding cash discounts and subtracting alteration costs.

ILLUSTRATIVE PROBLEM A hosiery department has an initial markup of 43 percent. Markdowns are 4 percent; shortages, 2 percent; cash discounts, 2 percent; and expenses, 34 percent. Find (a) the maintained markup percentage and (b) the gross margin percentage.

SOLUTION (a) Find the maintained markup percentage:

$$\begin{aligned}\text{Maintained markup \%} &= \text{Initial markup \%} - \text{Reduction \%} \\ &\quad \times (100\% - \text{Initial markup \%}) \\ &= 0.43 - 0.06 \times 0.57 \\ &= 0.43 - 0.0342 \\ &= 39.6\%\end{aligned}$$

(b) Find the gross margin %:

$$\begin{aligned}\text{Gross margin \%} &= \text{Maintained markup \%} + \text{Cash discount \%} \\ &\quad - \text{Alteration cost \%} \\ &= 39.6\% + 2\% \\ &= 41.6\%\end{aligned}$$

EXERCISES

1. Find the maintained markup percentage for a department with the following figures:

Initial markup	44%
Alteration costs	1%
Markdowns	5%
Shortages	1%

2. What is the gross margin percentage for a department having an initial markup of 45 percent, cash discounts of 3 percent, alteration costs of 1 percent, markdowns of 6 percent, discounts to employees of 1 percent, and shortages of 3 percent?

3. Find (a) the maintained markup percentage and (b) the gross margin percentage for a fur department with an initial markup of 54 percent, markdowns of 10 percent, alteration expenses of 3 percent, shortages of 2 percent, and cash discounts earned of 2 percent.

CHAPTER SUMMARY When merchandise is bought, it is marked up to its original selling price. This first markup is called the initial markup, and the hope is that the value of the merchandise will remain constant as the season progresses. This seldom happens, however. Retail reductions erode the initial retail value: slow-moving merchandise is marked down, discounts are given to employees and customers, and shortages occur.

The actual markup achieved on season purchases is referred to as the maintained markup. It is the difference between the gross cost and what the merchandise is finally sold for (net sales). Net sales are realized after retail reductions have been deducted from the original selling price. Thus the maintained markup is always less than the initial markup.

The maintained markup is equal to the gross margin, unless cash discounts and alteration costs are involved. Cash discounts are sometimes granted by manufacturers when retailers pay their bills on or before the due dates. They can easily add up to a significant amount and provide a profit cushion that may make the difference between an operating profit and an operating loss. Alterations are often necessary before merchandise can be effectively sold. Even though a store may charge for part or all of the alterations represented, alterations nevertheless are often an expense to the store. Cash discounts and alteration expenses make the difference between gross costs and total costs, and between maintained markup and gross margin. If the maintained markup is known, then the gross margin is obtained by adding cash discounts earned and subtracting the alteration costs.

It is more useful to express initial markups, maintained markups, and gross margins in percentages than in dollars because percentage comparisons with other stores are meaningful, whereas dollar amounts are often not. The initial markup is expressed as a percentage of the original selling price, whereas the maintained markup and gross margin are expressed as percentages of net sales. When working with percentages, these different bases must be recognized. Reductions in dollars may be subtracted from the initial markup in dollars to obtain the maintained markup. This simple subtraction is not possible when using percentage figures because of the difference in bases, and the loss in the cost value as well as the retail value of the goods must be considered.

QUESTIONS FOR REVIEW

1. What is the difference between the initial markup and maintained markup?
2. Name the three types of retail reductions.
3. Distinguish between a customer discount and an employee discount and explain why stores regularly give them.
4. How do you account for the marked increase in customer and employee pilferage in recent years?
5. What are the ways in which stores with which you are familiar have combated pilferage?
6. Explain the difference between gross costs and total costs.
7. In a men's clothing store is it possible for gross margin to be the same as maintained markup?
8. Why are manufacturers willing to give cash discounts to stores?
9. What are some store transactions that might involve alteration expenses?
10. Why is it not possible to subtract the retail reduction percentage from the initial markup percentage to obtain the maintained markup percentage?

DISCUSSION QUESTION

In a practical sense should consumers be concerned about the increased store losses due to shoplifting? Why?

PROBLEMS FOR REVIEW

1. A store realized net sales of $65,000 during the first year of operation. Markdowns totaled $5,000; discounts to employees, $500; and shortages, $1,300. What was the initial markup percentage if the cost of the merchandise was $40,000?
2. A department's planned purchases for a season are $26,000, to be retailed at $50,000. Markdowns are planned at $2,500 and shortages at $1,500. What will be the maintained markup percentage?
3. A buyer of boys' wear bought 100 dozen boys' dungarees at $25 a dozen for a special sale. They were retailed at $3.50 a pair. Most were sold during the sale, but markdowns amounting to $300 were necessary to clear out what remained. What was the initial markup percentage and what was the actual maintained markup percentage?
4. A fur department enjoyed record sales of $325,000 during the month of August. The gross cost of the merchandise was $160,000, but cash discounts earned amounted to $3,000. Alteration expenses were $1,000. What were the department's maintained markup and gross margin?
5. If a department's gross margin was $74,000, cash discounts were $1,200, and alteration costs were $800, what was the maintained markup?
6. The maintained markup of a department was $62,000. Cash discounts earned were $1,300, and expenses were $50,000. If net sales were $130,000, what was the percentage of gross margin and operating profit?
7. What was the initial markup percentage of a store with the following planned figures:

Operating expenses	35%	Cash discounts	2%
Operating profit	8%	Shortages	1%
Markdowns	5%	Employee discounts	1%

8. If the gross margin was 43 percent, markdowns were 5 percent, employee discounts were 1 percent, and shortages were 3 percent, what was the initial markup percentage?
9. The initial markup of a department is 52 percent. If markdowns are 7 percent, shortages are 2 percent, and alteration expenses are 1 percent, what is the maintained markup percentage?
10. Find the gross margin percentage of a department, given an initial markup of 54 percent, cash discounts of 2 percent, alteration expenses of 1 percent, and markdowns of 7 percent.

CASE PROBLEM

THE BROKEN RULE

Although sales at the ABC department store showed a healthy increase of 7 percent over the previous year, net profit was down. Store officials attributed this decline to many reasons, some of which were (1) a minimum wage increase that raised payroll costs, (2) huge markdowns taken in the apparel departments because dresses did not sell as anticipated, (3) a hefty increase in the cost of supplies, and (4) an alarming jump in losses due to theft.

In an effort to hold down spiraling costs, the store decided to wage an extensive austerity campaign. A special task force, made up of some of the store's chief executives, was appointed by the president to find ways to save money. Two of their recommendations have already been put into effect: (1) training sessions to teach sales personnel how to spot and handle shoplifters and (2) the replacement of some full-time sales people with part-time help.

At one of the task force meetings the controller comes up with an idea to reduce retail reductions. He suggests that they reexamine the policy of employee discounts. The policy is to allow a 20 percent discount on all store purchases and a 30 percent discount on personal clothing. The controller notes that this type of reduction has been running at about 1 percent of sales, which he feels is about twice as much as it should be.

Although each employee is issued a discount card for personal use only, it is common knowledge that discounts are also given regularly to friends and relatives. Supervisory personnel have grown lax in enforcing the discount rules. Just recently a new assistant buyer, conscientious and eager to follow store policy, was severely criticized for refusing to approve a discount for the mother of the head of the management division. The woman had become highly distraught when asked to produce a discount card and even more upset when the discount was denied because she could not produce a card.

The store finally decides to reduce employee discounts to 10 percent on all purchases except personal clothing, for which the discount will be 20 percent. In addition, it is decided that a three-month tabulation by employee name will be issued on total discounts given. If it can be proved that an employee has abused his or her discount privileges, the employee will be asked to forfeit his or her card and will be subject to other possible disciplinary actions.

1. Do you think that the store is right in reducing the discounts to employees and tightening the enforcement of the privilege?
2. What is a store's purpose in granting employee discounts?
3. Should store rules apply equally to everyone, or should store executives be granted special privileges?

6

HOW TO PLAN MARKDOWNS

KEY POINTS

1. A markdown reduces the retail value of goods and is most often taken when the merchandise fails to sell at its original price.

2. Early markdowns are usually favored by high-volume promotionally oriented stores and late markdowns by prestigious less promotionally oriented stores.

3. Three successive markdowns are usually sufficient to clear away most stocks of slow-moving goods.

4. A price-change form is used to effect a markdown, a markdown cancellation, or an additional markup.

5. Markdowns can be minimized if the buyer is skilled at applying the "five rights" of merchandising.

MARKDOWN DEFINED

A markdown is a *reduction* in the selling price of a piece of merchandise. It is often necessary when merchandise does not sell at the original price. Markdowns are one of three types of retail reductions, as explained in Chapter 5, that reduce the retail values of goods. They are usually expressed in terms of dollars and cents or as a percentage of net sales.

Markdowns are planned for an entire season just as the initial markup, sales, purchases, expenses, and profit are. However, markdown planning should not be thought of as a goal, but rather as a guide. If markdown estimates are too high, the initial markup will also be high, perhaps too high to meet local competition. Conversely, if markdown estimates are too low, the resulting initial markup may not be high enough to provide a sufficient gross margin to insure a satisfactory profit.

CAUSES OF MARKDOWNS

The causes of markdowns may be classified in many different ways, but it is useful to place them in three major groups: (1) errors in buying and selling, (2) as an operational device, and (3) as merchandising devices to promote sales.

Errors in Buying and Selling

Many markdowns can be avoided if buyers do not make errors in judgment when buying merchandise. Very often faulty sales planning causes too much merchandise to be bought. Sometimes buyers are not sufficiently sensitive to customer tastes and buy the wrong things. Inexperienced buyers may buy what they themselves like rather than what will actually sell. Bad timing is another frequent cause of markdowns. Goods may arrive too late for maximum sales exposure or too early for consumer purchase.

Buyers should see to it that their goods arrive at the right time. Buyers sometimes also do not inspect incoming shipments thoroughly and discover defects too late. Merchandise is often ordered in the wrong sizes because the buyers' size studies are not up to date.

The sales force also has an important influence on how many markdowns are taken. It is natural for sales people to show their own favorite merchandise first while other merchandise suffers from benign neglect. In spite of pressure from the buyer, some sales people fail to follow the "first-in, first-out" (FIFO) rule, thus causing future markdowns because some merchandise becomes aged and soiled. Some sales people, especially those on commission, use high-pressure sales tactics, which result in a high rate of returns and subsequent markdowns. Careless handling can often cause damage to merchandise, and sloppy housekeeping keeps merchandise from looking fresh and salable.

Operational Devices

Even if buyers and sales people do a near perfect job, some markdowns are inevitable. There are always remnants and odds and ends that must be cleared from stock. Merchandise gets shopworn, soiled, and damaged just from the normal wear and tear of doing business. Markdowns are taken on regularly bought merchandise that has been used for display purposes. Sometimes a markdown is necessary in adjusting a customer complaint that the merchandise is defective. Price adjustments are made to meet competition, and if a competitor's prices are lowered, markdowns are necessary. A buyer may decide to consolidate price lines, in which case it may be necessary to mark down some merchandise.

Some stores have found that the most successful way to eliminate remnants, odds and ends, shopworn, soiled, or damaged merchandise from their stock is to run monthly end-of-month (EOM) sales. Such one-day-only sales are usually advertised widely, and many customers wait for them each month to take advantage of the rock-bottom prices. Some buyers, on the other hand, purchase special promotional merchandise to work into their EOM items to take advantage of the heavy store traffic on the sale days.

Merchandise Devices to Promote Sales

If a store or department decides to run a special sale, regular merchandise is often taken from stock and marked down. When the sale is over, the merchandise is marked up again to its original price. Some buyers go one step further and try to sell the same merchandise to two types of customers. They take a long initial markup when the goods first arrive to attract those customers who care greatly about quality but little about price. Later, they mark the goods down to a more normal retail to attract the price-conscious customers.

Many stores use a multiple-sale policy to increase store traffic. For example, an item may be offered at 59¢ or two for $1.00. When the multiple-sale period is over, a markdown is necessary to adjust the total retail downward from 59¢ to 50¢.

Markdowns taken on remainders from job lots and special sale merchandise should be given a special classification, according to the *Markdown Manual* published by the Merchandising Division of the National Retail Merchants Association. This is done so that losses from special purchases are not confused with those resulting from broken assortments and remnants from regular stock.

MARKDOWN POLICIES

There is no general agreement as to when markdowns should be taken. In large, promotionally oriented department stores most buyers believe in early markdowns. As some merchandisers like to say, "the first bath is the cleanest." Once an item is discovered to be not selling, a markdown is immediately taken. An early markdown will insure that most of the merchandise will be sold, leaving enough time for another markdown later in the season, if needed. Early markdowns also generate open-to-buy, enabling the buyer to purchase additional goods. Many stores like to avoid huge clearance sales at the end of the season and prefer to clear out slow-selling merchandise as the season progresses. They want to give the impression that good buys are always available.

In spite of these advantages for taking early markdowns, buyers in so-called prestige stores and in smaller specialty stores often prefer to take late markdowns. Some of these stores feature only two big clearance sales a year, one in January and one in July, which bring in a different type of customer. The regular clientele of these stores tend to be more interested in style and quality than price, whereas the customers at clearance sales are more price conscious. Small store owners often feel it unnecessary to take many markdowns. They believe that there will be an eventual buyer for every piece of merchandise in stock, and they stretch the selling season as long as they can.

There is no firm rule on how large a markdown should be. The size of markdowns should be governed by the original retail prices of the items and the time when the reductions are taken. It is common practice to reduce the original retail price by 20 to 25 percent for the first markdown. A deeper markdown may be taken the second time, and if a third markdown is necessary, the retail price should be low enough for quick clearance. For example, a buyer may decide to mark down a group of $5.00 scarves that have been on the selling floor for more than six months, in which case the series of markdowns may well look like this:

	FROM	TO
First markdown	$5.00	$3.99
Second markdown	3.99	1.99
Third markdown	1.99	.49

End-of-season sale
SOURCE: Michael Ginsburg/Magnum

If some scarves still do not get sold at 49¢, they may be marked down to $.00 and given to charity. (Note: Most promotionally oriented stores use a 99¢ price ending for reduced merchandise, while prestige stores often stick with $.00 price endings for regular and reduced merchandise alike.)

A few stores have had success with an "automatic markdown" policy. Prices are reduced by a certain percentage at regular intervals regardless of how well the merchandise may be selling. Filene's department store in Boston uses the automatic markdown plan in their famous bargain basement. Merchandise obtained from fire and bankruptcy sales are mixed in with stock bought from famous stores like Saks Fifth Avenue, Neiman-Marcus, and Bonwit Teller; and items carrying such designer names as Pucci, Givenchy, and Bill Blass abound. Markdowns are taken according to a fixed schedule: a 25 percent reduction after twelve selling days, a 50 percent reduction after eighteen selling days, and a 75 percent reduction after twenty-four selling days. If an item is still on hand after thirty selling days, it is given to charity. Anyone who has witnessed the daily "mob scene" at Filene's basement will attest to the apparent success of this policy.

Once merchandise has been marked down, a question arises as to how to display the reduced items for maximum selling appeal. Should they be segregated or mixed in with regular merchandise? It is commonly believed that if markdowns are to be used for clearance or promotional events, they should be in separate displays where they can be spotted easily by the customer. Proper signs located in heavy-traffic areas are effective

Automatic markdown at Filene's basement
SOURCE: Cary Wolinsky/Grafia

attention-getting devices. On the other hand, if markdowns are used to "beef up" regularly priced assortments, they should be mixed in with the other items. If customer acceptance is low on a certain retail item, the item may be marked down and mixed in with other items that sell better. The purpose is to elicit delighted reaction from customers who feel that they are finding unadvertised bargains while doing their regular shopping.

THE MARKDOWN REQUEST

In order to effect a markdown, a price change form must be filled out. Although this form is normally used for markdowns, it may also be used for canceling a markdown or even for marking merchandise up. It is usually prepared by the buyers or their assistants and countersigned by the divisional merchandise manager and the marker, who physically changes the prices. The standard practice is to use a colored grease pencil or a pen with red ink to show the new retail price on the original price ticket so that customers will know that a markdown has actually occurred.

Figure 6.1 shows the stubs of price tickets attached to sale items. When the stores decided to mark the items down, the marker drew a line through the original retail and printed the new price in red ink. Most customers would now recognize these items as bargains.

New tickets may be ordered with the price change form, but in the absence of the original price tag astute customers may suspect that what is claimed to be a markdown is no markdown at all. If new tickets are ordered, therefore, under no circumstances should the season letter (which tells when the merchandise first arrived in the store) be changed.

As mentioned earlier, merchandise is sometimes taken out of regular stock and marked down for a promotional event. After the sale is over, the merchandise is marked up again to its original retail price. The latter price change is known as a *markdown cancellation*. Occasionally, a buyer may feel that the original retail price was not high enough, either because the competitive situation will allow even higher prices or because the vendor has issued a general price increase and there is still merchandise on hand at the former retail price. The buyer may then put through an *additional markup* to increase the price beyond the original retail. Both markdown cancellations and additional markups may be accomplished by means of the price change form, as illustrated in Figure 6.2.

It is important not to confuse a markdown with a *revision of retail downward*. A markdown reflects a depreciation in the value of the merchandise; a revision of retail downward does not. The latter is a correction of a mechanical error made in pricing merchandise, or a cancellation of additional markup, or a price reduction either to meet competition or to take advantage of a rebate from a vendor. In none of these cases is there a depreciation in the cost value of the stock.

Figure 6.1
TICKET STUB SHOWING MARKDOWN

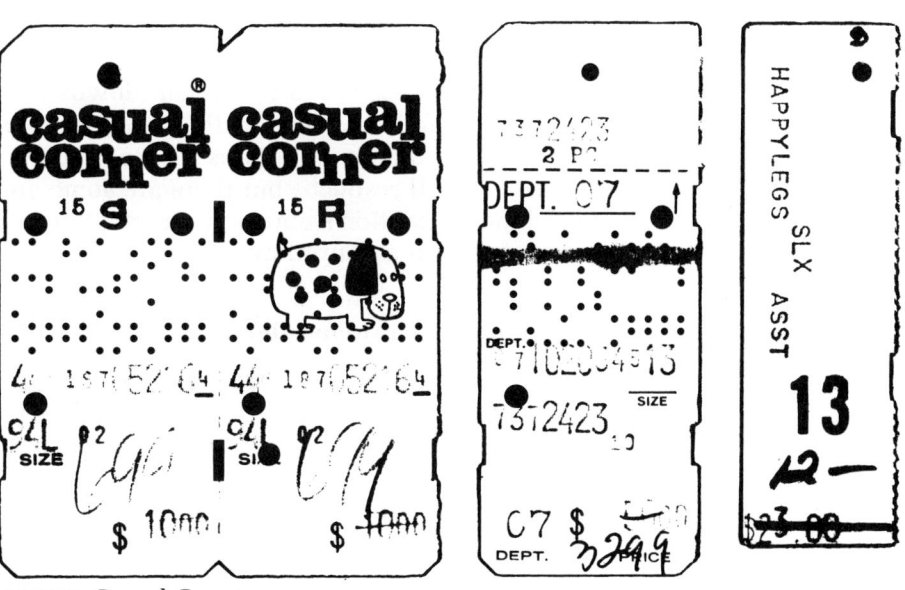

SOURCE: Casual Corner

Figure 6.2
PRICE CHANGE FORM

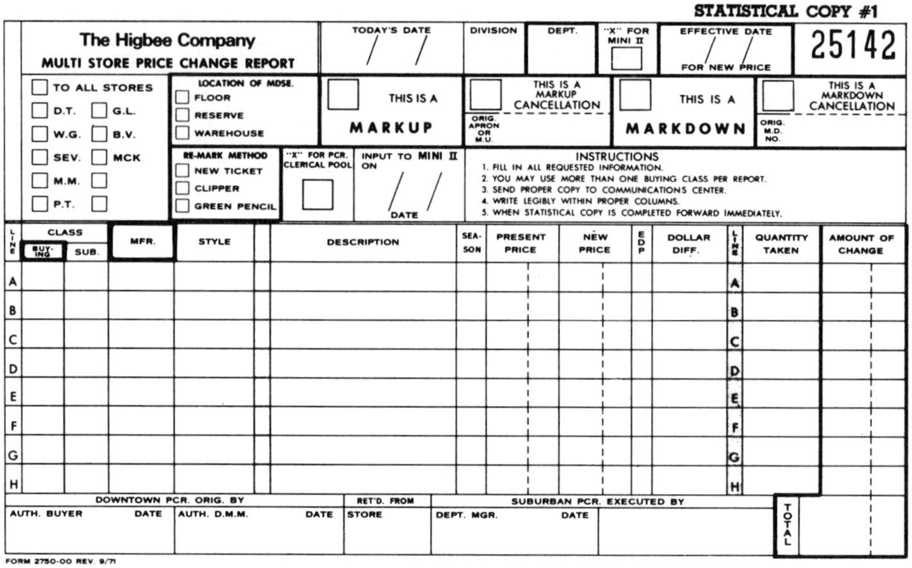
STATISTICAL COPY #1

The Higbee Company
MULTI STORE PRICE CHANGE REPORT

TODAY'S DATE / / | DIVISION | DEPT. | "X" FOR MINI II | EFFECTIVE DATE / / FOR NEW PRICE | 25142

TO ALL STORES
D.T. G.L.
W.G. B.V.
SEV. MCK
M.M.
P.T.

LOCATION OF MDSE.
FLOOR
RESERVE
WAREHOUSE

THIS IS A MARKUP
THIS IS A MARKUP CANCELLATION — ORIG. APRON OR M.U.
THIS IS A MARKDOWN
THIS IS A MARKDOWN CANCELLATION — ORIG. M.D. NO.

RE-MARK METHOD
NEW TICKET
CLIPPER
GREEN PENCIL

"X" FOR PCR. CLERICAL POOL
INPUT TO MINI II ON / / DATE

INSTRUCTIONS
1. FILL IN ALL REQUESTED INFORMATION.
2. YOU MAY USE MORE THAN ONE BUYING CLASS PER REPORT.
3. SEND PROPER COPY TO COMMUNICATIONS CENTER.
4. WRITE LEGIBLY WITHIN PROPER COLUMNS.
5. WHEN STATISTICAL COPY IS COMPLETED FORWARD IMMEDIATELY.

LINE	CLASS: BUYING	CLASS: SUB.	MFR.	STYLE	DESCRIPTION	SEASON	PRESENT PRICE	NEW PRICE	EDP	DOLLAR DIFF.	LINE	QUANTITY TAKEN	AMOUNT OF CHANGE
A											A		
B											B		
C											C		
D											D		
E											E		
F											F		
G											G		
H											H		

DOWNTOWN PCR. ORIG. BY: AUTH. BUYER — DATE — AUTH. D.M.M. — DATE
RET'D. FROM STORE
SUBURBAN PCR. EXECUTED BY: DEPT. MGR. — DATE
TOTAL

FORM 2750-00 REV. 9/71

SOURCE: The Higbee Company, Cleveland, Ohio

Another example of a price reduction that represents no depreciation is the *discount to employee or customer.* This reduction appears on the individual salescheck rather than on a price change form and is recorded in the accounting office.

CONTROL OF MARKDOWNS

Although it is impossible to avoid markdowns entirely, total markdowns can be substantially reduced with the correct application of the "five rights" of merchandising. Perhaps it is too much to expect a buyer to be always right in all respects, but there are some areas of common neglect that need more attention from many merchandisers if markdowns are to be kept under control and minimized.

Determination of Customer Demand

The first task of a buyer is to find out as accurately as possible what the customer wants. There are many ways in which this can be done: examining past sales records, conducting customer surveys through questionnaires and by talking with customers in the store, querying vendors, making use of reports by comparison shoppers, studying trade publications, and subscribing to private reporting services.

A favorite tool of many buyers which, if handled correctly, can help assess customer demand, is the *want slip.* At the end of a selling day each sales person is requested to attach a want slip to his or her sales tally listing the items customers asked for that the department did not have. There is space on the slip for listing what substitutes, if any, the customers took.

The want slip system can be effective only if the sales people take it seriously. If they fall into the habit of scribbling "no calls" on the slips each day, the system becomes useless. On the other hand, sales people must feel that their want slips are being given some attention in order to take them seriously, so buyers often announce purchases that have resulted from want slips.

Buyers must be sure that an actual demand exists before placing an order. Buying a little of this and a little of that at the merest suggestion, with no regard to stock depth, is called *delicatessen buying* and is not the best way to run a business. Buyers must also be sure that vendors anxious to sell their products have not encouraged friends and relatives to come to the store to create false wants.

In spite of its drawbacks, a want slip system, properly executed, can pay worthwhile dividends for the buyer and the store. Figure 6.3 shows a typical form used to record customer wants.

In most stores want slips are examined regularly by the buyer's divisional merchandise managers. Each merchandise manager wants to know what action, if any, the buyer has taken on customer requests and also how conscientious the sales people have been in filling out want slips. A buyer should never feel that this examination is a means for the merchandise manager to check on his or her buying efficiency.

Figure 6.4 shows how the contents of want slips can be summarized for submission to the divisional merchandise manager's office. Such summaries are usually prepared weekly, and space is provided for the buyer to make any comment deemed necessary. If merchandise is already on order, the order number should be given. Sometimes merchandise is carried in another department, and sometimes it is simply not available. The most popular response to items that appear on want slips is to state that there is insufficient demand to warrant an order.

Planning and Control of Stock

Buyers may be adept at selecting the right merchandise based on accurate knowledge of customer demand, but unless they know how much to buy and how to keep stocks balanced, they are nevertheless doomed to failure. Good record-keeping and planning are indispensable. Without them, stocks may become too heavy, turnovers may become slowed, and huge markdowns may result.

Developing Key Vendors

Every successful buyer needs several key resources. There must be firms that can be depended on for promised deliveries; the prices must be low; and styles must be attractive. Timing is also vital: if goods arrive too

Figure 6.3 WANT SLIP

CUSTOMER'S REQUEST FOR MERCHANDISE NOT IN STORE

L511-17 12M 5-72KA

This schedule is to help your department and show what wanted items are not in stock. Please be specific and clear in giving the information as indicated by heading below.

DATE _____ STORE _____

ITEM	DESCRIPTION	APPROX. PRICE	COLOR	SIZE	WHAT SUBSTITUTE IF ANY, DID CUSTOMER TAKE	NO. OF REQUESTS	SIGNATURE	BOUGHT	NOW IN STOCK	CANNOT FIND

Figure 6.4
WANT SLIP SUMMARY

WANT SLIP SUMMARY
FORM 3146 REV. 3/69

ATTACH ALL WANT SLIPS TO THIS REPORT AND TURN IN TO DIVISIONAL MERCHANDISE MANAGERS OFFICE BY TUESDAY OF THE FOLLOWING WEEK.

DEPT.__________ WEEK ENDING__________

TOTAL NUMBER OF SALESPEOPLE ENTIRE WEEK (Count each salesperson once for each day worked)__________

TOTAL NUMBER OF WANT SLIPS SUBMITTED BY SALESPEOPLE FOR ENTIRE WEEK . . . . .__________

TOTAL NUMBER OF WANT SLIPS WITH "NO REQUESTS" . . . . .__________

SUMMARY OF WANTS

ITEM	COLOR	SIZE	NO. CALLS	COMMENTS

BUYER'S SIGNATURE __________

early or too late, excessive markdowns are almost sure to follow. The merchandise must be right; consequently, many manufacturers build their reputation on quality and style. The cost must also be right so that merchandise can be sold at acceptable and profitable prices.

Analyzing Sales

A constant analysis of sales is necessary to take quick action on both fast and slow sellers. If an item is selling quickly, reorders should be placed promptly before the stock runs out. If an item is not selling, an immediate markdown may save larger markdowns later on. Monthly, weekly, and even daily stock reports showing the merchandise on hand by season letter must be reviewed carefully. When merchandise has not sold, the buyer should analyze the reasons for the failure in order not to repeat mistakes.

One way for a buyer to keep abreast of items that have proved to be runners—a *runner* is an item that sells very quickly and is reordered frequently—is to make up best-seller reports on the basis of weekly stock reports. Figure 6.5 shows such a report. Weekly sales are recorded for the main store as well as the branches. Since stock reports are forwarded to the merchandise managers, buyers should place reorders quickly to show their capacity for prompt action.

Figure 6.5 BEST SELLER REPORT

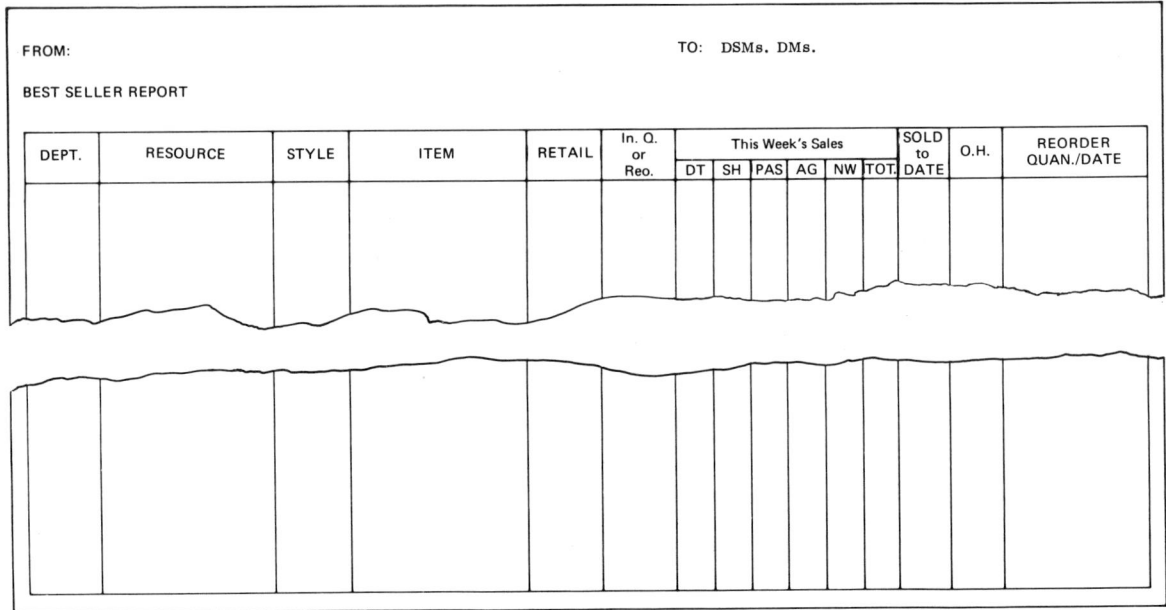

Improving Selling and Stockkeeping

The way merchandise is sold can have more to do with the frequency and depth of markdowns than some buyers realize. Sales people can be trained to keep stocks neat and clean to minimize markdowns resulting from damage and soilage. They can be trained to take accurate stock counts so that stocks can be better balanced; to show and display and therefore sell the slow sellers first to keep stocks fresh; to avoid high-pressure selling tactics so that returns, which often lead to markdowns, are minimized. These types of training are best undertaken by the buyers and their assistants and they must be ongoing.

MARKDOWNS BASED ON ORIGINAL RETAIL

Although net markdowns are usually expressed as percentages of net sales, they are sometimes given as percentages of the original retail prices *of the goods marked down*. In the latter case it is common to refer to them as *markdown off percentages*.

ILLUSTRATIVE PROBLEM	A gift buyer has a selection of vases currently retailing for $20 each. The vases have been in stock for more than six months, and the buyer wishes to mark them down by 20 percent of sales. How much markdown should be taken in dollars and in percentage of the original retail?

SOLUTION   Let sales be 100 percent. Then

$$100\% + 20\% = 120\% \text{ (the original retail)}$$

Therefore,

$$120\% = \$20$$

and

$$\text{Sales} = \frac{\$20}{120\%} = \$16.67$$

$$\text{Markdown} = \$20 - \$16.67$$
$$= \$3.33$$

$$\text{Markdown off \%} = \frac{\$3.33}{\$20.00}$$
$$= 16\ 2/3\%$$

EXERCISES
1. A group of fashion watches retailing at $40 will be marked down by 25 percent of sales. What will be the markdown in dollars, the markdown percentage of the original retail price, and the new retail price?
2. A collection of silk bow ties was not selling well at the retail price of $6.50 each. The buyer asked for a count and found that there were 503 on hand. It was decided to mark the ties down by 30 percent of sales. Determine the total markdown in dollars and the markdown percentage of the original retail.
3. A buyer of ladies' shoes has in stock a selection of Italian shoes that have been slow sellers at $60 a pair. He realizes that he must take some action, but he doesn't want to mark them down by more than 10 percent of sales. What will the new retail price be? Do you think that this is an effective clearance price? If not, what price would you recommend?

MARKDOWNS BASED ON SALES

As stated earlier, it is more useful to show markdowns as a percentage of net sales. The dollar sales figure is the most readily available, and most other planned figures are stated in terms of sales. Also it is easier to compare a store's markdown percentages with those of other retailing institutions if they are based on net sales.

ILLUSTRATIVE PROBLEM   A stationery buyer bought too many minicalculators and decided to reduce them by 20 percent for quick clearance. The present retail price is $100 each. What are the new retail price and the markdown percentage of net sales if all are sold?

SOLUTION   Let $100 = original retail. Then

$$\$100 \times 0.20\ (20\%) = \$20 \text{ (the markdown)}$$

And

$$\$100 - \$20 = \$80 \text{ (the new retail)}$$

Therefore

$$\text{Markdown \%} = \frac{\$20}{\$80}$$
$$= 25\%$$

EXERCISES

1. If a group of hats are reduced by 25 percent and all are sold, what is the markdown percentage?
2. A buyer of men's furnishings marked down his summer weight pajamas from $8.00 to $5.00 a pair in the middle of July. The markdown amounted to $260. Two weeks later he marked down the last 53 pairs to $3.00 each. The total summer pajama sales during the season amounted to $7,500. What was the markdown percentage?
3. An appliance store owner had four floor samples of color television sets on hand that had been in stock for nearly one year. Two of them were retailed at $500 each, and two at $600 each. He decided to take a heavy 30 percent markdown for quick clearance. If all four were sold, what was the markdown percentage on the samples?

CHAPTER SUMMARY

Markdowns are used to clear stocks of unwanted goods. There may be many reasons why merchandise does not sell at the original retail price: it may not have customer appeal, the retail price may be too high, the merchandise may be soiled, damaged, or shopworn, or there may be no seasonal demand for it. Sometimes a buyer simply buys too much, and markdowns become necessary to move surplus stocks.

Since a markdown reduces the retail value of merchandise, it is classified as a retail reduction. Markdowns are planned in advance of the selling season as are other merchandising figures, but it is considered a coup for a buyer if actual markdowns turn out to be less than anticipated. Markdowns are usually shown as percentages of net sales. If they are calculated as percentages of the original retail prices, they are called markdown off percentages.

Some stores believe in early markdowns; others save markdowns for semiannual clearance sales. The reason for early markdowns is to rid stocks of slow sellers quickly so that fresh merchandise can be brought in. Late markdowns are justified on the basis that perhaps there will be an eventual customer for every piece of merchandise so that total markdowns can be minimized.

Two or three successive markdowns are sufficient to move most sluggish sellers. Filene's of Boston has had notable success with an automatic-markdown system in its bargain basement. If merchandise has not been sold in thirty selling days during which time three markdowns have been taken, it is given to charity. In other stores it is common to reduce merchandise by 20 to 25 percent for the first markdown, with deeper cuts taken on subsequent markdowns if they are necessary.

There are a number of ways to control and minimize markdowns. Buyers should be adept at determining customer demand and planning the amount of stock necessary to meet this demand. Sales results should be analyzed to avoid repetition of buying mistakes. Key vendors should be cultivated so that the right merchandise can be obtained at the right time at the right price. Sales people should be trained to push slow sellers and to maintain good housekeeping habits.

QUESTIONS FOR REVIEW

1. What are the three major causes of markdowns?
2. Why is a revision of retail downward different from a markdown?
3. Explain the difference between a markdown cancellation and an additional markup.
4. What is an automatic-markdown policy?
5. What is the significance of a season letter?
6. Name some of the ways in which a buyer can help minimize and control markdowns.
7. Explain the difference between a markdown off percentage and a markdown percentage.
8. Why do promotionally oriented stores usually favor early markdowns?
9. What is the psychological advantage of using the old tickets rather than issuing new ones when markdowns are taken?
10. How does a manufacturer become a key vendor?

DISCUSSION QUESTION

Do you believe that it is ethical for a buyer to use the end-of-the-month sale as an opportunity for featuring specially bought promotional merchandise? Why?

PROBLEMS FOR REVIEW

1. A book buyer had net sales of $60,000 for the season. Net markdowns amounted to $4,000, and the original retail value of the goods that were marked down had been $12,000. What were the markdown off retail percentage and the markdown percentage?
2. All button-down white dress shirts were marked down from $5.00 to $4.00 each. The total markdown amounted to $200. Two months later the sixty remaining shirts were marked down to $2.00 each. The total white dress shirt sales for the period were $9,600. What were the markdown percentage and the markdown off retail percentage?
3. A buyer has an item in stock retailing for $24 that she wants to mark down by 20 percent of sales. What will be the markdown percentage off the original retail price?
4. The sweater department plans a markdown of 8 percent of net sales. If the original retail value of its stock is $18,000, what is the new retail value of the stock after the markdowns?
5. A buyer took all of his $5.00 boxed candy (350 boxes) and marked them

down to $4.00 each for a special sale. All but forty of the boxes were sold. After the sale the candy was marked back up to $5.00 a box. What was the markdown percentage on the transaction?

6. A buyer plans to specially price all of her jeans for an Anniversary Day sale, but she does not want the markdown to exceed 10 percent of net sales. What will be the amount of markdown in dollars if the present retail value of the jeans is $2,200?

7. A department has a planned markdown of 9 percent of net sales for the season. Determine the markdown percentage of the original retail and the new retail for an item that previously retailed for $15.00.

8. A fur buyer slashed the price of all of his mink stoles from $800 to $600 each for an August fur sale, and all were sold. What were the markdown off percentage and the markdown percentage?

9. A buyer reduced the price of 2,400 pairs of men's socks from $2.00 to $1.59 a pair for a special sale. They were all gone in a matter of hours, but before the end of the week 28 pairs were returned. The returns were later sold at the regular price. What was the markdown percentage on the sale socks?

10. A boutique owner has in stock a selection of midi-length dresses that she wants to mark down by 40 percent of sales for quick clearance. The dresses are presently retailing for $50 each. Determine the markdown percentage of the original retail.

CASE PROBLEM

FALLING SOCKS

One of the responsibilities assigned to Bill Jones, boys' wear buyer for the Fisher Department Store, was to buy for the Boy Scout department. The department contributed only a small percentage to total departmental sales, but Fisher's was the only store in the city to carry Boy Scout merchandise, and Mr. Jones was aware of the importance, for customer goodwill, of carrying a well-balanced inventory. He had given his head sales person, Mrs. Owens, authority to manage the department. She took frequent inventories and filled out reorder forms for items as needed. Mr. Jones signed the orders in a routine way, since Mrs. Owens had proved to be an efficient manager of the department for many years and customer complaints were almost nonexistent.

It was Mr. Jones's practice to carefully study the want slips turned in by his sales force at the end of each day. Although most of the time the listed items were fringe items that would never generate any real sales volume, sometimes the slips did indicate holes in basic stocks. On a few occasions the slips showed a definite trend of developing customer demand for items that the department did not carry. Mr. Jones took the want slips seriously and tried to make sure that his sales people did also.

During the past several weeks he had noticed a number of calls for Explorer scout garters. Upon questioning Mrs. Owens, he found that one customer seemed to have been responsible for many of the calls. Although the garters were an optional uniform item, he asked Mrs. Owens to get the customer's name, address, and phone number when he came into the department again.

About a week later Mrs. Owens came into Mr. Jones's office with the information requested. It turned out that the customer was a Mr. Wilson, who was scout master of a local troop of Explorer scouts. Wilson had been dismayed at not finding the wanted garters at Fisher's and had even encouraged his scouts to come into the store to ask for them.

That evening Mr. Jones called Mr. Wilson, and the latter reminded him that he had a responsibility to make sure Fisher's stocked all the items scouts would need to dress in full uniform, optional items included. When asked how many Explorer scouts there were in the city, Mr. Wilson replied that there were thirty in his troop and at least 150 more Explorer scouts in the area. Mr. Jones assured Mr. Wilson that he would take immediate action and that the garters should be in stock within three weeks. A trial order for fifteen dozen garters was placed, and the merchandise was on the shelf by the time promised.

About five months later Mr. Jones was supervising inventory-taking in his department and he happened to stop by the Boy Scout section to see how Mrs. Owens was doing. He noticed the Explorer scout garters on the shelf and asked Mrs. Owens how many had been sold since their arrival. Mrs. Owens checked her records and reported that not one pair had been sold since they were put in stock.

Perplexed, Mr. Jones decided to call Mr. Wilson. Mr. Wilson's phone was disconnected. Mr. Jones then called the local Boy Scout council headquarters and learned that Mr. Wilson had moved away from the city and that his troop of Explorer scouts had been disbanded.

1. What steps, if any, should Mr. Jones take to rid his stock of the scout garters?
2. Is markdown action feasible for an item of this type?
3. If some basic items are slow to sell, should merchandisers be concerned? Why or why not?

7

HOW TO USE THE RETAIL METHOD OF INVENTORY

KEY POINTS

1. If a store wants to find out the actual value of its stock on hand, a physical count or inventory is taken.

2. The perpetual or book inventory tells the store how much stock it should have on hand at a given time between physical inventories.

3. If the physical inventory is smaller than the book inventory, a shortage is reported. If the physical inventory is larger, which is rare, there is an overage.

4. Small stores tend to evaluate their inventories at cost, but the majority of large stores have adopted the retail method of inventory.

5. Retail deductions are subtracted from the total merchandise handled at retail to produce the book inventory. They consist of retail reductions plus net sales.

REASONS FOR TAKING INVENTORY

It is imperative that a store owner know the value of his or her stock at all times. Without this information, it is impossible to determine whether a profit is being made. The most accurate way of determining the value of the stock on hand is to physically count the merchandise. This procedure is known as *inventory taking*.

Some stores take a physical count of their merchandise once a year, but many do it twice a year, usually in late January and late July. It is customary to ask the employees to work overtime to accomplish this burdensome but necessary task. Only upon taking a *physical inventory* does a store owner know what the store *actually* has on hand.

During the period between physical inventories store owners need to know how much they *should* have on hand. Merchandising decisions must be frequently made as the season progresses, and stock adjustments are often necessary. The *perpetual inventory system* or *book inventory* provides a means of estimating how much stock should be on hand at any time. The book inventory may be kept in terms of units of merchandise and/or dollars, and it is based solely on store records, not on physical counts.

In addition to supplying the figures for calculating profit and loss, inventories also tell a merchandiser how old the stock is, because they list the merchandise according to the season letters, which tell when the merchandise first arrived in the store. Thus the merchandiser is able to identify aging merchandise at a glance and take corrective action to keep stocks fresh and salable.

Inventories also help merchandisers analyze their stocks by style, color, size, and other factors. Stock assortments can then be adjusted to reflect changes in customer demand. In recent years the computer has become an effective means of providing quick data derived from inventories. A computer can yield immediate information on what has been sold by style,

Physical inventory counting
SOURCE: Cary Wolinsky/Grafia

color, size, and other factors, and then proceed to print reorder forms to keep the stocks at desired levels. The use of the computer will be discussed more fully in Chapter 15.

Inventory taking can also be an educational process for store personnel. Through the physical counting and handling of the merchandise, they are reminded of all the items in stock. Sales people in particular can thereby refresh their memories and thus serve their customers more effectively.

METHODS OF INVENTORY VALUATION

Inventories may be valued at cost or at retail. In the early days of retailing, all records were kept at cost. It was easy enough to consider that the dollar amount received for an item above its actual cost represented gross margin. However, some items do not sell quickly or at all, and the cost method does not take into account the depreciation of cost value as times goes by. Also the cost of an item may fluctuate during the time that the merchandise is being sold. Nevertheless the cost method is still the most widely used and, in some ways, the simplest. The majority of small stores use this system, primarily because the retail method of inventory-taking is more complex and requires many more records.

Using a computer to keep a running inventory at the point of sale
SOURCE: Cary Wolinsky/Grafia

The newer method, however, is to evaluate the stock according to its retail value. Most large stores in particular have adopted the retail method of inventory. Physical inventories do not have to be taken as often as they do when cost methods are used, and departmental operating statements can be prepared monthly or even more frequently based on book inventory figures.

The Original-Cost Method

Some types of retail institutions still find that the original-cost method fits their needs best. This is often true with businesses where quick turnover is the norm and retail prices may change even during one selling day. Food stores, bakeries, and fruit stands find this method the simplest to use. Of course any store can use any method so long as it is used consistently. Since each method will yield a different value for a given inventory, the amount of profit shown will also differ according to the method used. For this reason the Internal Revenue Service prefers to have every store stay with one method. And the Treasury Department requires companies to use the same inventory method in reporting profits to stockholders as in reporting to the Internal Revenue Service. A change in method can be made, but it requires approval from the IRS.

When inventories are evaluated according to original cost, the problem arises as to how the original cost to the store of a listed item can be determined. One way is to use a cost code on the price ticket. As each item is listed together with its quantity the cost is decoded and also entered on the inventory sheet. There are many variations of cost codes. A popular one is *MONEY TALKS*: each of the ten letters stands for a different number from 1 to 10, where the letter M stands for 1, the letter O stands for 2, etc. With this code, an item originally costing $6.42 would have TEO printed on its ticket. Cost codes are changed frequently to prevent competing stores as well as customers from becoming aware of the actual costs.

Another way is to print a serial or reference number on the price ticket. A control card is kept in the controller's office for each serial or reference number used, and the appropriate costs are filled in on the inventory sheets after the physical inventory has been completed.

The Cost-or-Market-Whichever-Is-Lower Method

Many stores first value their inventory at both the original cost and the current market value and then use the lower figure for bookkeeping. In this way the book value of the inventory is kept at the minimum. Thus an article that cost the store $2.00 may have a replacement value of $2.50, in which case the lower cost figure is used because the appreciation of $.50 represents a paper profit only. There is real profit only after goods have been sold. This reasoning is justified because experience has shown that when goods are to be replaced, they are seldom sold at a higher price than originally intended until the replacements are actually made at higher costs, and not when it is rumored that the goods will cost more in the future. Thus profits are stated at a minimum.

There are several ways to determine the current market value of an item. Vendors' catalogs and price lists may be consulted, market quotations studied, or a professional appraiser hired. To make allowances for depreciation of the goods in stock, a depreciation schedule may be set up: for example, full cost for stock from one to three months old, 25 percent less than cost for three-to-six-months-old stock, 50 percent less than cost for six-to-twelve-months old stock, 75 percent less than cost for one-to-two-years-old stock, and zero value for older stock.

The Retail Method

As stated earlier, large department stores have found the retail method of inventory taking more suited to their needs, although other types of stores also use this method. A running book inventory is kept by department so that profit-and-loss statements can be prepared at any time without taking a physical inventory. Of course a physical inventory should be taken once or twice a year, at which times the goods are listed on the inventory sheets according to their current retail values. This eliminates the need for trying to find the original costs or the current market values at cost as required by the other methods. The current retail prices are really the market values at retail, because they reflect depreciation. The retail method is effective only when the merchandise is homogeneous. That is why large department stores have used it on such a large scale; it is very helpful in departmental control.

Figure 7.1
INVENTORY SHEET

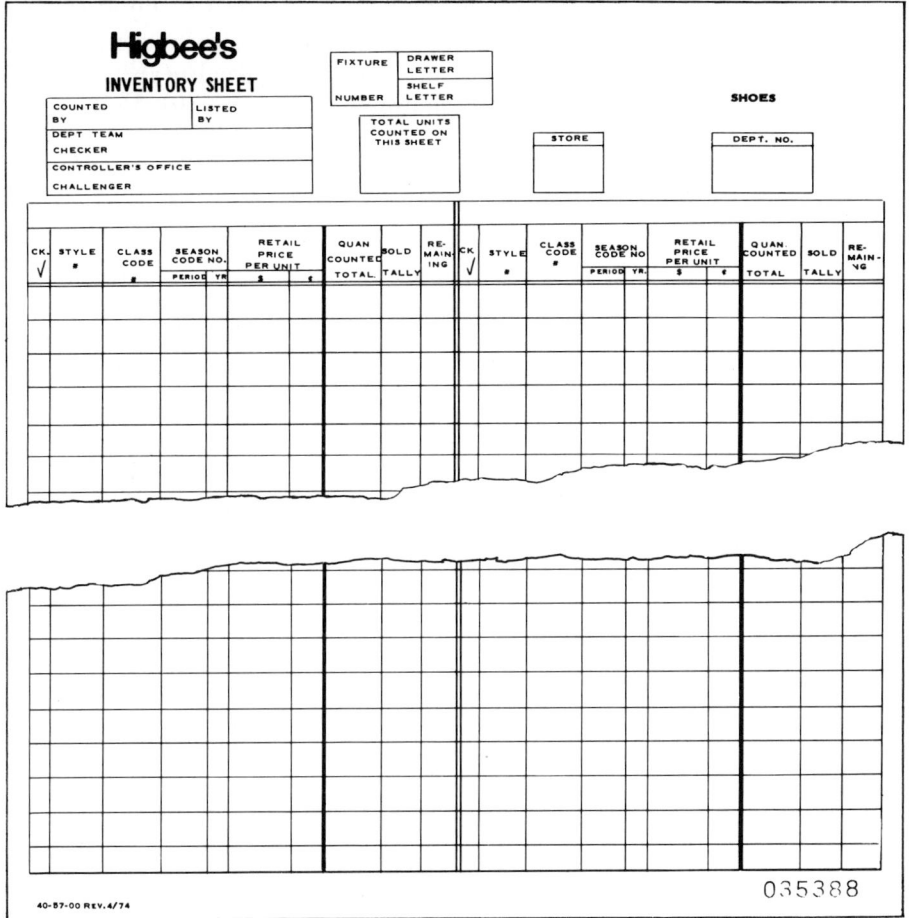

SOURCE: The Higbee Company, Cleveland, Ohio

Figure 7.1 shows a form that can be used for taking physical inventories, even while selling activity is still in progress, because it allows quantities of merchandise sold in the meantime to be deducted from quantities of merchandise already counted to give a remaining inventory figure. The season code is very important, since it enables the store to make an age analysis of the stock, for which purpose the bottom part of the inventory sheet may be used.

When the retail method is used, the cost value of the inventory may be found by applying the complement of the cumulative markup percentage at any given time to the retail inventory figure. The cumulative markup is the difference between the total cost and the original retail value of the goods that are to be sold.

ILLUSTRATIVE PROBLEM   After taking the January inventory a fabrics buyer found that she had merchandise on hand valued at $25,000 at retail. She had begun her season

METHODS OF INVENTORY VALUATION   **113**

with a stock of $15,000 at cost and $22,000 at retail. During the past six months she had purchased fabrics amounting to $50,000 at cost and $85,000 at retail. (a) What was the value at cost of the January inventory? (b) How much merchandise had been sold at retail?

SOLUTION (a) Find the value at cost of the ending inventory:

	COST	RETAIL
Beginning inventory	$15,000	$22,000
Purchases	50,00	85,000
Total merchandise handled	$65,000	$107,000

Therefore,

Cumulative markup % = $107,000 − $65,000
             = $ 42,000

Cumulative markup % = $\dfrac{\$42{,}000}{\$107{,}000}$
             = 39.3%

Ending inventory at cost = $25,000 × 60.7% (complement of cumulative markup %)
             = $15,175

(b) Then find the retail sales during the season:

Sales = Total merchandise handled − Ending inventory
   = $107,000 − $25,000
   = $82,000

EXERCISES

1. After one year of operation a stationery store owner took an inventory of his stock on hand. It amounted to $32,000 at retail. During the year he had kept accurate records, which indicated that he had purchased goods costing $63,000 with a retail value of $92,000. Determine his closing inventory at cost.

2. Find the market value of the closing inventory, given that the opening inventory was $30,000 at cost and $50,000 at retail, net sales were $175,000, and purchases during the season amounted to $80,000 at cost and $170,000 at retail.

3. A ski shop owner featured imported merchandise on which he took long markups. He had enjoyed a very successful season and counted merchandise worth only $8,500 at retail when he took his July 31 inventory. He had begun his season with merchandise worth $14,000 at cost and $35,000 at retail. His purchases during the season had been $80,000 at cost and $200,000 at retail. What was his July 31 inventory at cost?

FIFO AND LIFO METHODS OF INVENTORY VALUATION

In conjunction with the orthodox cost or retail methods of inventory valuation, many firms also use either the FIFO (first-in, first-out) or the LIFO (last-in, first-out) inventory systems in preparing corporate earnings statements. When using the cost and retail methods already explained, inventories are valued according to the FIFO approach. The idea is that the first items acquired are also the first to be sold. Most retailers use the FIFO system, since it seems to correspond logically with the natural flow of stock.

During periods of inflation, however, some firms have turned to the LIFO system. If the firms are big enough to make the system worthwhile, the LIFO system enables them to receive a significant tax break, as we shall explain very shortly. Even if the LIFO system is adopted by large companies in preparing corporate reports to stockholders, the traditional retail method of inventory taking is still commonly used to measure departmental operating results. The LIFO system has nothing to do with the usual physical flow of merchandise, as does the FIFO system; it lists the merchandise sold as that which was most recently purchased merely for accounting purposes.

The FIFO Method

Stores have long trained their sales force to sell first what has been on the shelves the longest. This keeps the stocks looking new and fresh. While this is the proper merchandising method, the FIFO method of inventory valuation does not work well in finding values at cost when cost prices are rising; it works very well only when costs are stable.

For example, consider the following situation. In February a buyer of girls' dungarees purchased 2,400 pairs at a cost of $4.80 a pair. She decides to sell them at $8.00 a pair. By June she finds that she needs more dungarees and orders an additional 2,400 pairs. In the meantime, however, there has been an increase in the price of denim goods, and the vendor has raised the price for dungarees to $4.90 a pair. The store's semiannual physical inventory taken on July 31 shows that there are 2,000 pairs of dungarees left in stock. The record for the entire season's shipments is as follows:

MONTH	QUANTITY PURCHASED	COST	TOTAL COST
February	2,400 pairs	$4.80	$11,520
June	2,400 pairs	4.90	11,760
Totals	4,800 pairs		$23,280

The average cost of a pair of dungarees during the season comes to $\frac{\$23,280}{4,800}$ or $4.85. Evaluation according to the FIFO method, however, will assume that the February shipment has all been sold as well as 400 pairs of the June shipment so that the remaining 2,000 pairs of dungarees listed on the inventory sheet will carry the higher value at cost of $4.90 a pair. Then the cost of most of the goods sold during the season will come out lower, thus inflating the profit with consequent higher taxes.

The LIFO Method

The LIFO method, on the other hand, assumes that the stock that arrives last is sold first. Although the assumption is contrary to recommended merchandising practice, according to which the oldest merchandise should be sold first, it does prevent profits from being overstated as a result of inflation.

A numerical comparison of the two methods of inventory evaluation is helpful. Using the girls' dungarees example, we have the following comparative figures:

	FIFO		LIFO
Retail sales (2,800 pairs at $8.00)	$22,400		$22,400
Cost of goods sold (2,800 pairs at $4.80)	13,440	(2,800 at $4.90)	13,720
Gross margin (profit)	$ 8,960		$ 8,680
Ending inventory value (2,000 pairs at $4.90)	$ 9,900	(2,000 at $4.80)	$ 9,600

The gross profit comes out to be higher when the FIFO method is used than when the LIFO method is used. Taxes, accordingly, will also be higher. Moreover, the ending inventory value also comes out to be higher with the FIFO method.

There is an advantage to using the LIFO method only when wholesale prices or costs are rising. When costs are falling, the advantage is reversed. When prices are stable, there is no difference between the two methods.

Companies that use the LIFO method like it obviously because it reduces present taxes. The reduction amounts to a permanent deferment of some taxes, because the tax does not have to be paid so long as the company remains in business and continues to use this method of bookkeeping.

BOOK VERSUS PHYSICAL INVENTORY
Book Inventory

As stated earlier, the book inventory is a running inventory and reflects how much stock the store or department should have on hand at a given time. When the retail method of inventory taking is used, it is standard procedure to prepare a profit-and-loss statement for each department every month. This enables merchandisers to keep a continuous watch on departmental operations.

The accuracy of a book inventory depends on two principal figures: total merchandise handled and retail deductions. When the latter is subtracted from the former, the remainder is the amount of stock left, which is the book inventory.

CALCULATION OF TOTAL MERCHANDISE HANDLED

The figure for total merchandise handled is made up of a number of important components. While it might seem sufficient merely to add the purchases during the season to the beginning inventory to obtain the total merchandise handled, this is too simplistic. Other factors also affect the final figure:

1. *Purchase returns and allowances.* Merchandise is returned to vendors for a variety of reasons. An item may be defective, it may be different from what was ordered, or it may arrive too late. Allowances are sometimes obtained for imperfect merchandise that the store decides to keep. Rebates are sometimes obtained when the cost declines and there has been a guarantee against such a decline. These returns and allowances must be subtracted from gross purchases valued both at cost and at retail to arrive at a net purchase figure.
2. *Transfers in and out.* There are times when it is advisable to transfer merchandise from one department to another or one store to another within the same organization. Slow-selling merchandise in one department or store may sell well in another location. Or merchandise may be transferred to round out the assortments in another department or branch. A *transfer in* is treated like a purchase, and a *transfer out* like a purchase return. For example, a men's furnishings department might decide not to carry men's belts in size 28 any longer. A transfer of the stock on hand to the boys' department is arranged, and the two departments agree upon suitable cost and retail values for the merchandise.
3. *Freight charges. Freight in* is the cost of transporting goods to the store, and it is added to the purchasing cost. In order to cut the purchase cost and improve markup, buyers are urged to persuade vendors to pay for the freight charges whenever possible. Thus an F.O.B. store (where the vendor pays all transportation costs and title does not pass until the goods reach the store) is considered superior to an F.O.B. factory (where the vendor pays only the shipping charges to a shipping depot, with the store paying the rest, and the title passes at the shipping point). Most merchandise, however, is still shipped F.O.B. factory or shipping point. Obviously freight charges have no retail value.
4. *Additional markups.* As stated in the previous chapter, an additional markup is sometimes taken after the goods have initially been put into stock when the buyer feels a higher retail is warranted. This price change adds to the retail value of the stock without affecting the cost.
5. *Revision of retail downward.* This adjustment of the retail value was also explained in the last chapter. We recall that it does not include markdowns, but is a correction of errors in the original retail prices of merchandise.

ILLUSTRATIVE PROBLEM A department's beginning inventory on February 1 was $50,600 at cost and $92,300 at retail. During the next six months goods valued at $82,000 at cost and $150,200 at retail were purchased. Merchandise worth $1,300 at cost and $2,430 at retail was returned to vendors. Freight charges amounted to $1,102. Additional markups totaled $184, revisions of retail downward came to $63. Merchandise valued at $230 at cost and $385 at retail was transferred out of the department, and transfers in were valued at $530 at cost and $936 at retail. Determine (a) the total merchandise handled at cost and at retail and (b) the resultant cumulative initial markup percentage.

SOLUTION (a) Find the total merchandise handled at cost and at retail:

	COST		RETAIL	
Beginning inventory		$50,600		$92,300
Gross purchases	$82,000		$150,200	
Less returns	1,300		2,430	
Net purchases		80,700		147,770
Freight in		1,102		
Additional markups				184
Transfers in	500		936	
Less transfers out	230		385	
Net transfers in		300		551
Revisions of retail downward				− 63
Total merchandise handled		$132,702		$240,742

(b) Find the cumulative initial markup percentage:

$$\begin{aligned} \text{Markup} &= \text{Retail} - \text{Cost} \\ &= \$240{,}742 - \$132{,}702 \\ &= \$108{,}040 \\ \text{Markup \%} &= \frac{\$108{,}040}{\$240{,}742} \\ &= 44.9\% \end{aligned}$$

EXERCISES

1. Given:

Transportation charges	$82
Retail inventory August 1	$10,230
Transfers out (cost)	$220
Transfers out (retail)	$350
Purchases at cost	$15,660
Purchases at retail	$29,880
Purchase returns and allowances (cost)	$280
Purchase returns and allowances (retail)	$800
Cost inventory August 1	$4,336

Find (a) the total merchandise handled at cost and at retail and (b) the cumulative initial markup percentage.

2. A small boutique took an inventory on July 31 and counted merchandise valued at $23,500 at cost and $52,300 at retail. Goods purchased after

July 31 came to $63,200 at cost and $121,382 at retail. Freight charges were $102. Additional markups amounted to $72. What was the cumulative initial markup percentage?

3. Given:

Opening inventory at cost	$ 8,882
Opening inventory at retail	$15,320
Transportation charges	$600
Net retail purchases	$8,400
Net cost purchases	$5,618
Revision of retail downward	$220
Cost transfers out	$300
Retail transfers out	$500
Cost transfers in	$1,200
Retail transfers in	$2,000

Find the cumulative initial markup percentage.

CALCULATION OF RETAIL DEDUCTIONS

Retail deductions consist of the retail reductions explained in Chapter 5 (markdowns and discounts to employees and customers) and net sales. It is important to distinguish between gross sales and net sales. If customers kept all the merchandise they bought, gross sales and net sales would be the same. But this is almost never the case, since customers usually bring back to the store some of the merchandise they bought earlier. If an even exchange is made, the sales figure remains the same. But if cash is given back or a charge account credited, the transaction must be treated as a return and subtracted from the gross sales figure. If an allowance is given to a customer, it must also be subtracted from the gross sales figure. An allowance is sometimes given when defects in merchandise are found *after* the sale has been made, as when a customer buys a light blue cashmere sweater and discovers later that the color has faded slightly as a result of exposure to hot light in a display case; instead of returning the sweater, the customer might want to keep it and accept a $5.00 allowance. In order to keep the stock records correct, this allowance must be recorded as a markdown because depreciation has taken place. Net sales are therefore obtained by subtracting *customer returns and allowances* from gross sales. When returns and allowances are expressed as a percentage, they must be shown as a percentage of gross sales, not net sales. A customer allowance should not be confused with a customer discount. An allowance is given sometime after the sale has been made, whereas a discount is given at the time of sale, usually as a gesture of good will.

ILLUSTRATIVE PROBLEM

An umbrella department's figures for the season are:

Total merchandise handled at cost	$25,000
Total merchandise handled at retail	$45,000
Gross sales	$30,500
Returns and allowances	$1,800
Discounts to employees and customers	$300

Net markdowns			$2,400

Determine the closing book inventory.

SOLUTION

		COST	RETAIL
Total merchandise handled		$25,000	$45,000
Retail deductions:			
Gross sales	$30,500		
Less returns	1,800		
Net sales	28,700		
Markdowns	2,400		
Discounts to employees and customers	300		
Total retail deductions			31,400
Ending book inventory			$13,600

EXERCISES

1. If a department had total merchandise in stock amounting to $35,000 at cost and $60,000 at retail during a season, net sales of $45,000, discounts to employees of $600, markdowns of $2,000, and markdown cancellations of $300, what was the closing book inventory?
2. A toy department had record sales of $203,000 for the season, but customer returns and allowances amounted to $34,000. Markdowns were $16,800, and employee discounts were $3,600. If the total merchandise handled was $285,000 at retail, what was the closing book inventory?
3. The initial markup percentage for the total merchandise handled at a cost of $60,000 was 40 percent. Net sales were $30,000, markdowns were $2,000, and discounts to employees were $800. What was the ending book inventory for the period?

Physical Inventory

The results of annual or semiannual physical inventories are compared with the book inventory. If the physical inventory is larger than the book inventory, the store records an *overage*. More commonly the physical inventory is smaller than the book inventory, indicating a *shortage*. Like most other merchandising figures, shortages are usually shown in dollars and/or as a percentage of net sales. A percentage figure is more meaningful because the shortage may be compared with similar stores doing a comparable volume. It should be noted that a closing *estimated* physical inventory can be taken at any time using an estimated shortage figure derived from past experience.

ILLUSTRATIVE PROBLEM

Using the figure in the last illustrative problem and assuming the physical inventory at the end of the season to be $12,200, calculate (a) the amount of the shortage, (b) the ending inventory at cost, and (c) the gross cost of the merchandise sold.

SOLUTION (a) Find the shortage:

Ending book inventory	$13,600
Physical inventory	12,200
Shortage	$1,400

(b) Find the ending cost inventory:
As explained in the solution of a previous problem, the ending inventory at cost may be found by multiplying the ending physical inventory by the complement of the cumulative initial markup percentage. Thus we have:

$$\text{Ending cost inventory} = \$12,200 \times \frac{\$20,000}{\$45,000} \text{ or } 44.4\%$$

$$= \$12,200 \times 55.6\%$$

$$= \$ 6,783.20$$

(c) Find the gross cost of merchandise sold:
Subtract the ending inventory at cost from the total merchandise handled at cost.

Total merchandise handled at cost	$25,000.00
Less ending inventory at cost	6,783.20
Gross cost of merchandise sold	$18,216.80

EXERCISES

1. The total merchandise handled during a six-month season was $24,000 at cost and $38,000 at retail. Net sales during the period were $14,000, markdowns were $900, and employee discounts totaled $330. A physical inventory taken at the end of the season showed a retail value of $23,070. What was the amount of the overage or shortage? the value of the physical inventory at cost?

2. The opening inventory for a department was $18,000 at cost and $32,000 at retail. Purchases were $15,000 at cost and $25,000 at retail. Net sales were $20,000, net markdowns were $1,000, and employee discounts were $500. A physical inventory at the end of the season showed stock worth $34,500. Determine the overage or shortage and the value of the inventory at cost.

3. A department recorded gross sales of $32,000 during a season. Markdowns were $2,000 and customer returns and allowances were $1,200. Gross purchases during the period were $24,000 at cost and $45,000 at retail, with vendor returns amounting to $1,000 at cost and $1,800 at retail. The department began the season with an inventory of $12,000 at cost and $20,000 at retail. A physical inventory at the end of the season showed a retail valuation of $30,000. Find (a) the shortage, (b) the value of the inventory at cost, and (c) the gross cost of the merchandise sold.

ILLUSTRATIVE PROBLEM

A small gift shop has an opening inventory of $15,000 at retail. Purchases during the season amounted to $29,000 at retail. Net sales were $30,500 and net markdowns amounted to $1,500. A physical inventory taken at the end of the season amounted to $11,500 at retail. Find (a) the book inventory and (b) the shortage in percentage.

SOLUTION (a) Find the book inventory:

Opening inventory at retail		$15,000
Purchases		29,000
Total merchandise handled		$44,000
Less retail deductions:		
Net sales	$30,500	
Net markdowns	1,500	
Total retail deductions		32,000
Closing book inventory		$12,000

(b) Find the shortage in percentage:

Book inventory	$12,000
Physical inventory	11,500
Shortage	$ 500

Dividing the shortage in dollars by the net sales, we have:

$$\text{Shortage in percentage} = \frac{\$500}{\$30,500} = 1.6\%$$

EXERCISES

1. Given the following:

Net sales	$50,000
Net markdowns	$2,500
Discounts to employees	$500
Opening inventory at retail	$42,000
Purchases at retail	$53,000
Physical inventory	$40,000

Find the retail shortage in dollars and percentage.

2. A ladies' dress shop keeps a record of all sales by auditing the sales checks. During the spring season a total of $65,000 in retail sales was recorded. Purchases at retail during the season amounted to $70,000. The opening inventory at retail was $20,000, and a physical inventory taken at the end of the season showed stock worth $24,675. What was the percentage of retail shortage?

3. If the total merchandise handled in a store was $60,000 at retail during a season, the book inventory was $10,000, and the physical inventory was $9,000 at retail, what was the percentage of retail shortage?

THE PROFIT-AND-LOSS STATEMENT

The various components of the profit-and-loss or operating statement have been discussed in this and preceding chapters. Like a jig-saw puzzle, the pieces can now be put together. Although the overall format will differ from store to store, the end result will be the same, that is, showing whether the store or department has made a net profit.

Is is *not* important that students be able to construct a profit-and-loss statement from memory. It *is* important that they know which figures should be added and which subtracted and what the figures mean. They should recognize which figures make up the total merchandise handled and the retail deductions as well as know how to compute the total costs of merchandise and thus arrive at a gross margin and how to use operating expenses to show a profit or loss.

A small store's hypothetical operating statement for a six-month period is presented in Figure 7.2. A departmental operating statement in a large store would stop with net operating profit, since the "other income" and tax deductions pertain to a store as a whole. The figures have been simplified to facilitate understanding.

Figure 7.2
OPERATING STATEMENT

	COST	RETAIL
Opening inventory	$60,000	$100,000
Gross purchases	$82,000	$144,000
Less purchase returns and allowances	2,000	4,000
Net purchases	80,000	140,000
Transfers in	3,000	5,000
Less transfers out	400	700
Net transfers in	2,600	4,300
Freight charges	2,400	
Additional markups		2,700
Revisions of retail downward		−1,000
TOTAL MERCHANDISE HANDLED	145,000	246,000
Gross sales		155,000
Less customer returns and allowances		5,000
NET SALES		150,000
Markdowns		16,000
Less markdown cancellations		1,000
Net markdowns		15,000
Discounts to employees and customers		1,000
TOTAL RETAIL DEDUCTIONS		166,000
CLOSING BOOK INVENTORY		80,000
CLOSING PHYSICAL INVENTORY	44,175	75,000
STOCK SHORTAGE		5,000
Gross cost of merchandise sold	100,825	
Less cash discounts earned	1,825	
Net cost of merchandise sold	99,000	
Plus alteration expenses	1,000	
TOTAL MERCHANDISE COSTS	100,000	
GROSS MARGIN		50,000
OPERATING EXPENSES	40,000	
NET OPERATING PROFIT		10,000
Plus other income		1,000
Net profit before income taxes		11,000
Less income taxes		3,000
NET PROFIT AFTER INCOME TAXES		$ 8,000

CHAPTER SUMMARY

The best way for a retail firm to find out the dollar valuation of its inventory is to take a physical count of the stock on hand. This valuation may be in terms of cost or retail price. Small stores tend to favor the older cost valuation methods, because they are easier to use and require less recordkeeping. Larger stores have widely adopted the retail method of inventory so that frequent departmental operating statements may be prepared through the use of a perpetual inventory system. It is not practical for large firms to take a physical inventory more than once or twice a year. Between physical counts, the book inventory is relied on for information on how much stock the store should have on hand.

The traditional cost and retail methods of taking inventory are based on the FIFO (first-in, first-out) method of valuation. This way of evaluating stock works well when costs are generally stable. However, during inflationary periods, many firms prefer the LIFO (last-in, first-out) valuation method, especially when preparing corporate earnings statements. By using this accounting device, profits can be understated so as to save the business many tax dollars.

One of the chief reasons that retailers use a perpetual inventory system is that this system makes it possible to uncover merchandise shortages. Physical inventory is compared with the book inventory. If it is smaller than the book inventory, then there is a shortage. The amount of shortage is one measure of the efficiency of the departmental or store operation.

Although an operating statement can become quite complex, a merchandiser should be aware of how the principal components of the statement are related to one another and therefore to the final profit or loss figure. Thus what is included in total merchandise handled, net sales, retail deductions, book inventory, gross margin, and operating profit or loss should be thoroughly understood.

QUESTIONS FOR REVIEW

1. Why is it so important for a store to maintain a perpetual inventory system?
2. What are the chief reasons for taking a physical inventory once or twice a year?
3. What is the purpose of having a cost code on the price ticket?
4. What are two serious weaknesses of the original-cost method of inventory valuation?
5. Although the FIFO method of merchandising keeps stocks looking fresh and salable, what effect does it have on the taxes a store must pay and why?
6. What is a compelling reason for using the LIFO method of inventory evaluation?
7. What are some of the ways in which a store can determine the market value of an item?
8. List the components that make up the figure for the total merchandise handled at cost and at retail.
9. Do stores usually find they have a shortage or an overage at the end of a fiscal year? Why?

10. Is it possible to derive an estimated physical inventory without actually counting the merchandise? If so, how is it done?

DISCUSSION QUESTION	If you were a stockholder of a large retailing corporation, would you prefer earnings to be reported with the FIFO or LIFO method of inventory valuation?

PROBLEMS FOR REVIEW

1. A buyer realized gross sales of $75,000 for the season, but returns totaled $3,000. He had begun the season with an opening inventory of $25,000 at cost and $40,000 at retail. During the six-month period, purchases were made at a cost of $35,000 and with retail value of $65,000. Determine (a) the closing inventory at cost and (b) the closing inventory at retail.
2. When a buyer took his January inventory, he discovered that he had merchandise in stock with a retail value of $65,000. He had begun the season with goods worth $35,000 at cost and $60,000 at retail. Purchases were made at a cost of $40,000 which were worth $70,000 at retail. Determine the closing inventory at cost.
3. A card shop began its new season with an inventory worth $25,000 at cost and $40,000 at retail. During the season new merchandise was purchased with a value of $15,000 at cost and $30,000 at retail. Freight costs were $150. Some merchandise, worth $300 at cost and $500 at retail, had to be returned to the vendor. Upon arrival one shipment of cards was inadvertently priced too high, resulting in a revision of retail downward amounting to $60. What was the total merchandise handled at cost and at retail?
4. The couture shop of a large department store showed an opening inventory of $35,000 at cost and $75,000 at retail. The new merchandise that arrived during the season was valued at $50,000 at cost and $112,000 at retail. Freight charges amounted to $800. A few dresses that came in were considered not suitable for the department and were transferred to the better-dress department at an agreed cost of $1,800 and retail value of $3,000. Find the department's cumulative initial markup percentage.
5. The total merchandise handled during the spring season in a girls' sizes-seven-to-fourteen department was $135,000 at cost and $250,000 at retail. Gross sales were $210,000, but customer returns amounted to $10,000. Net markdowns of $5,000 were taken, and discounts to employees totaled $2,000. What was the book inventory at retail?
6. A ski shop had a retail stock during the fall season totaling $83,000. Gross sales were $55,000, but customer returns and allowances were $5,000. Markdowns amounting to $5,000 were taken for an annual sale, but after the sale there were markdown cancellations worth $2,000. Determine the book inventory.
7. A cosmetics department recorded net sales for the season of $140,000. Markdowns totaled $8,000, of which $2,000 was later canceled. Discounts given to employees amounted to $1,000. The total merchandise

handled during the period was $180,000 at cost and $300,000 at retail. At the end of the season a physical inventory showed $165,000 worth of merchandise in stock. Determine (a) the shortage or overage and (b) the cost of the physical inventory.

8. The total merchandise handled in a fur department during a fall season was $200,000 at cost and $580,000 at retail. Total retail deductions were $380,000. Even though a physical count of the furs was made each day, the official physical inventory at the end of the period was $195,000. Find (a) the value at cost of the final physical inventory and (b) the gross cost of the merchandise sold.

9. A department takes a physical inventory and finds that it has stock with a retail value of $325,000. Net sales for the period just completed totaled $836,000, and markdowns were $40,000. According to store records, the department's book inventory should be $335,000. What is the shortage in dollars and in percentage?

10. According to the physical inventory just completed, a department has merchandise on hand worth $74,000 at retail. The opening inventory had been $45,000 at cost and $85,000 at retail. Net sales were $60,000, and total retail deductions were $65,000. Purchases amounted to $30,000 at cost and $55,000 at retail. Determine (a) the book inventory, (b) the shortage, (c) the gross cost of the merchandise sold, and (d) the shortage percentage.

CASE PROBLEMS

ONE MAN'S SHORTAGE

John Tanner was recently fired as the notions buyer for the Greene Department Store. He received his termination notice while sitting in his merchandise manager's office one afternoon in early February. Mr. White had called him in to review his January inventory results, and he had no idea the meeting would result in his getting a "pink slip."

Tanner had been buyer of notions for three years. The management had seemed to be pleased with the merchandise he bought, and everyone in the store liked him. He was a happy-go-lucky sort of person who was popular with stockboys and senior executives alike. He had formed some fine business relationships with vendors in the market and always seemed able to produce exciting promotional merchandise for major store events.

For a time, therefore, Tanner's future in the store seemed bright, although ever since he had become a buyer, the notions department was plagued with high inventory shortages. These shortages cut deeply into departmental profit. In fact, the previous storewide inventory taken in July showed such a discrepancy between the book inventory and the physical inventory in Tanner's department that another physical inventory had to be taken in his department only a week later. Although some errors were corrected, the results were still so bad that Tanner was given a warning that his shortage percentage would have to improve or he would be looking for a new job.

Since Tanner was paid a salary plus a percentage of his departmental profit, he was as anxious as the store to cut his shortages and thereby improve the profit picture. He suspected there were two chief reasons for his inventory troubles. His department, No. 6, was located next to the larger stationery department, designated as No. 5. Sales people were free to sell from both departments to give better customer service. While seasoned sales people seemed to appreciate the importance of ringing up merchandise on the correct cash register key or writing separate sales checks for merchandise from different departments, Tanner had noticed that sales help from the flying squad and the Christmas extras were not so careful and sometimes rang up complete sales on the No. 5 key or wrote only one sales check for several items to expedite the transaction. He also wondered whether customer theft in his department was unduly large because the way many items were displayed made it easy for someone to tuck them into a handbag, pocket, or shopping bag.

Mr. White, however, was not convinced by Tanner's theories. Even though the stationery department was running an overage, he felt that Tanner's shortage figure was too large to be tolerated any longer. Six months after the warning Tanner's shortage percentage was worse than ever. Mr. White told Tanner that he could continue with the store until April 1, but that a new buyer would be named to his post on that date.

1. Can a buyer have any real control over the shortage in his department? What could Tanner have done to reduce his shortages?
2. Can you think of other reasons for a stock shortage to occur?
3. Do you feel that the store was too hasty in discharging Tanner?
4. Construct a simple profit-and-loss statement to show what happens when sales are "given" to another department.

A WORN-OUT WELCOME

Zelda Peters has discovered a way to beat the high cost of living. With three active sons to feed and clothe, her husband's salary was barely enough to cover monthly expenditures for basic needs. The time had come to cut corners wherever possible.

In order to avoid interest charges for not paying bills on time, the Peters were in the habit of paying cash for most of their purchases. They have, however, maintained a charge account at Walker's, the city's largest department store, ever since they were married ten years ago. Mrs. Peters buys much of the family wardrobe at Walker's because she likes the store's styles, quality, and fit. Occasionally she does shop at a nearby discount chain, but she always goes back to Walker's if she can't find what she wants at the discount house.

Mrs. Peters often patronizes the boys' department in Walker's basement store, where the prices are more in line with her budget. The upstairs boys' department, however, carries the dungaree that she particularly likes; it is a nationally advertised brand with a double-knee guarantee. If the knees do not last the life of a garment, a new dungaree will be supplied free of charge. Mrs. Peters' sons, aged 6, 7, and 10, give their dungarees unusual punishment, and Mrs. Peters has become accustomed to returning worn-out dungarees to the store for free replacements. If a knee has not completely worn out, Mrs. Peters makes sure that it does. Moreover, she always looks for a young sales person, new to the department, when she goes to ask for replacements and she always asks for a size larger than the pair she returns—after all, her boys were growing. Thus for several seasons she has been able to keep her boys suppled with just one initial purchase of 10 pairs of the famous dungaree.

One spring day Mrs. Peters arrives again at Walker's armed with six pairs of badly worn dungarees. The knees were, as usual, in shreds. The department was very busy, and an older gentleman approached and introduced himself as Mr. Johnson, the buyer. Mrs. Peters explained that she wanted free replacements because of the company's guarantee. "What sizes would you like?" asked Mr. Johnson. "I need two pairs each in sizes 7, 8, and 11," replied Mrs. Peters. "We must measure the dungarees you are returning, since we can give you free replacements only in the same sizes," explained Mr. Johnson. "You mean you don't believe that I'm telling the truth?" shouted Mrs. Peters. "Sorry, madam, some of our customers have taken advantage of the manufacturer's liberal guarantee, and we must be very careful."

When Mr. Johnson measured the garments, it became evident that the returned dungarees were respectively one size smaller than those requested. "I'm afraid I can give you only sizes 6, 7, and 10," the buyer said. "Why, I've never been so insulted in my life," cried Mrs. Peters. "I've had a charge account at Walker's for ten years, and this is the thanks I get! I'm going upstairs right now to tell the president of the store about this!"

"Madam, please do that. Mr. Roger's office is on the fifth floor. If you take that elevator over there, you'll be there in no time."

Mrs. Peters stomped angrily out of the department. As she left, Mr. Johnson noted with a wry smile that she was headed for the down escalator.

1. Most stores try to follow the rule "the customer is always right." Do you agree with the buyer's treatment of Mrs. Peters?
2. Did the returned dungarees represent a loss to the store? Explain.
3. Do you believe that Mrs. Peters ever contacted the store president?

8

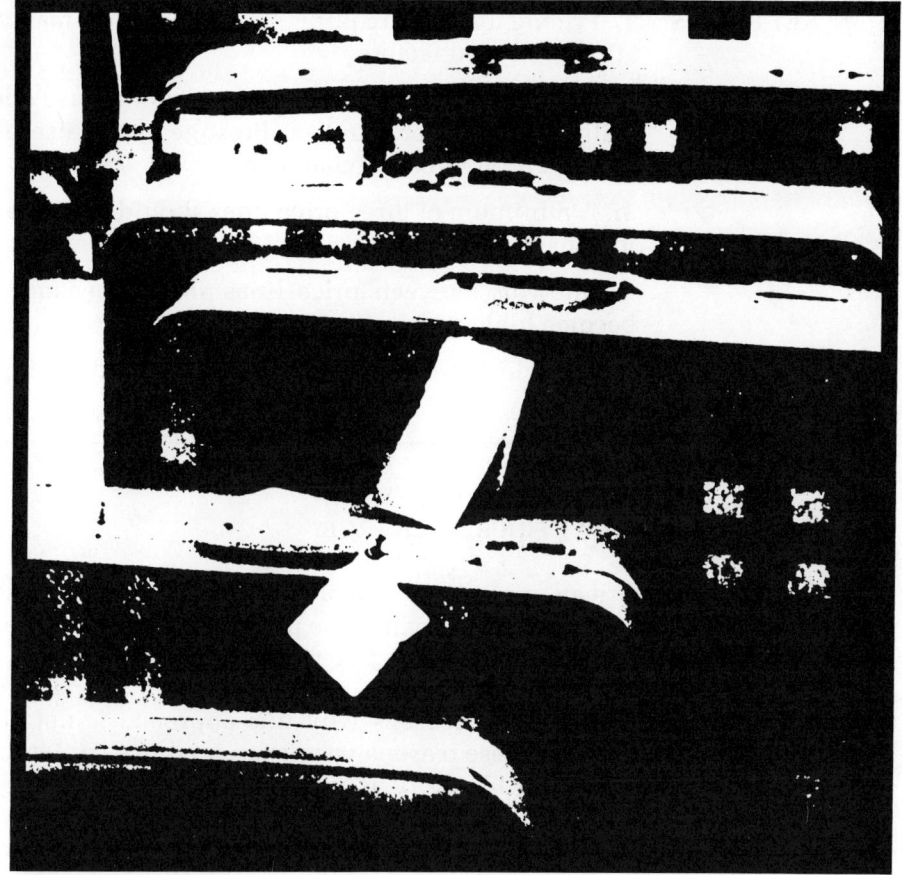

HOW
TO
PRICE
FOR
PROFIT

KEY POINTS

1. Pricing for profit requires skillful decision-making based on a consideration of several factors.

2. Promotionally oriented stores very often use odd price endings, especially for sale merchandise. Prestige stores use even price endings for almost all types of merchandise.

3. A minimum of three price lines should be offered in most categories of merchandise.

4. Intervals between price lines should become wider as retail prices become higher.

5. Price lining becomes more complicated during periods of galloping inflation.

WHAT PRICE TO CHARGE?

It may appear that one of the easiest tasks of merchandising is to decide what retail price should be placed on each article sold. After all, buyers are aware of their respective markup percentage goals, and it is easy to apply the departmental markup to each piece of merchandise. There are, however, several reasons why this approach is not always practicable, and some of these reasons were examined in Chapter 4.

Pricing for profit is not a simple matter. Be it an art or a science, it provides an interesting and exciting challenge to every retailer. In order to answer the age-old question, "What price shall I charge?" the following factors should be considered.

Profit

Before setting a retail price, the buyer must be quite sure it is going to be high enough to cover not only the original cost of the item but also other costs of doing business, such as expenses and retail reductions, and still leave a margin for profit. This margin of profit is often surprisingly low, but it must be there if the retail operations are to continue.

Competition

Retailing is a very competitive business. Stores spend millions of dollars trying to attract new customers and hold on to the old ones. A merchant who ignores his competition will not survive long. Some large stores maintain staffs of comparison shoppers to keep abreast of what their competitors are doing. When pricing branded staple merchandise, merchandisers usually have the competition in mind, and retail prices do not vary much from store to store. Many manufacturers preticket their merchandise and have suggested retails printed on their packages, but highly competitive stores often sell products for less than these suggested prices, hoping that customers will feel they are getting real bargains and therefore entertain goodwill toward the stores. There is considerably more leeway in pricing fashion merchandise, especially if the merchandise is not widely distributed.

Competition is generally considered a healthy thing, and some stores have received widespread publicity for their competitive spirit. The long-standing battle between Macy's and Gimbels at Herald Square in New York City is a prime example of intense competition that is beneficial to both stores.

Volume

One way to increase sales volume is to advertise the lowest possible prices. Some stores, most often discount retailers, prefer to offer few services along with low prices and thus operate on a small profit margin in order to build up volume. Other stores adopt a leader policy combining both high and low markups. Loss leaders do draw customers into the stores, but little or no profit is made on these items. The hope is that the customers thus drawn into the store may be enticed to buy other items carrying higher markups. If volume is high enough, low markups may prove to be more profitable than normal markups.

Type of Store

Buyers must be familiar with their store's clientele if they want to price their merchandise correctly. In a so-called prestige store, customers expect to pay more, but they also expect more services, nicer surroundings, and better treatment than in bargain stores. Often merchandise sold in a prestige store is exclusive to that store, so that long markups can be taken without worry about the competition.

Customer Demand

The demand for a product often affects pricing. If the demand is high and the supply is low, a higher price can be charged. Back in the 1950s, when the Davy Crockett craze was sweeping the country, a boy's white T-shirt could be sold for at least $1.00 more than usual simply by adding a Davy Crockett insignia. Once the demand tapered off, prices fell back to their original prices or even below. Generally, if the supply of merchandise is unlimited, more units of that item can be sold by lowering the price. *Price elasticity* is the measure of the relationship between price change and change in demand. For example, consider a store that sold 100 football blankets during a given month at $20 each. The next month the price was lowered to $15, and the store sold 200. The price had decreased 25 percent, but the demand had increased 100 percent. When a price reduction causes a unit sales increase of a greater percentage, the demand is said to be *elastic*.

Customer Habit

Some customer resistance is unavoidable when prices are changed. A mother may have become used to paying $5.98 for a pair of name-brand dungarees for her son. Then she will be upset to discover one day that she must now pay $6.50 for a pair of the same dungarees. Thus it is often wise to maintain the same retail on staple items for as long as possible, unless the wholesale price fluctuates widely. Customers feel secure with stable prices.

The Economy

In recent years consumers have become accustomed to paying ever-higher prices for the merchandise they buy. In periods of inflation prices can be raised with some confidence unless there is government intervention to freeze prices. In periods of recession, prices often go down, and price-cutting sometimes develops. Buyers must be sensitive to the state of the economy in adjusting their prices.

Government Regulation

Over the years federal and state governments have passed legislation governing the pricing of many commodities. Although the purpose of this legislation is usually to insure free and healthy competition among large and small stores alike, the effect has been to make the merchant's pricing policy less flexible. Two areas of legislation in particular have had considerable impact on the prices that can be charged for certain products.

RESALE PRICE MAINTENANCE

If a merchant does business in a state that has resale-price-maintenance laws, or *fair-trade* laws as they have become known, prices may be dictated by the manufacturer. The law says that if one retailer in the state signs a contract to sell a branded item at the retail specified by the manufacturer, all other retailers in the state must then charge the same price for that item. Critics of the law, which was passed during the Depression of the 1930s, maintain that it has outlived its usefulness especially with the current inflationary trend of the 1970s. There can be striking differences between prices charged for the same merchandise in states with fair-trade laws and those without these laws. The laws make it easy to make a profit by reducing price competition. Manufacturers counter that without the law there would be a lowering of quality standards. Also many small merchants would be driven out of business because, in order to remain competitive, they would have to lower their profit margins to a point where there would be no incentive to stock name-brand products.

In states where the nonsigner clause is in effect, where one signature enforces fair trade for all retailers, a manufacturer's product cannot be sold for less than the stipulated minimum retail price. However, even in these states only about 5 to 10 percent of the merchandise is fair-traded. Retailers may undersell if the trade mark or brand name has been removed from the product. Close-outs, damaged, or deteriorated goods are also exempt from the force of the law. Some states have ruled the nonsigner clause unconstitutional, but manufacturers and retailers nevertheless can agree to maintain fair-trade prices. If some retailers do not cooperate, the manufacturers may simply refuse to sell them more goods. There are other states that have no fair-trade laws at all.

In a state with fair-trade laws, if it is discovered that a retailer is not abiding by the fair-trade agreement, he or she can be sued for damages by the manufacturer. However, litigation is expensive and time-consuming, so that such court actions are limited. Policing is often poor, but some manufacturers make a real effort to find out whether retailers are charging what they should. Their sales representatives spot check prices for them. Figure 8.1 shows the form a representative might use to determine how well a store is living up to its fair-trade obligations.

UNFAIR-TRADE-PRACTICES ACTS

Many states have passed unfair-trade-practices acts aimed at preventing deep price-cutting that injures or destroys competition. For example, Minnesota's Unfair Sales Act requires retailers to add at least 8 percent to their invoice cost of goods and wholesalers to add at least 2 percent; the only exception is that lower prices may be charged to meet the legal prices of competitors.[1]

The unfair-trade-practices acts reduce the use of loss leaders, because they prevent the sale of merchandise at prices below their costs. They apply to both retailers and wholesalers, and to all products branded or unbranded. However, the laws have been difficult to enforce, and they seem to ignore the idea that the purpose of a business is to make a profit on total operations rather than on individual items.

PRICING TECHNIQUES

Price Endings

Does pricing have psychological aspects as well as practical ones? No studies have been made that prove that more women will buy a skirt priced at $12.98 rather than $13.00. Indeed, it would seem that especially after the sales tax has been added there is little difference between the two prices.

---

[1]Charles F. Phillips and Delbert J. Duncan, *Marketing*, 6th ed., Irwin, Homewood, Ill., 1968, p. 851.

Figure 8.1
SHOPPING REPORT

SALESMAN'S SHOPPING REPORT

Name & Address of Store: _____

Date & Time of shopping and purchase: _____

Item purchased: _____

Fair Trade Price: _____

Posted Price: _____

Advertised Price: _____

Price Asked: _____

Purchase Price: _____

Name of Salesman making purchase: _____

Conversation with customer: _____

Remarks*: _____

* How much product is on display. With this report, please send in sales slip if purchase is made.

Comment on whether outlet is a regular Whitman account. If not, determine, if possible, from where product was obtained.

SOURCE: Whitman Chocolate's Division, Philadelphia, Pennsylvania

Economy store showing odd-numbered price ending
SOURCE: Ray Ellis/Rapho, Photo Researchers, Inc.

Yet, historically, it has been assumed that price endings make a difference to customers and retailers alike, and it appears that many stores make use of this psychological assumption in marking their merchandise.

An examination of newspaper advertisements will reveal that promotional stores almost always use a $.99 ending on some sale and clearance items. Regular merchandise is often marked with a $.95 or $.98 ending. The belief is that a price just below an even dollar figure will increase sales. The use of multiple pricing is also common. Many stores have found that they can sell more knit tops at three for $20 than at $7.00 each. Prestige stores lean heavily toward even-dollar price endings ($.00) even when merchandise is marked down for clearance or for special sale items. On the other hand, some stores seem to retail merchandise with little regard to price endings. They apply a standard markup to all their items so that their prices may have even or odd endings. But in this case, too, psychology plays a big role. Merchandisers who use this technique hope that when a customer pays $10.32 for a shirt, for example, he will think that the lowest possible markup has been added to the cost.

Price Zones

There is widespread belief that customers can be grouped according to the range of prices they are willing to pay for a certain item. Very often the grouping is closely correlated with levels of income. A store may feel that

Price zones in luggage—a low-priced canvas line, medium-priced plaid cloth luggage, and an expensive leather group
SOURCE: Cary Wolinsky/Grafia

one group of customers will pay between $3.00 and $5.00 for pajamas, another group between $6.00 and $10.00, and still another group between $11.00 and $20.00. These ranges are called *price zones*. Sears, Roebuck, the largest-volume retailer in the world, implicitly acknowledges having price zones by describing some of their merchandise as "good," "better," and "best."

Price Lines

A *price line* is a single price level maintained for similar merchandise with slightly varying costs. Several price lines may be found within one price zone. Setting a price line that will be acceptable to customers is a very important function of the buyer.

Consider, for example, the case of a buyer of boys' wear for a discount chain who has been shopping for sports shirts in sizes three to seven in the $2.50-to-$3.50 price range. His departmental markup is 40 percent. After several days in the market, he has narrowed down his selections so that if the 40 percent markup is applied, the costs and retail prices of his wanted merchandise will appear as follows:

COST	RETAIL
$22.50 per dozen	$3.10 each
$21.50 per dozen	$2.85 each
$22.00 per dozen	$2.95 each
$23.00 per dozen	$3.25 each

It would be foolish of the buyer to offer to the public four groups of sports shirts in the same price range at four different retail prices. A single price line should be set up for all these shirts. In this instance $2.99 might be the best price, especially if his customers are accustomed to paying $2.99 for a little boy's sports shirt.

Buyers may find that in their eagerness to offer a large variety of merchandise to their customers, they are driven to establish too many price lines. Three price lines, however, are the absolute minimum for most merchandise, for rather obvious reasons. In the process of selling, items in the middle price line can be shown first. Then, depending on customer inclinations, more expensive or less expensive merchandise can be shown. When setting additional price lines, the intervals between each group should widen as retail prices become higher, because customers shopping in the lower price ranges are more price sensitive than those shopping in higher price ranges. Also dollar volume usually diminishes with increasing prices, so that it may not be profitable to offer a large selection of expensive, low-volume items.

Wise buyers will review their departmental stock often to see whether the price lines offered are the best possible to insure adequate variety and profitability. The policy of price lining should be under constant review. Its advantages are many, but there are also some inherent disadvantages.

ADVANTAGES OF PRICE LINING

1. *The decision-making process for customers is simplified.* Many shoppers are confused by the sight of too many items with different retail prices. Often sales are lost because customers cannot make up their minds. A few price lines representing a large variety of merchandise make shopping that much easier.
2. *Greater depth and better assortments are possible with fewer price lines.* A limited number of price lines will enable a buyer to keep a closer watch on the stock to insure that needed merchandise is always on hand. In this way, loss of sales resulting from out of stock can be minimized. Also stock turnover can be increased, thus reducing the risk of markdowns.
3. *Sales people can become familiar with the stock more readily.* Knowledgeable sales people are an asset to any store. They are more self-confident and are better able to use suggestion selling.
4. *Advertising and sales promotion become more effective when emphasis can be placed on a few price lines.* Customers come to know the

price lines a store is promoting and can be easily assured that wide assortments will be available.

5. *The buying job is made easier.* The buyer does not have to shop so many resources and therefore can concentrate on providing the best selections possible in each price line.

DISADVANTAGES OF PRICE LINING

1. *Some buyer flexibility is lost.* The buyer sometimes feels restricted by the price lines, and as a result the price lines may become more important than the merchandise itself.
2. *Selection must be limited to some degree.* Some customers may feel that the stock is not as complete as it should be. Stores that have built up reputations for wide selections may find that too much price lining will damage their image.
3. *The maintenance of certain price lines can be difficult when wholesale prices rise and fall by an appreciable amount.* This is especially true when costs are rising. Then ever-higher price lines must be established, and customer antagonism may develop, resulting in sales loss.

ANALYSIS OF PRICE LINES

A periodic analysis of price lines within a department is necessary to insure that consumer demand is being satisfied in the most profitable manner. If a price line is not generating a desired volume of sales and markup, it may be wise to drop it, unless competitive pressures work against such action. When setting price lines, the buyer should group merchandise into price zones according to what the store's customers can afford to pay and how much they are willing to spend. Price endings should conform with store policy. Care should be taken to increase the intervals between price lines as they go higher.

A price line analysis can be made using both original and reduced retails. However, markdowns usually speed the sale of merchandise so affected, and reduced items may appear more desirable than they actually are. Theoretically, then, a price line analysis should reflect customer acceptance before any markdowns are taken. Some markdowns are inevitable, of course, so sales at original retails can be segregated from those at reduced prices. Since markdowns are usually taken according to need, and there is so little consistency in price endings used, this text will show how to analyze original price lines only without regard to any possible markdown action.

ILLUSTRATIVE PROBLEM At year end a hosiery buyer is dissatisfied with the performance of her department. Her sales were down, and sales people and customers alike complained about missing sizes and shades in the stockings and pantyhose being sold. The buyer tried to cater to all types of customers by carrying the merchandise of four leading manufacturers. She suspects that she was spreading her stock too thinly and decides to trim the number of price lines offered. An analysis of last year's sales by price lines reveals the following:

PRICE LINE	PERCENTAGE OF SALES
$1.15	10%
1.35	20
1.50	5
1.65	8
1.95	25
2.25	3
2.50	8
2.95	6
3.35	2
3.50	8
3.65	1
3.95	4

What is the best way to consolidate the price lines, eliminating some and creating new ones if necessary?

SOLUTION The buyer decides to drop her least profitable vendor and cut the number of price lines down to seven so she can provide better depth in each line and still offer a wide assortment of merchandise. She decides on the new price lines on the basis of percentage of sales and comes up with the following price structure: $1.15, 1.35, 1.65, 1.95, 2.50, 2.95, and 3.50. Now she examines the intervals between price lines. The lower price lines appear to fit in well with price-lining principles, but the higher price lines seem to need adjustment upward if the principles are to be maintained. Nevertheless, the buyer is aware that more and more women are buying hosiery and pantyhose in discount houses, supermarkets, and drug stores, and often at retail prices less than $1.00. She decides to let the price lines stand, make $3.50 her top price, and watch her lower price lines carefully to see whether she should trade down even further in the future to remain competitive.

EXERCISES 1. A glove buyer decides that the merchandise in her department could be improved by eliminating some of the existing price lines. An analysis of last year's sales reveals the following:

PRICE LINE	PERCENTAGE OF SALES
$2.95	5%
3.00	18
3.50	6
3.95	10
5.00	30
5.50	3
5.95	4
6.95	8
7.25	2
8.00	2
8.95	12

How should she revise the price lines?

2. At present the ties in a men's furnishings department are sold at ten different prices. The buyer feels that there are too many prices. Last year's sales analysis shows the following:

PRICE LINE	PERCENTAGE OF SALES
$2.50	8%
3.00	6
3.50	15
4.00	12
5.00	28
6.50	19
8.00	5
9.00	2
10.00	4
15.00	1

Reduce the number of price lines to five according to valid price-lining principles.

3. The owner of a specialty shop, Pillow Talk, has increased his stock greatly in recent years. Now he feels that the number of price lines has gotten out of hand, and he wants to simplify his operation. An analysis of last year's sales by price lines indicates the following:

PRICE LINE	PERCENTAGE OF SALES	PRICE LINE	PERCENTAGE OF SALES
$2.00	4%	10.95	3
2.50	3	11.00	2
2.95	4	12.50	1
3.00	9	13.00	1
3.50	3	18.00	4
4.25	8	20.00	3
4.50	1	22.50	2
5.00	14	25.00	5
6.00	10	27.50	1
6.95	8	30.00	1
8.95	4		
10.00	9		

Reduce the number of price lines to ten with the help of valid price-lining principles. New price lines may be created if necessary.

Although an analysis of price lines according to sales volume is a good starting point for revising price lines, it is important to bear in mind that best sellers are not necessarily the most profitable. A study of the total markup achieved with each price line, including the rate of sale, should also be a part of the final decision.

ILLUSTRATIVE PROBLEM The owner of a fashionable boutique, Poise 'n Ivy, is currently carrying seven price lines of men's sports shirts. He decides that he has too many price lines and cuts them down to four in order to increase stock depth. Which of the following should he keep? Consider the profit margin along with sound price-lining principles.

PRICE LINE	AVERAGE COST	RATE OF SALE (12 MONTHS)
$ 3.98	$ 27.00 per dozen	140
5.98	42.00	200
7.98	54.00	160
12.98	84.00	120
15.00	102.00	80
20.00	132.00	200
25.00	180.00	220

SOLUTION It is important to know which price line yields the greatest dollar markup. This figure is the difference between the unit cost and the unit retail for the various price lines. The total markup is found by multiplying the unit markup by the number of shirts sold during the past year. Thus the following set of figures should be considered.

PRICE LINE	AVERAGE COST	UNIT COST	MARKUP	RATE OF SALE	TOTAL MARKUP
$ 3.98	$27.00	$ 2.25	$ 1.73	140	$ 242.20
5.98	42.00	3.50	2.48	200	496.00
7.98	54.00	4.50	3.48	160	556.80
12.98	84.00	7.00	5.98	120	717.60
15.00	102.00	8.50	6.50	80	520.00
20.00	132.00	11.00	9.00	200	1,800.00
25.00	180.00	15.00	10.00	220	2,200.00

If the four most profitable price lines were kept, the boutique would sell shirts at the prices of $7.98, 12.98, 20.00, and 25.00 each. The spread, however, is then the same between the two lower price lines as between the two higher. Also it is not wise to begin pricing the shirts at $7.98 each; 340 shirts were sold at $3.98 and $5.98 each. Nevertheless, the store has catered to very affluent customers. The most expensive shirt was also the most popular in terms of units sold as well as profit. Therefore, perhaps the store should have these price lines: $5.98, 12.98, and 20.00. Also it appears that the time is ripe to trade up and add a $30.00 price line. Its profitability would have to await analysis of sales results.

EXERCISES

1. The owner of the Paraphanelia Shop is currently carrying blouses in seven price lines:

PRICE LINE	AVERAGE COST	RATE OF SALE (WEEKLY)
$4.98	$36.00 per dozen	20
5.98	42.00	12
7.50	54.00	10
10.50	72.00	18
15.00	96.00	10
18.00	120.00	5
25.00	162.00	5

She decides to cut her inventory by reducing the number of price lines to four. Which four should she choose? Defend your answer in terms of abstract reasoning and dollars-and-cents figures.

2. A ladies' shoes department in a prestige store has ten price lines of better shoes in stock. The buyer decides to revise the price lines, eliminating those that are least profitable. What action should be taken on the basis of the following figures?

PRICE LINE	AVERAGE COST	RATE OF SALE (WEEKLY)
$25.00 per pair	$12.50 per pair	22
28.99	16.00	30
30.00	17.00	10
35.00	17.50	16
42.00	21.50	25
43.00	22.50	20
45.50	23.50	14
50.00	25.00	12
60.00	29.50	8
62.00	30.00	6

3. The buyer of housedresses in the lower level of a promotional department store is offering eight price lines in an effort to be very competitive. In order to give more depth to her stock, however, she decides to eliminate the three least profitable lines. Which three should she eliminate given the following figures?

PRICE LINE	AVERAGE COST	RATE OF SALE (WEEKLY)
$ 3.99	$2.50 each	120
4.99	3.00	70
5.99	3.75	180
6.99	4.25	54
8.99	5.50	92
10.99	6.75	130
12.99	7.50	84
13.99	8.00	60

CHAPTER SUMMARY Selecting the right retail price for every piece of merchandise bought is a continuing and formidable challenge to every retailer. The right price must be high enough to insure some profit yet low enough to meet competition. It must dovetail with the image the store hopes to maintain for itself, yet be such as to stimulate a high sales volume. It must be flexible enough to reflect shifts in the nation's economy, but sufficiently stable to preserve customer confidence. It must adhere to governmental regulations that may be in force. In short, pricing is not a simple matter. It is partly an art, with psychological overtones, and partly a science with tried and true formulas.

A prime concern of merchandisers is the price endings. Although there are no hard and fast rules, it seems that promotional stores favor $.95 and $.98 endings for regular merchandise and $.99 endings for sale merchandise. Multiple pricing is also widespread. Prestige stores generally use even price endings ($.00) for regular and sale merchandise alike. Of course, there are exceptions to the rules, just as it is difficult to label stores as promotional, semipromotional, or nonpromotional.

Price lining is a technique that makes shopping easier for the customer, provides better-balanced assortments, simplifies the sales person's and the buyer's jobs, and aids the sales promotion department. It is simply the setting up of a single retail price for groups of similar merchandise where costs differ by small amounts. It is important, however, not to streamline prices to such a degree that selections appear limited. Also buyers should not buy with very hard retail prices in mind. Moreover, with today's soaring inflation rates, it is almost impossible to hold onto established prices for very long.

Buyers find that too many price lines can quickly develop. Some prefer to price their merchandise within definite price zones. The intervals between prices in the lower price zones should be smaller than in the higher price brackets, where customers think more about quality than price. In no case, however, should there be so many price lines that stock depth suffers.

QUESTIONS FOR REVIEW
1. What are the factors to be considered when deciding on a retail price of an item?
2. Are loss leaders usually profitable in a store with low volume?
3. Why does a store located in a shopping center often encourage competing stores to locate in the same center?
4. What is an elastic demand?
5. Do price endings have any psychological importance?
6. Why do most stores employ the multiple-pricing technique?
7. What is a price zone? Which large retailer has made use of this concept?
8. Why are three price lines considered the minimum for most categories of merchandise?
9. What are the advantages and disadvantages of price lining?
10. Are high-volume sellers the most profitable? Why or why not?

DISCUSSION QUESTION In the absence of government intervention, should a retailer always price his goods as high as he thinks the traffic will bear? Why or why not?

PROBLEMS FOR REVIEW

1. Due to heavy demand, a business machines store stocked a large variety of pocket calculators. At the end of the fiscal year, the owner found that the calculators had sold as follows:

PRICE LINE	PERCENTAGE OF SALES
$ 41.00	6%
42.50	20
52.00	2
59.00	1
60.00	28
62.00	1
69.00	24
73.00	3
96.50	10
100.00	2
200.00	3

In order to reduce his inventory, the owner decided to stock only five calculators. According to sound price-lining principles, which ones should he keep?

2. A leather goods store yielded the following statistics on sales of men's wallets during the past year:

PRICE LINE	PERCENTAGE OF SALES
$ 5.50	18%
8.00	22
12.00	13
15.00	26
20.00	10
27.50	5
32.00	6

In an effort to trim the inventory, the buyer decided to place future orders in four price lines only. Which price lines should be maintained?

3. A handbag buyer for a fashion store stocks leather bags in the following price lines and with the following rates of sale:

PRICE LINE	AVERAGE COST	RATE OF SALE (WEEKLY)
$19.50	$10.00 each	12
25.00	12.00	18
40.00	20.00	4
42.00	20.00	10
45.00	21.00	20
60.00	32.00	15
65.00	35.00	8
80.00	38.00	14

To provide greater depth of stock, she decides to eliminate the two least profitable price lines. What should be her new price structure?

4. A department store plans to discontinue selling bicycles on a volume basis because of increased competition from mail-order houses and discount stores. It decides to keep three numbers for customer convenience and good will. An analysis of sales during the past six months reveals the following:

PRICE LINE	AVERAGE COST	RATE OF SALE (WEEKLY)
$ 50.00	$30.00	6
65.00	40.00	14
80.00	50.00	10
92.50	60.00	6
105.00	62.00	8
119.00	70.00	1
135.00	80.00	3

Which three price lines have been most profitable and therefore should be retained?

CASE PROBLEM

UNHAPPY ENDINGS

Ruth Wolcott is the lamp buyer for a large department store in the Midwest noted for its quality merchandise and fine service. Her lamp shade business has fallen off in recent years, and Ms. Wolcott feels that she is losing too much business to competing stores. During the past year she bought merchandise from several new vendors in an attempt to stock shades that were truly distinctive and unusual. She was in the habit of applying an initial markup of 50 percent to each shade with little regard to price endings. She also purchased job lots and promoted the shades at special sale prices in order to stimulate customer traffic.

At the end of the year Ms. Wolcott is dismayed to find that her sales have slipped even farther. Her profit margin has also fallen. To make matters worse, her merchandise manager accuses her of delicatessen buying, and there were many customer complaints. An analysis of her want slips indicates that many sales were lost because shades were not available in wanted colors and styles, and customers were often unwilling to wait for special orders to arrive.

After the January inventory results have come in, Ms. Wolcott meets with her merchandise manager to discuss ways of improving the profit picture for her department. Lamp shades at the following retail prices are currently in stock:

$3.33	$5.99	$7.60	$14.98	$28.99
3.99	6.35	8.00	16.59	32.00
4.29	6.82	9.50	17.00	35.00
5.00	7.12	11.33	23.50	36.54
5.75	7.25	13.27	27.00	39.00

As a first step, both Ms. Wolcott and her merchandise manager agree that a price-line analysis is sorely needed.

1. How would you go about price lining the merchandise if you were Ms. Wolcott?
2. Do you think that Ms. Wolcott took her competition into consideration when pricing her lamp shades?
3. Do you think that Ms. Wolcott is using good price endings? How would you improve them?

9

HOW TO CALCULATE STOCK TURN

KEY POINTS

1. Stock turn tells the retailer how fast the stock is selling.

2. A meaningful stock turn figure depends on accurate sales and average-stock figures.

3. Although a high stock turn is usually desirable, a healthy balance between sales and stocks must be maintained.

4. The stock-sales ratio tells the retailer how much stock is available at a particular time to meet customer demand.

5. The return on merchandise investment (ROI) shows the relationship between profit and what has been invested in the business.

THE MEANING OF STOCK TURN

One of the prime concerns of every retailer is to keep stock moving. Although buyers may be highly satisfied with their merchandise selections, they will be happier if the goods are purchased quickly by customers. As soon as merchandise is bought by the buyer, it should be sold so that new merchandise can be brought in to take its place.

Merchants find out how fast their stock is selling by means of a measure called *stock turn* or *stock turnover*. Stock turn may be defined as the number of times the *average* stock for a period is sold and replaced. Stock turn may be stated in terms of a week, a month, a season, a year, or any other period of time. The common practice, however, is to consider yearly turnovers. If a monthly turn is available, the yearly rate is simply twelve times that figure. Similarly, given a six-month seasonal turn, we can get the yearly rate by multiplying the given figure by two.

Stock turn is usually given in terms of a retail base because most stores today use the retail method of inventory. However, if a store bases its merchandising figures on cost, stock turn should also be shown in terms of the cost of the goods.

CALCULATING STOCK TURN

There are three basic formulas to remember for calculating stock turn:

1. At retail

$$\text{Stock turn} = \frac{\text{Net sales}}{\text{Average retail stock}}$$

2. At cost

$$\text{Stock turn} = \frac{\text{Cost of goods sold}}{\text{Average cost stock}}$$

3. In units of merchandise

$$\text{Stock turn} = \frac{\text{Unit sales}}{\text{Average unit stock}}$$

Stock turn at cost is always higher than stock turn at retail because the cumulative markup between the cost and retail of the stock is greater than the maintained markup on net sales.

ILLUSTRATIVE PROBLEM

The watch section in a jewelry store sold 240 watches, resulting in net retail sales of $12,000 for the year just ended. The merchandise had cost the store $4,800. The average stock of eighty watches was valued at $2,000 at cost and $6,000 at retail. What was the stock turn at retail, at cost, and in units of merchandise?

SOLUTION

At retail, we have:

$$\text{Stock turn} = \frac{\text{Net sales}}{\text{Average retail stock}}$$
$$= \frac{\$12,000}{\$6,000}$$
$$= 2$$

At cost, the turnover is:

$$\text{Stock turn} = \frac{\text{Cost of goods sold}}{\text{Average cost stock}}$$
$$= \frac{\$4,800}{\$2,000}$$
$$= 2.4$$

And in units of merchandise, it is

$$\text{Stock turn} = \frac{\text{Unit sales}}{\text{Average unit stock}}$$
$$= \frac{240}{80}$$
$$= 3$$

EXERCISES

1. A stationery department realized sales of $24,000 for the month. The merchandise had cost $14,400. The average retail stock was $4,000 at cost and $8,000 at retail. What was the monthly stock turn at retail?
2. A paint store sold 630 cans of spray paint at $1.00 each during the past year. The cans had cost the store 60¢ each. The average stock carried was 200 cans. What was the yearly stock turn in units of merchandise?
3. A leather goods department sold 800 initialed coin purses at $15 each during the spring and summer six-month season. The merchandise had cost $7.50 each. The average stock maintained was $2,000 at cost and $5,000 at retail. What was the yearly stock turn at (a) cost and (b) retail?

Average Stocks

The key to an accurate calculation of stock turn is finding a realistic average-stock figure. Perhaps the simplest way to find an average stock is to take the stock at the beginning of a period, add it to the stock at the end of the period, and divide the sum by two. For example, the average may be of the stocks at the beginning of the merchandising year (February 1) and at the end of the year (the following January 31). However, stocks are usually at a low point in February. Christmas buying and January clearance sales often deplete the supply of merchandise on hand in most departments, and since customer traffic is usually slow in February, stores do not build up stocks for spring selling until later. Thus using a February stock figure may result in an unrealistically low average-stock figure and so inflate the stock turn.

In order to obtain a more accurate picture of stock conditions during the entire year, it may be advisable to report stock figures at the beginning of each month, beginning on February 1 and ending on the following January 31. The sum of these figures, however, should be divided by thirteen instead of twelve to yield the average, because the twelfth stock figure will be that for January 1, whereas the fiscal year does not end until January 31, so that a thirteenth stock figure for January 31 must be included. In this way the ending stock figure for one year will also be the beginning stock figure for the next year.

Stocks often drop at the end of each month and peak during the middle of the month. Many stores advertise end-of-month clearance sales to get rid of slow sellers and reduce the size of the stock at the end of each month. Therefore, if still more accuracy is desired, stocks can be reported at the beginning of each week. If a store decides to do this, the total stock figure must be divided by fifty-three, not fifty-two, to include the final week of the year. Of course, even daily stock figures could be used to compute stock turn, but the task then becomes too cumbersome for most stores to be practical.

ILLUSTRATIVE PROBLEM

A ladies' specialty shop, The Hen's Den, reported the following data for the six-month period beginning February 1 and ending July 31. What was the yearly rate of stock turnover?

STOCK ON HAND		NET SALES	
February 1	$13,000	February	$ 8,000
March 1	18,000	March	10,000
April 1	17,000	April	11,000
May 1	16,000	May	10,000
June 1	15,000	June	9,000
July 1	14,000	July	9,000
July 31	12,000		

SOLUTION

(a) Find the net sales by adding the figures for the six-month period. The total is $57,000. (b) Find the average stock by adding the stock-on-hand figures and dividing by seven. The average is $15,000. (c) Apply the formula:

$$\text{Stock turn} = \frac{\text{Net sales}}{\text{Average stock}}$$
$$= \frac{\$57{,}000}{\$15{,}000}$$
$$= 3.8$$

(d) Multiply the semiannual turn by two (3.8 × 2), giving a yearly stock turn of 7.6.

EXERCISES

1. A toy buyer had an inventory at the beginning of August amounting to $65,000, which shrank to $55,000 by the end of the month. Net sales were $15,000 for the month. What were (a) the monthly stock turn and (b) the yearly stock turn?

2. A fur store reported the following figures for the fiscal year beginning February 1 and ending on January 31. Find the stock turn (a) at retail and (b) at cost.

	Inventory			Net Sales	
	COST	RETAIL		COST	RETAIL
February 1	$17,000	$35,000	February	$ 6,000	$12,000
March 1	16,000	35,000	March	5,000	10,000
April 1	20,000	45,000	April	5,500	10,000
May 1	25,000	50,000	May	4,500	8,000
June 1	18,000	40,000	June	4,000	7,000
July 1	30,000	60,000	July	3,000	5,000
August 1	38,000	80,000	August	25,000	50,000
September 1	35,000	70,000	September	18,000	40,000
October 1	30,000	60,000	October	20,000	40,000
November 1	32,000	65,000	November	23,000	45,000
December 1	35,000	70,000	December	34,000	65,000
January 1	20,000	40,000	January	12,000	22,000
January 31	10,000	30,000			

3. A record department had net sales of $4,000 in September and $6,000 in October. The retail stock on September 1 was $6,000, that on October 1 was $8,000, and that on November 1 was $10,000. What was the annual rate of stock turnover?

Stock Turn Ratio

The basic stock turn formula

$$\text{Stock turn} = \frac{\text{Sales}}{\text{Average stock}}$$

can be very useful in planning sales or forecasting stock needs. By transposition we see that the equation can be written as follows:

$$\text{Sales} = \text{Average stock} \times \text{Stock turn},$$
$$\text{Average stock} = \text{Sales divided by Stock turn}$$

These triple relations may be more easily grasped if numbers are used. Let Sales = 10, Average stock = 5, and Stock turn = 2. Then

$$\text{Stock turn (2)} = \frac{\text{Sales (10)}}{\text{Average stock (5)}}$$
$$\text{Sales (10)} = \text{Average stock (5)} \times \text{Stock turn (2)}$$
$$\text{Average stock (5)} = \frac{\text{Sales (10)}}{\text{Stock turn (2)}}$$

ILLUSTRATIVE PROBLEM A new merchant decides to open a small stationery store. He needs to know approximately what his sales volume might be during his first year of operation. He has $20,000 to invest in merchandise that can be retailed for $35,000. He discovers that a store of his size and type usually has a stock turn of four. If his average stock remains at $35,000, what might his first-year sales volume be?

SOLUTION
$$\begin{aligned}\text{Sales} &= \text{Average stock} \times \text{Stock turn}\\ &= \$35{,}000 \times 4\\ &= \$140{,}000\end{aligned}$$

ILLUSTRATIVE PROBLEM A departmental buyer plans sales of $50,000 for the month of December. If a stock turn of two is typical for her department at that time of year, how much average stock will be required to operate her department successfully?

SOLUTION
$$\begin{aligned}\text{Average stock} &= \frac{\text{Sales}}{\text{Stock turn}}\\ &= \frac{\$50{,}000}{2}\\ &= \$25{,}000\end{aligned}$$

EXERCISES
1. A smoke shop planned a stock turn of six during the year. If the average stock for the year was pegged at $14,000, what would be the net sales?
2. A hosiery department planned sales totaling $150,000 for a six-month period. A stock turn of three was typical for the period. What should the average stock be?
3. Last year a candy department showed sales of $40,000 with a stock turn of five. If the buyer plans a 10 percent increase in sales with the same number of stock turns, what should the average stock be?

Finding an Average Stock Turn

After the stock turns of individual departments or sections of a store have been found, retailers may want to find the average stock turn for the store as a whole. In a large store with many departments, this task is naturally more complex than in a smaller store with fewer departments. For our purpose it suffices to show how a small store might find its average stock turn.

ILLUSTRATIVE PROBLEM   A boutique, Uppers and Lowers, was divided into three departments with the following net sales and stock turns for the fiscal year:

	NET SALES	STOCK TURN
Department 1	$240,000	4
Department 2	160,000	4
Department 3	320,000	2

What was the average stock turn for the entire shop?

SOLUTION   (a) Find the average stock for each department:

$$\text{Average stock} = \frac{\text{Sales}}{\text{Stock turn}}$$

$$\frac{\$240,000}{4} = \$60,000 \text{ (Dept. 1)}$$

$$\frac{\$160,000}{4} = \$40,000 \text{ (Dept. 2)}$$

$$\frac{\$320,000}{2} = \$160,000 \text{ (Dept. 3)}$$

Therefore,

$$\text{Total average stock} = \$260,000$$

(b) Find total net sales for the boutique:

$$\text{Total net sales} = \$240,000 + \$160,000 + \$320,000$$
$$= \$720,000$$

(c) Find the average stock turn for the boutique:

$$\text{Stock turn} = \frac{\text{Total net sales}}{\text{Total average stock}}$$
$$= \frac{\$720,000}{\$260,000}$$
$$= 2.8$$

EXERCISES   1. A drug store with two departments showed the following sales and stock turns for the year just ended:

	NET SALES	STOCK TURN
Department A	$60,000	3
Department B	$350,000	5

What was the average stock turn for the store?

2. The manager of the men's division of a department store wants to know the average stock turn for the entire division. The general departments showed the following sales and stock turns:

	NET SALES	STOCK TURN
Shoes	$ 350,000	5
Hats	$ 30,000	6
Sportswear	$1,200,000	3
Furnishings	$2,400,000	4
Clothing	$1,500,000	5

What was the divisional stock turn?

3. A store with four departments reported the following data:

	DEPARTMENT 1	DEPARTMENT 2	DEPARTMENT 3	DEPARTMENT 4
Net sales	$50,000	$60,000	$80,000	$20,000
Stock turn	5	4	2	4

What was the average stock turn for the store?

ADVANTAGES AND DISADVANTAGES OF RAPID STOCK TURN

It is often believed that the quicker the stock turn, the more profitable the department. This may or may not be true. But no matter how quickly the stocks are moved, there must be a healthy balance between sales and stocks. The stock turn reflects the efficiency with which the department or store is being run. To increase this efficiency is a challenge that faces every buyer interested in building the reputation of the store and increasing sales at a profit.

Generally, therefore, retailers strive for ever-higher stock turnovers. An excellent way to reach this aim is to reduce stocks without adversely affecting sales. For example, if a department with $100,000 in sales reduces average stocks from $25,000 to $20,000, the stock turn will increase from four to five. A reduction in stock may be accomplished by reducing the number of price lines carried, avoiding duplications in styles and brands, and reducing the size and color assortments. It is always a good idea to stock heavily the so-called *heart sizes*, where the demand is greatest, and to stock lightly if at all the *fringe sizes*. These methods of stock reduction can be employed without materially affecting sales volume.

Advantages of Rapid Turnover

1. *Reduces markdowns.* An important reason for striving for rapid turnovers is to make markdowns less necessary. If goods are moved quickly

in and out, they have less chance to get soiled, shopworn, and aged. Fresh-looking merchandise entices customers to buy and is more easily sold at the original retail prices.
2. *Increases sales.* Customers tire of seeing the same merchandise for a long period of time. They continually seek the unusual and different. The quicker the turnover, the easier it is for a store to bring in brand new items to stimulate customer interest. Sales people also become more enthusiastic; and if the merchandise is wanted, sales are bound to rise.
3. *Increases the return on merchandise investment.* Merchandise is an important part of store investment. Unless it is sold, the investment is not productive. Merchandise that stays on the shelf cannot yield profits, so it makes sense that a rapid stock turn improves investment return.
4. *Decreases certain operating expenses.* Cost of space is reduced because a smaller average inventory takes up less selling and stockroom space. There are also savings in insurance costs and in taxes due to lower inventory investment. Interests on capital are reduced because the merchant can pay back a loan faster if the inventory is smaller.

Disadvantages of Rapid Turnover

1. *Increases difficulty in maintaining balanced stocks.* A rapid stock turn can quickly deplete stocks. Unless reorders are placed immediately, serious gaps in stock structures may develop, resulting in lost sales. An

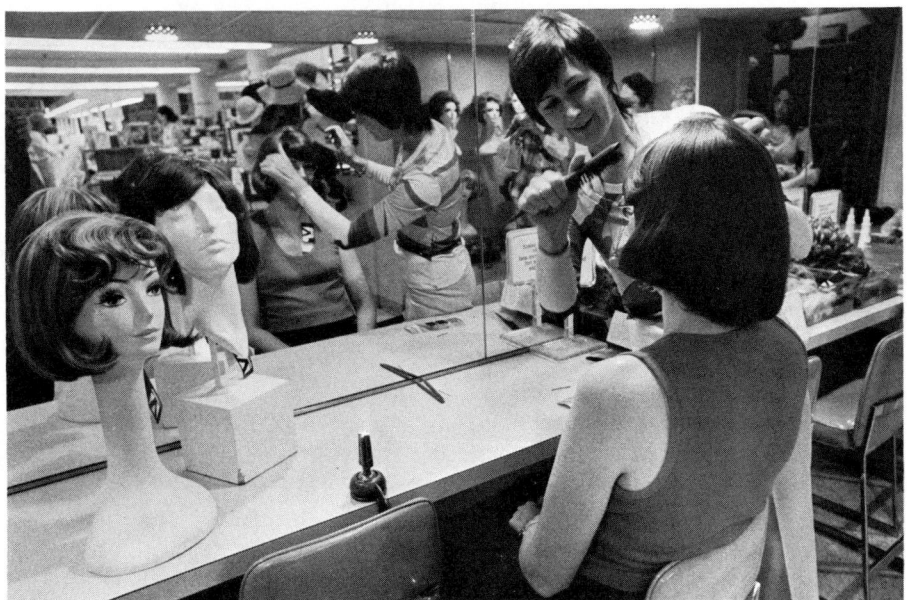

Wigs—example of fast stock turn
SOURCE: Cary Wolinsky/Grafia

out-of-stock situation is especially serious with basic stock items such as baby blankets or boys' dungarees.

2. *Increases merchandise expense.* Frequent reorders to make sure that stocks are kept balanced necessarily result in higher merchandise costs. When buyers order just enough to cover short-term needs, they are doing *hand-to-mouth* buying, which is expensive. Quantity discounts cannot be taken advantage of, clerical costs are increased because there are more orders to process, and transportation charges increase, as do receiving and marking costs.

Stock Turn Goals

What constitutes a good turnover rate depends greatly on the type of merchandise in question and its price. A good turnover in one department may be considered poor for another. The Financial Executives Division of the National Retail Merchants Association furnishes annual stock turnover figures by departments for department and specialty stores, according to sales volume so that turnover rates may be compared and studied. Stock turn goals, which represent a performance level better than that achieved by 75 percent of the stores surveyed, are also published. Figure 9.1 shows stock turn goals for representative departments in department stores with yearly sales in excess of $50 million. We note that very expensive items, such as furs and fine jewelry, tend to turn over slowly, while most apparel departments enjoy higher turnovers.

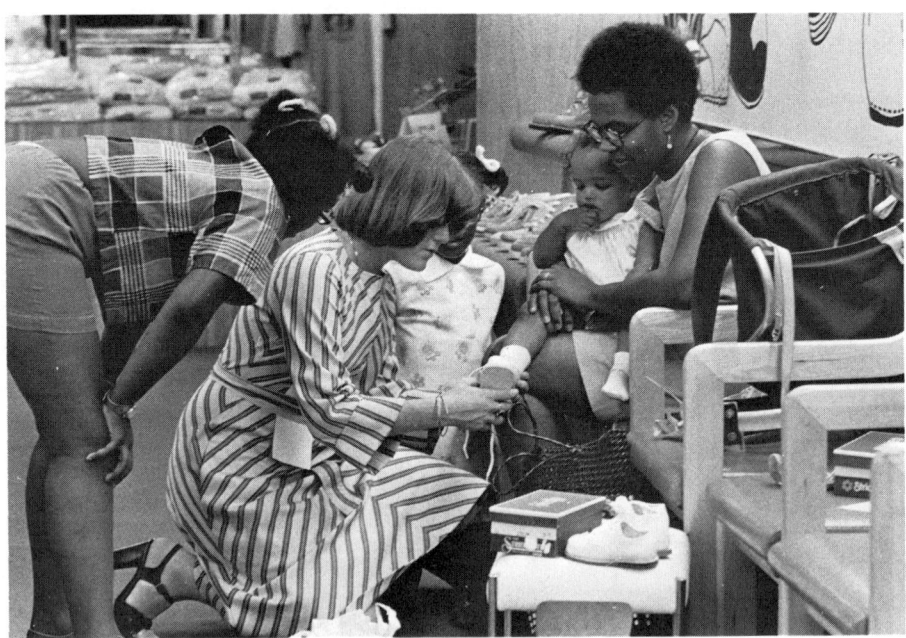

Children's shoes—slow stock turn items
SOURCE: Cary Wolinski/Grafia

Figure 9.1
STOCK TURN GOALS

DEPARTMENT	STOCK TURN GOAL (YEARLY)
Furs and fur garments	2.3
All dresses	5.3
Maternity clothing and accessories	3.8
Corsets and bras	3.3
Daytime lingerie	3.7
Sleepwear and robes	5.3
Fine jewelry and watches	1.8
Women's hosiery	3.7
Women's gloves	4.1
Hats, hairpieces, and trimmings	6.9
Men's clothing	3.3
Men's furnishings	3.9
Girls clothing 3 - 6X and 7 - 14	4.9
Boys' clothing 2 - 16	3.4
Children's footwear	1.8
Cosmetics, toiletries, drugs	3.7
Toys	3.6
Luggage	2.8
Sporting goods	2.1
Floor coverings	2.7
Chinaware and glassware	1.9
Silverware	2.2
Lamps and lighting fixtures	2.1
Christmas decorations	4.2

SOURCE: *Merchandise and Operating Results*, National Retail Merchants Association, New York, 1972.

CAPITAL TURN

Capital turn differs from stock turn in that in this case the net sales are divided by the average stock at cost instead of the average stock at retail. It indicates turnover on the invested capital itself. Merchandisers find stock turns to be more meaningful, but outside financiers often have to rely on capital turn because average stock figures at retail are not available. However, sales and stock figures at cost can usually be obtained from store balance sheets and income statements.

Capital turnovers are always higher than the corresponding stock turnovers. If both the capital turnover and the stock turnover are known, the initial markup on the average stock can be easily found.

ILLUSTRATIVE PROBLEM

A children's shoe department had an inventory at cost amounting to $140,000 on February 1. On the following January 31 the inventory at cost amounted to $180,000. Net sales during the year were $320,000. What was the capital turnover?

SOLUTION

$$\text{Capital turn} = \frac{\text{Net sales}}{\text{Average stock at cost}}$$
$$= \frac{\$320,000}{\$160,000}$$
$$= 2$$

ILLUSTRATIVE PROBLEM A silverware department had a capital turnover of 8 and a stock turnover of 4. What was the initial markup percentage on the average stock?

SOLUTION (a) Find the average stock at cost and at retail. We let sales = $100. Then using the formula above, we have:

$$\text{Average stock at cost} = \frac{\text{Sales}}{\text{Capital turn}}$$
$$= \frac{\$100}{8}$$
$$= \$12.50$$

$$\text{Average stock at retail} = \frac{\text{Sales}}{\text{Stock turn}}$$
$$= \frac{\$100}{4}$$
$$= \$25.00$$

(b) Then

$$\text{Initial markup} = \text{Average stock at retail} - \text{Average stock at cost}$$
$$= \$25.00 - \$12.50$$
$$= \$12.50$$

(c) Finally,

$$\text{Initial markup \%} = \frac{\text{Initial markup}}{\text{Average stock at retail}}$$
$$= \frac{\$12.50}{\$25.00}$$
$$= 50\%$$

EXERCISES

1. The opening inventory of a handbag department was $12,000 at cost and $20,000 at retail. The ending inventory totaled $10,000 at cost and $19,000 at retail. Net sales for the period amounted to $33,000. What was the capital turn?
2. The capital turn in a candy department was ten, and the stock turn was six. What was the initial markup percentage?
3. On August 1 the inventory in a china department was $35,000 at cost and $72,000 at retail. During the month purchases amounting to $123,000 were made. Net sales amounted to $110,000, and markdowns totaled $1,500. On September 1 the department inventory showed a total stock of $43,000 at cost and $85,000 at retail. What was the capital turn?

STOCK-SALES RATIO

Although the stock turnover gives a merchant an idea of how fast his or her stock is selling, it does not indicate how much stock should be carried during the week or month ahead, because it deals with average stocks. It is the *stock-sales ratios* that show how much stock should be on hand at a given time. As the words imply, the stock-sales ratio is found by dividing the stock by the sales. It is common to state the ratio for one-month periods, but weekly ratios may also be useful if the merchandise has an unusually high stock turn.

The stock figure used for this ratio may be that at the beginning of the month (B.O.M.) or the end of the month (E.O.M.). The beginning-of-the-month stock figure is more useful, because it shows how much stock is available to meet the demand during the month. The end-of-the-month figure is useful only in planning for the following month's sales. Unless stated otherwise, therefore, we will assume that the B.O.M. figure is being used.

ILLUSTRATIVE PROBLEM A carpet department had a September B.O.M. stock totaling $250,000 and an E.O.M. stock of $225,000. Sales for the month of September came to $125,000. (a) What was the B.O.M. stock-sales ratio? (b) What was the E.O.M. stock-sales ratio?

SOLUTION (a)

$$\text{B.O.M. stock-sales ratio} = \frac{\text{B.O.M. stock}}{\text{Sales}}$$
$$= \frac{\$250,000}{\$125,000}$$
$$= 2$$

(b)

$$\text{E.O.M. stock-sales ratio} = \frac{\text{E.O.M. stock}}{\text{Sales}}$$
$$= \frac{\$225,000}{\$125,000}$$
$$= 1.8$$

EXERCISES

1. A buyer had a stock at the beginning of the month amounting to $26,000. Sales during the month totaled $13,000. What was the stock-sales ratio?
2. Planned sales in a stationery department were $24,000 for the month of November. The planned stock-sales ratio was three. How much stock should have been on hand at the beginning of November?
3. According to a retail trade association, the stock-sales ratio in a camera department for the month of December should be four. The planned stock on December 1 was $120,000. What were the planned sales for the month?

RETURN ON MERCHANDISE INVESTMENT

Another figure that tells the merchant something about his or her efficiency is the *return on merchandise investment* or R.O.I. (return on investment). It is important that stores be rated, not only on the relationship of profit to sales, but also on the relationship of profit to merchandise investment. The latter is obtained by dividing the profit in dollars by the average merchandise investment (average inventory at cost).

The amount of merchandise investment necessary to operate a successful business has grown in recent years. There are many new products on the market that must be stocked. The rush to the suburbs has accelerated the opening of branch stores. The depreciation of the dollar has called for more capital to be invested.

In order to attract more capital, many retailers have gone public and invited outside investors in the form of stockholders. Stockholders, however, demand a high return on their investment, so that corporate stores have found it necessary to maintain their operations at peak efficiency.

CHAPTER SUMMARY

It is important for merchandisers to know how efficiently their departments or stores are being run. Whether a report is being submitted to stockholders or to the store management, it should show that profitable use is being made of the capital invested.

Two significant measures of operating efficiency are stock turnover and capital turnover. Stock turnover shows how rapidly the average stock at retail is being sold and replaced. Capital turnover shows the same thing for average stock at cost. The triple relations among sales, average stock, and turnover are very useful for planning future sales and stock needs.

Another method of determining efficiency rests on the relation between net profit and the amount invested in merchandise. The R.O.I. (return on investment) is of particular interest to shareholders who have invested capital in the business.

Stock turnovers refer to average stocks, so that they do not tell the retailer how much stock will be needed at a particular time. It is the stock-sales ratio that gives this information, and this ratio is especially helpful at the beginning of each month because it shows how much stock is available to meet customer demand during the month.

Merchandisers strive for a high turnover, but fast-moving items require constant attention. Lost sales and unhappy customers are possible consequences of an uneven balance between sales and stocks.

QUESTIONS FOR REVIEW

1. Define "stock turn." What are three ways in which it may be calculated?
2. When computing the average stock for a year given the monthly figures, why must the total stock be divided by thirteen instead of twelve?

3. What are some advantages of rapid turnovers? What are some of their disadvantages?
4. How does capital turn differ from stock turn? Which one is always higher than the other?
5. What is stock-sales ratio? Why is it better to use a stock-sales ratio at the beginning of the month rather than at the end of the month?
6. Why is a stock-sales ratio more helpful in sales and stock planning than a stock turn figure?
7. Is it possible for a merchant to compare his stock turns with other stores of similar volume and type?
8. How can a retailer be sure that enough stock of an item with high turnover will be on hand to satisfy customer needs?
9. What is the difference between capital turn and return on merchandise investment and how is each obtained?
10. What are heart stocks, fringe stocks, and hand-to-mouth buying?

DISCUSSION QUESTION Why is a candy department more likely to have rapid stock turns than a children's shoes department?

PROBLEMS FOR REVIEW

1. A candle shop, Beeswax 'n Things, had a December B.O.M. stock of $15,000 and an E.O.M. stock of $17,000. Net Christmas sales amounted to $8,000. What was the stock turn for the month of December?
2. A beach shop had stocked heavily for the summer season and showed a beginning inventory on June 1 of $12,000 at cost. Late shipments boosted the cost inventory to $16,000 by the end of the month. The books showed that the cost of the merchandise sold during the month was $14,000, with a retail value of $30,000. Determine the June stock turn at cost.
3. The men's shirts department of Famous Department Store reported sales of 5,600 shirts during the six-month period ending July 31. The average stock was $40,000 at cost and $75,000 at retail, which represented 4,400 shirts. Based on these figures, what was the yearly stock turn?
4. The Feather Boa, a boutique, obtained the following figures for its first six months of operation. What was the stock turn (a) at cost and (b) at retail?

	Inventory		Net Sales	
	COST	RETAIL	COST	RETAIL
March 1	$12,000	$20,000	$ 8,000	$14,000
April 1	14,000	24,000	9,500	15,000
May 1	14,000	26,000	10,000	17,500
June 1	15,000	28,200	11,500	20,000
July 1	13,200	24,000	8,000	14,500
August 1	12,800	22,000	5,000	11,000
September 1	10,000	18,900		

5. The average stock for the month of March was $3,200 in a record department. If the stock turn was 0.5, what were the net sales for the month?
6. The net sales in a cosmetics department were $88,992 for the six-month period ending January 31. If the stock turn during that period was 3.6, what was the average stock?
7. With the new display cases in his department the buyer of boys' furnishings feels that he can increase his stock turn from five to six with the same amount of average stock. If his average stock remains at $200,000, by how much in dollars and cents will his net sales have to increase to achieve the higher turnover?
8. A men's specialty store was divided into five departments. The manager was given the following figures and was asked to determine the stock turn for the entire store. What did he report?

	NET SALES	STOCK TURN
Furnishings	$150,000	3.0
Sportswear	120,000	2.0
Shoes	50,000	2.5
Clothing	105,000	1.5
Hats	5,000	1.0

9. A picture frame shop had an inventory amounting to $8,400 at cost and $16,000 at retail on February 1. A year later the inventory was $10,200 at cost and $22,800 at retail. Sales during the year had amounted to $27,900. What was the capital turn?
10. An umbrella department had a B.O.M. stock for the month of October amounting to $13,000 and an E.O.M. stock of $15,000. Given that the October sales were $9,000, determine (a) the B.O.M. stock-sales ratio, and (b) the E.O.M. stock-sales ratio.

CASE PROBLEMS

ONE GOOD TURN DESERVES ANOTHER

Beverly Simon is the buyer of ladies' hosiery for a prestigious specialty store in the midwestern part of the country. The store has become world famous on account of its unusual merchandise offerings, high quality, and wide selections. Its Christmas catalog is awaited eagerly each year for its many extraordinary gift suggestions.

Ms. Simon has operated a successful hosiery department for many years. She has stocked complete lines of nylon hosiery with four nationally advertised brands as well as the store's private brand. During the past holiday season she made hosiery news by buying genuine silk stockings from Italy. The silk stockings became a much talked about feature in the Christmas catalog.

During the past several years Ms. Simon's department has been overstocked. As a result, the stock turn has slipped from 4.2 to 3.5 to 3.2, and finally, according to the latest year-end statistics just in, to 2.8. Since stock turns for departments of her size should fall between three and four, she realizes that corrective action must be taken.

Ms. Simon has noticed much change in the hosiery business during the time that she has been buyer. More and more women, especially younger ones, are buying pantyhose instead of regular stockings. Also her customers seem reluctant to pay for branded hosiery and prefer to buy their pantyhose and stockings at supermarkets, drug stores, discount houses, and other outlets where prices are very low and brands are not important.

Since her stock has not been moving as well as planned, Ms. Simon has been forced to take some heavy markdowns. She has even persuaded her key vendors to take back some unwanted stock. Although the silk stockings created a sensation, they were only a mediocre seller.

At a meeting with her merchandise manager Ms. Simon is asked to submit to her an outline of the steps she plans to take to increase her stock turn.

1. What can Ms. Simon do to improve her stock turn?
2. Even if the silk stockings were not a big seller, is there an advantage to promoting an item of this type? Why?

STITCH 'N SAVE

Jim Lebsack, a retailing teacher at Sandhills Community College, became enthusiastic about franchising after a visit to his brother-in-law, Steve. Steve had acquired a franchised drive-in hamburger restaurant only three years ago and had already paid off his investment loan. He was now making plans for the purchase of a second unit. Steve had had very little prior knowledge about the restaurant business, having been a former automobile salesman.

Mr. Lebsack, therefore, began gathering information on various types of franchises. He was surprised to note that even the most successful were less than twenty years old. Most franchisers seemed to offer basically the same type of "package." Though it varied, the franchise fee usually ranged from $1,500 to $25,000, with $10,000 being the average. Other major costs included a royalty between 2 and 5 percent and advertising expenses of 1 to 3 percent of gross sales. Both these fees were collected monthly by the franchiser.

In return for the fees, franchisers offered a variety of services, including comprehensive training, continuing management aids, basic building plans and specifications, accounting controls, lease negotiation, construction supervision, traffic counts, site selection, equipment placement, financing arrangements, and a package insurance plan.

One brochure received in response to a newspaper advertisement was of particular interest to Mr. Lebsack. It outlined the program for a national chain of fabric stores called Stitch 'n Save. Mr. Lebsack felt that with today's inflationary pressures, more and more women would turn to home sewing. Stitch 'n Save stores featured a wide selection of fabrics along with a complete line of sewing accessories. The stock was obtained directly from one fabric manufacturer who maintained several large warehouses.

Owners of Stitch 'n Save stores could thus buy fabrics at a much lower cost and still get a big selection of the newest materials. Best of all, an owner would run his own store and yet be backed by a company with a nationally advertised name, proven promotional programs, and the management experience of a successful franchiser. Mr. Lebsack also knew that his experience as a textiles teacher would aid him in his merchandising efforts.

The Stitch 'n Save package required an initial cash outlay of $12,000, half of which would represent the prepaid franchise fee with the other half going toward the purchase of the initial stock. Mr. Lebsack would lease both property and building from an area investor who would build a store to company specifications in return for a lease guarantee of twenty years.

After sending in his completed Confidential Qualification Report that had come with the brochure, Mr. Lebsack was soon contacted by a company representative who further explained to him the franchise package offered by Stitch 'n Save. The representative stated that at present the average store grossed $125,000 after one year's operation. Several profit-and-loss statements showed a minimum net profit before taxes of 20 percent. Mr. Lebsack was assured that Stitch 'n Save represented one of the best investments in the franchise business today. Stock turnover was rapid in Stitch 'n Save stores because customers were offered quality fabrics at bargain prices. The representative further stated that the area in which Mr. Lebsack was interested was a prime market for this type of business, and the company would guarantee a trading area populated by 100,000 persons.

1. What other information should Mr. Lebsack obtain before deciding on whether or not to buy the franchise?
2. What are the benefits he could obtain as a franchisee?
3. What other types of franchises exist today?

10

HOW TO PLAN SALES

KEY POINTS

1. Accurate and realistic sales forecasting is necessary to keep sales and stocks balanced.

2. A sales plan is usually prepared for a six-month season, but it must be flexible enough to allow adjustments to changes in the economy, consumer tastes, store policy, and other factors.

3. Sales should be recorded daily and compared with those of previous years to anticipate the development of trends.

4. In periods of high inflation, sales planning is very difficult. Among the better gauges of sales success are the number of transactions and the size of the average sale.

5. Changes in the number of selling days and the calendar date of Easter must be considered when planning sales.

IMPORTANCE OF SALES FORECASTING

The importance of accurate sales forecasting cannot be underestimated. The existence of a store depends on making sales. Well-stocked shelves of attractive merchandise, inviting window displays, and provocative advertisements are of no importance if goods are not sold. Since sales are the very heart of a retailing enterprise, their planning requires sound judgment based on adequate knowledge. (A little crystal-ball gazing does not hurt, either.)

Sales are usually planned for two six-month periods in a year: the fall-winter season (August 1 to January 31) and the spring-summer season (February 1 to July 31). Sales are projected for each month on the basis of a plan, variously referred to as a *sales plan, merchandise plan, sales and merchandise plan,* or *merchandise budget*. In this text we shall refer to it as the sales and merchandise plan. Whatever name is used, however, a buyer begins to work on it at least four months before the beginning of each season. The plan is actually initiated in the controller's office, because it is here that all the figures of the previous year are kept and recorded. The controller enters last year's figures on the plan and also submits other information that might aid the buyer in planning her or his sales. The dates of last year's promotions, of holidays, the number of selling days in each month, and changes in store policy that might affect sales are also given to the buyer. When the buyer completes the planning, the merchandise manager reviews what has been done, and then the plan is submitted to the controller for final approval. In smaller stores the procedure is less complicated, but the aim is the same: to set a realistic sales goal.

It is difficult to make day-to-day comparisons within the framework of six-month projections, since calendar months differ on account of leap years. Therefore, some stores prefer to use a 4-5-4 control, which keeps four-week and five-week months consistent from year to year. The year is divided into four quarters of thirteen weeks each with a total of fifty-two weeks.

Figure 10.1 shows a typical sales and merchandise planning sheet. After the sales have been forecast, the buyer must determine the inventory requirements to make sure there will be enough merchandise on hand to meet the planned sales. He or she must then plan the initial markup necessary to cover the estimated retail reductions, as well as the maintained markup and gross margin to cover expenses and profit. Cash discounts and alterations expenses must also be anticipated because they make the difference between maintained markup and gross margin. The stock turnover goal and retail purchases must also be planned. The overall plan then becomes a guide for merchandisers to follow in making sure that sales and stocks remain balanced. All of the planned figures are important because each has a part in determining whether in the final analysis there is a profit or a loss.

We note that sales planning requires four lines on the planning sheet. Last year's sales are entered first, then the planned sales. The actual sales figures are watched closely during the season. If the sales of a department or store begin to run well ahead of projection, a buyer may wish to revise the sales plan upward. Conversely, if sales do not come up to expectations, the buyer will probably revise the plan downward and cut back on buying to avoid overstocking. The line for the adjusted plan is to be used for such a purpose.

Figure 10.1 shows last year's sales for the six-month spring-summer season to have begun with $80,000 for February and ended with $65,000 for July. The season's total sales of $500,000 are recorded in the last column. In this particular case, the buyer apparently feels that the steady growth of her departmental sales coupled with rising retail prices due to inflation justify a 10 percent increase in planned sales. Ten percent of $500,000 is $50,000, so that the planned total sales figure for the year in question is $550,000.

The monthly contributions to total sales for last year's spring-summer season were as follows:

MONTH	SALES	PERCENTAGE OF TOTAL
February	$80,000	16%
March	90,000	18%
April	110,000	22%
May	85,000	17%
June	70,000	14%
July	65,000	13%
Total	$500,000	100%

Here the percentages are found by dividing the monthly sales by the season's total. Thus February's share of the total comes to $80,000/$500,000 or 16 percent.

Figure 10.1 SALES AND MERCHANDISE PLAN

SALES AND MERCHANDISE PLAN

Season: Spring
Department No.: 2

	Last Year	Plan	Actual		Last Year	Plan	Actual
Initial Markup %	43.3	43.4		Gross Margin %	38.4	39.3	
Reductions %	10.0	9.0		Operating Expense %	36.0	36.0	
Cash Discount %	1.8	2.0					
Alteration Expense %	1.0	1.0		Season Turn	2.5	3	
Maintained Markup %	37.6	38.3		Net Profit %	2.4	3.0	

	FEB / AUG	MAR / SEPT	APR / OCT	MAY / NOV	JUNE / DEC	JULY / JAN	TOTAL
SALES							
Last Year	80,000	90,000	110,000	85,000	70,000	65,000	500,000
Plan	88,000	104,500	115,500	93,500	82,500	66,000	550,000
Adjusted Plan							
Actual							
RETAIL STOCK (B.O.M.)							(Average Stock)
Last Year	151,670	215,666	235,666	210,666	195,666	190,666	200,000
Plan							
Adjusted Plan							
Actual							
RETAIL STOCK (E.O.M.)							
Last Year	215,666	235,666	210,666	195,666	190,666	200,000	
Plan							
Adjusted Plan							
Actual							
REDUCTIONS							
Last Year	7,500	5,000	5,000	11,000	9,000	12,500	50,000
Plan							
Actual							
RETAIL PURCHASES							
Last Year	151,496	115,000	90,000	81,000	74,000	86,834	598,330
Plan							
Adjusted Plan							
Actual							
COST PURCHASES							
Last Year	85,898	65,205	51,030	45,927	41,958	49,235	339,253
Plan							
Adjusted Plan							
Actual							

The buyer looked at her calendar and saw that Easter will be in March this year. Last year it was in April. Since Easter means increased business, there must be a revision of the percentage breakdown for March and April. Also the store's traditional "Bargain Bee" promotion is being shifted this year from July to June. Thus the planned sales for June need to be higher and those for July must be lower. In this way the buyer arrives at the following plan:

MONTH	PERCENTAGE OF TOTAL		TOTAL SALES		MONTHLY SALES
February	16%	×	$550,000	=	$ 88,000
March	19	×	550,000	=	104,500
April	21	×	550,000	=	115,500
May	17	×	550,000	=	93,500
June	15	×	550,000	=	82,500
July	12	×	550,000	=	66,000
Totals	100%				$550,000

The planned sales for this year are then entered on the sales and merchandise planning sheet.

FACTORS TO CONSIDER

Accurate sales forecasting requires a great deal of expertise along with some luck. There are several factors that can greatly influence future sales, and the retailer should take all of them into consideration in anticipating the future.

Sales Trends

Many merchandisers transfer sales figures from a daily sales report into a book often referred to as the "beat yesterday" book. The book shows how the day's sales compare to the day before and the same day last year. Such comparisons can send the buyer or the department manager or the merchandise manager into a state of euphoria or utter dismay. The book leaves a margin next to the sales figures to enable the buyer to enter explanations for victories or defeats and indicate the weather conditions of the day. Some merchandise managers ask their buyers to submit detailed sales reports at the end of each season, and jottings from the "beat yesterday" book can be invaluable in preparing these reports. The book may also yield helpful information for planning special promotions and sales for the following year.

In addition to comparing the sales statistics with those of the immediately preceding year, retailers should examine the sales results of like periods during the past several years. A department or store may have been on an upswing for several years, and one year of disappointing sales may not indicate that a steady decline has set in. The "beat yesterday" book provides spaces for merchandisers to record sales over a six-year period.

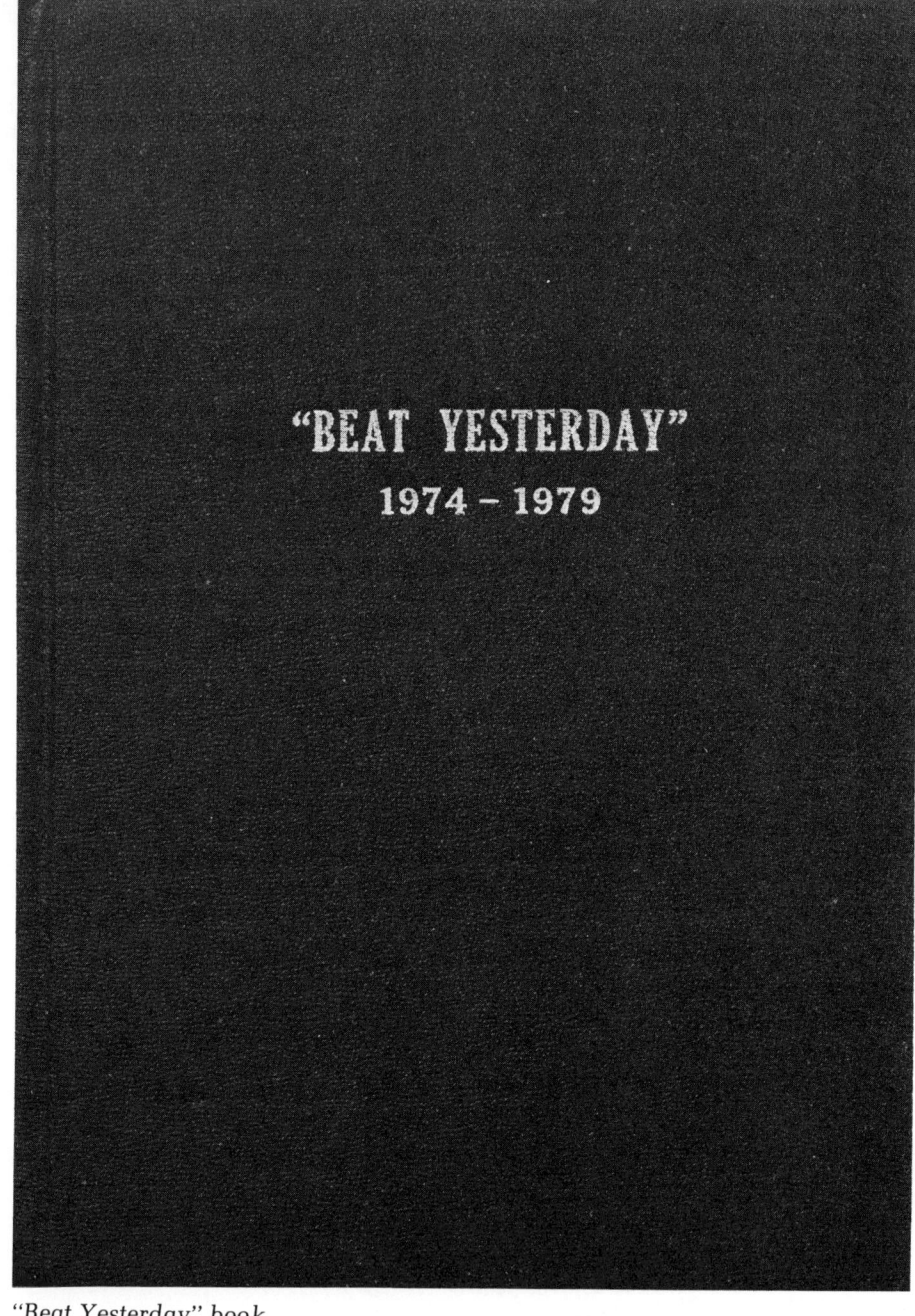

"Beat Yesterday" book
SOURCE: Sales Record Publishing Company, Holyoke, Massachusetts

JANUARY

		1974	1975	1976
Mon.				
Tues.	1			
Wed.	2		1	
Thurs.	3		2	1
Fri.	4		3	2
Sat.	5		4	3
Sun.	6		5	4
Week				
Mon.	7		6	5
Tues.	8		7	6
Wed.	9		8	7
Thurs.	10		9	8
Fri.	11		10	9
Sat.	12		11	10
Sun.	13		12	11
Week				
Mon.	14		13	12
Tues.	15		14	13
Wed.	16		15	14
Thurs.	17		16	15
Fri.	18		17	16
Sat.	19		18	17
Sun.	20		19	18
Week				
Mon.	21		20	19
Tues.	22		21	20
Wed.	23		22	21
Thurs.	24		23	22
Fri.	25		24	23
Sat.	26		25	24
Sun.	27		26	25
Week				
Mon.	28		27	26
Tues.	29		28	27
Wed.	30		29	28
Thurs.	31		30	29
Fri.			31	30
Sat.				31
Sun.				
Week				
Mon.				
Tues.				
Month				
Year				

FACTORS TO CONSIDER

Economic Conditions

The state of the economy can have a decisive effect on future sales. When employment and wages are high, stores naturally do well. But when a nearby plant closes down or an industry leaves town, the local economy suffers and retail business is affected immediately. Sales volume can be a deceptive figure. The current world-wide inflation means that higher prices are being paid for goods at all levels of distribution. Sales volume can rise by 5 percent or more just on account of inflation.

Shortages of goods and services can have a devastating effect on sales. The gasoline shortage of the early months of 1974 had a serious impact on retail sales in suburban stores. Shoppers were not able to visit shopping centers as easily as before, and even after gasoline supplies became more plentiful it took weeks for sales to rise again. During the same year the Easter sales of jelly beans declined because of a shortage of sugar and plastic wrappers.

Changes in Consumer Tastes

As every merchandiser knows, fashion does not stand still. Consumers are always on the lookout for new and interesting products. Likes and dislikes change, and merchandisers must keep abreast of these changes. A "hot seller" in one season can become an unwanted item in the next.

The "blue-jeans explosion" of the early 1970s gave a sales lift to sportswear departments and boutiques across the land. Faded dungarees, which cost no more than $10 when new, were recycled and adorned with embroidery and sold for $26 a pair at fashionable stores. This "washed-out look," however, was hurting the dress business. Young women in particular were becoming full-fledged members of the jeans generation, and many older women came to prefer pant suits to dresses. Dress departments took a beating, and stores had to adapt quickly to these changes by setting up new departments and reducing the inventory and space of others.

Competition

Competition from other retailers often has a negative effect on sales, but sometimes it also helps. If an area is already saturated with stores, another store is bound to be bad for business. The pie is only so large for everyone to share. However, new shopping centers like to attract a few large, competitive stores and many small ones. A competitive situation draws shopping crowds and helps sales.

It is difficult for a store to maintain a healthy sales volume in a deteriorating area once other stores have begun to abandon it. Many central-city shopping areas have succumbed to this fate: stores have been forced either to move to the suburbs or to build branches in order to survive. Some branch stores now do larger volumes of business than their parent stores downtown. Other stores have found *twig operations* very successful. A twig is a small branch store that stocks only one classification of merchandise or a few related ones. Bloomingdale's store in Manhasset, New York, is an example of a twig carrying extensive selections of only home furnishings.

Some well-known retailers have found branch operations so profitable that they have expanded well beyond their original trading areas. Lord and Taylor, the New York based fashion store on Fifth Avenue, operates six branches in the metropolitan New York area. It has also opened branches in such widely dispersed areas as Boston, West Hartford in Connecticut, Atlanta, Chicago, Dallas, and Houston. Lord and Taylor stores are also found near Philadelphia and Washington, 'D.C. Neiman-Marcus, the world-famous Dallas emporium, has opened branches outside Texas in Bal Harbour, Florida, Atlanta, and St. Louis, and is planning a new store in San Francisco to open in 1977.

Changes in Store Policy

A change in store policy can affect sales dramatically. A store may decide to *trade up* by adding higher-priced lines of merchandise to its stock. If the units of sale remain constant, then trading up will raise total sales volume. J. C. Penney, the nation's largest general merchandise chain, has experienced notable success in its trading-up policy in many merchandising

Lord and Taylor's Oak Brook branch outside Chicago
SOURCE: Lord and Taylor, New York, New York

areas. Alternatively, a supermarket may decide to drop trading stamps and lower prices in an attempt to attract more business. A and P's WEO (where economy originates) promotion has had a beneficial affect on the sales of that supermarket chain.

Changes in Space Allocation and In-Store Activities

More space should mean more sales, and buyers compete for precious square-footage. However, the space allocated to each department must be productive. Thus one measure of the efficiency of a department is its sales-per-square-foot ratio. Annual sales of $100 per square foot is considered a good figure.

The location inside a store can also be crucial to satisfactory sales performance. Studies have shown that space on the main selling floor and in areas near store entrances, elevators, and escalators are the most productive. Thus, if a department is enlarged or moved to a location with greater customer traffic, its sales should be planned upward accordingly.

Store renovation can help sales too. It seems that in some stores remodeling never stops. Also changes in consumer tastes constantly dictate the creation of new departments and abandonment of old ones.

Unusual displays can increase sales
SOURCE: Van Bucher/Photo Researchers, Inc.

Changes in the Merchandising Calendar

Because holidays and the number of selling days are different from year to year, sales forecasters must take these changes into account. For example, there may be more selling days in the month of December this year than last year. And since each day in December before Christmas should be a heavy selling day, sales should be adjusted sharply upward. The date of Easter has a strong effect on Spring business in apparel departments. Easter may be in late March one year and mid-April the following year. One might think that the two months could be planned together. However, records indicate that if Easter is late, the two-month business is usually much better than if Easter arrives early. April weather seems more conducive to the purchase of spring wardrobes than the blustery and often cold month of March.

An Easter special
SOURCE: Frank Siteman/Stock, Boston

Changes in Promotional Plans

Most stores, especially the promotion minded, plan several storewide selling events each year. These major promotions are given such names as Anniversary Day sales, Founder's Day sales, Bargain Days, and Harvest Days. Other promotions such as end-of-month sales and Assistant Buyer's Day sales or individual departmental specials have less impact, but they can all contribute to a store's selling success. Some stores feature fairs or festivals when foreign goods are displayed and promoted. One large department store recently ran a two-week British Fair at which merchandise from England and Scotland was given special emphasis. Special exhibits and demonstrations were arranged, resulting in increased sales volume and much customer goodwill.

If a major promotion is shifted to another month or canceled altogether, the change must be taken into account in sales planning. Also if a brand-new storewide event is planned, sales must be adjusted upward for that period.

SALES PLANNING FOR BRANCH STORES

When a store has one or more branch operations, the sales of each branch must be planned separately. Since the flagship store acts as the center for merchandise planning, the departmental buyers must forecast sales for all branches and include them in the master sales plan. In order to prepare realistic sales goals, buyers should consult with the branch store manager familiar with their departments.

The sales potentials of branch stores should not be underestimated. Since some branch stores sell as much or more merchandise than the flagship store, they should be stocked accordingly.

Figure 10.2 shows a sales and merchandise planning sheet containing sales plans for branch stores. Here each branch is indicated by a special letter code.

Stores may find it advantageous to show planned and actual sales for each department that combine the sales of the downtown store with those of the branches in one form. When this is done, the downtown store is in effect considered as just another branch.

Figure 10.3 shows comparative sales plans and results for eight stores by the month and year-to-date.

SALES PLANNING WHEN PRICES ARE STABLE

Planning seasonal sales with monthly percentages. Planning sales is an easier task when retail prices do not fluctuate widely. A steady growth in sales volume is hoped for, and this overall growth pattern is expected to affect each month of the new season in the same proportion as the monthly sales percentages of previous years.

Figure 10.2

BRANCH STORE PLANS

SALES AND STOCK PLAN
(UH-W-BV-CS)

Season Spring   Department No. 2

			FEB	MAR	APR	MAY	JUNE	JULY	TOTAL
			AUG	SEPT	OCT	NOV	DEC	JAN	
Sales	UH	Last Year							
		Plan							
		Adjusted Plan							
		Actual							
	W	Last Year							
		Plan							
		Adjusted Plan							
		Actual							
	BV	Last Year							
		Plan							
		Adjusted Plan							
		Actual							
	CS	Last Year							
		Plan							
		Adjusted Plan							
		Actual							
Retail Stock (B.O.M.)	UH	Last Year							
		Plan							
		Adjusted Plan							
		Actual							
	W	Last Year							
		Plan							
		Adjusted Plan							
		Actual							
	BV	Last Year							
		Plan							
		Adjusted Plan							
		Actual							
	CS	Last Year							
		Plan							
		Adjusted Plan							
		Actual							

Figure 10.3 DEPARTMENTAL SALES REPORT

DEPARTMENTAL SALES REPORT

DEPT. _____ NO. _____
YEAR _____
BUYER _____ DIV. _____

MO.	DOWNTOWN				WESTGATE				SEVERANCE				MIDWAY				PARMA				GREAT LAKES				BELDEN VILLAGE				McKELVEY'S			
	LY	PLAN	TY	%	LY	PLAN	TY	%	LY	PLAN	TY	%	LY	PLAN	TY	%	LY	PLAN	TY	%	LY	PLAN	TY	%	LY	PLAN	TY	%	LY	PLAN	TY	%
FEB																																	
MAR																																	
YTD																																	
APR																																	
YTD																																	
MAY																																	
YTD																																	
JUN																																	
YTD																																	
JUL																																	
YTD SEAS																																	
AUG																																	
YTD																																	
SEP																																	
YTD																																	
OCT																																	
YTD																																	
NOV																																	
YTD																																	
DEC																																	
YTD																																	
JAN																																	
YTD																																	
FALL																																	

FORM 3713

SOURCE: Higbee Company, Cleveland, Ohio

ILLUSTRATIVE PROBLEM A hosiery buyer realized sales of $250,000 for the six-month period August through January last year. This year, taking into account normal growth conditions, she believes she can increase her sales volume by 10 percent. The controller's office gives her a percentage breakdown based on the five previous years' sales as follows: August, 8 percent; September, 10 percent; October, 16 percent; November, 20 percent; December, 40 percent; and January, 6 percent. What should her sales plan be for each month of the new season?

SOLUTION The buyer hopes to increase her sales volume by $25,000 (10 percent of $250,000) to achieve total sales of $275,000 for the season. Her monthly sales breakdowns should appear as follows:

August	$22,000 (8% of $275,000)
September	27,500 (10% of $275,000)
October	44,000 (16% of $275,000)
November	55,000 (20% of $275,000)
December	110,000 (40% of $275,000)
January	16,500 (6% of $275,000)
Total	$275,000

Planning sales on the basis of current activity to date. Even when prices remain stable and a normal rate of growth is planned, something unforeseen may happen to cause sales to jump or fall beyond expectations. When this occurs, an adjustment to planned sales should be made for the remaining months of the season.

ILLUSTRATIVE PROBLEM As the fall season progresses, the hosiery buyer of the last illustrative problem finds that her sales are running ahead of plan as follows:

	LAST YEAR	PLANNED THIS YEAR	ACTUAL THIS YEAR	ADJUSTED PLAN	INCREASE OVER LAST YEAR
August	$ 20,000	$ 22,000	$24,000		20%
September	25,000	27,500	30,000		20
October	40,000	44,000	50,000		25
November	50,000	55,000			
December	100,000	110,000			
January	15,000	16,500			

The buyer attributes the healthy increase in sales to the introduction of a new pantyhose into her department. She is now concerned that she may not have enough stock to take care of Christmas business. How should she adjust her planned sales to insure that she will have sufficient stock on hand during the holiday season?

SOLUTION   The buyer had no way of knowing that the new pantyhose would be accepted so quickly by her customers. Thus her original sales plan turned out to be much too conservative. Assuming that she can get quick deliveries of needed merchandise and given the sales trend, it appears that she can count on a 30 percent increase over last year for the remainder of the season. Her adjusted planned sales for November, December, and January should look like this:

	ADJUSTED PLANNED SALES
November	$65,000 (130% of $50,000)
December	130,000 (130% of $100,000)
January	19,500 (130% of $15,000)

Important Note. As stated in Chapter 2 in our discussion of figuring a percentage increase over a previous year, it is important that the previous year's figure be used as the *base*. For example, the August sales increase turned out to be $4,000. The percentage increase is $4,000 divided by the August sales of last year:

$$\frac{\$4,000}{\$20,000} = \frac{1}{5} = 20\%$$

Planning sales when selling days vary. All else being equal, a gain or a loss of one or more selling days in a month can affect sales volume for that month. This is particularly true during certain months that enjoy unusually brisk business. To illustrate the importance of even one extra day of selling activity, some stores have begun to open on Memorial Day and Labor Day.

ILLUSTRATIVE PROBLEM   November sales of a toy department totaled $320,000 last year. This year sales are expected to rise by 5 percent under normal business conditions. However, there will be only twenty-four selling days in the month this year instead of twenty-five as last year. What should the planned sales be for November of this year?

STEP 1:
Find the projected 5 percent increase:

$$5\% \text{ increase} = \$320,000 \times .05 = \$16,000$$
$$= \$320,000 + \$16,000 = \$336,000$$

STEP 2:
Find planned sales with one less selling day:

$$\text{Planned Sales} = \frac{24}{25} \times \$336,000$$
$$= \$322,160$$

Planning sales when Easter falls on a different date. Today, Easter finery is not as important to as many people as it once was. The trend toward more casual clothing, the young consumer's attitude toward "dressing up," and unsettled economic conditions have lessened the impact of the Easter buying period at least in apparel departments. Nevertheless, the date of Easter still has a decided effect on sales volume during the months of March and April. An early Easter generally means a drop in business for the two-month period, and a late Easter portends an upswing in selling activity that often carries over to Mother's Day.

ILLUSTRATIVE PROBLEM The buyer of millinery is planning her sales for the spring season. Due to the increased popularity of hats and a late Easter, she is planning a 20 percent increase over last year. Her sales last year amounted to $10,000 in March and $15,000 in April. Easter falls on April 14 this year. The last time this happened was ten years ago, when March sales were $8,000 and April sales were $16,000. What should the planned sales for March and April be?

SOLUTION STEP 1:
Find the projected 20 percent increase:

$$20\% \text{ increase} = (\$10,000 + \$15,000) \times 0.20 = \$5,000$$
$$= \$25,000 + \$5,000$$
$$= \$30,000$$

STEP 2
Find the relative proportions of March and April sales in the year when Easter falls on April 14:

$$\text{Total sales} = \$8,000 \text{ (March)} + \$16,000 \text{ (April)} = \$24,000$$

$$\text{March sales} = \frac{\$8,000}{\$24,000} = \frac{1}{3}$$

$$\text{April sales} = \frac{\$16,000}{\$24,000} = \frac{2}{3}$$

STEP 3
Find the planned sales for March and April in accordance with the relative proportions of ten years ago:

$$\text{Planned sales for March} = \frac{1}{3} \text{ of } \$30,000 = \$10,000$$

$$\text{Planned sales for April} = \frac{2}{3} \text{ of } \$30,000 = \$20,000$$

EXERCISES 1. Sales for the coming season in a rug department are planned at $225,000. Using the following expected monthly sales percentages, plan the sales for each month:

February 12%	May 20%
March 15%	June 20%
April 20%	July 13%

2. The owner of a small shoe store in a shopping center was disappointed over his spring sales. A gasoline shortage apparently caused large reductions in his sales volume. He realized the need to make some adjustments in his planned sales for the remainder of the season, even though the April sales finally reached the same level as last year, due to a late Easter. What should his planned sales be for May, June, and July, based on the following data?

	LAST YEAR	THIS YEAR
February	$3,000	$2,000
March	5,000	4,000
April	4,000	4,000
May	3,000	
June	2,000	
July	1,500	

3. Last year a children's department reported November sales of $160,000 with twenty-five selling days. This year, due to an increase in space, the department expects to record a sales increase of 20 percent. Also there will be twenty-six selling days this year. How should the November sales be planned?

4. A men's boutique in New Orleans noted that its February and March sales were strongly affected by the date of Mardi Gras. This year Mardi Gras falls on March 6. The last time Mardi Gras was in early March was eight years ago, when February sales were $8,000 and March sales were $12,000. Sales this year should be about 40 percent greater than eight years ago. What should the planned sales for this February and March be?

SALES PLANNING WITH FLUCTUATING PRICES

It seems that inflation is here to stay, so that the question is not whether there will be inflation, but how steep it will be. When future sales are being planned, two indicators of growth or decline are more meaningful than the total sales volume. They are the number of transactions that take place and the amount of the average sale. During periods of inflation, the size of average sale should go up, and if there is also a rise in the number of transactions, then a healthy sales increase will develop. The formula we use is:

Total dollar sales = Average sale × Number of transactions

ILLUSTRATIVE PROBLEM A fur buyer expects a 10 percent increase in wholesale prices, which she will pass on to her customers next season. However, due to fashion changes, she expects her number of transactions to drop by 4 percent. Last year she realized sales of $250,000 for the season, with a $1,000 average sale. How should she plan the sales for next season if the average sale increases by 10 percent?

SOLUTION

$$\text{Number of transactions} = \frac{\text{Dollar sales}}{\text{Average sale}}$$
$$= \frac{\$250{,}000}{\$1{,}000}$$
$$= 250$$

But transactions will decrease by 4 percent:

$$\begin{aligned}\text{Transactions} &= 250 - (0.04 \times 250)\\ &= 250 - 10\\ &= 240\end{aligned}$$

And the average sale is expected to increase by 10 percent:

$$\begin{aligned}\text{Average sale} &= \$1{,}000 + (0.10 \times 1{,}000)\\ &= \$1{,}000 + 100\\ &= \$1{,}100\end{aligned}$$

So that

$$\begin{aligned}\text{Planned sales} &= \text{Average sale} \times \text{Number of transactions}\\ &= \$1{,}100 \times 240\\ &= \$264{,}000\end{aligned}$$

ILLUSTRATIVE PROBLEM

Retail prices in a camera shop are expected to increase by 8 percent next season due to increased costs both at home and abroad. It is expected that the number of transactions will drop by about 5 percent as a result. If these changes do take place, by how much in percentages will the average sale go up or down?

SOLUTION

Let last year's sales = $100 and the number of last year's transactions = 100. Then

$$\begin{aligned}\text{Planned dollar sales} &= \$100 + (0.08 \times \$100)\\ &= \$108\\ \text{Planned number of transactions} &= 100 - (0.05 \times 100)\\ &= 95\end{aligned}$$

$$\begin{aligned}\text{Last year's average sale} &= \frac{\text{Dollar sales}}{\text{Transactions}}\\ &= \frac{\$100}{100}\\ &= \$1.00\end{aligned}$$

$$\begin{aligned}\text{and this year's planned average sale} &= \frac{\$108}{95}\\ &= \$1.14\end{aligned}$$

Therefore, the percentage increase in this year's planned average sale over last year's average sale is:

$$\% \text{ increase} = \frac{\$1.14 - \$1.00}{\$1.00}$$
$$= \frac{\$0.14}{\$1.00}$$
$$= 14\%$$

We note that as prices increase and the number of transactions decrease or remain constant, it becomes increasingly important for sales people to use better selling techniques. Suggestion selling, say in the illustrative problem above in the form of selling the customers rolls of film, flash attachments, and other equipment, can raise the average sale. Similarly, trading up can also raise the average sale.

ILLUSTRATIVE PROBLEM

A boutique owner has just learned that she will have to pay 12 percent more for jeans due to an increase in denim goods. She cannot absorb the increase by herself, so she expects to raise her retail prices by the same amount. Her average sale will go up by 10 percent as a result. How will this affect the number of her transactions, as a percentage of last year's number of transactions, in this category of merchandise?

SOLUTION

As before, let last year's sales equal $100, last year's average sale equal $1.00, and last year's number of transactions equal 100. Then

Planned dollar sales = $100 + (0.12 × $100) = $112
Planned average sale = $1.00 + (0.10 × $1.00) = $1.10

$$\text{The number of transactions} = \frac{\text{Dollar sales}}{\text{Average sale}}$$
$$= \frac{\$112}{\$1.10}$$
$$= 101.82$$

Therefore,

$$\text{Percentage increase in the number of transactions} = \frac{101.82 - 100}{100}$$
$$= \frac{1.82}{100}$$
$$= 0.0182 \text{ or } 1.82\%$$

EXERCISES

1. A stationery store expects a 15 percent increase in the average sale and a 10 percent decrease in the number of transactions. If sales last year were $180,000, how much should the planned sales be for this year?
2. What may à pet shop expect its average sale to be this year if the number of transactions increases by 6 percent and dollar sales go up by 20 percent? Last year's average sale amounted to $18.00.
3. What is the percentage change in the number of transactions that may be expected in a card shop if the dollar volume is expected to go up by 15 percent, but the average sale will increase by only 5 percent?

CHAPTER SUMMARY

Planning future sales is a tricky but essential part of every buyer's or store manager's job. A sales plan will show how a department or store is expected to perform, and enough merchandise must be purchased to make the attainment of that performance goal possible.

In most stores sales plans are formulated well in advance of the beginning of a six-month season. In the case of a multi-unit operation, branch store sales should be planned separately. Once the season has begun the sales plans may require adjustments depending on the current sales trend.

There are many factors to consider when developing the sales forecast for a new season. Past sales records are very helpful, and such factors as weather and promotional effort must be considered. The number of selling days has an impact on sales volume, especially in the month of December. The date of Easter affects selling activity in apparel and some other departments. The health of the local and national economy must be examined. Fashion changes need to be followed closely, and departments with a fresh and attractive appearance tend to be more productive in sales than others. Competition from other stores may have a beneficial effect on sales if it draws more customers into a shopping area. Changes in store policy can boost sales volume.

Sales planning in times of fluctuating prices takes more skill than when prices are stable. Also changing prices make sales figures misleading. A sales increase of 6 percent may be due entirely to inflation. The number of transactions that take place and the size of the average sale are often better indicators of sales success.

QUESTIONS FOR REVIEW

1. Why is it so vital for a store to plan its sales in advance of the selling season?
2. Once a retailer has forecast sales for each month of the next season, should he or she be bound by those figures? Explain your answer.
3. Why is it important for a buyer to make notations in his "beat yesterday" book to explain the selling success or failure for each day?
4. Which is a better gauge of sales success: total dollar volume or units sold? Explain your answer.
5. What is meant by trading up?
6. Would a typical department store welcome the arrival of a large general-merchandise chain operation in the block across the street? Explain your answer.
7. Why do most stores benefit from a late Easter?
8. How can suggestion selling increase the amount of the average sale?
9. Should sales figures be compared with those of the previous year only when forecasting sales?
10. Give some examples of how changing consumer tastes can affect the sales in certain departments and stores.

DISCUSSION QUESTION

When a store notices a precipitous drop in sales due to weather conditions, a transportation strike, a gasoline shortage, large industrial layoffs, or other factors, should management take immediate action to reduce expenses (in the form of services, personnel, and so forth) and cancel outstanding purchase orders if possible? Explain your answer.

PROBLEMS FOR REVIEW

1. Last year a toy buyer recorded sales during the month of December of $684,000. This year, due to inflation and a favorable sales trend, he believes he can show an increase of 15 percent in sales. How should his December sales be planned?
2. During the spring and summer season ending July 31 last year, a record department posted sales of $800,000. June sales contributed 20 percent and July 22 percent to the total. If sales are planned upward by 5 percent this year, what are the planned sales for these two months?
3. The owner of a boutique located in a beach community opens only five months a year, May through September. May and June were unseasonably cold this year, and her sales fell 20 percent below last year's figure for the two months. According to *Farmer's Almanac*, the rest of this summer will be cool, too. In order to avoid a serious overstock, how should she adjust her planned sales for July, August, and September if last year's figures were $60,000, $50,000, and $30,000, respectively?
4. A sportswear department showed sales of $260,000 last May with twenty-six shopping days. This year the department hopes for increased sales because the store will be open on Memorial Day so that there will be twenty-seven shopping days. Due to sluggish business conditions, sales are not expected to rise otherwise. How large will May sales be?
5. A dress buyer had a disappointing Easter season last year when Easter fell on March 27. Her March sales were $150,000 and April sales were $180,000. This year Easter falls on April 7, and she is planning a 10 percent increase in sales. When Easter fell on the same day ten years ago, March sales came to $150,000 and April sales were $250,000. How large will this year's March and April sales be?
6. Due to price increases, a gasoline station expects an increase of 20 percent in average sale, but the number of transactions is expected to decrease by 5 percent. If total sales for a three-month period last year were $90,000, what sales volume can be expected for a like period this year, given that the average sale last year was $6.00?
7. A curio shop expects a banner tourist season this year with a 10 percent rise in average sale and 5 percent increase in the number of transactions. If sales during the season last year were $80,000, what sales volume can be expected for this season?
8. Although the retail prices in a furniture store are expected to go up by 10 percent, the number of transactions is expected to decline by only 2 percent. By what percentage will the average sale decrease or increase?
9. Due to inflated prices, a florist expects her average sale to increase by 10 percent and her sales volume by 8 percent. By what percentage will the number of her transactions increase or decrease?
10. What will a department's new average sale be if sales rise by 18 percent

and the number of transactions increases by 9 percent? Last year's average sale was $16.00.

CASE PROBLEM

A SLIGHTLY BENT TWIG

Robert Jenkins was the men's clothing and sportswear buyer for Bentley's, a major department store in a large midwestern city. Jenkins was responsible for buying merchandise for the downtown store and three branch stores as well. He also bought merchandise for a twig store located in Collegeville. Collegeville was the site of the state university and boasted a striking Tudor-style shopping district adjacent to the campus. Bentley's outlet there was called The University Shoppe and carried only men's clothing, sportswear, furnishings, shoes, and a few gift items. In addition to Jenkins, the buyers of men's furnishings and shoes also provided stock for this small store.

For many years the three buyers tried to find merchandise that would appeal to the male students of the university. They bought suits and sports jackets of the three-button conservative variety, button-down shirts, and wing-tipped shoes. Periodically, Jenkins and the other two buyers would visit campus stores in New Haven, Princeton, and other eastern university cities, and when they returned they would try to emulate the so-called Ivy League look. In recent years, however, when the Ivy-League style began to lose popularity, the three buyers experimented with more casual clothes. But their emphasis was always on quality and a dressed-up image.

Late in 1973 Jenkins's merchandise manager asked him to prepare a tentative sales plan for his department for the 1974 merchandise year ending January 31, 1975. Although all of the 1973 figures were not in, Jenkins was able to estimate yearly sales with some accuracy. He decided to examine the sales figures for the past five years to see whether a sales trend could be detected. The following figures were furnished by the controller's office:

Year	Dollar Sales				
	DOWNTOWN	SOUTHSIDE	HAMPTON	GREEN VALLEY	UNIVERSITY SHOPPE
1969	$880,000	$735,000	—	—	$180,000
1970	925,000	760,000	$700,000	—	170,000
1971	900,000	850,000	763,000	$542,600	140,000
1972	870,300	917,200	800,200	584,000	110,000
1973*	935,000	943,000	825,000	623,000	90,000

*Estimated

Jenkins noted that his department downtown was just holding its own. Since prices were higher, the number of transactions was obviously down. However, the branch stores were making up for any loss downtown, and the department at the oldest branch, Southside, was beginning to outsell that in the downtown store. The newer stores, Hampton and Green Valley, were also doing very nicely.

With some alarm, however, Jenkins studied the sales figures for The University Shoppe. Even with higher retails, sales dropped by 50 percent during the five-year period. If this trend should continue, the store would have to be closed. After checking with the other two buyers, Jenkins found that they were also having difficulty there, although the declines were not as dramatic. Clearly something had to be done if the twig was to be saved. Their merchandise manager had already called a meeting for the following week to discuss the situation, and Jenkins wanted to be prepared with some constructive suggestions.

1. What is a twig store?
2. What are some of the possible causes of the twig's poor performance during the past five years?
3. How should the merchandise policy be changed to improve sales?
4. Assuming normal business conditions during 1974, how would you plan the sales for the five stores?

11

HOW
TO
PLAN
STOCKS

KEY POINTS

1. Realistic stock planning is essential to avoid overstocking.

2. It is not necessary to increase or reduce stocks in direct proportion to variations in sales in order to maintain adequate merchandise assortments.

3. When planning stocks, merchandisers must consider sales trends, availability of merchandise, merchandise priorities, and previous store records.

4. Most formal methods for deriving stock figures are based on stock turnover, so it is important that the stock turn figure be accurate.

5. Planning should not be so inflexible that buyers are prevented from taking advantage of an exceptional buy or stocking a promising new item.

IMPORTANCE OF STOCK PLANNING

In the last chapter the value of sound and realistic sales planning was stressed. Correct stock planning is just as vital, for without the proper supply of stock, sales potentials cannot be fully realized. How sweet it would be if the right merchandise assortments in the right quantity were always available so that sales were never lost. But this is rarely the case.

After the planned sales figures have been entered on the seasonal sales and merchandise plan, the next logical step is to figure how much stock will be necessary to insure that sales goals can be met. Figure 11.1 shows the same sales and merchandise planning sheet as Figure 10.1, but here the stocks planned for the beginning and end of each month have been entered. Note that the beginning stock of any month is the same as the ending stock of the previous month. There is a line for adjusting stocks when sales are revised upward or downward in the course of the season. In this chapter we will explain four methods of calculating the beginning stock figure (B.O.M.). Both the beginning- and end-of-the-month stock figures in Figure 11.1 were obtained by means of the basic-stock method.

Although it is the buyer who first plans the stock, all the figures on the plan are of course carefully reviewed by the merchandise manager and then the controller, who releases the monies to be spent on new merchandise. By the nature of their responsibilities controllers tend to be more conservative in fiscal matters than merchandisers. It is their job to control and supervise budgets. Since they are, in effect, guardians of the store's funds, they keep an ever-watchful eye on the extravagances of buyers. Conflict is thus almost inevitable; buyers often feel that too much emphasis is placed on the control of expenditure and, as a result, imagination is stifled and sales are held down unnecessarily. Controllers feel that they must cut corners wherever possible to keep the stock and other merchandising variables in line so that a satisfactory level of profit can be maintained.

Figure 11.1 SALES AND MERCHANDISE PLAN

SALES AND MERCHANDISE PLAN

Season: Spring
Department No. 2

	Last Year	Plan	Actual		Last Year	Plan	Actual
Initial Markup %	43.3	43.4		Gross Margin %	38.4	39.3	
Reductions %	10.0	9.0		Operating Expense %	36.0	36.0	
Cash Discount %	1.8	2.0					
Alteration Expense %	1.0	1.0		Season Turn	2.5	3	
Maintained Markup %	37.6	38.3		Net Profit %	2.4	3.0	

	FEB / AUG	MAR / SEPT	APR / OCT	MAY / NOV	JUNE / DEC	JULY / JAN	TOTAL
SALES							
Last Year	80,000	90,000	110,000	85,000	70,000	65,000	500,000
Plan	88,000	104,500	115,500	93,500	82,500	66,000	550,000
Adjusted Plan							
Actual							
RETAIL STOCK (B.O.M.)							(Average Stock)
Last Year	151,670	215,666	235,666	210,666	195,666	190,666	200,000
Plan	179,666	196,166	207,166	185,166	174,166	157,666	183,333
Adjusted Plan							
Actual							
RETAIL STOCK (E.O.M.)							
Last Year	215,666	235,666	210,666	195,666	190,666	200,000	
Plan	196,166	207,166	185,166	174,166	157,666	183,333	
Adjusted Plan							
Actual							
REDUCTIONS							
Last Year	7,500	5,000	5,000	11,000	9,000	12,500	50,000
Plan							
Actual							
RETAIL PURCHASES							
Last Year	151,496	115,000	90,000	81,000	74,000	86,834	598,330
Plan							
Adjusted Plan							
Actual							
COST PURCHASES							
Last Year	85,898	65,205	51,030	45,927	41,958	49,235	339,253
Plan							
Adjusted Plan							
Actual							

FACTORS TO CONSIDER

Sales Trends

If a store or department is enjoying an upward sales trend, it is natural to raise the planned stocks accordingly. Buyers are usually optimistic people, and one of their worst fears is to run out of merchandise. Nevertheless, it is important to keep stock levels from becoming too high. It is never wise to increase stocks by the same percentage as the present or planned sales increase, because adequate selections of merchandise can be maintained without doing so.

Availability of Merchandise

On account of strikes, economic conditions, price fluctuations, or scarcity of raw materials, buyers may sometimes feel that they should procure in large quantities to protect themselves against possible merchandise shortages. This buying philosophy recalls the housewife who reads that there will be a paper shortage and therefore drives to the supermarket and loads up her car with cartons of toilet tissue and paper towels. *Scare buying* rarely works to a store's advantage because a serious overstocked position can easily develop, which may lead to heavy markdowns at sometime in the future. Also too much money may get tied up in a small number of items, leaving insufficient open-to-buy for other merchandise. Further, storage may be a problem. On the other hand, if a buyer learns of impending price increases and buys heavily at the present lower prices, there is an opportunity for improving markups when wholesale prices do go up.

Merchandise Priorities

In a department that offers a variety of staple merchandise, stocks must be planned high enough to make sure that the assortments are balanced according to style, size, and color. Staples are often referred to as *never out items* for the very good reason that stores must never be out of them. Stores build their reputations on the supply of these staples as well as the *bread and butter lines* that are regularly stocked in full assortments. For example, men's black dress socks might be considered a staple. However, a store would also want to carry a full assortment of men's dress socks in other colors as well; these are the bread and butter lines. Adequate supplies of both staples and bread and butter merchandise must take priority over others in the planning of stocks. Monies must also be set aside for fashion merchandise, especially if a store is noted for fashion leadership. In some areas of merchandise, fashion merchandise is much more important than staple merchandise, and balanced assortments are again necessary. But there is much more risk involved in buying fashion merchandise, as will be explained in Chapter 13.

If a store is promotionally oriented and wants to create a high-volume business, it usually plans departmental and storewide sales on a regular

Merchandise priority—wide assortments within one category of merchandise
SOURCE: David A. Krathwohl

basis. Special promotional merchandise must be bought for these events, and stock plans must allow for these purchases. Finally, a buyer should have the option to buy an interesting fad that may come along, but this type of merchandise should take the lowest priority in building stocks.

Stock Turn and Stock-Sales Ratios

A stock planner should always keep in mind two barometers of success in merchandising: the stock turn and the stock-sales ratio. As explained in Chapter 9, the stock turn reflects the efficiency with which the department or store is being run. It tells whether there is a healthy balance between sales and stocks. If the stock turn is too low, generally the stocks are too heavy. If the stock turn is too high, the stocks may be too thin and probably have broken sizes and colors.

Many merchandisers prefer to work with the stock-sales ratio when planning their stocks. This ratio is easily obtained, as was seen in Chapter 9. The stock at the beginning of the month is simply divided by the sales for that month. It is not even necessary to find an average stock as in the case of stock turn.

STOCK PLANNING FOR BRANCH STORES

Due to the huge increase in selling activities in suburban areas during the past twenty years, particular attention must be given to stocking branch

Merchandise priority—many categories of merchandise with narrow assortments in each
SOURCE: David A. Krathwohl

stores. The traditional tendency has been to understock the branches and to consider the flagship store in the center city as the base for all merchandising operations. Although most buying is done by the main store, the store itself should be thought of as just another selling unit. If some of the branches are outselling the flagship store, they should be stocked accordingly. After all, branch operations contribute between 50 and 80 percent of the total sales of some stores.

Merchandisers have learned that customer tastes can be quite different in the suburbs than in the heart of the city. There may be a greater demand for casual clothes, hobby items, sporting goods, and home-care products. A branch may be located in an area of high average income, in which case expensive and better-quality merchandise is needed. Departments that cater to young people may do especially well. The astute buyer studies the demographics (population characteristics, such as size, income, age, marital status) of each trading area before ordering and sending out merchandise to the branch store in that area.

Because consumer demand varies so greatly from branch to branch, buyers must cultivate a close relationship with branch department managers. A competent and cooperative branch manager can contribute much to a buyer's success. Depending on the number of branches involved, frequent visits to them are important. Stock levels and floor displays require checking, and transfer of merchandise may be necessary. The branch manager should be encouraged to visit the flagship store, too. A constant flow of information back and forth will insure that the branch gets the merchandise it needs.

Between store visits, buyers and branch department managers should keep in close contact on the telephone and by means of weekly reports. A typical department manager's report is shown in Figure 11.2. With such a report the manager can tell the buyer which classifications of merchandise are the most active, which classifications need restocking to meet demand, the style numbers that are selling fast and should be reordered, those that are slow sellers, and the staple stocks that need fill-ins to be brought up to basic stock levels.

Even when the channels of communication between buyers and branch department managers are open and functioning, many buyers still fail to recognize the real stock needs of the branches. There may be a persistent feeling that the flagship store should carry the most complete merchandise assortments. Since suburban customers shop in the same stores more frequently than do their city cousins, stocks seem to lose their freshness early. Sometimes not enough merchandise is on hand when advertisements break, and staple merchandise is not stocked at the proper levels. Too many branch customers have heard the familiar statement "If you'll wait a minute, I'll find out if downtown has it."

Branch store merchandising has become so important that in many stores an assistant buyer cannot be named buyer without some branch store experience. The logical executive progression becomes assistant buyer→ branch department manager→buyer. The idea is that future buyers must fully appreciate the special needs of the branch stores.

STOCK-PLANNING METHODS

In the planning of stocks buyers usually begin with the consideration of how much merchandise is needed to take care of basics, fashion items, and merchandise for special promotions. Then come the price lines, colors, and sizes. The decisions are based on past store records and personal experience. The buyer hopes that the resulting figures will be accepted by the merchandise manager and controller. Very often, they are not. The controller is likely to use one of the four methods explained below to determine the proper stock levels and frequently will find the proposed figures too high. The buyer must then defend the plans. If they are convincing enough, the plans will be approved. If not, the planned stocks must be reduced to levels more in keeping with the results of the controller's mathematical computations. The four methods that a controller may use to keep stocks and sales balanced are the basic-stock method, the percentage-variation method, the week's-supply method, and the stock-sales ratio method.

Basic-Stock Method

In this case planned sales for each month are added to a basic stock (no relation to a model stock) to yield the stock level for the first of each

Figure 11.2
DEPARTMENT
MANAGER'S
MERCHANDISING
REPORT

DEPARTMENT MANAGER'S MERCHANDISING REPORT

FOR WEEK ENDING _____   DEPT. MGR'S. SIGNATURE _____

The following report is important to your department. If properly filled out, it will enable your department to produce more sales. This report is to be made solely from YOUR OWN observation in your selling department, and there is to be no reference to any Buyer's Unit Control Records or any conference with your Buyer. Be accurate and resourceful, for this report will be used to indicate your merchandising ability.

Please complete this report in duplicate and give both copies to your Division Manager, on Thursday. Your Division Manager will review this report and forward both copies to the Store Director who will also review this report and will forward one copy to the appropriate Merchandise Manager.

1. What are the most active classification of merchandise that the customers are buying this week.

   DEPARTMENT #   CLASSIFICATION   PRICE

2. On which of these active classifications is the department stock inadequate to take care of customer demand.

   DEPARTMENT #   CLASSIFICATION   PRICE   APPROX. QUANTITY
                                                              IN STOCK

3. What are the styles that are selling fast and should be reordered?

   DEPARTMENT #   STYLE #   MANUFACTURER   CLASSIFICATION   PRICE

4. What are the styles that are selling slowly and should be marked down?

   DEPARTMENT #   STYLE #   MANUFACTURER   CLASSIFICATION   PRICE   APPROX. QUAN.
                                                                       (in stock)

5. What are the basic stock numbers that need fill-in to basic stock level?

SOURCE: Alexander's, New York, New York

Figure 11.3
BASIC STOCK METHOD

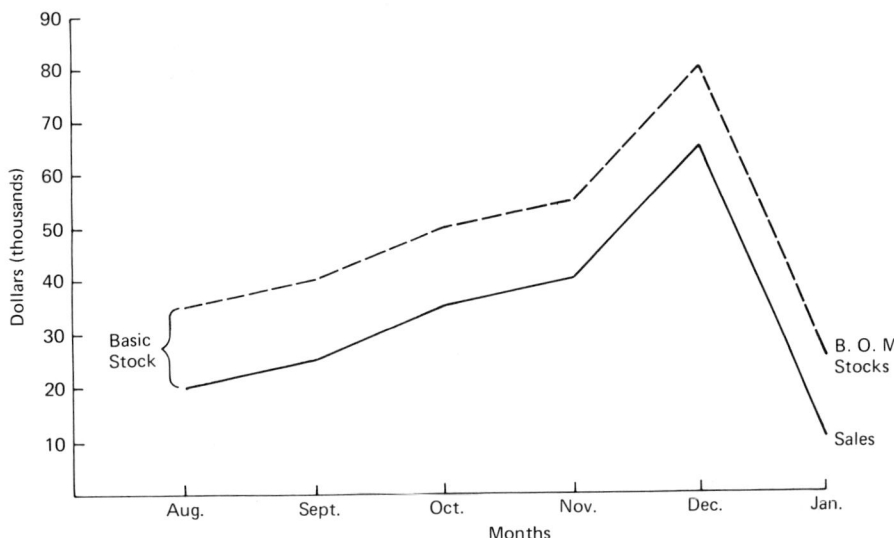

month season. Sales are estimated at $100,000. February (four weeks) merchandise that should be on hand even at the slowest time of the year. It is found by subtracting the average monthly sales from the average stock:

Basic stock = Average stock for season − Average monthly sales for season

Then

B.O.M. stock = Basic stock + Planned sales for month

Perhaps the relation between the stock at the beginning of the month and the planned sales will be clearer when depicted as a graph (Figure 11.3). Note that as beginning-of-the-month stocks rise and fall, the planned sales also rise and fall by the same amount. The constant difference ($15,000 in this case) is the basic stock. Even if the planned sales were zero, the basic stock would still remain at $15,000.

The basic-stock method of calculating stock levels should be used only when the yearly stock turnover is six times or less. If the stock turn is as high as twelve times a year, the basic stock will become a negative figure and thus not meaningful.

ILLUSTRATIVE PROBLEM A boys' department had planned sales of $150,000 for the spring and summer season. The planned sales for April were $60,000 with three stock turnovers. What stock levels should be planned for the beginning of April?

SOLUTION STEP 1
Find (a) the average monthly sales and (b) the average stock:

(a) $$\text{Average stock} = \frac{\text{Sales for the season}}{\text{Stock turnover}} \quad \text{(see Chapter 9)}$$
$$= \frac{\$150,000}{3}$$
$$= \$50,000$$

(b) $$\text{Average monthly sales} = \frac{\text{Sales for season}}{\text{Number of months}}$$
$$= \frac{\$150,000}{6}$$
$$= \$25,000$$

STEP 2
Find the basic stock:

$$\text{Basic stock} = \text{Average stock for the season} - \text{Average monthly sales for the season}$$
$$= \$50,000 - \$25,000$$
$$= \$25,000$$

STEP 3
Now we can find the beginning-of-the-month stock for April:

$$\text{B.O.M. stock} = \text{Basic stock} + \text{Planned sales for the month}$$
$$= \$25,000 + \$60,000$$
$$= \$85,000$$

When the stock turns over three times a season or six times a year, the average weekly sales are used instead of the average monthly sales. This makes sense since when stocks are being sold and replenished more frequently, stock levels must be more flexible. Weekly averages will allow for more flexibility.

ILLUSTRATIVE PROBLEM A record department plans to have five stock turns during the six-month season. Sales are estimated at $100,000. February (four weeks) is expected to contribute $10,000 of that amount. How should the stock level be planned for the beginning of February?

SOLUTION STEP 1
Find the (a) average stock for the season and (b) average weekly sales for the season:

(a) $$\text{Average stock} = \frac{\text{Sales for the season}}{\text{Stock turnover}}$$
$$= \frac{\$100,000}{5}$$
$$= \$20,000$$

(b) $$\text{Average weekly sales} = \frac{\text{Sales for the season}}{\text{Number of weeks}}$$
$$= \frac{\$100,000}{26}$$
$$= \$3,846$$

198 HOW TO PLAN STOCKS

STEP 2
Find the basic stock:

Basic stock = Average stock for the season
                − Average weekly sales for the season
                = $20,000 − $3,846
                = $16,154

STEP 3
Finally, we find the February beginning-of-the-month stock:

B.O.M. stock = Basic stock + Average weekly sales for the month
$$= \$16,154 + \$2,500 \; \frac{(\$10,000)}{4}$$
$$= \$18,654$$

EXERCISES

1. A men's boutique plans to realize fall and winter sales amounting to $180,000 with two stock turnovers for the season. If December sales are budgeted at $80,000, how should the stock level be planned at the beginning of December?
2. A stationery department plans four annual turnovers with total sales of $240,000. If January sales are pegged at $8,000, what should the stock level be at the beginning of January?
3. A candy store has planned yearly sales of $156,000 with eight stock turns. If December has a control period of five weeks with sales planned at $80,000, what should the stock level be at the beginning of December?

Percentage-Variation Method

This method is best used when the annual stock turnover is six or more and the seasonal turnover is three or more. It relies on the reasoning that the percentage difference of planned monthly sales from average monthly sales should not bring about the same percentage difference in the stock. A buyer, for example, may note that his or her planned June sales are 40 percent higher than the average monthly sales for the season and thus try to justify a 40 percent increase in stock for the beginning of June. As mentioned earlier in this chapter, however, such a policy is not necessary, still less is it wise, because a balanced selection of merchandise can be maintained without so large an increase in stock.

According to the percentage-variation method, the increase or decrease in stocks should be one-half the planned increase or decrease in sales. Experience has shown that this is a sufficient adjustment in stock, but it is only a rule of thumb figure, not an absolute. Thus the buyer mentioned above should increase the June stock at the beginning of the month by only 20 percent over the average stock.

ILLUSTRATIVE PROBLEM   A drug department plans sales of $300,000 for the fall and winter season with four stock turnovers. October sales are planned at $60,000. What should the stock level be at the beginning of October?

SOLUTION It should first be determined whether the October planned sales are more or less than the planned average monthly sales and by what percentage. The October beginning-of-the-month stock should then differ from the average monthly stock by one-half the percentage difference between the two planned sales figures.

STEP 1

Find (a) the average monthly sales and (b) the average stock:

(a) Average monthly sales $= \dfrac{\text{Sales for the season}}{\text{Number of months}}$

$= \dfrac{\$300,000}{6}$

$= \$50,000$

(b) Average stock $= \dfrac{\text{Sales for the season}}{\text{Stock turn}}$

$= \dfrac{\$300,000}{4}$

$= \$75,000$

STEP 2

Find the percentage variation between the planned October sales and the planned average monthly sales and apply one-half of this percentage to the average stock figure to obtain the October beginning-of-the-month stock.

SALES		STOCK	
October sales	$60,000	Average stock	$75,000
Average monthly sales	50,000	B.O.M. Stock	$75,000 + 10%
Dollar increase	$10,000	(½ of sales increase)	
Percent increase	$\dfrac{\$10,000}{\$50,000}$[1] $= \sfrac{1}{5}$ or 20%	B.O.M. Stock $= \$75,000 + \$7,500$ $= \$82,500$	

[1] It is important always to use the average monthly sales figure as the base when calculating the percentage variation.

ALTERNATE
SOLUTION

B.O.M. stock $= \text{Average stock} \times \tfrac{1}{2}\left(1 + \dfrac{\text{Sales for month}}{\text{Average monthly sales}}\right)$

$= \$75,000 \times \tfrac{1}{2}\left(\dfrac{11}{5}\right)$

$= \$75,000 \times \dfrac{11}{10}$

$= \$82,500$

EXERCISES

1. Sales in a bookstore are planned at $360,000 for the year. January, the slowest month, is expected to yield only $6,000 in sales. If the planned annual stock turn is nine, what should be the stock level at the beginning of January?
2. A sporting goods department has the following sales plan: fall and winter sales, $240,000 with three stock turnovers; September sales,

$15,000. Determine the proper stock level for the beginning of September.

3. A toy department does 60 percent of its total yearly volume in December. If yearly sales are planned at $600,000 with six stock turnovers, what should the December beginning-of-the-month stock be?

Week's-Supply Method

As the name implies, this method is to be used when sales and stocks are planned on a weekly instead of monthly basis. The desired number of weeks' supply of stock depends on the planned stock turn, and the amount of stock carried varies directly with planned sales.

This method is more suitable for some staple merchandise than for general departmental stock. When sales are high, stocks rise; when sales are low, stocks drop proportionately. There is no provision for a minimum basic stock when sales are low. Its danger is that stock levels may become too high when sales are up and not enough stock may be on hand when sales are down.

ILLUSTRATIVE PROBLEM The men's underwear department in a large store carried mostly staple items. Average weekly sales were planned at $5,000 with five turnovers during the six-month period. How much stock should be planned?

SOLUTION The following formula should be used when planning stocks according to the week's-supply method:

Planned stock = Average stock weeks' supply × Planned weekly sales

We have already seen that

$$\text{Average stock} = \frac{\text{Sales}}{\text{Stock turnover}}$$

To find the weeks' supply, we have:

$$\text{Average stock in weeks' supply} = \frac{\text{Sales in weeks' supply}}{\text{Stock turnover}}$$

and

$$\text{Average stock in weeks' supply} = \frac{26}{5} \text{ (weeks in six month period)}$$
$$= 5.2$$

where twenty-six is the number of weeks in a six-month period. Therefore,

$$\text{Planned stock} = 5.2 \times \$5,000$$
$$= \$26,000$$

EXERCISES 1. Average weekly sales of $6,000 were planned for a department with four stock turnovers during the six-month period. What is the amount of stock that should be carried?

2. A candy store plans average weekly sales of $500. If the annual stock turn is five, how much stock should be planned?
3. Planned average weekly sales of a flower shop are $2,000 during the busy season, and only $500 during the slow season. Planned annual stock turns are ten during the busy season and only four when business drops. What is the planned stock (a) during the busy season and (b) during the slow season?

Stock-Sales Ratio Method

The stock-sales ratio has already been discussed in Chapter 9. It was stressed that the beginning-of-the-month stock-sales ratio is more valuable than the end-of-the-month ratio because the former shows how much stock should be on hand at the beginning of the month in order to meet planned sales requirements.

We recall that

$$\text{B.O.M. stock-sales ratio} = \text{B.O.M. stock divided by the Sales}$$

Therefore,

$$\text{B.O.M. Stock} = \text{B.O.M. stock-sales ratio} \times \text{Sales}$$

SHORTCOMINGS OF THE STOCK-PLANNING METHODS

Although the four methods described above are very useful in planning stocks, they are by no means completely dependable. The first three methods are based on the figure for planned stock turns, and it would be a grave mistake to put too much emphasis on this factor alone. The last method is dependent on variations in the sales volume, which also can be misleading.

If these mathematical methods are used with little or no regard for the uncertainties or intuitive feelings that make merchandising so exciting, then stock planning can become too rigid. Sometimes a buyer may spot a new item or line of merchandise that he or she is sure will be a winner. Planning should be flexible enough to allow stock levels to be adjusted for such unplanned purchases. Also a buyer may be offered a very attractive job lot, and it may not make sense to turn it down just because planned stocks do not permit the purchase. Some categories of merchandise need to be bought in unusually large assortments of sizes and colors. They, too, may lift stock figures above normal requirements. A department may find it has carried over too much slow-selling stock. Such carry-overs should not be allowed to interfere unduly with the purchase of new stock. These are all reasons for taking great care in applying the formalized stock-planning methods.

CHAPTER SUMMARY

Stocks are the stuff of which sales are made, so they must be planned carefully. Buyers do not often use mathematical formulas in calculating their stock needs. They rely more on past sales records and experience. Buyers' interests are in making sure that basic stocks are maintained at the desired levels, there is sufficient depth in fashion merchandise, and there is enough stock to cover departmental and storewide promotions. They also want the stock levels to be high enough so that branch stores can be supplied with the merchandise assortments they need.

Since buyers have a tendancy to overstock in their zeal to satisfy all customer wants, there are formal financial methods for calculating stock levels to act as a brake if necessary. Most of these methods make use of stock turn goals. If a buyer's estimates of stock needs agree with the results obtained by means of the formal methods, the stock plans will be approved quickly by the merchandise manager and the controller. If they exceed the mathematical estimates by a significant amount, the buyer will be asked to defend his or her plan. If enough sound reasons cannot be given for inflated stocks, the plan will likely be cut back. The control of expenditure, however, should not be so rigid as to prohibit a buyer from occasionally investing in unplanned stocks that he or she believes will be productive.

If a store has one or more branches, stock planning becomes a bigger challenge. Because branch stores do a major share of the total business today, they must be adequately stocked. Stock requirements vary from store to store, and the demographics of each trading area must be studied. Continual communication between branch department managers and the buyer is necessary to insure that the five rights of merchandising are obtained for the branch store operation as well as the parent store.

QUESTIONS FOR REVIEW

1. Explain why buyers and the store controller may differ in their estimates of stock needs.
2. If sales have increased by 40 percent over the previous year, should stocks also be increased by 40 percent? Why?
3. What is meant by bread and butter business?
4. Describe some of the storewide promotional events with which you are familiar.
5. Describe the four formal methods of stock planning.
6. What makes the basic-stock method very different from the other three?
7. Why is it such a mistake for buyers to send identical assortments of merchandise to all branch stores?
8. It is imperative that buyers visit their branch operations frequently. Why?
9. What are some of the reasons that a buyer may find merchandise in short supply?
10. How should the basic-stock method be modified for situations where the stock turns over more than six times a year?

DISCUSSION QUESTION A young college graduate has inherited some money and decides to open a children's apparel shop. His sales goal for the first year of operation is $200,000. He plans to open on March 1 and expects sales of $15,000 during the first month. How can he determine the amount of merchandise needed for opening day?

PROBLEMS FOR REVIEW

1. A delicatessen has planned sales of $52,000 for the upcoming six-month season. The stock is expected to turn over eight times. If March sales (five-week control period) are planned at $5,000, what should the stock level be at the beginning of March, according to the basic-stock method?

2. A men's hat department plans a sales volume of $60,000 for the year and only four annual stock turnovers. If September sales are expected to be $3,000, what, according to the basic-stock method, should be the stock level at the beginning of September?

3. A department has six stock turnovers and planned sales of $240,000 for the six-month period ending January 31. If November sales are planned at $25,000, what should the stock level be at the beginning of the month? Use the percentage-variation method.

4. Sales in a neighborhood drugstore are planned at $300,000 for the year with eight stock turnovers. If August sales are expected to be $30,000, how much stock, according to the percentage-variation method, should be planned for the beginning of August?

5. A staple-merchandise department plans weekly sales of $6,000 for the six-month period with two seasonal stock turnovers. According to the week's-supply method, how much stock should be available?

6. If a department carrying mostly staple items plans weekly sales of $8,000 and a stock turn of four during a busy season lasting four months, and weekly sales of $3,000 and a stock turn of two during the rest of the season, how much stock should be carried (a) during the busy season and (b) during the slow season? Use the week's-supply method.

7. A hosiery store plans weekly sales of $4,000. How much stock should the store carry if there are six annual stock turnovers?

8. An appliance store has budgeted for sales of $12,000 during the month of September. If the stock-sales ratio is 2.5, what should the stock level be at the beginning of the month?

9. The planned sales in a department are $18,000 for the month of May with a stock-sales ratio of 0.9. What are the stock requirements for the beginning of the month?

10. Using the appropriate stock-planning method, determine the stock requirements for the beginning of June if sales for the month are expected to be $85,000. Sales for the six-month period are planned at $510,000 with five seasonal stock turnovers.

CASE PROBLEMS

THE SMELL OF SUCCESS

Bill Stevenson, buyer of men's sportswear for the Woodward Company, a medium-sized department store in the Northeast, has been feeling the flush of success for the past three years. His departmental sales at Woodward's two branch stores have zoomed, and even the flagship store downtown has held its own. Profits are also up in his department, and Stevenson has become the star of the men's merchandising division. He attributes his success to the "jeans revolution," more aggressive promotion, and better departmental displays.

Stevenson has just completed his sales and merchandise plan for the upcoming spring and summer season. Since his sales for the current season have mushroomed 25 percent over the like period a year before, he plans another hefty sales increase, this time 30 percent. Although he knows he is treading on dangerous waters, he plans a stock increase of 25 percent, he thinks with good reason. He anticipates a major fashion change in his department—the acceptance of the "leisure suit"—and wants to be prepared with plenty of stock. A sample order of 100 such suits was all sold within a week. A quickly placed reorder is expected to arrive in a few weeks.

The leisure suit, consisting of a jacket and slack ensemble to be worn without a tie, is taking the men's market by storm. Sometimes called the easy suit, the safari suit, or the western leisure suit, it is being made to retail for $40 up to $200. The less expensive suits are shirt-weighted sportswear models with finished bottoms, but the more expensive numbers are fully constructed tailored models with unfinished bottoms. Stevenson plans to buy heavily from sportswear firms making the leisure suit to retail from $40 to $80.

A week later Stevenson finds himself reviewing his six-month plan with Steve Gray, his divisional merchandise manager, and Harold Miller, the store's controller. Even though Stevenson has been riding on the crest of success, Mr. Miller is shocked to see such large sales and stock increases. He is especially upset by the 25 percent increase in stock levels. Stevenson explains that the increased stock is necessary to bring in 3,000 leisure suits, which he is sure he can sell. Mr. Miller says, on the other hand, that he is afraid the leisure suit will go the way of the Nehru jacket, which flopped miserably some years before and cost the store very serious markdowns. He then proceeds to show Stevenson mathematically that even by increasing the stock-sales ratio and the stock turnover, the request for a 25 percent increase in stock cannot be justified.

Stevenson has been trapped by Mr. Miller's mathematical computations before. He feels very strongly, however, that the leisure suit is not just a gimmick and that it has real long-range potential. It is a way for younger men in particular to be well dressed for business situations and yet feel relaxed and comfortable. He is not about to be stymied by Mr. Miller, an ultraconservative who has never spent one day as a buyer and who is constantly buried in his figures. But sensing that he is losing his case, Stevenson looks at his merchandise manager hoping for help.

Mr. Gray has listened to the conversation between the two, knowing that a tough decision has to be made. He has great respect for Stevenson's ability to smell out a new fashion trend and does not want to dampen his buyer's enthusiasm. On the other hand, he is not sure that the leisure suit really represents many extra sales. According to the reports he has read, leisure suits are cutting deeply into the sports coat business. Sports coats are bought by Jim Terry, the clothing buyer, who has been fighting declining sales for sometime. Wide acceptance of leisure suits will probably make Terry's sales and stock position even worse. Mr. Gray, therefore, decides to make several recommendations for solving the conflict between his buyer and the controller.

1. What recommendations can Mr. Gray make in order to insure that the Woodward Company would be well covered in the area of leisure suits?
2. Is it wise for two buyers in the same division or in the same store to compete for the same market?

UP THE LADDER

Georgina Smith is the general merchandise manager at Cushman's, a prestigious specialty store in the Northeast. Cushman's stocks high-quality men's and women's apparel, children's wear, women's accessories, and several other categories of merchandise, but it has no hard lines, such as furniture, appliances, or sporting goods. One day the president of the store calls Ms. Smith into his office to remind her that the firm's first branch store is due to open in four months. A staff for the new store is needed, and the first executive to be named will be the store manager. The president believes that the manager should be an experienced merchandiser so the new branch will be merchandise oriented. Ms. Smith is asked to recommend one of her three divisional merchandise managers to the post. Since the branch will be big, the step from divisional merchandise manager to branch store manager will be considered a major promotion. The president wants to have Ms. Smith's recommendation within a week.

Ms. Smith returns to her own office to mull over the qualifications of the three persons. They are all able, so the decision will not be easy. She takes out a piece of paper and begins to jot down what she knows about them. When she has finished, her notes look like the following:

Dick Bechtold: four-year college graduate, joined Cushman's eight years ago and became a buyer after only one year as an assistant buyer; has merchandised women's and children's apparel for three years with highly satisfactory results; is very bright, has a pleasing personality, makes a good appearance, and meets the public well; Ms. Smith likes to reminisce with Bechtold about their days at Cornell, from which they both graduated, and they try to attend two or three Cornell games together each fall in the company of their spouses; Bechtold is 35 years old.

Jane Comerford: a two-year college graduate with twelve years' service with Cushman's; also an effective merchandiser, and her accessories and other main-floor departments have enjoyed steady gains in sales volume and profits; became a buyer after three years as assistant buyer; is now in her fourth year as a departmental merchandise manager and is very popular with her buyers; possesses an unusual amount of drive and inventiveness; Comerford is 40.

Levy Hartog: is from the "old school"; is a high school graduate with over thirty-two years of service with the store; is 50 and has worked his way up through the ranks; began as a stockboy, sold men's furnishings for five years, became an outstanding assistant buyer, and was promoted to buyer of men's wear eight years later; served as buyer for ten years and was then promoted to his present position as merchandise manager of the men's and boy's wear division; his three buyers like him although they find him a hard taskmaster; has become very sure of himself through the years and sometimes argues with Ms. Smith and other store executives about the way things should be done; somewhat lacking in polish and makes mistakes in grammar, but certainly knows his merchandise, and his departments are the top profit makers in the store.

By the end of the week, Ms. Smith has made her decision. Bechtold will get the job. She feels that Bechtold is the man with the most potential. While recognizing that Comerford is a real go-getter and deserves a promotion and Hartog has seniority and, though deficient in tact, his personality is not poor enough to be a serious drawback, Ms. Smith feels that for the position of store manager Bechtold has to be the best choice. Although the promotion will not be officially announced for sometime, Ms. Smith plans to tell Bechtold about her recommendation confidentially when they sit together at the Cornell game the next afternoon. Before the promotion is announced, Ms. Smith must also interview both Comerford and Hartog to tell them of her decision. She knows that she will have no problem with Comerford, but she is not sure how Hartog will take the news. She does not want to ruffle Hartog's feelings because Hartog is her most seasoned merchandise manager and the most successful.

1. How do you think Hartog will react when he finds out Bechtold has received the promotion?
2. Did Ms. Smith use good personnel strategy in choosing the new store manager?

12

HOW TO PLAN PURCHASES AND OPEN-TO-BUY

KEY POINTS

1. A chief function of the sales and merchandise plan is to provide for monthly purchases of stock.

2. Planned monthly purchases and open-to-buy figures are usually not the same because buyers may have previous orders still outstanding.

3. Open-to-buy may be calculated in terms of dollars and cents or in units of merchandise and can be obtained for any time during the month.

4. A model stock represents a balanced merchandise mix based on customer demand. Model stocks may be set up for both staple and fashion merchandise.

5. If a buyer is out of open-to-buy, there are ways of getting some more, although it is vital to avoid feeding an already overstocked position.

PLANNING PURCHASES

All of the planned figures that we have considered for the sales and merchandise plan so far are needed for the final computation of planned monthly purchases. It is this final figure that tells the buyer how much merchandise to buy to keep sales and stocks balanced. Since most stores use the retail method of inventory and all of the figures included in the plan are based on retail, purchases at retail are planned first. Purchases at cost are derived easily by using the planned initial markup. The procedure was explained in Chapter 3.

The formula for planned purchases is:

Planned purchases = Planned E.O.M. stock + Planned sales + Planned reductions − Planned B.O.M. stock

The formula indicates that purchases must be made to cover anticipated needs: a remaining stock at the end of the month plus sales and reductions (markdowns, shortages, employee discounts). From these needs can be subtracted the merchandise already on hand at the beginning of the month.

In order to illustrate how purchases are planned, we shall examine once again the same sales and merchandise plan shown in Chapters 10 and 11. (See Figure 12.1) Using the formula above, we can see that the February planned purchases at retail come to:

```
      $196,166 (planned E.O.M. stock)
  +     88,000 (planned sales)
  +      9,900 (planned reductions)
      $294,066 (total merchandise available)
  −    179,666 (planned B.O.M. stock)
      $114,400 (planned purchases)
```

Figure 12.1 SALES AND MERCHANDISE PLAN

SALES AND MERCHANDISE PLAN

Season: Spring   Department No. 2

	Last Year	Plan	Actual		Last Year	Plan	Actual
Initial Markup %	43.3	43.4		Gross Margin %	38.4	39.3	
Reductions %	10.0	9.0		Operating Expense %	36.0	36.0	
Cash Discount %	1.8	2.0					
Alteration Expense %	1.0	1.0		Season Turn	2.5	3	
Maintained Markup %	37.6	38.3		Net Profit %	2.4	3.0	

	FEB / AUG	MAR / SEPT	APR / OCT	MAY / NOV	JUNE / DEC	JULY / JAN	TOTAL
SALES							
Last Year	80,000	90,000	110,000	85,000	70,000	65,000	500,000
Plan	88,000	104,500	115,500	93,500	82,500	66,000	550,000
Adjusted Plan							
Actual							
RETAIL STOCK (B.O.M.)							(Average Stock)
Last Year	151,670	215,666	235,666	210,666	195,666	190,666	200,000
Plan	179,666	196,166	207,166	185,166	174,166	157,666	183,333
Adjusted Plan							
Actual							
RETAIL STOCK (E.O.M.)							
Last Year	215,666	235,666	210,666	195,666	190,666	200,000	
Plan	196,166	207,166	185,166	174,166	157,666	183,333	
Adjusted Plan							
Actual							
REDUCTIONS							
Last Year	7,500	5,000	5,000	11,000	9,000	12,500	50,000
Plan	9,900	4,950	4,950	9,900	4,950	14,850	49,500
Actual							
RETAIL PURCHASES							
Last Year	151,496	115,000	90,000	81,000	74,000	86,834	598,330
Plan	114,400	120,450	123,950	92,400	70,950	106,517	628,667
Adjusted Plan							
Actual							
COST PURCHASES							
Last Year	85,898	65,205	51,030	45,927	41,958	49,235	339,253
Plan	64,750	68,175	70,156	52,298	40,158	60,289	355,826
Adjusted Plan							
Actual							

To find February planned purchases at cost, we multiply the retail by the complement of the planned initial markup percentage:

February planned purchases at cost = Retail × (100% − MU%)
= $114,400 × (100% − 43.4%)
= $114,400 × 0.566
= $ 64,750

To check the accuracy of the February planned purchases at retail, we make the calculations to see that the March beginning-of-the-month stock is $196,166, as shown in the plan:

Planned February B.O.M. stock	$179,666
plus planned retail purchases for February	114,400
Total merchandise available	$294,066
− planned February sales and reductions	97,900
Planned March B.O.M. stock	$196,166

It is important to understand how planned reductions are computed in order to obtain the correct planned purchases. Total reductions last year amounted to $50,000, representing 10 percent of sales. The monthly distribution of these reductions was as follows:

MONTH	REDUCTIONS	PERCENTAGE OF TOTAL
February	$ 7,500	15%
March	5,000	10
April	5,000	10
May	11,000	22
June	9,000	18
July	12,500	25
Total	$50,000	100%

Planned reductions for this year are only 9 percent of sales or 0.09 × $550,000 = $49,500. The monthly distribution of these planned reductions is slightly different from the actual distribution last year:

MONTH	PERCENTAGE OF TOTAL	TOTAL REDUCTIONS	MONTHLY REDUCTIONS
February	20%	$49,500	$ 9,900
March	10	49,500	4,950
April	10	49,500	4,950
May	20	49,500	9,900
June	10	49,500	4,950
July	30	49,500	14,850
Total	100%		$49,500

OPEN-TO-BUY

Very simply, open-to-buy is what the buyer plans to purchase less what is already on order; it is the merchandise needed less what the store already has. What the store already has includes the following: actual stock on hand, merchandise already received but not yet on the selling floor, merchandise in transit (on its way to the store), and merchandise outstanding (ordered but not yet shipped). In summary:

TOTAL MERCHANDISE NEEDED	TOTAL MERCHANDISE AVAILABLE
Planned sales	Beginning stock
Planned reductions	Merchandise received
Planned ending stock	Merchandise in transit
	Merchandise outstanding

If the total merchandise needed is greater than the total merchandise available, the buyer is *open to buy*. Conversely, if the merchandise available is greater than the merchandise needed, the buyer is overbought and no open-to-buy may be forthcoming until stocks have been reduced.

Open-to-buy is dear to every buyer's heart. It is what it takes for a buyer to do his or her job. If one is without it, he or she will try to find a way to get it.

Dollar Open-to-Buy

Open-to-buy may be given in terms of dollars and cents or in units of merchandise. Although buyers purchase in units, they are always anxious to know how many retail dollars they can spend. Open-to-buy may be calculated for the beginning of a season or month or at any given time during the season.

FINDING THE OPEN-TO-BUY AT THE BEGINNING OF THE MONTH

It is most common to figure how much a buyer has to spend on new merchandise as of the beginning of each month. This open-to-buy figure represents a starting point; adjustments may need to be made as the month progresses to keep sales and stocks balanced.

ILLUSTRATIVE PROBLEM — A cosmetics department has merchandise in stock amounting to $24,000 on March 1. The stock level planned for the end of the month is $28,000. March sales are expected to be $10,000 and $1,000 worth of markdowns are planned for the month. There are outstanding orders totaling $4,000, and a keystone markup of 50 percent is planned. What is the open-to-buy at cost and at retail?

SOLUTION — Merchandise needed:
    Planned E.O.M. stock $28,000
    Planned sales   10,000
    Planned reductions   1,000
    Total merchandise needed $39,000
Merchandise available:
    Stock on hand $24,000
    Stock on order   4,000

Total merchandise available	$28,000
Open-to-buy March 1 (retail)	$11,000
Open-to-buy March 1 (cost)	$ 5,500

$$C = R \times (100\% - MU\%)$$
$$C = \$11,000 \times .50$$
$$C = \$5,500$$

EXERCISES

1. Sales in the pro shop at a golf club are planned at $3,000 for the month of May. The stock at the beginning of the month amounts to $8,000, and the estimated ending stock is $6,000. No markdowns are planned, but discounts to employees are expected to total $500. If the merchandise on order amounts to $800, what is the open-to-buy as of May 1?
2. The inventory in a bridal shop on June 1 has a value of $18,000. Sales during the month are expected to be $10,000. The stock level planned for the end of the month is $12,000. Assuming that there will be no markdowns, what is the June 1 open-to-buy, if outstanding orders amount to $5,000?
3. A department in a discount house has the following plans for the month of August: sales, $45,000; end-of-the-month stock, $80,000; markdowns, $5,000; and shortages, $500. The stock on August 1 is worth $100,000, and outstanding orders total $18,000. What is the open-to-buy at retail and at cost, if the planned initial markup is 40 percent?

FINDING THE OPEN-TO-BUY AT A SPECIFIC TIME DURING THE MONTH WHEN STOCK ON HAND IS KNOWN

A buyer may wish to be more precise in estimating his or her merchandising needs and not wait until a month is over before seeing what the new open-to-buy will be. Sales may be running well ahead of plan for a variety of reasons, and the buyer wants to be prepared for continued good sales. A number of factors could cause a sharp decrease in sales, also, and the buyer may wish to take quick action to reduce the amount of stock on hand. A physical inventory will give the most accurate open-to-buy figure. However, a physical inventory is usually not practical during the season, so the buyer will usually rely on the running book inventory furnished by the controller for information on the stock situation on a given day.

ILLUSTRATIVE PROBLEM

Several new important novels were published during the past week, and the book buyer wonders on April 20 whether she still has some open-to-buy so that she can purchase the new novels in quantity. Her planned sales for April are $12,000, and she has recorded actual sales through April 20 of $10,500. Planned markdowns are $1,000, of which $800 have already been taken. She began the month with a retail stock of $25,000 and was planning to end the month with an inventory of $27,000. Her stock on April 20 is $18,000. There are outstanding orders amounting to $8,000, which should arrive before the month is over. If she operates on the basis of a keystone markup of 50 percent, what is her open-to-buy at retail and at cost on April 20?

SOLUTION Merchandise needed for the balance of the month:

Planned E.O.M. stock		$27,000
Planned sales for April	$12,000	
Actual sales, April 1 - 20	−10,000	
Balance planned sales		2,000
Planned, markdowns for April	1,000	
Actual markdowns, April 1 - 20	− 800	
Balance, markdowns		200
Total merchandise needed		$29,200

Merchandise available for the balance of the month:

Stock on hand, April 20	$18,000	
Outstanding orders,[1] April 20	8,000	
Total merchandise available		−26,000
Open-to-buy at retail, April 20		$ 3,200
Open-to-buy at cost, April 20		$ 1,600

EXERCISES

1. A buyer of luggage needs an open-to-buy figure as of November 12. He has the following figures at his disposal:

Planned sales for November	$28,000
Planned E.O.M. stock for November	50,000
Actual sales, November 1 - 12	15,000
Actual stock, November 12	55,000
Planned markdowns for November	2,000
Actual markdowns, November 1 - 12	1,500
Outstanding orders, November 12	6,000

What is the buyer's open-to-buy as of November 12?

2. Using the following figures, determine whether the buyer in question is still open to buy as of July 22.

Planned sales for July	$ 60,000
Actual sales, July 1 - 22	45,000
Planned markdowns for July	6%
Actual markdowns, July 1 - 22	3,000
Planned E.O.M. stock	100,000
Actual B.O.M. stock	130,000
Stock on hand, July 22	120,000
Outstanding commitments, July 22	10,000

3. The manager of a boutique is anxious to buy a line of handpainted dolls, but she is not sure whether she has any open-to-buy left as of January 15. Determine her open-to-buy at retail and at cost as of that date, using the following figures:

---

[1] The amount of outstanding orders is much too high for this time in the month. The buyer must exert more pressure on her vendors to deliver needed merchandise; otherwise she will find herself in a seriously understocked position.

Planned initial markup percentage		60%
Planned reductions		3%
Actual markdowns, January 1 - 15	$	500
Actual shortages, January 1 - 15		50
Planned E.O.M. stock, January 31		75,000
Planned sales for January		30,000
Actual sales, January 1 - 15		16,000
Orders outstanding, January 15		1,000
Actual stock, January 15		86,000

FINDING THE OPEN-TO-BUY AT A SPECIFIC TIME DURING THE MONTH WHEN STOCK ON HAND IS NOT KNOWN

If a physical count is not taken or the book inventory figure cannot be obtained for a certain date, it is still possible to determine the open-to-buy. The procedure for finding the quantity of merchandise needed is the same. However, the quantity of merchandise available is computed by using the beginning-of-the-month stock figure and then adding on the merchandise receipts up to the given date and subtracting sales and markdowns up to the same date because they take away from the value of the merchandise. Again, it is not usually practical to take a special physical inventory between regular inventory times unless the stock to be counted is very small.

ILLUSTRATIVE PROBLEM The owner of a sporting goods store is selling more merchandise in June than he anticipated because of unseasonably warm weather. Wanting to place some quick fill-in orders, he decides to find out whether he has some open-to-buy on June 18. June sales were planned at $35,000, but he has already recorded sales of $24,000. The plan calls for a stock level of $90,000 at the end of the month, while his beginning-of-the-month stock was $95,000. Between June 1 and June 18 he received merchandise amounting to $8,000, and he still has outstanding commitments of $3,000. What is his open-to-buy as of June 18?

SOLUTION

Merchandise needed for the balance of the month:

Planned E.O.M. stock		$90,000
Planned sales for June	$35,000	
Actual sales, June 1 - 18	24,000	
Balance, planned sales		11,000
Total merchandise needed		$101,000

Merchandise available for the balance of the month:

B.O.M. stock, June 1	$ 95,000
Orders received, June 1 - 18	+ 8,000
Total merchandise handled, June 1-18	$103,000
Actual sales, June 1 - 18	− 24,000

Stock on hand, June 18	79,000
Outstanding orders, June 18	+ 3,000
Total Merchandise Available	−82,000
Open-to-Buy, June 18	$19,000

EXERCISES

1. A record buyer wants an open-to-buy figure as of December 10. The following figures are available to him:

Planned sales for December	$ 80,000
Actual sales, December 1 - 10	35,000
Planned reductions for December	6,000
Actual reductions, December 1 - 10	4,000
Planned E.O.M. stock	120,000
December B.O.M. stock	160,000
Orders received, December 1 - 10	20,000
Orders outstanding, December 10 - 31	25,000

    Has the buyer any open-to-buy, and if so, how much?

2. A buyer hopes that he still has some open-to-buy so he can place an order for a new item that a vendor has just shown him. He puts together the following figures, which are valid as of October 17:

Planned E.O.M. stock	$34,000
B.O.M. stock for October	32,000
Merchandise received, October 1 - 17	9,000
Commitments outstanding, October 17 - 31	7,000
Planned October sales	13,000
Actual sales, October 1 - 17	7,400

    Markdowns of $1,000 are planned, but none has been taken. What is the buyer's open-to-buy?

3. On November 11 a buyer decides to have a new open-to-buy figure. His planned initial markup is 48 percent. Since he hopes to bring in a new line, he wants to know how much he can spend at cost. Based on the following figures, how large should his purchases be at cost?

Planned sales for November	$120,000
Actual sales, November 1 - 11	45,000
Planned markdowns for November	8,000
Actual markdowns, November 1 - 11	2,000
Planned E.O.M. stock	300,000
November B.O.M. stock	249,000
Purchases received, November 1 - 11	130,000
Orders outstanding, November 11 - 30	21,000

Unit Open-to-Buy

When buyers visit their markets, they are armed with buying plans that tell them how many *units* of each item they can buy. These buying plans are a necessity if the buyers make infrequent trips, because under the circumstances they cannot afford to make mistakes. Buyers who have ready access to their respective markets and visit them once a week or even more often seldom bother with formal buying plans, but they, too, must know how many units of each item they can buy.

The formula for planning purchases in units of merchandise instead of dollars is exactly the same as before:

$$\text{Unit planned purchase} = \text{Unit E.O.M. stock} + \text{Unit sales} \\ + \text{Unit markdowns} - \text{Unit B.O.M. stock}$$

Open-to-buy in units of merchandise are thus equal to units of planned purchases less units on order. This formula works well for fashion merchandise, where the beginning and ending stock figures can be obtained by physical counts and the units sold can be recorded by analyzing sales checks, merchandise stubs, or by means of the computer. A more detailed discussion of the buying plan and the relations that hold among open-to-buy, unit control, and fashion merchandise will be given in the next chapter.

Finding open-to-buy in merchandise units in the case of staple and bread and butter merchandise is a little different. Staple merchandise in particular should *always* be in stock in the right quantity, assortment, size, and color. Usually to make sure the store is well supplied, a reserve stock is set up to allow for shipping delays, strikes, or sudden changes in the rate of sale. Minimum and maximum stocks, delivery time, and reorder frequency all work together to insure an almost foolproof system of keeping staple stocks up to desired levels.

Buyers must know their open-to-buy before visiting the market.
SOURCE: Mimi Forsyth/Monkmeyer Press Photo Service

In order to understand how this method of stock replenishment works, the student should become familiar with the following terms:

1. *Minimum stock* is the amount of stock that *should be* in a department at reordering time. It should be high enough to include a reserve (often referred to as the safety factor) as well as to cover the probable sales during the delivery period.
2. *The reserve* (safety factor) is stock that is kept on hand to cover any unforeseen change in the rate of sales or undue delays in shipping. It is made up of a basic stock, which is the smallest quantity of merchandise in an assortment of sizes, colors, and styles to satisfy customer demand, plus one week's extra stock.
3. *Maximum stock* is the sum of the minimum stock and the amount of the reorder at the time of reorder.
4. *Delivery period* is the length of time between the ordering of the new stock and the receipt of that stock.
5. *Reorder period* is the frequency with which a particular item is ordered; it may be weekly, monthly, every two months, or longer intervals.

The importance of the reserve stock may be illustrated by the following example. A mother enters the girls' department to buy a basic white cotton blouse for her daughter who is to attend a private school in Switzerland where a white blouse is part of the school uniform. She decides to buy enough blouses to last her daughter for one year. Such a purchase may very well deplete the store's basic stock in that size. Without the safety factor of a week's supply of extra stock, the store will run the risk of losing some sales before a new shipment of blouses arrives.

The basic formulas to remember are:

Minimum stock = Reserve + (Delivery period × Weekly rate of sales)
Maximum stock = Minimum stock + (Reorder period × Weekly rate of sales)
Open-to-buy = Maximum stock − (Stock on hand + Stock on order)

ILLUSTRATIVE PROBLEM   A men's specialty store has been selling an average of 120 pairs of stretch socks a week. In order to keep an adequate assortment in fancy patterns and solids, a reserve of 240 pairs is required. A reorder is placed every two weeks, and it takes an average of two weeks for shipments to arrive. On July 1 there are 510 pairs of socks in stock and 84 on order. Determine how many pairs should be ordered next time.

SOLUTION   STEP 1
Find the minimum stock:

Minimum stock = Reserve + (Delivery period × Weekly rate of sales)
             = 240 + (2 × 120)
             = 240 + 240
             = 480 units

STEP 2
Find the maximum stock:

Maximum stock = Minimum stock + (Reorder period
                 × Weekly rate of sales)
              = 480 + (2 × 120)
              = 480 + 240
              = 720 units

STEP 3
Find the open-to-buy:

Open-to-Buy = Maximum Stock − (Stock on hand
              + Stock on order)
            = 720 − (510 + 84)
            = 720 − 594
            = 126 units[2]

EXERCISES

1. An infants' wear buyer estimates that she sells 800 Chux diapers each week. She keeps a reserve stock of 2,000. On October 15 she takes a count and finds 2,440 in stock with 1,200 on order. The reorder period is one week, but it takes two weeks for a shipment to arrive. What will be her open-to-buy in units at the time of the next order?
2. One of the hottest sellers in a hosiery department is one-size panty hose. In order to keep up with the demand, the buyer takes a weekly count and places a weekly order, but it takes three weeks for the merchandise to arrive. She maintains a reserve of 100 dozen in assorted shades. When she took a count on January 7, she found she had a stock of 2,680 with 840 in outstanding orders. How many should she order next time if weekly sales are running at approximately 900?
3. Although the sales of men's ready-tied black bow ties are very limited, a department decides to keep them in stock at all times. Weekly sales average only 20, and a safety factor of 60 is maintained. As of June 22, there are 78 in stock with 48 on order. Due to the low turnover, reorders are placed at four-week intervals, but delivery time is only one week. How many new bow ties should the buyer order?

THE MODEL STOCK PLAN

A model stock plan is just what the name implies: a model to be followed so that the store can best satisfy customer demand in terms of the assortments wanted at the lowest inventory investment possible. It gives the *minimum* quantity of sizes, colors, styles, and prices that the store should have on hand even during the slowest selling periods. It can be set up for either

---

[2]Men's socks are usually ordered by the dozen. Thus 126 pairs would represent an order for 10 and ½ dozen. Many buyers prefer to order in even dozens, so that this particular order would probably be eleven dozen.

fashion or staple merchandise. Model stock plans for fashion merchandise tend to be quite flexible, as we will see in the next chapter. Those for staples, however, are expected to be followed rigidly. Once a model stock plan has been set up and approved, the filling in of needed stock becomes a mechanical process, although still very important. Those responsible for the maintenance of the model stocks must be sure that counts and reorders are done regularly. They must also be able to analyze changes in the rate of sale so that the model stocks can be adjusted if necessary.

The formula given for open-to-buy in units of merchandise can be used in ordering staple stocks on a periodic basis. Once we have determined the reserve, delivery period, reorder period, and the weekly rate of sales, we know the maximum stock, and this quantity remains constant. The only variable will be the amount of stock on hand, which is affected by sales and returns.

In Figure 12.2, the model stock structure for a staple item, men's boxer shorts, is shown. A physical count of the merchandise on hand is taken at periodic intervals. The difference between the physical count and the model stock represents the quantity to be ordered in half dozens. If the buyer was short of open-to-buy and wanted to order conservatively, the order would probably look like Figure 12.2.

Figure 12.3 shows the suggested model stocks for four different stores covering pajamas, robes, and lounge wear, set up by a nationally advertised men's pajama manufacturer. The quantities are given in dozens with no regard to sizes or colors. An entire program presented this way tells the retailer what the initial and seasonal commitments are likely to be in retail dollars. Size and color preferences would be given to the vendor when the order was prepared.

If any of the numbers in the program sold well enough to be included in the department's basic stock, a reorder cycle by color and size could be instituted.

HOW TO INCREASE OPEN-TO-BUY

Buyers feel uncomfortable when they have no open-to-buy and even worse when they are *overbought*. Of course, there are times when a buyer would use the lack of open-to-buy as a convenient excuse to get rid of a pestering vendor. This kind of refusal is familiar to every sales representative.

Figure 12.2
REORDER CYCLE

MEN'S BOXER SHORTS
ASSORTED SOLIDS, GRIPPER STYLE

Sizes	28	30	32	34	36	38	40	42
Model Stock (doz.)	6	12	18	20	16	10	8	5
On Hand 2/15/75	53	89	136	142	116	54	62	39
Order (6/12)	$1^{6/}$	$4^{6/}$	$6^{6/}$	8	$6^{6/}$	$5^{6/}$	3	$1^{6/}$

Figure 12.3 MODEL STOCK PROGRAM

WELDON'S PAJAMA, ROBE & LOUNGEWEAR PROGRAM (In Retail Dollars)

	Retail Price	Store "A" Doz.	Dol.	Store "B" Doz.	Dol.	Store "C" Doz.	Dol.	Store "D" Doz.	Dol.	TOTALS Doz.	Dol.
A. Palmer Terry Program											
Shave Coat	$16.	5	$960	4	$768	3	$576	2	$384	14	$2688
Short	8.50	4	408	3	306	2 6	255	1 6	153	11	1122
Sarong	7.50	4	360	3	270	2 6	225	1 6	135	11	990
Scuff	7.	4	336	3	252	2 6	210	1 6	126	11	924
Robe	22.50	3 6	945	3	810	2	540	1 4	360	9 10	2655
Total		20 6	$3009	16	$2406	12 6	$1806	7 10	$1158	56 10	$8379
Total 3 turns =			$9027		$7218		$5418		$3474		$25137
Solid Dacron & Cotton Program											
Long Sleeve Long Leg	$12.	8	$1152	6	$864	4	$576	2 6	$360	20 6	$2952
Robe	15.	4	720	3	540	2	360	1 6	270	10 6	1890
Longs	13.50	2 6	405	2 6	405	1 6	243	1 6	243	8	1296
Extra Sizes	14.50	1	174	1	174	6	87	6	87	3	522
Total		15 6	$2451	12 6	$1983	8	$1266	6	$960	42	$6660
Total (3 turns =)			$7353		$5949		$3798		$2880		$19980
Basic Fancy Program											
Drawstring Pin Stripe	$10.	3	$360	2 9	$330	1 6	$180	1 6	$180	8 9	$1050
Window Pane Check	10.	3	360	2 9	330	1 6	180	1 6	180	8 9	1050
Gingham Check	13.	3	468	2 6	429	1 6	234	1 6	234	8 9	1365
Longs	12.	2 6	360	2 6	360	1 6	216			6 6	936
Extra Sizes	12.50	1	150	1	150	6	75			2 6	375
Total		12 6	$1698	11 9	$1599	6 6	$885	4 6	$594	35 3	$4776
Total (3 turns =)			$5094		$4797		$2655		$1782		$14328
Fancy Pajama Program											
First Range	$10.	12	$1440	8	$960	5	$600	3	$360	28	$3360
Second Range	12.	8	1152	6	864	3	432	1 6	216	18 6	2064
Third Range	13.	6	936	4	624	2	312	1 3	195	13 3	2067
Fourth Range	15.	4	720	2	360					6	1080
Total		30	$4248	20	$2808	10	$1344	5 9	$771	65 9	$9171
Total (2 turns =)			$8496		$5616		$2688		$1542		$18342
Flannel Pajama Program											
Solid	$10.50	8	$1008	6	$756	3	$378	1 6	$189	18 6	$2331
Fancy	10.50	12	1512	8	1008	5	630	3 6	378	28 6	3525
Long	12.50	2 6	375	2 6	375	1 6	225	1 6	225	8	1200
Extra Sizes	13.	1	156	1	156	6	78	6	78	3	468
Total		23 6	$3051	17 6	$2295	10 6	$1311	6 6	$870	57 6	$7527
Total (even)					$2295		$1311		$870		$7527
Napsack Program											
Fancy	$10.	3	$360	2 6	$300	2	$240	1 6	$180	9	$1080
Fancy	10.	3	360	2 6	300	2	240	1 6	180	9	1080
Total		6	$720	5	$600	4	$480	3	$360	18	$2160
Total (2 turns =)			$1440		$1200		$960		$720		$4320
Fashion Program											
Benchwarmers - Western											
Patchwork - 1st Niter		50	$7200*	35	$5040	20	$2880	15	$2160	120	$17280
Country Club - Red Flannel											
Total			$7200		$5040		$2880		$2160		$17280
Sale Group	$8.	75	$7200	60	$5760	50	$4800	25	$2400	210	$20160
Total			$7200		$5760		$4800		$2400		$20160
Total (Initial Commitment)			$29577		$22491		$14772		$9273		$76113
TOTAL (Season Commitment)			$48861		$39895		$24510		$15828		$106914

SOURCE: Stanley Slotnick, Vice President, Weldon, Inc.

When buyers find themselves with no open-to-buy, there are nevertheless steps they can take to generate purchasing power. Some of these should be routine practice; others should be used only as a last resort. Buyers should never feel completely hamstrung if they feel sure that additional purchases are warranted. Occasionally, an item has such an appeal that money must be found to stock it. At other times competition makes it imperative to stock certain merchandise that was not part of a buying plan. Buyers must be willing to take a chance now and then, and their merchandise managers should back them up when requests for additional open-to-buy seem reasonable.

The following are the ways by which open-to-buy can be increased.

1. *Increase planned sales.* This is the most obvious way to give a buyer more money to spend. If actual sales are running ahead of plan, it is practical to raise the sales goals. However, if sales are just at the planned level or lagging, then obviously it makes no sense at all to increase the sales goal.
2. *Increase planned markdowns.* This is a favorite ploy of buyers. Heavier markdowns take away from the retail value of the merchandise and hence increase open-to-buy. Larger markdowns may be perfectly legitimate for purposes of speeding the sale of slow-moving merchandise. However, buyers should remember that markdowns adversely affect profits, and departments with excessive markdowns are not looked upon with favor when performance evaluation time rolls around.
3. *Cancel outstanding orders.* This is a sure way to increase open-to-buy, but it may not be ethical. If the vendor is doing his or her part to supply merchandise, the buyer should not refuse to live up to the terms of the purchasing agreement. If the vendor cannot meet delivery dates as set forth or cannot ship the merchandise exactly as ordered, the buyer can then cancel the order.

    A sure way of increasing open-to-buy is to cancel outstanding balances on purchases already received. Manufacturers often short-ship, and the buyer should take frequent trips to the receiving room to cancel the balance due. Although the balances on individual orders are often small, when there are many orders they add up to large sums, and the advantage is worth the paperwork involved.
4. *Transfer outstanding orders to a later month.* This method can provide immediate open-to-buy if the buyer thinks that the merchandise will be delayed. Alternatively, if the merchandise is not needed in the store during the month it was ordered for, vendors are often willing to postpone delivery to a later date. In either case a well-placed telephone call to the vendor can reap big dividends in open-to-buy for the buyer.
5. *Increase planned ending stock.* The buyer may be justified in using this approach if it appears that sales will be better than anticipated. Sudden influxes of people into an area can occur, in which case stock levels should be raised accordingly.
6. *Return goods to vendors.* This practice is seldom ethical unless the

Checking for incomplete shipments can provide more open-to-buy.
SOURCE: Shelton/Monkmeyer Press Photo Service

merchandise is defective or there is a previous agreement that unsold goods can be returned. There are buyers who try to show their buying muscle by taking advantage of suppliers in this way to make room for newer merchandise. Sometimes buyers from large organizations can get away with it, but the practice is to be deplored.

CHAPTER SUMMARY

Finding planned purchases at retail and at cost is the last step which completes the seasonal sales and merchandise plan. These figures show how many dollars the buyer can spend at the beginning of each month for new merchandise and are affected by all the other components of the sales and merchandise plan.

In fact, buyers do not purchase all their needed merchandise at the beginning of each month. Furthermore, some merchandise does not arrive at the proper time; delivery may be too early or too late. In the course of a month or a season, buyers often need to know exactly how much money can be spent for the balance of the month or season. These figures are their open-to-buy and represent the difference between what the stores need and what they already have. What they need are the planned purchases, and what they have includes all the merchandise already on order for delivery. Some of this merchandise may already be in the stores, some may be in transit or not yet shipped. If the merchandise ordered for a certain month does not arrive until the following month, the open-to-buy is reduced by that amount the following month.

Open-to-buy may be calculated for any time during the month or season on the basis of book inventory figures. (It is usually not practical to take a physical inventory each time an open-to-buy figure is needed.) Even when book inventory figures are not available, it is still possible to determine the open-to-buy at any time by using the beginning-of-the-month inventory, sales, markdowns, and merchandise receipts up to a certain date.

Most stores report merchandising figures at retail, so that open-to-buy is usually given at retail. But its value at cost is easily obtained by multiplying the retail value by the complement of the planned initial markup percentage. Since buyers buy in units of merchandise, open-to-buy is also given in terms of such units on buying plans.

Model stock plans are often set up for many classifications of merchandise. A model stock is the ideal assortment of sizes, colors, prices, and styles to satisfy anticipated customer demand. Such plans may be developed for both fashion and staple goods. Because fashion can change rapidly, model stock plans in fashion departments undergo constant revision. Model stocks for staple items are more stable, but they, too, must be reviewed frequently. The proper maintenance of model stocks for basics (staples) is of particular importance, because these items should never be out of stock.

Buyers feel impotent without open-to-buy. So they try to produce it by revising the sales and merchandise plan, canceling outstanding orders, transferring outstanding orders to a later month, or returning merchandise to vendors.

QUESTIONS FOR REVIEW

1. What is open-to-buy?
2. Is there a difference between planned purchases and open-to-buy? Explain your answer.
3. Distinguish between merchandise in transit and merchandise outstanding.
4. Explain how a buyer can become overbought.
5. Why do buyers sometimes want to know their open-to-buy status in the middle of a month?
6. If a buyer wants to know his or her open-to-buy for a certain date, is it necessary for the calculations to be based on a complete physical inventory of the stock on that date? Explain your answer.
7. Why is the safety factor so important in planning open-to-buy in units of merchandise?
8. Explain the difference between the delivery period and the reorder period.
9. What is a model stock?
10. Explain six steps that a buyer could take to increase his or her open-to-buy.

11. Name two circumstances when a buyer might be justified in going to his or her merchandise manager and asking for more open-to-buy.

DISCUSSION QUESTION

Should the reserve factor in planning open-to-buy in merchandise units be of equal size for staple items such as men's white handkerchiefs and white underwear when they sell at the same rate?

PROBLEMS FOR REVIEW

1. A department plans sales of $8,000 and reductions of $1,000 for the month of March. The stock at the beginning of the month is $15,000, and the inventory at the end the month is planned at $10,000. If there are outstanding orders of $2,000, what is the open-to-buy?

2. A buyer has a retail stock of $17,000 on May 1, and the planned ending stock for the month is $15,000 at retail. The planned sales are $8,000 and planned markdowns are $1,000 for the month. The initial markup is planned at 45 percent. If the merchandise on order is worth $3,000 at retail, what is the open-to-buy as of May 1 (a) at retail and (b) at cost?

3. According to *Farmer's Almanac*, there will be heavy snows in March. Therefore, a buyer estimates that his sales for the month will be only $7,500. His stock at retail on March 1 is $20,000, and he has a stock of $8,000 at retail on order. Markdowns are expected to total $700 and the stock on March 31 will be $19,000. What is the buyer's open-to-buy status?

4. A discount buyer wants to determine his open-to-buy as of March 15. His stock on that date is $9,000. The stock planned for the end of the month is $10,000. Purchases received between March 1 and March 15 have totaled $1,500, and additional merchandise that will retail at $455 is on order. Planned sales for March are $6,000; actual sales to date are $4,500. Planned markdowns for March are 4 percent; actual markdowns so far come to $180. The initial markup is 37½ percent. What is the buyer's open-to-buy (a) at retail and (b) at cost?

5. A buyer has a retail stock of $17,000 on May 1, and the stock planned for the end of the month is $15,000 at retail. The planned sales are $8,000, and total markdowns of 10 percent are expected. He has stock on order worth $3,000 but has recently asked a vendor that delivery amounting to $1,000 be postponed until June. What is his open-to-buy as of May 1?

6. Determine the open-to-buy as of September 20, given the following data:

Planned September sales	$ 9,000
Actual sales, September 1 - 20	6,700
Planned September markdowns	600
Actual markdowns, September 1 - 20	400
Stock on hand at retail, September 20	18,000
Planned E.O.M. stock at retail, September 30	23,000
Merchandise received at retail, September 1 - 20	5,000
Outstanding orders at retail, September 20	4,500

7. Determine the open-to-buy as of July 15, given the following data:

B.O.M. stock	$25,000
Planned E.O.M. stock	23,000
Actual sales, July 1 - 15	5,000
Planned July sales	8,000
Planned July markdowns	600
Actual markdowns, July 1 - 15	200
Orders outstanding, July 15	3,000
Orders received, July 1 - 15	6,000

8. Based on the following data, what can you say of the buyer's open-to-buy as of February 16 at (a) cost and (b) retail?

B.O.M. stock	$80,000
Planned E.O.M. stock	70,000
Planned initial markup percentage	52%
Merchandise received, February 1 - 16	16,000
Outstanding commitments, February 16	4,000
Planned sales for month	30,000
Actual sales, February 1 - 16	18,000
Planned markdowns for month	1,000
Actual markdowns, February 1 - 16	800
Planned employee discounts for month	600
Actual employee discounts, February 1 - 16	200

9. A boys' wear buyer has been selling bell-bottoms in size 12 at the rate of 80 pairs a week. She feels that she should have a reserve of 150 pairs. Her bell-bottoms are ordered from Los Angeles and take four weeks to arrive. Reorders are made out every two weeks. At present she has 300 pairs on hand and 12 dozen on order. How many dozen should she reorder in size 12?

10. Due to their popularity, a toy buyer decides to make his $25 backgammon sets a basic stock item. At present he is selling an average of 120 sets a week, including the branch store sales. He decides to stock 300 sets as a safety factor since he will reorder only every four weeks. The delivery time is two weeks. There are now 475 sets in stock and 150 sets on order. How large should the next order be?

CASE PROBLEMS

AN OPEN-TO-BUY SQUEEZE

Mel Decker has been the buyer of men's furnishings for Pomeroy Department Store in a large western city for the past five years. He has fine working relations with his merchandise manager, Mr. Stoltz. In fact, they are both avid golfers, and they try to meet at the links when they can both get away from the store at the same time. The wives also like each other, and the four of them often go to concerts, plays, and parties together.

Decker flies to New York four times a year to buy merchandise for his department. Before leaving he usually presents a detailed buying plan to Mr. Stoltz for review. Decker shows his boss how much money he plans to spend by item and classification. By now Mr. Stoltz trusts Decker's judgment and seldom makes any changes in the buying plan. Occasionally he makes valuable suggestions, which Decker seems to appreciate. Men's furnishings have enjoyed steady gains in sales and profit ever since Decker took over.

Decker is now completing his market trip to buy merchandise for the upcoming spring season; in fact, it is his last day in New York. He has spent practically all his open-to-buy after leaving behind a small portion with which to cover reorders for basic merchandise. He is at his desk in the resident buyer's office wrapping up loose ends when he receives a telephone call from one of his key vendors. Due to overproduction, the vendor has an outstanding collection of men's short-sleeve sports shirts that he will sell to Decker for immediate delivery. He insists that Decker hurry over to his showroom to see the shirts.

When Decker arrives at the showroom, the vendor is plainly excited. He shows Decker the collection and offers it to him for $33.00 per dozen only if the entire lot of 500 dozen is taken. Decker makes a quick calculation and figures that he can retail each shirt for $4.99, which will give him a healthy 45 percent markup. The shirts are obviously of fine quality, and Decker has similar ones in his regular stock selling at $8.95 and $10.95. Best of all, the shirts will give considerable weight to the annual Anniversary Days sale in May.

The vendor senses Decker's pleasure and pulls out an order book to write up the confirmation. It occurs to Decker, however, that he has little open-to-buy left, certainly not nearly enough to cover the $30,000 investment at retail required by these shirts. He asks the vendor to hold off writing up the order until he has placed a long-distance call to his merchandise manager for permission to buy the shirts. The call is put through, but the store informs Decker that Mr. Stoltz has just left for the weekend and cannot be reached.

The vendor grows impatient and tells Decker that he must have an answer now or he will be forced to give the shirts to someone else. Decker is fully aware what an unusual buy the shirts are and is not about to let the deal slip through his fingers. He jumps up and tells the vendor to write up the order and ship the shirts immediately. Then he signs the order and leaves the vendor's showroom with a worried look on his face.

1. Did Decker do the right thing? Did he have any alternatives? Will there likely be any repercussions when he returns to the store?
2. If you were the merchandise manager, what action, if any, would you take against Decker?
3. Is it a good idea for Mr. Stoltz to socialize with his buyers? Discuss the pros and cons.

TOO MUCH INDEPENDENCE

"It's true I'm having a problem with Jean Barkley. Thanks for flying up to discuss the situation with me."

Marty Newman, who merchandises the upstairs children's departments for Trimbel's department store, one of the largest in New England, had been concerned almost from the very beginning with Jean Barkley's performance as children's outerwear buyer. Three years ago, when he needed a new outerwear buyer, he was delighted to get Ms. Barkley, who had served as an assistant in ladies' budget dresses with distinction, and the buyer there had given her a glowing recommendation. At the time Newman felt lucky to get her. Since then he had not been so sure the promotion was deserved.

"I'm not surprised Jean's figures are so poor," said Gil Stewart as he sank into a chair. "She just won't take any advice. When she comes to New York, she acts as if she knows it all. She's never invited me to go into the market with her. I see her in the office occasionally, but she has made it clear she doesn't want any help."

Stewart has been buyer for children's wear in the resident buying office with which Trimbel's has been associated for twelve years. He has seen many buyers come and go, and generally they are eager for his assistance. He is hardworking and conscientious, has good rapport with vendors, and keeps abreast of the latest fashion trends. He sends out excellent bulletins to member stores describing new ideas in outerwear and offers of outstanding job lots and special merchandise. Stewart is also noted for his research studies.

"Where does Jean seem to be having problems?" asked Stewart. "Here, look at these figures," said Newman. "Her sales have declined three years in a row. Her gross margin is below the average for other departments in the division. Her markdown percentage is one of the highest in the store. Since you have seen her in action in New York, I thought perhaps you could shed some light on why she can't make a decent showing."

"Let me take a look at my records and see what I can find," said Stewart. "You'll hear from me in a few days."

After returning to New York Stewart dug out his files. Upon reviewing Barkley's purchases for the past season, he found that she had done practically no business with manufacturers that the resident buying office considered as "key vendors." In fact, one-third of her open-to-buy had been spent with one vendor. According to the vendor analysis done by Trimbel's, that particular vendor had a history of large markdowns. He also found that Barkley had completely ignored his newsletter that outlined what he considered proper commitments by classification. For example, his office had recommended that 10 percent of the opening fall and winter stock be composed of pile fabrics, and Barkley had ordered 45 percent. He had suggested that 40 percent of new outerwear be trimmed models and 15 percent tailored; Barkley had ordered only 12 percent trimmed and nearly 37 percent in tailored models.

Stewart sat down and wrote Newman a long letter, informing him of all that he had found out. He also told Newman that while passing through

Barkley's department on the way out of the store the other day he had noticed how unattractive the department looked; there had been no imaginative displays and the housekeeping had been poor.

1. How should Mr. Newman handle the problem with Jean Barkley?
2. Why do you think Barkley might have been so independent when she visited the New York market?

13

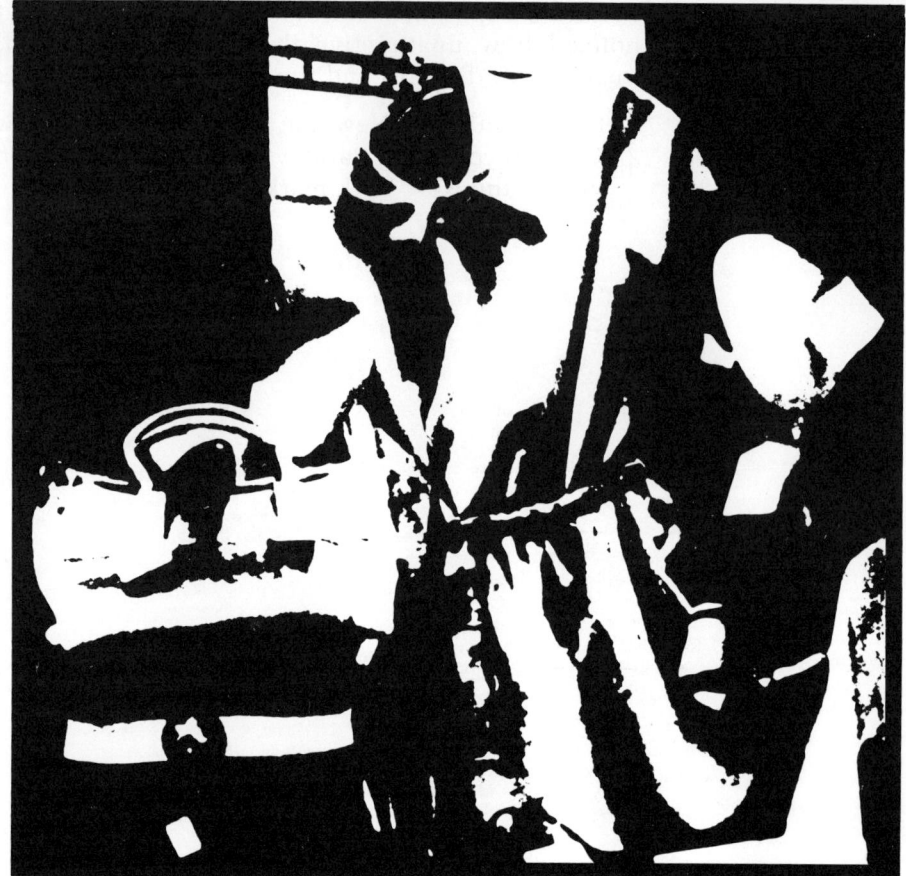

HOW TO PLAN AND CONTROL FASHION MERCHANDISE

KEY POINTS

1. Fashion does not mean the same thing to everyone, but retailers agree that fashion changes boost sales volume.

2. Fashion designers no longer dictate what people will wear to the extent they did in years past.

3. In spite of the rising importance of other fashion centers in this country and abroad, Paris is still considered the fashion capital of the world.

4. A fashion buyer needs a special expertise and creative flair particularly if employed by a store known as a fashion leader.

5. Because fashion merchandise is so fast-moving, sales and stocks must be controlled daily. The computer has been utilized very successfully in this area.

UNDERSTANDING FASHION

The word *fashion* has been used many times in this text. It was loosely defined as an item that has appeal for a large number of people over a period of time. It should not be confused with the word *style,* which refers to those characteristics that make one item different from another. But what really is fashion? Experts cannot seem to agree on the concept except that it includes innovation, change, and obsolescence. Fashion is certainly good for business. There is little in what is called fashion that is really new—almost everything has been tried in one form or another—and fashion has an interesting way of repeating itself.

The Changing Role of the Fashion Designer

What has changed is the role of the fashion designer, especially the couture designer, in shaping the course of fashion. The men and women who design and practice the fine art of dressmaking in their own houses, most often in Paris, used to be able to dictate public taste in clothing. Today, however, people dress anyway they want to, and *they* dictate the fashion. In June of 1974 the eminent Paris couturier Yves St. Laurent was quoted in *Women's Wear Daily* as saying "the couture is in decline—it won't last another seven years." He went on to say that fashion was not as important these days as it had once been. "The pure couture is an art of the past—and that was a very happy period."[1]

Only time will tell whether St. Laurent's prognosis is correct. Paris has certainly lost ground as the fashion capital of the world. Some rich and famous women still gather at the *haute couture* (high fashion) houses, such as Chanel, Dior, Cardin, Givenchy, and St. Laurent, to buy their expensive handmade original creations—creations that used to set fashion trends as

[1] "St. Laurent: The couture won't last," *Women's Wear Daily,* June 10, 1974, p. 4.

soon as they were worn. But the couture clothes have a splendor and extravagance that seem out of place in the modern-day world. Also haute couture is simply not very profitable anymore; materials and labor have become too expensive. The reasons for its remaining in existence are to act as a laboratory for new designs and to serve notice what might be in fashion during the coming season. Even so, couture collections still make fashion news. Store buyers the world over visit Paris twice a year to buy their favorite numbers. Then they go home to have them mass produced. A copy of a couture original can be bought by an American woman for a fraction of its original price.

There are couturiers from other countries, too. American designers such as Bill Blass, James Galanos, and Pauline Trigere are highly respected, as is Valentino of Italy. But it was in Paris that the couture business was founded and flourished for so many years. The point, however, is that no matter where the designer works now, he or she is no longer the powerful fashion arbiter as before.

How Does Fashion Happen?

CURRENT EVENTS

Changing times make fashion. The conclusion of World War II quickly put an end to the rationing of materials, so Dior's "New Look" became very popular. Skirts became longer, shoulders were padded, and lapels widened. In men's wear, cuffs were put back on trousers and hats featured wide brims. The Eisenhower jacket, patterned on the military uniform, was widely accepted. Then the continuing movement of people to the suburbs

Paris fashion show
SOURCE: Ellis Herwig/Stock, Boston

created a huge growth in casual wear. The coming of the space age has made lighter-weight clothing desirable, and items such as the jump suit have appeared for both men and women.

TECHNOLOGICAL DEVELOPMENTS

The invention of man-made fiber has had a tremendous impact on fashion. Wash and wear clothing was developed, with its quick-dry, wrinkle-proof qualities. Nylon hosiery has become a practical necessity, and stretch garments made of synthetics have removed the worry about size disparities. In these respects we have truly entered the age of the test tube, and chemists, engineers, and stylists have learned how to produce fabrics that offer all of the performance, look, and feel of silk, linen, cotton, or wool.

IMITATION OF THE FAMOUS

Setting fashion trends used to be private preserve of royalty and the very wealthy. Today a famous person, wealthy or not, can make fashion news. The clothes worn by a movie star, a military man, a president's wife, or a professional football player are often widely copied. Rock musicians often influence what the young will wear. Indeed, anyone who is admired and gets maximum exposure in the media is likely to affect fashion.

MOVIES AND PLAYS

The nostalgia craze of recent years stemmed in part from movies and plays about the 1920s, 30s, and 40s. Popular movies such as *Bonnie and Clyde* and *The Great Gatsby* can change the public tastes in clothing. Broadway hits such as *Irene* and *No, No Nanette* can influence men to wear knickers, argyle sweaters, and two-tone shoes. Some of these entertainment spectacles merely bring about fads; others have more long-lasting effects on fashion.

REBELLION AGAINST CONVENTION

Much of what is new and exciting in fashion today comes from youth. Young people like to dress differently from their parents, and they are affluent enough to support a new fashion trend. The accent on youth, especially strong in the United States, has actually persuaded many older people to change their own clothing habits in order to look younger themselves.

What Does Fashion Mean?

Fashion, that elusive and mysterious force, takes on different meanings for different people.

TO YOU AND ME

To the ordinary person, fashion is in the eyes of the beholder. What may be fashionable for one person may be out of date for another. All one has to do is attend a public function to observe the variety of dress being worn and the diversity of fashion tastes. A young lady was seen recently sitting in the orchestra section of the Metropolitan Opera House in New York City wearing a pair of denim overalls. In her opinion, she was in fashion!

"Kooky" clothes have become big business. Retailers have set up special departments to take advantage of the bonanza to be derived from the "way out" look. The young, in particular, are big buyers of the different and unusual. However, some stores have received complaints from regular customers who cannot find attractive clothes at sensible prices. Merchandisers must not be so anxious to stock fad items that they overlook the needs of their bread and butter customers.

TO THE ECONOMIST

To those who look at fashion from the economic angle, fashion is closely linked to planned obsolescence. Economists say that people often buy new things not because they need them but because what they have has gone out of fashion. Vance Packard claims in his book *The Waste Makers* that the American economy is based on planned obsolescence. It is said that manufacturers no longer produce goods of real quality because they are bad for business. Nevertheless, not many Americans wear out their clothes today. New purchases are made because fashion has changed. How many narrow-width men's ties are hanging on racks today waiting to be worn once more?

TO THE SOCIAL SCIENTIST

The sociologist perceives fashion as a form of status seeking. The age-old question, "Why do women dress well?" has never been fully answered. To please men, to please other women, or to please themselves? Even clothing labels have significance. Watch a group of women at a bridge party with their coats thrown casually over a chair so that the labels show! The men's wear industry has tried to promote sales by such slogans as "You can tell a man by what he wears," or "Dress smart, be smart." The suggestion is that somehow you can make a better impression by dressing in the latest fashion or that the clothes you wear can make you more nearly like what you want to be than what you actually are.

TO THE PSYCHOLOGIST

The psychologist sees fashion in still another light. What people wear may be indicative of their psychological states. Thus when young women began to shed their bras, they were saying, "I'm free at last—no more bondage." The immense popularity of the mini-skirt seemed to reflect women's sexual liberation as well. Men often wear their clothes as a sexual expression, too. Tight-fitting pants, muscleman T-shirts, and see-through shirts are worn as expressions of virility in order to attract the opposite sex.

The Fashion Cycle

No matter what the nature of a particular fashion is or how it begins, like life itself, it inevitably comes to an end. The cycle may last only one season, as often happens with a hat or a handbag; it may last several seasons, as in the case of a coat or a dress; or it may last many years, as with furniture.

Figure 13.1 shows the stages through which a fashion develops, from its inception to its demise.

WHERE TO BUY FASHION MERCHANDISE

When one speaks of fashion, clothing most often comes to mind. However, fashion may be found in almost everything people buy. Fancy patterned sheets, oddly shaped sun glasses, pink refrigerators, even colored thumb tacks all have elements of fashion. Since fashion changes are most noticeable in clothing, however, and since clothing buyers need a special expertise and flair, in this book we will narrow the field of fashion buying to men's, women's, and children's apparel only.

The American Market

New York City is the center of the American fashion industry. In fact, the apparel business is the largest industry in New York City and New York State. There are several reasons for this:

1. New York City has close proximity to the New England woolen mills and the cotton mills in the South.
2. There has been a good supply of labor as a result of the heavy immigration of skilled tailors from eastern Europe around the turn of the century. Lately, however, Puerto Ricans and blacks have made up a large percentage of the work force.
3. Vendors' showrooms are located in a compact area known as *Seventh Avenue*, bounded roughly by 34th and 42nd Streets and 6th and 9th

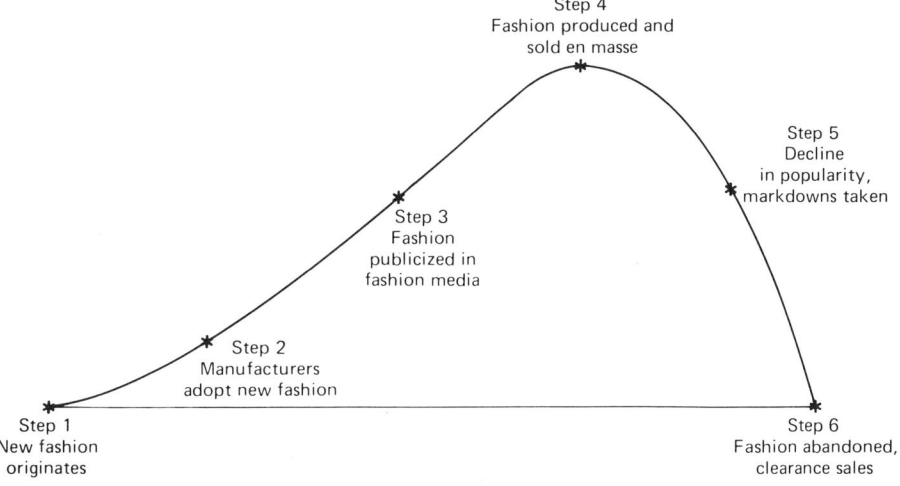

Figure 13.1
THE FASHION CYCLE

Avenues. This concentration allows buyers to save time by doing their purchasing with a minimum of travel.
4. Many auxiliary businesses are also located in New York, for example button manufacturers, embroidery houses, trimming suppliers, and so forth.
5. Fashion-conscious people live in New York City in greater numbers than anywhere else. It is also a city of immense wealth.

California is the fastest-growing manufacturing area for ready-to-wear clothes. Its market is best known for swimwear and sportswear for both men and women. There are also reasons for this development:

1. Californians seem very alert to new trends in fashion, especially in the area of casual dress.
2. Some designers like to work and live in California on account of its climate and casual atmosphere.
3. Designing for the movies and television has long been a big business and has attracted top talents to California.

Other fashion centers in the country are: Dallas (misses and women's sportswear), St. Louis (shoes and junior apparel), Chicago (all types of apparel), Miami (resort wear), Philadelphia (men's and boys' wear), and Rochester, New York (men's wear).

The garment industry is dominated by small businesses. Less than 5 percent of the firms employ 250 workers or more, and close to half the manufacturers and jobbers have individual sales volumes of under $1 million.[2] The industry is controlled by a model union, the International Ladies Garment Workers Union, which became powerful after the disastrous Triangle fire of 1911. That fire, which took 146 lives, signaled the end of the sweatshop era. Since 1920 industry-wide strikes have been almost nonexistent although there was a brief walkout during the spring of 1974.

Most volume manufacturers today consider themselves lucky if they can make a 2½ to 3 percent profit after taxes. Labor and fringe benefits are the major manufacturing costs. The average hourly wage of a worker in the New York City dress industry has increased at just about the same rate as the city's consumer price index. The average wage was $2.64 an hour in 1964. By 1973 it was 55 percent more or $4.09 an hour. During the same period, the cost of living in New York City increased by 51 percent.[3]

Figure 13.2 shows how a piece of fabric costing $4.30 becomes a dress with a wholesale price of $59.75. When it reaches the retailer the price rises to $110. The profit of the retailer ($2.00) is only 1.8 percent. It is interesting to note that the estimated loss due to pilferage is also $2.00.

---

[2]Jeanette Jarnow and Beatrice Judelle, *Inside The Fashion Business*, 2nd ed. Wiley, New York, 1974, pp. 115 - 116.

[3]"Many Things Happen to That $4 in Fabric on Way to a $110 Tag," *New York Times*, April 23, 1974, p. 46.

Figure 13.2
BEHIND THE PRICE TAG OF A $110 SUMMER DRESS

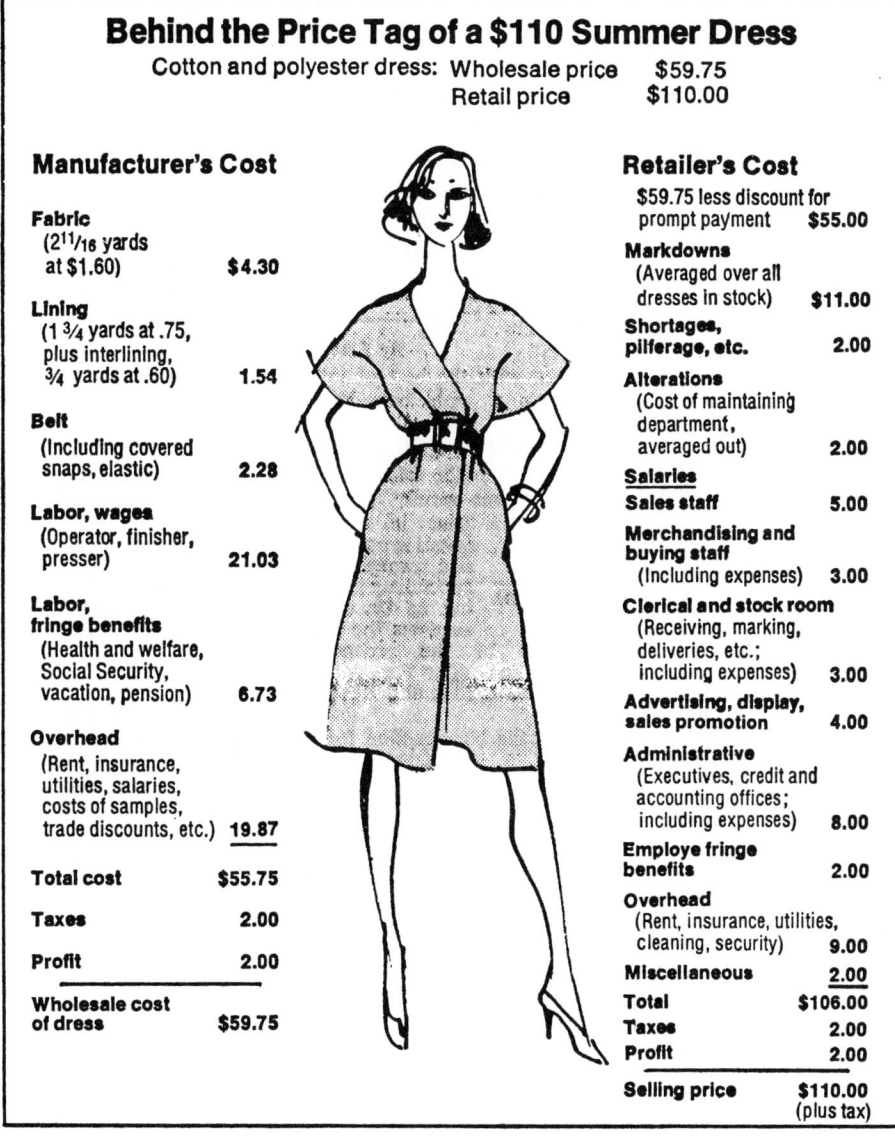

SOURCE: © 1974 by The New York Times Company. Reprinted by permission.

Foreign Markets

THE FRENCH

As we noted earlier, the Paris couture business is declining. Faced with rising costs, the couturier has had to look to other sources of income to remain solvent. Some of these sources are:

1. *Licensing agreements.* Famous couturiers sell their names to producers who make fashion-related items. For example, the House of Dior has sold worldwide licensing agreements to manufacturers of perfume, sweaters, handbags, gloves, and men's wear. The Dior label spurs sales because it represents quality and high fashion. St. Laurent has carefully licensed such diverse products as bath towels, perfume, and wallpaper. The designs are his, but the manufacturing is done by someone else. Givenchy and Chanel are other designer names widely seen on items of merchandise other than couture originals.
2. *Government subsidies.* It is common for the French government to give a couture house a subsidy. An agreement might stipulate that 80 percent of the fabrics used by the house be bought from French producers.
3. *Outside money.* "Angels" invest money in a couture house if it appears the investment will pay off. In 1961 a wealthy Atlanta businessman invested one million dollars in setting up St. Laurent in his own couture house. It was a wise investment, because St. Laurent has been a top couturier ever since.
4. *Ready-to-wear.* The *prêt-à-porter* business has been the salvation of many couturiers. The clothes are designed by the couturier but made in factories. They are sold in boutiques either in the couture house or in other locations.

French ready-to-wear has become a very important source of fashion innovation. Before the 1960s no country in the world could duplicate the American mass production of clothing. Since then, however, the French prêt-à-porter industry has been growing rapidly, but in terms of dollars and cents it cannot compare with Seventh Avenue. In 1973 French exports of ready-to-wear totaled seventy million dollars, while the New York garment makers shipped some seven billion dollars worth of goods.[4] The difference between the two countries' clothing industries lies in creativity. The French ready-to-wear designers have stolen the show from the couturiers, and the world has been looking to them for fashion leadership. Until Seventh Avenue begins to value creativity as highly as commercial success, the French will probably continue to provide many of the new ideas in fashion.

OTHER COUNTRIES

Although France has been noted for fashion leadership since the days of the Louis's, other countries also make important contributions to fashion. England has become a fountainhead for new ideas, and names such as Carnaby Street and Mary Quant have become synonomous with fashion. The Scandinavian countries are envied for their beautiful sweaters, many of them handmade. Italy is justly famous for women's accessories, such as handbags and shoes, and an Italian knit dress or suit is a treasured commodity. The Spaniards do wonderful things with leather, as do the Bel-

---

[4]Bernadine Morris, "7th Ave. ready-to-wear: still playing follow the leader," *New York Times*, June 9, 1974, p. 60.

gians with lace. Germany has a thriving fashion industry, and Dusseldorf ranks second only to Paris as a fashion center in Europe. The Far East has a silk industry that is unparalleled, and exports include all types of clothing. The list could go on and on, and store buyers have become accustomed to scouring the far corners of the world for fashion merchandise.

HOW TO BUY FROM FOREIGN MANUFACTURERS

1. *Foreign market trips.* Imported fashion merchandise has become so important to many stores that seasoned buyers make regular trips abroad. Because so much territory must be covered, it is important to adhere to strict schedules and make advance appointments with vendors. American buyers must be able to adapt to a less hurried atmosphere. There are of course also language problems in dealing with foreigners.
2. *Foreign resident buying office.* An overseas office similar to an American resident buying office is of great help in overcoming language barriers and in placing orders with foreign manufacturers. If under foreign management, the resident buyer is called a commissionaire; if under American management, a purchasing agent. The office charges the store a certain percentage of the purchases made in the foreign country for services performed.
3. *Store-owned foreign office.* An American retail organization may operate a foreign office for its own use. Most store ownership groups maintain at least one foreign office. In order to economize, it is common for one buyer in a chain of stores to buy foreign merchandise for all of the stores in the chain. For example, the boys' wear buyer from the May Company in Cleveland might take a trip to Europe and buy boys' wear for all of the May Company stores. The following year the buyer from the Los Angeles store might do the same thing.
4. *Importer.* An importer is an individual or company located in the United States specializing in foreign goods. The importer buys in quantity and takes all of the risks. A small retailer who cannot afford to send a buyer overseas finds it best to rely on the importer to obtain merchandise made abroad.
5. *Foreign export selling house.* This institution acts like an importer but is located overseas. A buyer may save considerable time and effort by visiting this selling house to view the merchandise assembled under one roof. If a trip abroad cannot be taken, it is nevertheless possible for the buyer in the United States to use a catalog published by the export house.

ADVANTAGES OF FOREIGN MERCHANDISE

1. *Exclusiveness.* Foreign merchandise gives a store the opportunity of stocking and advertising merchandise not found in most other stores. Some foreign merchandise is even handmade—an almost extinct commodity in the United States due to high labor costs. Stores such as

Alexander's and Ohrbach's in New York City have had considerable success in buying exclusive couture clothes in Paris and copying them in this country for mass distribution.

2. *Higher markup.* Because foreign merchandise is not usually branded and does not have to compete with American goods, high markups are possible. Thus even though transportation costs are higher with imports, the high markups usually allow for gross margins large enough to yield handsome profits.

3. *Prestige.* Foreign merchandise gives a store an aura of prestige and status. To many American consumers, there is magic in the word "import." Stores often conduct storewide promotions of imported goods. For example, a store may feature a Scandinavian Fair with merchandise imported from Norway, Sweden, and Denmark in almost every department, and special events such as fashion shows, cheese-making, sweater-knitting, and liquor-tasting demonstrations making for an exciting week of fun, profit, and goodwill.

DISADVANTAGES OF FOREIGN MERCHANDISE

1. *Slow delivery.* Foreign merchandise is often manufactured only after an order has been placed. Since delivery is usually by sea, a lead time of at least six months is necessary. If a buyer wants goods to arrive for spring and summer selling, he must visit the foreign markets in the preceding fall.

2. *Difference in product standards.* Items made abroad are not always suitable for American use without some modifications. For example, sizing is often quite different. Thus European shoe lasts are not the same as American lasts. Cuts of clothing vary, and electrical appliances often need special adapters.

3. *Little chance for reorders.* Due to delivery lag, reorders are almost impossible, especially with fashion merchandise. Thus the importance of gauging the salability of an item takes on special significance.

4. *Returns are difficult.* Because of time lags, it is not feasible to return foreign merchandise with the hope of obtaining a satisfactory replacement. Even when merchandise is returned for credit, the refund may be delayed, thus tying up store funds.

5. *Landed cost can be high.* Although merchandise purchased abroad may be good buys initially, many other costs must be incurred on the way to the store. The final cost to the retail store is called *landed cost.* It includes transportation charges, duties, insurance, packing, commissions, and other fees. Goods are usually shipped F.O.B. factory, which means that the retailer must pay all the freight, both on land and sea. The form shown in Figure 13.3 may be used by a foreign vendor to quote total landed cost to the store. The difference between the F.O.B. factory shipping cost (line 1) and the total landed cost (line 7) can often be quite considerable.

Figure 13.3
QUOTATION SHEET

MESSRS:			
			DATE

QUOTATION SHEET

DESCRIPTION		PACKING	
		INSIDE	
		C/T	
		CFT.	
		WGT.	

MAKER:			
1.	FOB:		EX-FACTORY
2.	OCEAN FREIGHT:		RATE:
3.	INSURANCE: (1% on FOB)		
4.	DUTY:		RATE:
5.	5% GENERAL CHARGE: (on FOB)		
6.	INLAND FREIGHT:		
7.	TOTAL L/C.		

DELIVERY

THE NATURE OF FASHION BUYING

Fashion Merchandise Policy

Before any fashion merchandise is bought, management should decide whether the store will be a fashion leader or a follower. If the former, the store must realize that there is much more risk involved in being first with a new look. Much high-fashion merchandise is not suitable for mass consumption. A famous trend setter may find a particular dress just perfect for her, but its style or color may be totally unsuitable for the average woman. Thus the original market is small, and the high-fashion buyer must be able to pick winners and pick them early. Just as important is the ability to recognize a mistake quickly so that an early markdown can be taken. In view of the awesome responsibility in being a fashion leader, buyers in stores such as Neiman-Marcus in Dallas, I. Magnin on the West Coast, and Lord and Taylor and Bergdorf Goodman in New York must be unusually creative. Their successes have made what they say and do carry considerable weight in the market.

The majority of stores prefer to follow the fashion. Their customers often cannot afford to pay the price of original creations. These stores are interested in fashion volume, which involves much less risk because the winners have already been sorted out by the leader stores and by the manufacturers. Hence their retails are lower, as are their markdowns.

Determining Customer Demand

Buyers cannot go to the market to purchase fashion merchandise without some idea of what the customers want. Past sales records can be relied on for buying staple items; and basic stock plans and regular reorders are absolutely necessary, as we showed in the last chapter. Buying fashion merchandise on the other hand is a much more dramatic and dynamic business. Detailed past sales records simply cannot be used as effectively as with staples because fashions change so rapidly. There is seldom any repeat business on a specific item unless it is a runner. So even though past sales records can help, buyers also rely on the following as guides to their purchases.

CONSUMER SURVEYS

A survey may be conducted by means of a questionnaire through the mail or by personal interviews. Customers may be asked about the size, color, type of material, style, and price of the dress they plan to buy the next season. It is interesting that with older women, what they say they will buy and what they actually do buy are often quite different. Information on the growth or decline of a fashion trend can be obtained by means of a *fashion count,* where surveyors located in areas of heavy customer traffic tabulate the clothing worn by passersby according to color, style, pattern, material, and so forth.

VENDORS

Manufacturers can be of great help in forecasting what customers will buy. Most vendors can be trusted to give honest information. Buyers should be wary, however, of those manufacturers who are merely trying to unload losers.

STYLEOUTS

This is an effective way to see why some items are selling and others are not. Merchandise that is selling well is placed on one rack, while items that are not moving are placed on another. The buyer physically handles the merchandise and usually finds that there is a developing trend that affects sales. Future orders are based on the information derived from the styleout.

THE RESIDENT BUYER

Resident buyers should be consulted because they are in the market nearly every day. Smart buyers depend on their advice and help. Figure 13.4 shows a flyer distributed by a large resident buying office to all the member stores. The flyer describes a merchandise offering that the resident buyer feels has great sales potential. All necessary information, i.e. vendor, color, size range, and delivery, is given so the store buyer can place a covering order. The resident buyer will arrange a sample order shipment if the store buyer wishes to inspect the merchandise.

FASHION PUBLICATIONS

Fashion buyers should read as many of the trade papers and magazines as their busy schedules permit. Certainly, women's and children's wear

Figure 13.4
RESIDENT BUYING
OFFICE FLYER

amc market evaluation
ASSOCIATED MERCHANDISING CORPORATION • 1440 BROADWAY, NEW YORK, N.Y. 10018

July 2, 1974

THE ALABASTER SHORT COAT -- FUR TRIMMED

POTENTIAL ITEM FOR FALL 1974

The combination of Alabaster (grey) with natural grey rabbit trim has had early consumer acceptance with Natalie Green.

These fur trimmed short coats were first shipped in early June and instant checkouts were reported wherever received.

While the big volume colors will still be camel and beige, we feel that our stocks should have some additional colors for customer selection.

This light grey color, a fashion neutral, has good volume potential.

The best styles:

    3938/70.75 -- wool plush, 34" waist mark, belt detail, grey rabbit collar and cuff

    1897/68.75 -- wool plush 32", double breasted, strap detail, grey rabbit collar and cuff

    4990/79.75 -- wool plush 34", shirred waist, grey rabbit collar and cuff

The color: Alabaster Grey

Sizes: 8 to 16

Delivery: A/R 4 weeks

Resource: Natalie Green 500 7th Avenue, NYC

If you are not covered on this fashion story, we urge you to act quickly and be first in your community to present Alabaster for Fall 1974.

Please contact us if you want us to place sample orders.

                                        Merchandise Representative

TO: BUDGET AND BETTER COAT BUYERS
       DIVISIONAL MERCHANDISE MANAGERS

SOURCE: Associated Merchandising Corporation and Natalie Green.

buyers should never miss a copy of *Women's Wear Daily*. Men's and boys' wear buyers read another Fairchild publication, the *Daily News Record*. Magazines such as *Vogue, Harper's Bazaar, Mademoiselle,* and *Glamour* are also very important in the women's field, and *Gentlemen's Quarterly* and *Esquire* are important men's fashion magazines. These publications spend very lavishly on researching public tastes, so wise buyers make use of their results.

Figure 13.5
REPORTING SERVICE

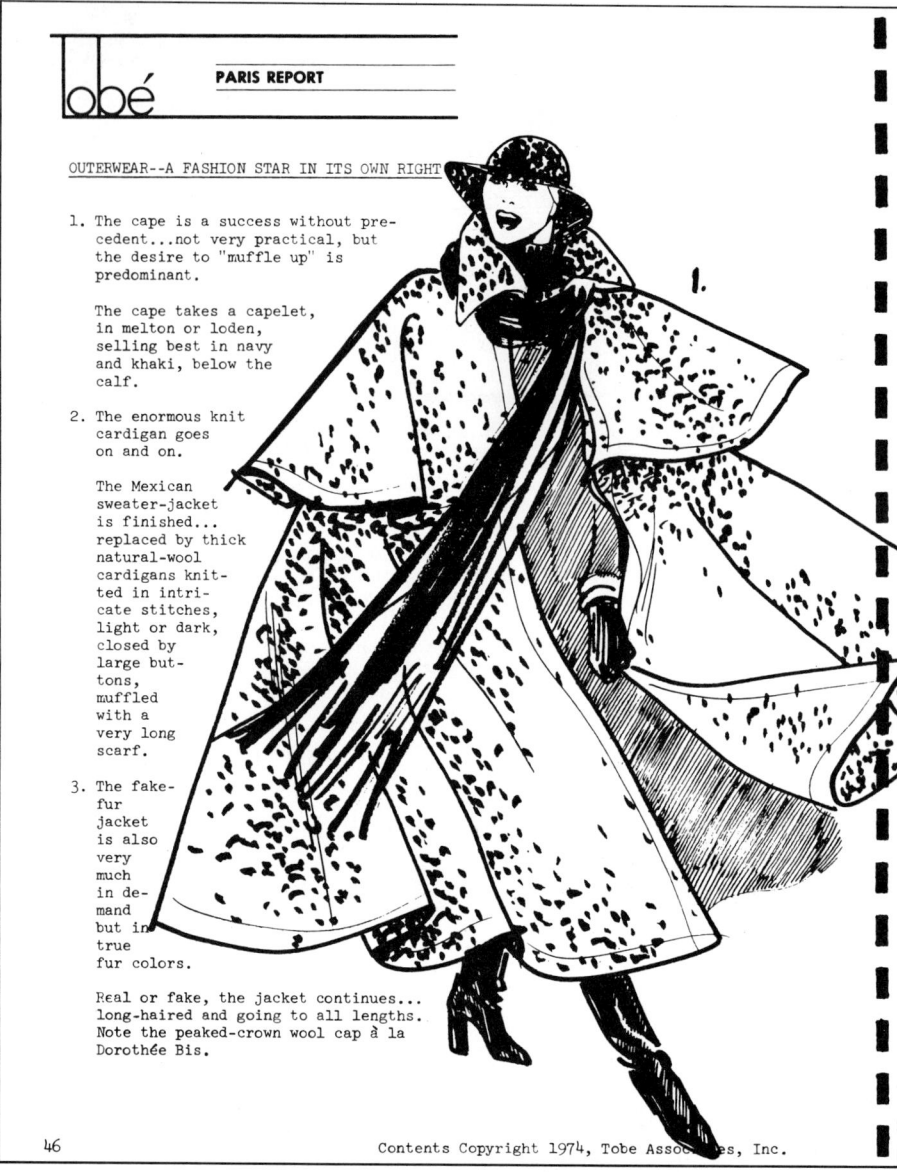

SOURCE: Courtesy Tobé Associates, Inc.

PRIVATE REPORTING AGENCIES

These organizations research the domestic and foreign fashion markets to determine what is selling best and why. Store buyers and resident buyers, as well, find the results to be useful when planning what to buy, and subscribe to weekly or monthly fashion reports published by them. One reporting service, "Coatvertising Weekly," reprints coat ads that have pulled especially well throughout the country. The Fairchild organization

244 HOW TO PLAN AND CONTROL FASHION MERCHANDISE

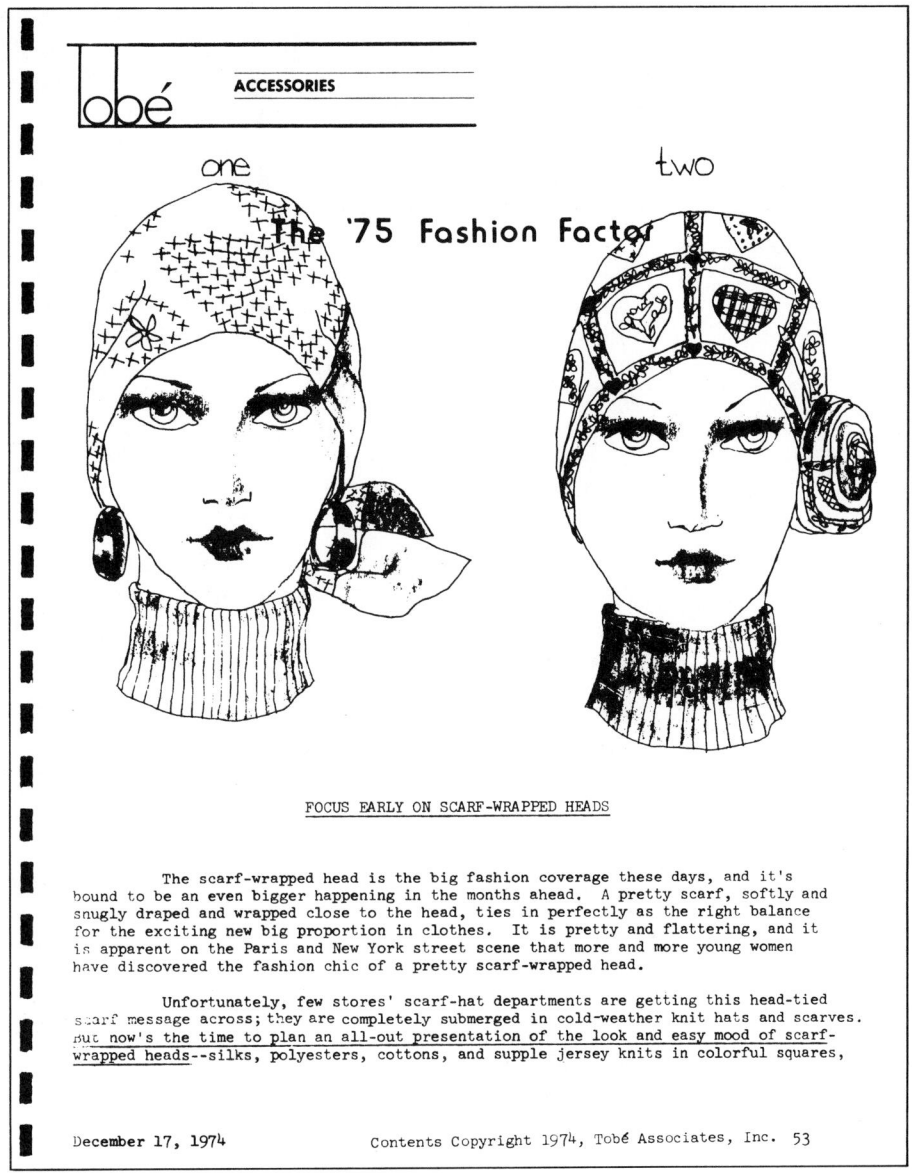

employs a staff of fashion reporters who continuously send in information telling what is happening on the fashion scene world-wide.

One of the best-known and most respected fashion-reporting and analyzing organizations is Tobé. Retailers who subscribe to the "Tobé Reports" find they help gauge customer demand and accurately forecast fashion trends. Excerpts from a "Tobé Report" are shown in Figure 13.5. One reports on best sellers in Paris and the other describes an important new fashion development in headwear.

PRETESTING

Fashion shows are held in stores very early in the season. At these shows the buyers can watch for customer reactions and place reorders accordingly. This is an excellent way to spot a runner. Sometimes employee fashion shows are held for the same reason. The shows can be morale builders and give buyers needed information at the same time. Some buyers invite selected customers to *trunk shows,* which are private showings of manufacturers' entire lines and at which customers may order whatever they wish. Buyers compare what the customers are buying with what they have ordered and hope that the two coincide. *Sampling* is another method of pretesting. If a buyer is very unsure of an item, she or he may order only a small quantity at the beginning of the season. Sales records are watched closely, and if the item seems to be gaining acceptance, a quick reorder is placed.

CONSUMER PANELS

Groups of people may be asked to come into a store to give their opinions on styles, colors, and other merchandise features. They may also be asked to give their opinions of the store's policies, services, and other factors. These "advisers" are often given a free luncheon or a shopping discount card for the day.

ELEMENTS OF FASHION MERCHANDISE

The characteristics of staple merchandise are very predictable. Their sizes, colors, materials, and styles do not change frequently, so that the maintenance of a basic staple assortment is one of mechanics.

With fashion merchandise, there is much less predictability and the challenge facing a fashion buyer is accordingly larger. Nevertheless, there are established guidelines based on past history that can be used in planning and controlling fashion stocks. Thus the following merchandise characteristics provide a framework within which fashion items can be successfully merchandised.

Classification

Most stores and departments stock many different kinds of merchandise. It is necessary to divide a department according to separate and distinct categories of merchandise so that their strengths and weaknesses can be more easily studied. These divisions are called classifications. For example, a boys' department may contain the following classifications: shirts, underwear, hosiery, pants, pajamas, outerwear, and accessories.

Size

Size ranges have become increasingly complicated as retailers strive to satisfy every customer want. It is common to offer men's suits and coats in regular, short, long, and stout sizes. Men's trousers are often found with either short or long rises. Women's sizes include regular, junior, petite, and half, among others. A buyer should be supplied with a size chart for each classification of merchandise. For example, if a boys' wear buyer wants to order 100 dozen sports shirts in sizes 8 through 20, he must know how many of each size to order. The size chart has been developed from frequent size studies based on past sales. The chart should be adjusted periodically, since size percentages do change and may differ considerably from store to store. Thus a men's clothing store located in a university town would use a very different size chart than a men's store located in a downtown shopping district. Recent studies show that average sizes are getting larger. People are taller and have larger hands and feet than customers fifty years ago. In order to satisfy the needs of bigger people, stores featuring merchandise for very tall people (and also very fat people) have proliferated in recent years.

To show how complicated sizing can become, a fifty-dozen size scale for men's dress shirts is illustrated in Figure 13.6. Twenty-nine different sizes must be reckoned with. Wise buyers concentrate their purchases on the *heart sizes*: neck 15, 15½, and 16, in sleeve lengths of 32, 33, and 34. The *fringe sizes* are ordered sparingly.

Color

Color is another element that can be fairly stable from season to season. Some colors have become historically basic: for example, navy, white, beige, and grey for spring; brown, purple, orange, green, and wine for fall. These colors may be reordered on the basis of past demands. However, each season has its share of *high shades*, which are new fashion colors with highly promotable tags, such as "shocking pink," "creamy white," "jonquil yellow," "apricot," or "avocado." Since these high shades cannot be forecast, the buyer must depend on fashion publications and other sources to decide which colors to order.

Material

Based again on past records, buyers will probably buy various percentages of wools, silk, linen, cotton, and man-made fibers. Open-to-buy must be set aside for any new fabric that may appear on the market such as Qiana, an

Figure 13.6

SUGGESTED SIZE SCALE FOR MEN'S DRESS SHIRTS

Popular Price National Brand
50 Dozen Scale

SLEEVE LENGTHS	NECK SIZES								
	14	14½	15	15½	16	16½	17	17½	18
32	8/12	3	4	4	1 4/12				
33	1	3	5	6	4	1 4/12	4/12		
34	4/12	1	3	3	2	8/12	4/12	4/12	4/12
35		8/12	1	1	1	8/12	4/12	4/12	4/12

uncrushable nylon with a silken look used extensively now in both men's and women's wear.

Price Lines

Price lines were discussed in Chapter 8. Depending on the rate of inflation, they may remain stable for several seasons. After a department has been divided into classifications, the next breakdown is likely to be of each classification into appropriate price lines. Buyers hesitate to change price lines too frequently since customers become used to paying a certain price for a given item and are apt to develop resistance when retails fluctuate wildly.

Vendor

Brand loyalty can be a very important ingredient in merchandising. Although brands are not always as important in fashion goods as with staples, branded merchandise nevertheless makes up a sizable proportion of most fashion departments. A man may wear nothing but Hathaway shirts, a boy's mother may insist on Farah slacks, or a young woman may prefer Capezio shoes. Even if the vendor's name is not too important to the customer, the vendor is important to the buyer because some vendors' lines are profitable while others are not. A vendor analysis should be made at the end of each season to determine how well each vendor has done in respect to sales volume, markdowns, turnover, and maintained markup. All else being equal, those vendors who contribute the largest volumes and highest markups are the ones from whom purchases are most often made and who become the buyer's *key vendors*.

CONTROL OF FASHION MERCHANDISE

Whether by hand or by electronic computer system, or a combination of the two, there must be a unit control that shows sales and stocks on hand daily. These figures are especially important in fast-moving fashion departments. As we shall see in Chapter 15, much of the manual labor necessary for the proper maintenance of unit control has been taken over by the computer in large stores.

In stores without a computer the following types of unit control systems are still being used.

Perpetual Inventory

This system, which relies on an accurate recording of daily sales, is very effective for women's, children's, men's, and boys' ready-to-wear. Sales information is taken from price ticket stubs, sales checks, or control cards (as with women's hosiery). The sales are recorded on a stock sheet such as shown in Figure 13.7, which is for a tailored rayon blouse retailing for

Figure 13.7 UNIT CONTROL STOCK SHEET

	MARCH				APRIL				MAY			
	OO	R	S	OH	OO	R	S	OH	OO	R	S	OH
1								50				12
2							9	41			2	11
3											2	9
4							2	40				
5							4	36			1	8
6												
7							6	31				
8												
9							3	28				
10		12		12								
11			6	6			1	27				
12	50						1	26				
13							1	25				
14			2	4			4	21				
15												
16							4	17				
17			2	2								
18							1	16				
19												
20												
21												
22												
23							2	14				
24												
25							2	12				
26			1	1								
27												
28							1	11				
29												
30							1	12				
31		50	1	50								
T		62	12	50			38	12				

CLASS
012
RETAIL
9.98
RESOURCE NO.
058
RESOURCE
H. Whiting
STOCK NO.
2134
ITEM
Blouse
MATERIAL
Rayon
PATTERN
Tailored

COST
5.75
TERMS
8/10

	5	7	9	11	13	15
26		XXX	XXX	XXX	XX	X
35	XX	XX	XX	XX	X	X
28	X	X	X	X		
12		XXX	XX	XXX	XXX	X

$9.98. The top section of the sheet contains information on exactly how many blouses are in stock every day of the month. The first column (OO) shows how many are on order. The second column (R) shows when they are received. The third column (S) is for recording sales, and OH designates quantity on hand. Here the buyer began with twelve blouses on March 10 and ended with eight on hand on May 5. The tiny slash indicates that a blouse was returned to stock on April 4. The bottom section of the sheet contains information on how many blouses are in stock according to size and color. The size numbers (5 through 15) are listed in the top row and the color codes (26, 35, 28, and 12) are listed down the side. When a blouse is sold, the slash mark becomes an X. Thus on May 5 there were three blouses left in size 5, three in size 9, and two in size 11.

Periodic Inventory

When stocks are small, stores sometimes use periodic stock control for fashion items. Sales are not recorded as they occur, but stock counts are taken on a regular basis to determine what has been sold. Although time-consuming, this system is much less expensive than maintaining a perpetual inventory. Not all the fashion stock should be counted at one time. It is advisable to count one classification one week, another the next week, and so forth.

The formula to be used with the periodic inventory of stock control is:

Stock at last count + Receipts − Stock at present count = Sales

---

ILLUSTRATIVE PROBLEM A dress buyer wants to know how many cocktail dresses were sold during the month of December. She asks her head of stock to take a count of what is on hand now (January 2). It is determined that 132 dresses are in stock, 24 dresses arrived in December, and the stock count on December 1 was 243. How many cocktail dresses were sold?

SOLUTION

Stock on hand (December 1)	243
Receipts	+ 24
Total merchandise available	267
Stock on hand (January 2)	−132
December sales	135

Reserve Requisition Control

This system is effective for packaged fashion goods, such as men's underwear, and when most of the stock is kept in the stockroom so that as stock becomes low on the selling floor, it is replenished from the stockroom supply. Only the stockroom supply is counted. The amount of stock sent to the selling floor is considered to be the amount sold and reorders are based on this quantity.

Visual Control

If fashion merchandise is displayed on a rack, a board, or in bins (which is rare), visual control may be used. When the merchandise appears low, it is reordered. Sometimes called *eyeballing* the stock, this is a rather haphazard way of controlling fashion merchandise. At best, it can give the buyer only a general impression of how fast merchandise is selling.

MODEL STOCKS

A model stock plan for fashion merchandise need not be as rigid as one for staples, as we mentioned in the last chapter. The elements of fashion merchandising can all be incorporated into the plan, but because fashion is so volatile, demand by classification, price, size, and other factors will likely change as the season progresses. The plan, then, becomes only a model and should be considered as a guide and nothing more.

A typical model stock plan for a bra and foundations department is shown in Figure 13.8. The stock is broken down according to classification, and the percentages reflect what portion of planned purchases to allot to each one. Price lines, sizes, materials, and the like are worked out as the buyer buys the merchandise.

Figure 13.8
MODEL STOCK PLAN
BRAS AND
FOUNDATIONS

BRASSIERES		BODY FASHIONS	
Soft cup and contemporary	9%	Briefs	5%
All contour bras	15	All pull-on panty girdles	9
All padded bras	6	All zipper panty girdles	3
All regulation underwire and bras with wide set straps	19	All girdles, pull-on and zipper	3
All longline bras	5	All-in-ones	10
Miscellaneous (Strapless, mastectomy pads-bras, bust pads)	5	Straight bottom (1) Brief leg (6) Regulation leg (3)	
Total	59%	Miscellaneous (Surgical corsets, garter belts, chafeeze, liquid soap	3
SWIMWEAR			
For cruise-wear selling, bring in limited group for November and December			
For regular swimwear business, start bringing in stock February 1. Stocks should be peaked by mid-April.		Total	33%
Total	8%		

THE BUYING PLAN

Once the fashion buyers have accumulated as much knowledge as possible on what has been sold in the past and what customers will want in the future, they are ready to formulate their buying plans. Model stocks that have been designed for their respective departments will steer them in the right direction. There are many different forms for use in setting up buying plans, but the one illustrated in Figure 13.9 is typical.

Suppose a boys' wear buyer is planning to buy some wash and wear dress slacks in sizes 8 through 12 as one item on the spring buying plan. The following figures are at her or his disposal:

Planned unit sales for season	145
Planned ending stock	140
Stock on hand	140
Stock on order	36

We recall that

Open-to-buy = Total units needed − Total units available

Thus the total units needed equal the planned unit sales (145) plus planned ending stock (140), or 285. The total units available equal the stock on hand (140) plus the stock on order (36), or a total of 176. The open-to-buy is then 285 less 176, or 109 units. These figures are shown clearly on the buying plan in Figure 13.9. Unit costs and retail prices as well as the sales history and total retails are also included. Although the open-to-buy for this item is 109 pairs, slacks are purchased in one-dozen lots as a rule. Therefore, the plan to buy in units will be 120 pairs or ten dozen.

A buying plan with a different format is shown in Figure 13.10. This buying plan covers a three-month period, and space is provided to show purchases for special events in addition to reorders. The open-to-buy is figured in the next-to-last column (planned purchases minus what is already on order).

CHAPTER SUMMARY

Although experts do not seem to agree on the meaning of fashion, retailing would be a dead and uninteresting business without it. Fashion is most often associated with apparel, but it is in fact found in most merchandise. In some categories of goods, fashion changes every season, but in others a fashion may last for decades.

For many years a small group of men and women who created original clothing designs in Paris dictated the course of fashion. Paris is still considered the center of world fashion, but the couturiers, as they are known, have lost much of their influence. Today people dress pretty much as they please.

New York City is the hub of American fashion, and Seventh Avenue ships out some seven billion dollars worth of goods annually. California boasts the fastest-growing ready-to-wear industry, and Dallas, Miami,

Figure 13.9 BUYING PLAN

BUYING PLAN
JORDAN MARSH The Stores With The Florida Flair

Current Period _Spring_ as of _Mar. 31_
(11) Est. Sales Bal. of Period
(13) Planned Stock End of Period
(16) Stock and Invoices
(17) Outstanding Orders
(18) Allowable Purchases

Next Month _____ as of _____
(23) Planned Purchases
(24) Outstanding Orders
(25) Allowable Purchases

REMINDERS
Orders Routed?
Advertising Allowance Available?
Key Resources Covered?
Discount Loaded?
Selling Facts Noted?
Delivery Date Specified?

Dept. No. _12_
Date Prepared _4/10/75_
Planned Mark-up _45.8_ %
Required Discount _____ %
Estimated Transportation _____
Delivery Period _____

ITEM	$ UNIT COST	$ UNIT RETAIL	UNIT SALES SEASON TO DATE This Year	Last Year	LAST YEAR BY MONTHS April	May	June	July	Planned Unit Sales To July 31	Planned Ending Unit Stock	Total Needs Units	STOCKS On Hand Units	On Order Units	Total O.H. and O.O. Units	OPEN TO BUY UNITS	PLAN TO BUY UNITS	TOTAL RETAIL $	TOTAL PURCHASED UNITS
Boys Slacks 8-12 Wash 'n Wear Assorted Plaids	5.50	10.00	38	30	35	20	27	18	145	140	285	140	36	176	109	120	1,200	
Total Units or Dollars																		

THIS PLAN MUST BE COMPLETED BEFORE TRANSPORTATION REQUEST WILL BE APPROVED

Signed _____ Dept. Manager _____ Approved _____ Mdse. Manager

Form 149J

SOURCE: Jordan Marsh, Florida

Figure 13.10 BUYING PLAN

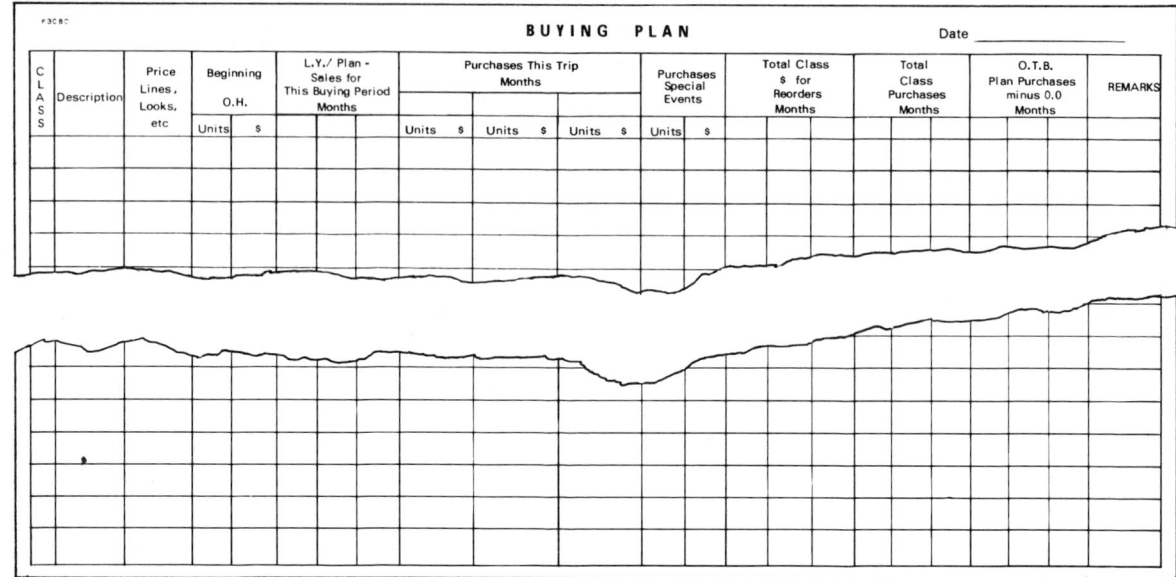

SOURCE: The Higbee Company, Cleveland, Ohio

Chicago, and Philadelphia are increasingly important fashion centers. Due to the increasing costs of doing business, many apparel manufacturers have found it difficult to make a profit, and a large number of Seventh Avenue firms have closed in the past several years.

Fashion buyers travel the world over in search of unusual and profitable merchandise. Big stores send buyers abroad several times a year, and some firms maintain their own foreign resident buying office. In spite of the inherent disadvantages to buying foreign goods, stores like the suggestions of exclusiveness and prestige, and the long markups that can be applied to merchandise made overseas.

A store must decide whether it will be a fashion leader or a fashion follower. Most stores are interested in high volume and prefer to follow fashion trends. This policy also involves less risk and fewer markdowns.

It is important to keep the sales and stocks of fashion merchandise under daily scrutiny because fashion changes so rapidly. A satisfactory unit control system must be found, and big stores are making use of the computer with great success. In stores with much smaller stocks some of the older control methods are still being used.

Buying plans for fashion goods are prepared only after the buyers have accumulated as much information as can be obtained on what the customers will want to buy. Model stock plans will help the buyers to distribute their purchases according to classifications, price lines, colors, materials, and sizes. And the buying plans show the buyers how many units of each item they are open to buy and thus help them stay within their budgets.

QUESTIONS FOR REVIEW

1. Why is the couture business in a state of decline?
2. What are some of the factors that make fashion happen?
3. Why does fashion seem such a mysterious force to so many people?
4. What is planned obsolescence?
5. Why do so many young people prefer to dress down?
6. It is said that fashion is found everywhere. Can you think of any kinds of goods that are completely devoid of fashion?
7. Name some reasons why New York City is the center of the American fashion industry.
8. Since couturiers are having difficulty operating in the black, what are some of their other sources of income besides the couture business?
9. Explain how an American buyer can buy foreign merchandise.
10. What is the difference between a purchasing agent and a commissionaire?
11. What is landed cost? What does it include?
12. What is a runner?
13. Explain the difference between a styleout and a sampling.
14. Are there aspects of fashion merchandise that are more predictable than others? Explain your answer.
15. What is brand loyalty? Is it more important in men's wear or women's wear?
16. Which system of unit control is best for fashion sheets and pillowcases? Why?
17. Why should the model stocks set up for fashion merchandise be flexible?
18. What is meant by eyeballing the stock?
19. Explain the difference between basic colors and high shades. What are some of the high shades popular at the present time?
20. Why is a well-constructed buying plan important to a buyer?

DISCUSSION QUESTION

In your opinion, is there a correct way to dress for certain occasions? Defend your answer by giving examples.

CASE PROBLEMS

THINK SNOW?

Carol Jordan is a buyer for O.T. Givemore, a chain of over 1,800 stores operating in all fifty states. She has an office in the firm's central buying headquarters in New York City. Due to the chain's huge volume, Ms. Jordan has been assigned the responsibility of buying only one category of merchandise—women's sweaters. She is now well into her second year as sweater buyer after having served as an assistant to the women's handbag buyer for three years.

The company was satisfied with Ms. Jordan's performance at the end of her first year except for her inability to meet her planned average markup. Costs had risen in the sweater industry, but Ms. Jordan had found it necessary to hold most of her established retail prices stable to meet stiff competition. Although her planned average markup had been 46 percent, the year-end statistics showed her actual markup to have been 44 percent.

About six months ago Ms. Jordan took her first buying trip to Europe. She spent about half her time in the Scandinavian countries shopping for ski sweaters. One Danish vendor showed her a magnificent line of handknits, which she could sell at a reasonable price and still take a long markup. She found another line in Norway that was equally attractive. Even with the transportation, packing, duty, and other fees involved, the ski sweaters promised to be excellent buys. So Ms. Jordan jubilantly placed large orders, feeling that she had found a way to increase her average markup. She decided to put markups of 60 percent or more on the sweaters.

The sweaters began to arrive and looked indeed beautiful. However, Ms. Jordan soon became alarmed because it appeared that all delivery dates were not going to be met. In fact, the Norwegian vendor wired that his shipment of sweaters would be delayed about six weeks. Ms. Jordan knew that the sweaters must arrive on time because they had to be distributed to her largest stores all over the country. She hesitated to cancel any orders because they represented a substantial share of her fall and winter commitments, and she had high hopes of increasing her average markup.

1. In addition to the possibilities of long markup, what are some other advantages of buying foreign merchandise?
2. What are some of the pitfalls to be aware of when buying merchandise overseas?
3. If many of the ski sweaters arrive very late in the season, what should Ms. Jordan do with them?

POOR TIMING

Reed's, a fashion-oriented specialty store on the West Coast, has had great success with customer advisory groups. Once a month a group of twenty women are invited to the store to discuss store policies, services, and merchandise assortments. The women are chosen at random from Reed's charge account customers, and after each Saturday morning meeting they are treated to a free lunch and given a 10 percent discount shopping pass for the day. The women are eager to voice their opinions, and the store has benefited greatly from their comments.

One criticism echoed over and over again is that the store is rushing the seasons. As a result, customers must plan and buy their winter wardrobes in July and August, and their summer wardrobes right after Easter. As one woman puts it, "in August I'm still at the beach in my bikini, and I don't feel like shopping for a winter coat. When I come into Reed's in October to buy my coat, there is no selection, and the sales people act as though I've lost my marbles." Another customer comments that she likes to come into Reed's when she actually needs something, and often the pickings are lean if she has missed the early shipments. Still another says she is too busy to sit down and plan her wardrobe months in advance: "I refuse to change my buying habits to suit stores like yours. We will just have to pressure you to have clothes suitable for the season in *that* season."

The merchandisers at Reed's know that it will be difficult to get off a merry-go-round that has been going on for years. Stores attribute early deliveries to manufacturer's production schedules, but the manufacturers reply that delivery dates are set by the stores. Will it ever be possible for stores and manufacturers to adjust the delivery schedule to the selling seasons? Frankly, the merchandisers at Reed's doubt it. But after listening to concerned customers, they are aware that an adjustment should be made. A definite change in buying patterns seems to have appeared, and the store managers feel that markdowns can be reduced if they do not rush the seasons.

1. What are some of the reasons for customers' dislike of buying clothes far in advance of their needs?
2. How will stores benefit from longer and more timely selling seasons?

14

HOW TO NEGOTIATE WITH VENDORS

KEY POINTS

1. One of the marks of an effective buyer is his or her ability to negotiate advantageous terms of purchase.

2. As a result of years of negotiation, many discount terms have become standardized.

3. Since markup is figured on the basis of gross cost, loading the invoice increases the retail price for consumers.

4. Although vendor aids often help the retailer sell goods more efficiently, they have a cost that is built into the cost of the goods.

5. The buyer's order is a legal document, the terms of which both the buyer and the seller should adhere to.

THE NEED TO NEGOTIATE

In Chapter 1 we discussed the qualifications needed to become an effective buyer. These qualifications are all important, but one deserves special attention. The buyer must be a *trader*.

A buyer's job would be much simpler (but not as challenging or rewarding) if it involved only shopping the market, making merchandise selections, having them shipped to the store, and then seeing that they were properly displayed and sold. The buyer must also make sure that his or her purchasing price is the lowest possible as well as taking advantage of any vendor helps that may be available. This does not mean that a buyer should be a chiseler and be overly impressed with the power of the pencil. It does mean that there is an interplay between the buyer and the seller triggered by the profit motive. In order for any sale to be satisfying, both parties must benefit, and it takes a certain amount of give and take to make this possible.

Generally, stores in this country operate on a one-price retail policy; that is, all customers pay the marked price. Many vendors insist that they have a one-price policy as well. However, the originally quoted vendor price can nearly always be shaved. How much reduction it can take depends on how badly the vendor wants to sell the merchandise and how important the buyer is. It would not be realistic to think otherwise. Here is where experience and talent pay off. A buyer must learn through the "school of hard knocks" how to negotiate for the best price and terms possible. If a buyer does not take the time for such negotiations, then he or she is not acting in the best interest of the store.

ELEMENTS OF NEGOTIATION

There are four factors to consider in negotiating with a vendor. Each is important. They will all affect how much profit (or loss) the store will make on a particular shipment of merchandise. The elements to consider are:

1. Quoted cost price
2. Discounts and dating
3. Transportation charges
4. Vendor aids

Quoted Cost Price

When a buyer walks into a vendor's showroom to look at a line of merchandise, price is not usually discussed immediately. The buyer first wants to see whether the merchandise is of the type and quality needed for her or his department or store. If interested, the buyer will most often estimate how much the merchandise is worth. This estimate is based on past experience as well as what has been seen in other showrooms. Seeing that the buyer is showing some interest, the vendor may ask, "How much are you willing to pay for this?" The buyer should never state his estimate first. It may be too high, in which case the vendor would be only too happy to sell at that price. It may be much too low, in which case the buyer might be held to ridicule.

The bargaining process, then, is somewhat akin to a game of poker. Both sides are reluctant to show too much enthusiasm or reveal their limits. The vendor will usually quote a price first, and it is often the published wholesale price. If there are trade discounts available, the wholesale cost can be reduced considerably, as we will see shortly. But it must be emphasized that some vendors are not open to negotiation no matter how important the buyer may be. However, the buyer must at least try to reduce the quoted price and drive a good bargain. Depending on the type of merchandise, the season, the quantity bought, and some other factors, more often than not he can be successful.

After the buyer has refused to accept the quoted price, the bargaining process continues. The buyer should be able to defend the top price he or she is willing to pay. For example, the merchandise may be needed for a promotion, or the buyer may be having trouble meeting the markup goal. The buyer should not try to force down the price of every single item in a line. If an assortment of goods is bought, the vendor is often willing to make concessions where he can, but due to certain manufacturing costs, there may be items that cannot be reduced.

The difference between the quoted price and what the buyer is willing to pay is gradually narrowed until a compromise is reached. The result is the agreed on gross wholesale price.

Discounts and Dating

After the gross wholesale price has been established, the buyer will try for further discounts. Years ago discounts amounted to anything the buyer could squeeze out of a particular vendor. One buyer might get a discount of 3 percent where another might insist on 10 percent. Eventually many discounts were stabilized, and certain percentages became standard in different trades as the result of years of negotiation between buyers and sellers.

Because of this standardization of discounts, vendors now build the discounts into their costs and quote their prices accordingly. Thus the manufacturer who allows a retailer the standard discount is really doing no more than giving back to the buyer the extra charge he has built into his price for that purpose.

When the wholesale price is reduced, the consumer benefits because markups are based on the billed gross wholesale prices. However, cash discounts are kept by the store as a profit cushion, as was explained in Chapter 5.

Even though some discounts have been standardized, many have not. The following types of discounts are commonly used when goods are bought for resale to the consumer.

TRADE DISCOUNT

A trade discount is a single discount or a series of discounts from the *list price,* which is the manufacturer's published catalog price. Since the list price is published, you may think it is a firm price. However, it is far from that because the discounts allowed can vary as much as the manufacturer desires. Thus the *net price,* or the price after the discounts have been subtracted, can be any amount. It is common to allow different buyers different trade discounts. Discount sheets are confidential, and it is difficult for competitors to discover what someone else is paying.

The list price is often the same as the suggested retail price. If so, the trade discounts are in reality the markup achieved for the item.

ILLUSTRATIVE PROBLEM The owner of a hardware store bought a lawn mower from a manufacturer for the list price of $100 less trade discounts of 20 percent, 10 percent, and 5 percent. If no other discounts were allowed, what was the net price?

SOLUTION The discounts must be deducted *one at a time* as a percentage of the previous balance, not of the original amount. Thus we have:

List price	$100
Less 20%	$100 × 0.20 = $20
	$100 − $20 = $80
Less 10%	$80 × 0.10 = $8
	$80 − $8 = $72
Less 5%	$72 × 0.05 = $3.60
Net price	$72 − $3.60 = $68.40

ALTERNATE SOLUTION Subtract in your head each of the percentages from 100 percent and multiply the difference to the dollar amount one at a time:

List price	$100
Less 20%	$100 × 0.80 = $80
Less 10%	$80 × 0.90 = $72
Les 5%	$72 × 0.95 = $68.40
Net price	$68.40

QUANTITY DISCOUNT

Quantity discounts are sometimes given to encourage buyers to purchase bigger lots of merchandise. Manufacturers save money by selling in larger quantitites; they save in packing, production, selling, and shipping costs. Quantity discounts, which are subtracted from the wholesale prices, seem to favor the large retailers because the orders they place can be much bigger than those placed by small retailers. Thus the Robinson-Patman Act was passed by Congress in 1936 to curb this special favor to large retailers which also benefits large manufacturers. Quantity discounts, accordingly, are legal only so long as the manufacturer can prove that the discounts given do not exceed the savings enjoyed.

Both large and small retailers often earn quantity discounts by placing *blanket orders*. Used most often with staple merchandise, a blanket order is an order large enough to satisfy stock requirements for a long period of time, perhaps as long as an entire season. The whole order is not usually shipped to the store at one time; rather, the store requisitions against the order as stock is needed. Manufacturers like blanket orders because with them they can better budget their production and selling costs. Stores like blanket orders because quantity discounts make the goods less expensive, and the manufacturer assumes part of the storage function.

Quantity discounts may be either noncumulative or cumulative. *Noncumulative* discounts are based on the quantity purchased at a single time for delivery at a single place. Thus a manufacturer might set up a discount schedule as follows:

QUANTITY	DISCOUNT
1 - 10 dozen	0
11 - 25 dozen	1%
26 - 50 dozen	2%
Over 50 dozen	3%

Cumulative discounts are based on the total volume purchased over a period of time for delivery to a single place or to several destinations. The discount schedule might then look like this:

TOTAL SEASONAL PURCHASES	DISCOUNT
Less than $200	0
$200 - $500	1%
$501 - $1,000	2%
$1,001 - $5,000	3%

ILLUSTRATIVE PROBLEM
A glove buyer placed an order for 100 dozen kid leather gloves priced at $60 per dozen. Because of the size of the order, the vendor granted a quantity discount of 2 percent. What was the net cost of the order?

SOLUTION

100 dozen gloves at $60/dozen	$6,000
Less 2% discount	120
Net cost	$5,880

SEASONAL DISCOUNT

A seasonal discount is sometimes offered to a buyer for purchasing goods out of season. For example, a swimsuit manufacturer might give a seasonal discount on a large order placed after the summer season is over. If the retailer has sufficient storage space and if basic styles are involved, the lower price might be advantageous. If there is danger of fashion change or deterioration or if storage costs are high, then it will not make sense to buy out of season. Manufacturers who deal with seasonal goods allow such discounts because they help them even out production schedules and reduce problems involved in massive changes in personnel needs.

CASH DISCOUNTS

A cash discount is a deduction from the wholesale price for paying the invoice within a specified period of time. A cash discount is never given simply because the bill is paid in cash. When figuring the net amount of an invoice, other discounts that may have been granted are deducted before the cash discount.

Standard cash discounts are common in some industries. For example, in the women's ready-to-wear field, an 8 percent cash discount is usually granted for bills paid within the time period allowed.

ILLUSTRATIVE PROBLEM Cash discount terms of 2/10, n/30 were allowed on an invoice for merchandise amounting to $3,600. The invoice was dated on April 14 and paid on April 21. How much should have been paid?

SOLUTION The terms of sale, 2/10, n/30, mean that a 2 percent cash discount would be allowed if the bill was paid within ten days of the issuance of the bill. The full amount (if the cash discount is not taken advantage of) must be paid within thirty days. (After thirty days the retailer might be subject to an interest charge on the delinquent invoice. The retailer's credit rating would also suffer.) Since the invoice was paid within the ten-day period, the 2 percent discount should have been deducted:

Invoice amount	$3,600
Less 2% discount	72
Net amount due	$3,528

DATING

Dating refers to the length of time that the vendor gives the buyer (store) to pay for goods purchased. There are many variations in dating and in cash discounts for paying earlier. The following types are often encountered:

Regular Dating
This is the most common method of dating, according to which a store is allowed a discount if the bill is paid within the time periods specified. For example, a discount term that reads 2/10, 1/20, n/30 means: a 2 percent discount is allowed if the bill is paid within ten days after the date of the invoice; a 1 percent discount may be deducted if the bill is paid within

twenty days; and the net amount without discount must be paid within thirty days.

E.O.M. Dating
Here a store may take a cash discount if the invoice is paid within ten days *after* the end of the month in which the invoice is issued.

ILLUSTRATIVE PROBLEM	A drugstore owner purchased 200 hair brushes at $5.00 each with terms of 3/10 E.O.M., n/60. The invoice was dated May 16. If he paid the bill on June 5, what was the amount of his remittance?
SOLUTION	Since end-of-the-month terms always provide for payment to be made ten days after the end of the month in which the invoice is dated, the due date in this case would be June 10. The store owner paid the bill five days before the due date, so the discount would be allowed. If the remittance had been made after June 10, the owner would have had sixty days after May 16 to pay the full amount.

Invoice amount	$1,000 ($5.00 × 200)
Less 3% discount	30
Net amount due	$ 970

Receipt of Goods (R.O.G.) Dating
A term of sale reading "3/10 R.O.G." means that a 3 percent discount will be allowed if the invoice is paid within ten days after the goods are received in the store.

Extra Dating
Sometimes a store may ask for more time for receiving a cash discount. If the extra time is granted, it is called extra dating and is denoted by a capital X.

ILLUSTRATIVE PROBLEM	The operator of a music store bought sheet music amounting to $580 with terms of 2/10, 60X, n/90. What payment is indicated if the invoice is dated September 8 and paid on October 28?
SOLUTION	Here the terms state that a 2 percent discount is allowed if the invoice is paid within ten days of the date of the invoice. However, the vendor is allowing an extra (X) sixty days in which the store can take the 2 percent discount. The full net amount must be paid within ninety days. In reality the music store operator has seventy days from September 8 to pay the invoice and qualify for the cash discount. The due date for the cash discount is therefore November 17:

Days remaining in September	22 (30 − 8)
Days in October	31
Total number of days in September and October	53
Due date	70 days − 53 days = 17 (November 17)

Since the invoice is paid well before the discount due date of November 17, the remittance should be $568.40 ($580 less $11.60).

Postdating

It is common in the clothing trades to extend the cash discount period for an extra month when the invoice is dated on or after the twenty-fifth of the month and end-of-the-month terms are given. For example, if an invoice is dated August 30 with terms of 8/10 E.O.M., the store will normally have only until September 10 to qualify for the discount. With postdating, the store will be given until October 10 to pay the bill and receive the discount. The invoice, then, is dated September 30 or a month after the goods are actually shipped.

ILLUSTRATIVE PROBLEM

An invoice dated April 26 for a shipment of ladies' dresses amounts to $2,500 with terms of 8/10 E.O.M. If postdating is allowed, what is the last day on which the payment can be made to qualify for the cash discount?

SOLUTION

Since the invoice is dated after the twenty-fifth of the month and end-of-the-month terms are given, postdating will give the store until June 10 instead of May 10 to receive the cash discount of $200.

EXERCISES

1. A French provincial chair has a list price of $200. A series of trade discounts of 30, 20 and 10 percent are offered to the buyer. What is the net price?
2. What payment should be made on April 7 on an invoice dated March 25 for $200 worth of stationery with terms of 3/10 E.O.M., n/60?
3. How much should a store pay on an invoice for $5,000 worth of ladies' hosiery dated May 4 with terms of 8/10, n/30 if remittance is made on May 8?
4. What payment is indicated on an invoice for $300 dated March 4 with terms of 2/10, n/30 R.O.G. if the goods are received on March 20 and paid for on March 31?
5. What is the discount due date for a shipment of goods invoiced at $100 with the terms 3/10, 60X if the date of the invoice is May 5?
6. An invoice for ladies' blouses amounting to $500 was dated August 26 and paid for on September 10. If the terms were 8/10, n/60, how much should have been paid?

ANTICIPATION

Although it is common practice for a store to receive cash discounts for paying its bills within specified time periods, many retailers ask for an extra discount if they pay *before the expiration of the cash discount period*. This extra bonus is called *anticipation* and usually amounts to ½ percent a month or 6 percent a year. By reason of anticipation the vendor gets the use of the store's money ahead of time, and the anticipation is nothing more than the store's interest charge on that money. As the prime interest rate has risen, more and more stores are asking for more than ½ percent per month, and many now receive ¾ percent or 9 percent a year. Some stores have been requesting a rate as high as 1½ percent monthly. As a result, vendors are finding anticipation very costly, and some have instituted policies of refusing anticipation altogether.

When anticipation is allowed, it is usually deducted from the original bill, not from the cost after the cash discounts. It will be assumed in this text that 6 percent a year is allowed for anticipation and 360 is the number of days in a year.

ILLUSTRATIVE PROBLEM A buyer of lingerie negotiated terms of 8/10 E.O.M. plus anticipation with one of her key vendors. An invoice from this vendor was dated June 4 and was paid by the store on July 2. If the amount of the bill was $6,000, how much did the store remit?

SOLUTION The store had until July 10 to qualify for the 8 percent cash discount. Thus there were eight days' worth of anticipation.

STEP 1
Find the anticipation:
The easiest way to find the anticipation is to multiply the principal to the rate and then to the length of time. In this case the principal was $6,000. The length of anticipation was 8 days. Using the 6 percent per year rate, we have:

$$\frac{\$6{,}000}{1} \times \frac{6}{100} \times \frac{8}{360} = \$8 \text{ anticipation (after cancellation)}$$

STEP 2
Find the cash discount:

$$\text{Cash discount} = \$6{,}000 \times 0.08$$
$$= \$480$$

STEP 3
Find the net amount of the invoice:

$$\text{Net amount} = \$6{,}000 - (\$480 + \$8)$$
$$= \$6{,}000 - \$488$$
$$= \$5{,}512$$

LOADING THE INVOICE

A buyer may ask the vendor to *load the invoice* in order to receive a higher percentage of cash discount than before. As we have shown, cash discounts are very important to the store because they act as profit cushions. The cushions may actually make the difference between an operating loss and an operating profit.

When it appears that a buyer is not receiving at least the standard rate of cash discount for the particular trade, there may be pressure from store management to increase the discount. The vendor is usually willing to accommodate so long as he or she receives the same amount of money for the goods. In other words, the vendor will not object to increasing the quoted wholesale price (the billed cost price before deducting the cash discount) in order to allow for a greater discount.

Since markups are figured on the basis of the quoted price and not the final net cost to the store, the consumer is the victim of loaded invoices. For example, if a keystone markup is applied to a quoted price of $5.00, the customer will pay $10.00 for the item. If the invoice is loaded and the quoted price is increased to $5.50, then the customer will have to pay $11.00.

ILLUSTRATIVE PROBLEM

A boy's furnishings buyer has been buying a cowboy shirt for several years at a quoted wholesale price of $5.00 on terms of 2/10, n/30. His merchandise manager feels that he should be getting terms of 5/10, n/30. The buyer then contacts the vendor and asks him to load the invoice to reflect the 5-percent cash discount. If the vendor agrees, what will be the new quoted cost price?

SOLUTION

STEP 1:
Find the net price:

$$\text{Net price} = \text{Quoted cost less cash discount}$$
$$= \$5.00 - 0.10 \ (\$5 \times 0.02)$$
$$= \$4.90$$

STEP 2:
Find the new quoted cost price:
The new quoted cost price must equal 100 percent. Then the net price is $4.90 or 95 percent (100 percent − 5 percent) because the vendor will increase the discount to 5 percent. Therefore, to determine the new quoted cost, divide $4.90 by 95 percent:

$$\text{New quoted cost} = \frac{\$4.90}{0.95}$$
$$= \$5.16$$

CHECK YOUR ANSWER

$$\text{Net price} = \text{New quoted cost less new cash discount}$$
$$= \$5.16 - 0.26 \ (\$5.16 \times 0.05)$$
$$= \$4.90$$

Note: So long as the cowboy shirt maker receives $4.90 net, it is immaterial to him whether the store receives a 2 percent or a 5 percent cash discount.

EXERCISES

1. An invoice for women's coats amounting to $3,000 was dated October 18 and paid on November 15 with terms of 8/10 E.O.M., 60X. How much should have been remitted if anticipation was allowed?
2. What payment is indicated on an invoice for $2,000 worth of women's

shoes dated May 26 with terms of 8/10, n/30 if the bill is paid on June 2? Allow anticipation.

3. A slipper buyer placed on order amounting to $1,000, getting terms of 3/10 E.O.M., n/60. The invoice was dated July 15 and paid on August 1. How much did the vendor receive if anticipation was granted?

4. An invoice was issued on July 26 for $8,000 worth of evening gowns with terms of 8/10 E.O.M., n/60. The bill was paid on August 14. If both postdating and anticipation were allowed, what was the net amount?

5. A domestics merchandise buyer bought $5,000 worth of towels from one of his top resources. Terms of 5/10, n/30 plus anticipation were allowed. The invoice was dated October 18. If the invoice was paid on October 25, what was the net amount?

6. A buyer bought a blouse listed at $12 from a new vendor last year and received a cash discount of 2/10. Her controller thought this was very strange since 8/10 was typical for women's wear. This year the buyer bought the same blouse and asked the vendor to load the invoice. What will the new list price be?

7. A men's wear buyer purchases 2,000 sweaters at a quoted cost of $10 each with terms of 2/10, n/30. The store's controller requested permission to load the invoice to allow terms of 5/10, n/30. What will be the new total cost of the order before any discounts are taken?

Transportation Charges

Shipping costs are very high, so buyers always try to persuade vendors to assume some of the cost and liability of sending goods. Most goods are shipped *F.O.B. factory* (free on board), which means that the title passes at a shipping point just outside the place where the goods are made. The store thus pays for the transportation charges and assumes the liability in transit. If, on the other hand, the vendor agrees to pay for transportation and assume liability until the goods reach the store, the goods are said to be shipped *F.O.B. store*. The title then passes when the store accepts delivery at its own receiving dock. The reason that shipments F.O.B. store are not more common is that due to price discrimination laws, if a vendor agrees to such an arrangement, he or she must make it available to all buyers. A third way is for the vendor to ship goods and assume all liability until the goods reach the store with the understanding that the store will later reimburse the vendor for all shipping costs. In this case the title passes when the store accepts delivery, as with F.O.B. store, but the shipment is said to be *F.O.B. store, charges reversed*.

If a store must pay for shipping, it will try to find the most economical carrier and route. One way to save money is to use a *freight forwarder*. A freight forwarder collects various shipments that individually will not fill up an entire railroad car or truck and consolidates them into *carload lots*. Shipping in carload lots is less expensive than in less than carload lots (L.C.L.). The freight forwarder selects the route, and although a fee is charged for his services, it is still less than shipping in L.C.L. Using *piggyback* rates is still another way to reduce shipping costs. Truck trailers are loaded and put aboard specially designed railroad flat cars. When the destination is reached, the trailer is put back on a truck at the railroad yard. Piggyback is ideal for sending merchandise long distances. If truck trailers are loaded on barges for a long haul, the procedure is called *fishyback*.

Most merchandise is shipped by truck or railway. Railroads are less expensive than trucks and are best for long-distance shipments where speed is not important. However, since Amtrak has taken over most of the nation's railroads, some train service has been discontinued. Trucks have, then, become more important. They are more flexible, can reach more towns, and are faster and more convenient.

A store may also use Railway Express. This is an agency owned by railroads that offers reliable service and the convenience of pick-up and delivery. Railway Express is suitable for small expensive packages that need special handling.

There are occasions when merchandise needs to be shipped by air to cover an advertisement that is about to break or replenish fashion stocks quickly. Items such as cut flowers or seafood are highly perishable and should be shipped by air. Air Express is the most expensive method of shipping. Merchandise is sent on regularly scheduled airlines. The cost has been reduced somewhat by the introduction of the 747 jumbo jets, but air express should be used only in cases of real emergency. Air Freight is less expensive because cargo planes are used.

Piggyback shipping
SOURCE: American Association of Railroads

ELEMENTS OF NEGOTIATION **269**

Vendor Aids

After the buyer has negotiated the lowest possible cost price, agreed on discount terms, and tried to get the vendor to pay for shipping costs, he is ready to discuss vendor aids. There are many different kinds of vendor services that may be offered. Some are promotional in nature, which are outside the purview of this text. Others involve marking, financing, and risk taking.

Buyers should understand that vendor aids cost the manufacturer money, which must be absorbed into the price paid for goods. Therefore, they would do well to examine how efficiently their own stores can perform the same function represented by vendor's aid. For example, if a store's advertising department is well staffed and noted for its creativity, then it will not be necessary to make use of advertising materials prepared by the vendor.

The following are a few of the vendor helps that a store might take advantage of:

1. *Preticketing.* If the vendor agrees to ticket the merchandise before it arrives at the store, the store will be saved considerable time and money. Preticketing is especially important for fashion goods where no time should be wasted in getting the shipment to the selling floor. Sometimes a store will send the vendor the necessary tickets and the vendor will simply attach them. At other times a store or buyer will furnish all the needed ticket information so that the vendor can print the tickets as well. Some vendors attach their own tickets with a suggested retail price, so that if store tickets show a lower price, customers will feel they are getting a bargain.

   Many large stores have marking done by freight consolidating companies. In addition to their primary job of physically distributing merchandise, freight consolidators will mark merchandise using the store's price tags. The goods are then ready for immediate sale when they reach the store.

2. *Consignment.* Merchandise bought on consignment may be returned to the vendor if not sold. The title stays with the manufacturer, and the store pays for only that portion of the goods that has been sold. When the merchandise is sold, the title shifts directly to the customer.

   Consignment buying is a good way for a buyer to try out new items with no risk to the store. It can tone up assortments and lend new interest. It is also an excellent means with which inexperienced buyers can learn about the needed quantities of merchandise. Best of all, there are never any markdowns. However, the store is usually bound to sell the goods at any retail price the vendor chooses. Consignment goods may take up too much storage space, the goods are not always desirable, and relations between the buyer and the vendor may become strained when returned merchandise is found to be damaged or soiled.

3. *Sale with a return privilege.* Unlike consignment buying, in this case the title to the merchandise shifts to the store as soon as the goods are

Merchandise preticketed by the manufacturer
SOURCE: Cary Wolinski/Grafia

shipped. However, the vendor agrees to take back any merchandise that does not get sold within a specified time period. If the vendor later refuses to take back the merchandise, the store may sue. The distinct advantage of this method over consignment buying is that the store may retail the merchandise at any price it chooses.

THE BUYER'S ORDER

After the buyer has made his or her merchandise selections and completed all the negotiations, there still is the purchase order to be written. The order is a legal agreement between the vendor and the purchasing store that says the vendor will deliver merchandise according to the specifications outlined in the order. In 1676 the English Parliament passed a statute requiring that certain contracts be in writing in order to be enforceable. It was called the *statute of frauds,* because its aim was to prevent fraudulent claims of the existence of oral contract or some details of oral contract. The statute of frauds has become a part of American law and states that any order over $50 must be in writing to be enforceable. However, the statutory minimum fixed by any state is subject to change by the state legislature, and the minimum may be as high as $500.

Although oral orders for goods not exceeding $500 in value may be enforceable in a court of law in some states, it is a good idea to put all orders into writing to avoid any misunderstanding as to the terms of sale and to provide a record for the store when the merchandise arrives. If a buyer orders merchandise over the telephone, it is important to give the vendor an order number, then write out the order and send in the confirmation. Even without a written order, a store may still accept shipment, in which case the receiving room prepares a memorandum upon receipt of the merchandise; but the buyer must still write a covering order if the merchandise is in fact wanted. If the merchandise is returned, there must be a very good reason even though the order was an oral one.

Order forms vary somewhat from store to store, reflecting variations in what is important to a store in insuring an efficient flow of merchandise into it. As major stores open more and more branch units, order forms have necessarily become more complex. Figure 14.1 shows a typical order form for a large metropolitan store with branches.

There must be at least three copies of the order. The vendor receives the original, and the receiving room and the buyer get the other two for their respective files. If merchandise has been ordered for branch stores, each branch should also receive a copy. In some cases, the resident buyer also receives a copy for purposes of delivery follow-up.

Since the buyer is acting as an agent for the store, his or her signature makes the order binding. In some stores the merchandise manager is required to countersign the order, especially if the value of the merchandise is over a certain amount. Although it may seem to be a good idea for the merchandise manager to sign all orders to keep close control over the buyers' spending, many buyers resent this requirement as an indication of lack of trust. Furthermore, when a buyer is in the market writing up many orders, it is not practical to have the merchandise manager cosign them.

When the vendor receives an order, it is customary for him or her to send an order confirmation back to the buyer to signify vendor acceptance of the order, thus making it binding on both parties. In the absence of such written acceptance, the actual shipment of the merchandise indicates acceptance.

In many cases orders are written up in the vendor's showroom on the vendor's order form. Such orders, however, are not considered legal contracts, but merely memoranda of what the buyer wants to order. The information needs to be transferred onto the regular store order form in order to make the orders binding agreements between the two parties.

However the order is finally written, its importance cannot be underestimated. Great care must be taken to insure that it is accurate and reflects exactly what the buyer wants. Buyers are under great pressure from vendors to write orders while they are in the market. If a buyer has many classifications of merchandise to buy, he or she may wish to shop one classification at a time, write up the necessary orders, and then go on to the next classification. For example, a boys' wear buyer might buy suits first, then sport coats, then outerwear, then long-sleeved sports shirts, and so

Figure 14.1 STORE ORDER FORM

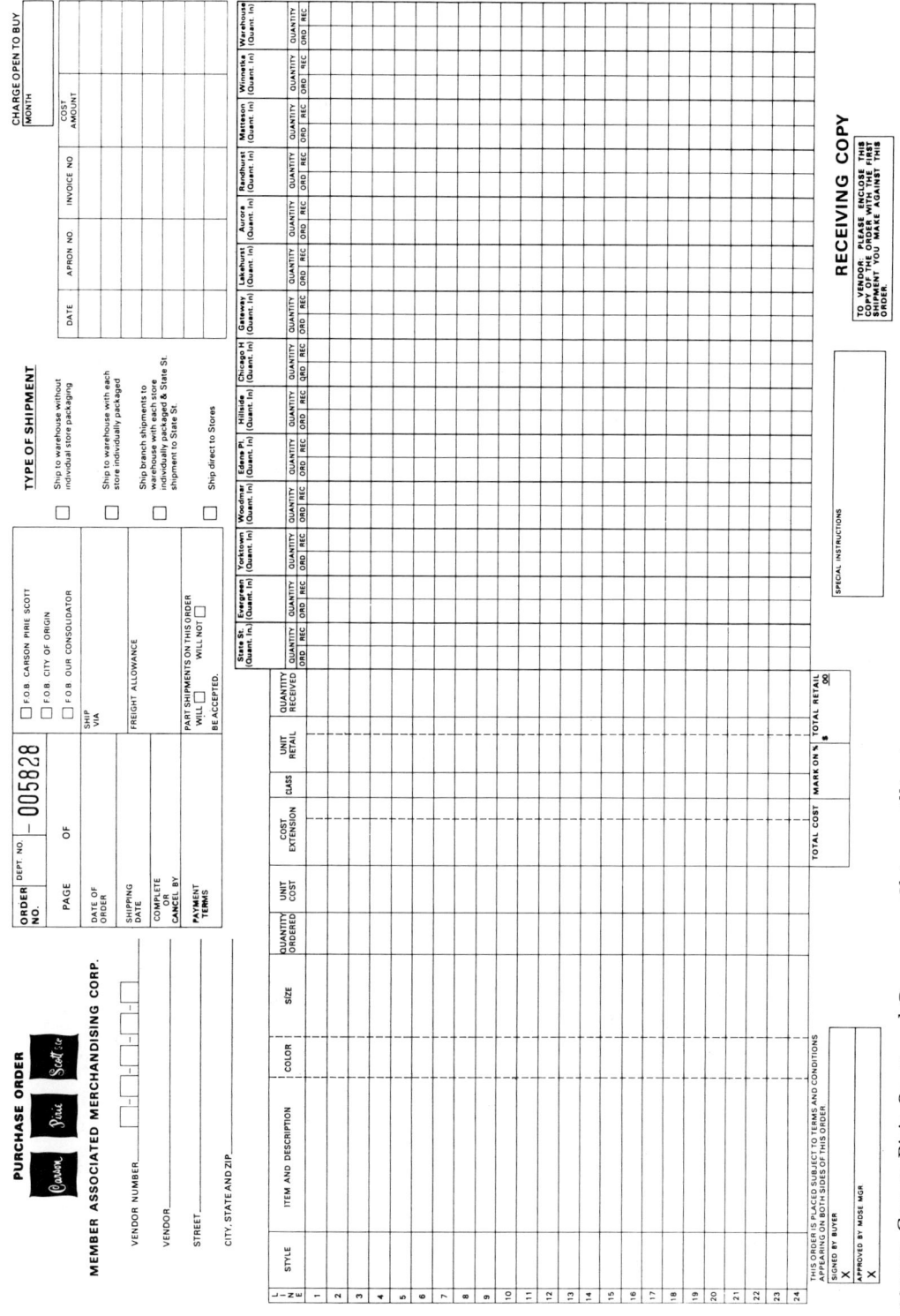

SOURCE: Carson Pirie Scott and Company, Chicago, Illinois

THE BUYER'S ORDER

forth. Some buyers prefer to wait until they have returned to their home stores before writing up any orders at all. In this way they can avoid vendor pressure and also enlist the aid of their assistants in completing the necessary paperwork.

Since the store order form represents a legal contract between the vendor and the buyer, a store may return the merchandise ordered if the vendor has not fulfilled his part of the agreement. Merchandise is most often returned because the vendor has:

1. Shipped goods that were not ordered
2. Shipped goods after the due date
3. Made substitutions in colors, sizes, and style numbers
4. Overshipped
5. Billed at the wrong price

Of course, merchandise is also returned because it was bought on consignment or with a right to return. There are also special cases where the store has oral or written permission to return goods.

Many stores have had to institute strict return policies when a vendor has violated the terms of the purchase order. The cost of returning goods has risen sharply as have the number of returns. If is now common for a store to impose upon an erring vendor a minimum handling charge ranging from $5 to $25 for each returned shipment. This handling charge is in addition to transportation costs that result from the return and must be borne by the vendor. Stores hope the handling charge will reduce the necessity for returns, most of which are caused by vendors shipping after the cancellation date.

Under no circumstances, however, should a buyer return merchandise simply because he or she bought too much, made a mistake in buying, or the merchandise is not selling. Vendors and buyers need each other, and neither should try to take advantage of the other.

CHAPTER SUMMARY

Negotiating contracts requires special skills and experience and is an integral part of every buyer's job. A buyer can be an excellent merchandise selector, but unless she or he learns how to negotiate with the vendors, the store's profit potential may not be fully realized.

Some manufacturers insist that they operate on a one-price policy. The insistence may be sincere, but buyers can usually find ways to buy merchandise for less, depending on how important they are to the vendor. If the quoted vendor price cannot be shaved, various discounts may nevertheless be obtained, beneficial transportation terms may be available, or vendor aids may be taken advantage of.

In addition to cash discounts and dating terms (many of which have been standardized in certain trades), stores often ask for anticipation as a reward for paying their bills early. Manufacturers can benefit from anticipation, too, unless the rate is exorbitant, because it in effect allows them to use the store's money. Retailers may also request increases in the percentages of cash discounts. This is known as loading the invoice; the stores take the cash discounts earned and use them as a contribution to profit.

Most merchandise is shipped F.O.B. factory, which means that the title to the purchased goods passes to the store at a shipping point in the factory; the store also pays shipping costs and assumes liability in transit. The vendor, however, may agree to pay for shipping the goods initially and be liable until the goods reach the store. If the store later reimburses the vendor for the transportation charges incurred, then the shipping is said to be F.O.B. store, charges reversed.

Vendor aids are designed to help the retailer stock and promote the given manufacturer's line of merchandise more efficiently. They may seem to be free, but of course their costs are built into the price that the vendor charges. Many stores prefer to buy merchandise for less and ignore most of the vendor aids.

A purchase order is a binding legal document that both the buyer and vendor are expected to honor. Even though oral orders for as much as $500 worth of merchandise may be enforceable in some states, orders should always be in writing. Oral orders lead to confusion and sometimes unethical conduct. A purchase is not a good one unless both the buyer and the vendor benefit from it, and neither should try to take advantage of the other. Returns and cancellations should be used only for valid reasons.

QUESTIONS FOR REVIEW

1. Why is it important for a buyer to be a good negotiator?
2. Does the consumer benefit more by having the wholesale cost reduced or by stores receiving bigger discounts? Explain your answer.
3. What is a trade discount? How can the list price be the same as the suggested retail price?
4. Why is a manufacturer eager to receive blanket orders?
5. Explain the difference between a quantity and a seasonal discount.
6. If a cash discount is not given for a bill that is paid in cash, then what is it?
7. Do stores usually prefer to have R.O.G. dating? Explain your answer.
8. What is the difference between extra dating and postdating?
9. If stores have adequate funds on hand, will they be more or less likely to take advantage of anticipation?
10. Explain how loading the invoice builds up a store's profit cushion.
11. What does a freight forwarder do?
12. What is the difference between shipping F.O.B. factory and shipping F.O.B. store? Which is the more common practice?
13. If a carload of men's underwear is to be shipped from a manufacturer in New York to a store in California, which mode of transportation is best and why?
14. Why is preticketing such an eagerly sought vendor aid?
15. What is an important difference between selling on consignment and selling with a return privilege?
16. What does the statute of frauds say about oral and written purchase orders?

17. If merchandise arrives at a store without a covering order, will the shipment be automatically returned to the vendor?
18. If a buyer makes a mistake and orders too much merchandise, is the store legally bound nevertheless to take the merchandise?
19. What are some of the reasons for which a buyer may return merchandise?
20. Why do some buyers wait until they have returned home from the market trip before writing any orders at all?

DISCUSSION QUESTION The XYZ department store in Anytown has a firm policy that every purchasing order must be countersigned by the appropriate merchandise manager. Discuss the advantages and disadvantages of adhering to this policy.

PROBLEMS FOR REVIEW

1. A stereo set has a list price of $650. Trade discounts of 20, 10, and 5 percent are offered to the buyer. What is the net price?
2. An invoice for ladies' blouses amounting to $4,000 was dated September 11 and paid on October 4 with terms of 8/10 E.O.M., 60X. If anticipation was allowed, (a) what was the cash discount due date, and (b) how much should have been paid?
3. What payment is indicated on August 15 on an invoice for $100 worth of chewing gum dated May 20 with terms of 2/10, 60X?
4. How much should be paid on an invoice for $3,000 worth of ladies' hosiery dated May 28 with terms of 8/10, n/30, if payment is made on June 2? Allow anticipation.
5. A buyer of sporting goods orders $100 worth of fishing reels. The invoice is dated April 18 with terms of 8/10 E.O.M. If the store pays the invoice on May 1 and anticipation is allowed, what is the net amount of the invoice?
6. A major appliance dealer bought two color television sets with a list price of $400 each. She was allowed a series of trade discounts of 30, 20, and 15 percent. The terms of sale were 6/10, n/30, and she paid the invoice within the cash discount period. What was the net amount of the invoice?
7. A hardware store bought 200 air conditioners on August 15 and received a seasonal discount of 2 percent. Each air conditioner carried a list price of $150 with a trade discount of 40 percent. The terms of sale were 2/10 E.O.M. If the invoice was paid on September 5, what was the net amount of the bill?
8. An invoice for $1,000 worth of ladies' scarves was dated January 28 with terms of 8/10 E.O.M. If the invoice was paid on March 1, how much was remitted if both postdating and anticipation were allowed?
9. A stationery buyer bought 1,000 folding chairs at $10 each. He received terms of 3/10, n/30. Due to pressure from his merchandise manager, he asked the vendor to load the invoice and give him the chairs on terms of 5/10, n/30. If the vendor agreed, what would be the new gross price?
10. A basic wool sweater priced at $15 had been bought by a sportswear

buyer for many years from the same manufacturer. The terms had been 8/10 E.O.M., n/60. Due to the large volume of sweaters purchased over the years, the store management felt justified in asking for terms of 10/10 E.O.M., n/60. If the manufacturer loaded the invoice accordingly, what would be the new cost of the sweater?

CASE PROBLEM

WRITER'S CRAMP

Lillian Scott was buyer of girls' coats, sizes 7 through 14, for a large department store in a western city for the past eight years. When first appointed to her job, she had been responsible only for her department in the parent store downtown. During the past five years, however, four branch stores opened in suburban areas, and buying for these stores added greatly to Ms. Scott's workload.

Ms. Scott made five or six market trips to New York City each year. During her first few years as buyer, she would spend many hours viewing coat lines in showroom after showroom, and when she was sure she had seen the best the market had to offer, she would ask the manufacturers to send her favorites to the resident buying office for final review. No purchase order would be written until Ms. Scott had seen the coat numbers twice. She was less rigid about promotional merchandise, but she combed the market for outstanding specials with great determination and zeal.

As her buying responsibilities increased, she began to learn a few tricks of the trade. She knew her key resources—the manufacturers who were reliable and offered her the best prices and terms. She no longer bothered to shop the market thoroughly but would depend on these manufacturers and on tips from her resident buyer. Since she trusted her key vendors so much, she would sometimes tell them she needed 200 coats in a certain style and price line, hand over her size scale, and say, "Give me the best you've got."

Ms. Scott found another way to save time. She had always written her own orders to make sure they were absolutely correct. In her early years as buyer, she had spent many exhausting hours in her hotel room trying to get her orders out before leaving New York. Sometimes she would finish writing her orders on the plane going home. She was the first to admit that this was the part of the job she most disliked. Lately, Ms. Scott began to minimize her order writing by letting each vendor write up her selections on the vendor's order form. These orders were then carried back to the store and turned over to Ms. Scott's assistant with instructions to write up the confirmation on the store's own order form. Ms. Scott thought that this was valuable experience for her assistant, and it certainly saved her a great deal of paper work.

Ms. Scott also discovered an easy way to increase her markup percentage. Every year the store management had increased her markup goal, and she was finding it increasingly difficult to maintain the necessary markup. When she was in a markup bind, Ms. Scott would request some of her vendors to bill her merchandise on a net basis. By deducting the customary cash discount before the invoice was made out, Ms. Scott was able to reduce the cost price and thus improve her markup. Of course, the store would not receive as much cash discount, but Ms. Scott didn't really care since her department never got credit for cash discounts anyway.

Ms. Scott felt she was really on top of her job. She had learned how to eliminate some of the bothersome details that used to give her headaches.

1. Do you think Ms. Scott is doing a more efficient buying job? Why?
2. Would any of Ms. Scott's practices described in this case result in a severe reprimand?

15

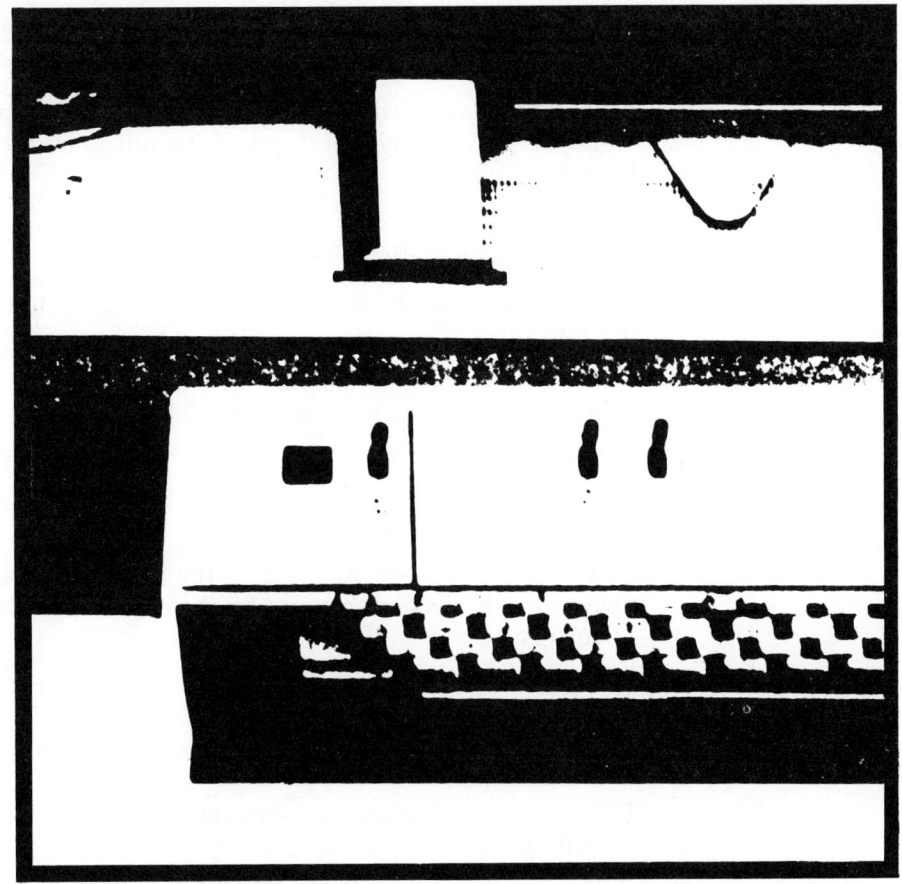

MERCHANDISING AND THE COMPUTER

KEY POINTS

1. The computer can provide a wealth of merchandising information on a daily basis.

2. The most important characteristics of the computer are speed, efficiency, and accuracy, but the machine must be properly programmed by a human being.

3. The computer is capable of storing vast quantities of information that can be used for statistical analysis at any time.

4. Data collected for a computerized retail system ideally begins at the point of sale.

5. Because computer systems are very expensive to install and operate, many companies rent computer time based on their individual needs.

WHAT THE COMPUTER CAN DO

Fifteen minutes after closing time the president of a large store decides to review the store's performance for the day. He has the following data at his fingertips:

1. The total sales volume, including the number and amount of cash and charge sales recorded.
2. The total number and amount of refunds, returns, and customer adjustments made.
3. An analysis of what was sold according to price, style, size, color, and department.
4. A record of items received into stock, returned to the vendor, and ordered for future delivery.
5. The net change in the value of the store's inventory.
6. The amount of merchandise each sales person sold during the day.
7. The status of each customer charge account.
8. The net profit or loss after the last sale was made.

Sound impossible? Not if the computer is put to work. The electronic computer is capable of yielding all this information and much more. Before the advent of the computer, the accumulation of such a quantity of data even on a weekly basis would have been a formidable task. Today the computer can easily supply merchandisers with such information on a daily basis. These data enable store management to make merchandising decisions more quickly and skillfully.

Because of its remarkable capacity, the computer is bound to play an increasingly larger role in the daily operation of a retail business. In fact, it is difficult to conceive of any individual connected with retailing today who has not encountered some form of computerization even in smaller stores. It is imperative, then, that every would-be retailer possess a general knowledge of the computer, its purpose, operation, and potential. In this chapter we will introduce the concept of the computer and provide a basic explanation of how a computer functions in the retailing environment. We will illustrate the use of many of the devices developed by computer technology and some of the terminology connected with computer work.

THE ELECTRONIC COMPUTER

The computer is one of today's least understood technological developments yet it is one of the most powerful computational devices known to man. For many, the computer is highly complex, mathematically oriented scientific equipment. It is often thought to be a cold, inhuman, calculating monster.

Fortunately, the computer is not like this at all. It is complex, but no more so than many of the machines already familiar to everyone in society. A computer can be accurately described as an extremely high-speed adding machine. Of course, it can also subtract, divide, multiply, and perform many other types of calculation. It is especially useful for repetitive tasks. In retailing, where stores have grown ever larger with accompanying increases in record-keeping, the computer has reduced mountains of paperwork to manageable proportions without adding to the payroll cost.

Computer Characteristics

The computer is noted for its speed, accuracy, and efficiency. Speed is perhaps its most astonishing characteristic. Computations can be made at speeds of over one-millionth of a second (macro-second), and speeds of one-billionth of a second (nano-second) are often attained. Because of its speed, the computer is capable of performing thousands of calculations in one second, far beyond what a human being can ever do manually. It thus becomes an invaluable time-saving device to the retailer.

Another invaluable characteristic of the computer is its accuracy. Despite numerous anecdotes about computer foul-ups, the computer is very reliable. Once data have been correctly entered into a computer, they can be recalled error-free any number of times. Computers also do not get fatigued, need no coffee breaks, and are not bored by performing the same task over and over again.

The efficiency of computers has been well documented. A computer can perform, single-handedly, tasks that used to be assigned to many clerks, and perform them at many times the speed of human beings. Upon completion of one task, the computer can be programmed for another. The efficiency of the computer has saved business billions of dollars.

Notwithstanding these amazing capabilities, the computer, it must be recognized, is only as effective as the person who feeds information and gives instructions to it. Computers will never completely replace the human being because they are not creative. They need human beings to feed them the information to be processed. Store buyers have seen their role change dramatically with computers removing much of the guesswork from their jobs. But buyers and manufacturers will always be needed to create new merchandise ideas, publicize them, and sell them. These the computer can never do.

The Basic Computer Cycle

The computer is a complex mechanical and electronic device. The UNIVAC 90/30 computer system with its full complement of supporting devices looks very complicated, indeed. However, the basic concept behind the operation of a computer is relatively simple. Three elements are involved in the operation of a computer: input, processing, and output.

Input is the placement of data into a computer system. *Processing* is the manipulation of the data within the system, including both arithmetic operations, such as addition and subtraction, and logical operations, such as the comparison of data to other numbers and limits. For example, a logical operation may be in answer to the question "Is the number of hours worked equal to forty or less?" aimed at determining whether an employee has worked overtime. Upon the completion of data processing, there is an *output* in the form of new data given in a predetermined format. The format is programmed to reflect the requirements of the users of the new data. Thus, if the data must be presented in the form of a neatly packaged report, the computer is given the proper instruction and the output is exactly as ordered. This is another example of how the computer must be directed by human beings. The computer can never decide by itself how the data should be presented; the computer programmer must do that.

To get a fuller understanding of the basic computer cycle, a new component must be included in our consideration: the computer's storage capability. The internal storage capacity of a computer is called *main storage*, which is an integral part of a larger area referred to as the *central processing*

The Univac 90/30 Computer System
SOURCE: Courtesy of Sperry Univac, a division of Sperry Rand Corporation

Figure 15.1
THE COMPUTER CYCLE

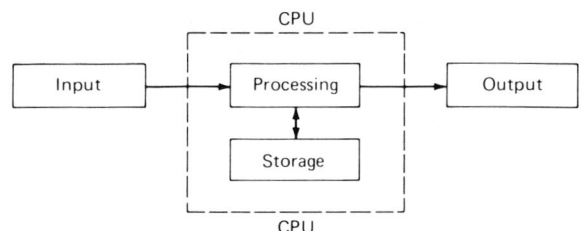

unit, or CPU. All processing must be performed within and under the control of the CPU. Data moved from one part of the system to another are transferred under control of the CPU also.

Figure 15.1 depicts the mutual relations of the three basic elements of the computer cycle. The storage component is also shown, and the dashed line indicates how all and any processing must occur in the CPU.

When the given data are ready for processing, they are held in the main storage, thus making possible the speedy retrieval of data, which is one of the greatest strengths of a computer system. It is evident that the larger the main storage, the greater is the quantity of data that can be stored and thus made readily available for processing.

The basic unit of storage of the computer is the *byte*. It is the smallest unit of storage inside the CPU and is capable of storing one item of data. That is, one character or one number can be stored in one byte. Thus the alphabetic letter *A* can be stored within one byte, whereas the characters L7 will require two bytes of storage. The CPU will efficiently store data while accurately recording the contents of each byte of main storage.

DATA HANDLING

There are several different types of computer systems. They differ according to the manner in which they handle the input and output of data. The devices that are used in the input/output (I/O) operations are generally referred to as *peripheral* devices. The materials or media employed to transmit data may range from paper cards and tapes to magnetically prepared surfaces.

When using either peripheral devices or specially prepared materials, the following facts should be kept in mind.

1. The more sophisticated the peripheral device or exotic the material to be used to process data, the greater is the cost.
2. A large CPU is required to support the use of sophisticated peripheral devices.
3. The cost of a computer system is directly proportional to the size of the CPU and the quality of peripheral devices employed.

The cost of a computer system employing sophisticated peripheral devices may be prohibitive for smaller stores. Even large stores that require a large CPU may find the cost so high as to be not economically feasible to install systems of their own. Also, computer systems become quickly outdated as new and better ways to collect, store, sort, and tabulate merchandising information are found. Thus it may be advantageous to rent computer time instead of owning a system outright. Stores can subscribe to a time-sharing service whereby computers are hooked into a store for use on an hourly basis. They can also make use of the services offered by professional computer centers staffed with programmers and operators. For a fee these centers will supply any type of output wanted from a given set of data. It is possible, then, for stores both large and small to avail themselves of the miracles performed by the computer without actually buying one.

In this chapter we will consider various types of media and peripheral devices ranging from the relatively inexpensive and simple to the very costly and complex. The more conventional forms of paper media will be discussed first.

The Punch Card

The first medium employed in computerizing data was the paper punch card designed by Dr. Herman Hollerith in the 1880s. The basic design and

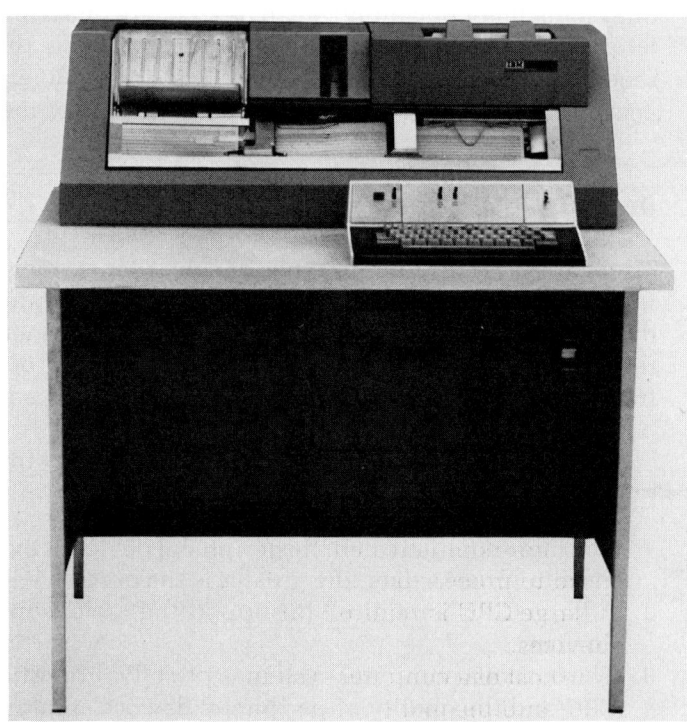

Keypunch machine
SOURCE: Courtesy of International Business Machines Corporation

card configuration has not changed much since then. The punch card is divided vertically into eighty card columns (consecutively numbered 1 through 80) and horizontally into twelve rows. Data are recorded onto the card column by column by a device known as a keypunch. Figure 15.2 shows a card that has been punched with alphabetic and numerical characters. The data are recorded onto the card in the form of rectangular holes (called punches) according to a code called the Hollerith code. This code permits the placement of only one character of data into one one-card column.

The punch card can be used for both the input and the output of data. During the input operation, data are electronically read from the card, fed into the CPU, and processed. For output the computer punches the results of data processing directly onto the card.

The Dual Card

Though the punch card has a standard size, its configuration may be altered to suit a company's specific data-processing needs. The dual card is an example of a punch card that has been modified for purposes of recording data (input) and providing data to the user (output).

One example of a dual card is the stock control card shown in Figure 15.3, which is put in a box of hosiery. The data recorded on the card include the style number, color, size, and number of pairs in a box. These data are considered the input. When the first pair of stockings in the box is sold, the card is placed in a special container for weekly outgoing mail by the sales person to be sent to the hosiery company for reordering purposes. When the hosiery company receives the card and others like it, the cards are processed issuing a reorder, which is the output.

The Stub Card

The stub card, another form of the punch card, enables the recipient of the card to retain a portion of it as a record of some transaction and to return the

Figure 15.2
STANDARD PUNCH CARD

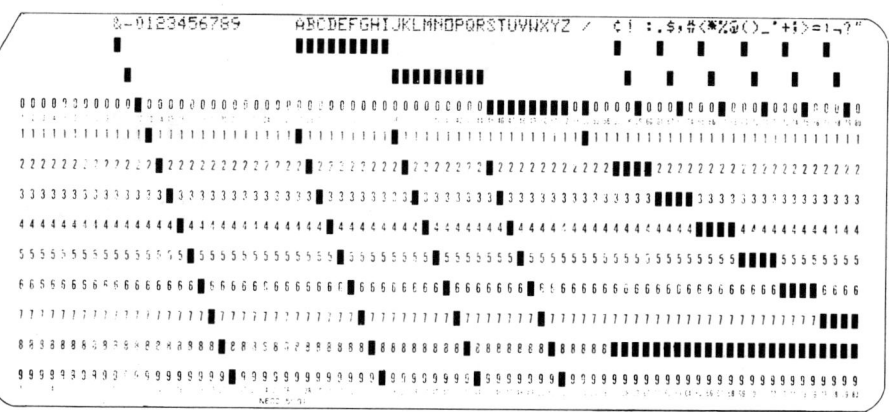

DATA HANDLING **285**

stub portion to the manufacturer or store. The stub card is used frequently by stores in their charge account operations. The monthly statement is a stub card with the stub returned to the store with the customer's payment. Other examples of stub cards are utility bill cards and credit card charges.

Magnetic Ink Character Recognition (MICR)

Dual and stub cards may be used in conjunction with a unique data-handling technique involving the use of magnetic ink and a specially designed number format. The special ink contains metallic flecks that are easily sensed by a reading device called an optical scanner. When the card or stub is returned to the company, it is fed through the optical scanner, and the data in stubby figures that were magnetically inked are sensed and transmitted to the computer for processing. A common use of MICR is in the processing of bank checks. The squat figures at the bottom of a personal check represent an individual's checking account number. After a check is cashed the bank records the amount of the check (in magnetic ink) immediately following the account number. The optical scanner serially records the checking account number and the amount of the check. After transmission to the computer, the data are posted directly against a specific account and subsequently appear in that customer's monthly statement.

Paper Tapes

Another type of material used successfully in the computerization of data is the paper tape. As shown in Figure 15.4, data are punched onto the tape in the form of a series of round holes according to a code. The punched-tape reader receives data in the form of electrical impulses through the holes and the data are processed by the computer. An advantage of tapes is that they are a more compact recording medium than the cards; they are, however, more costly than cards, and the computer must be specifically adapted to handle them.

Figure 15.3
DUAL CARD

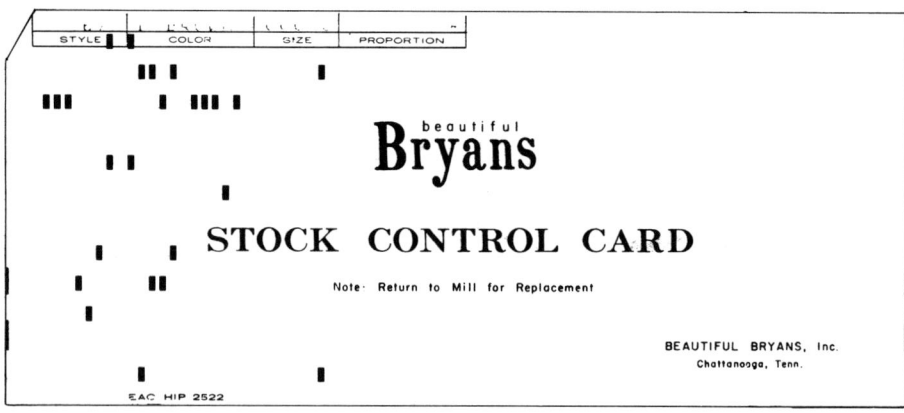

SOURCE: Beautiful Bryans, Inc.

Figure 15.4
PAPER TAPE

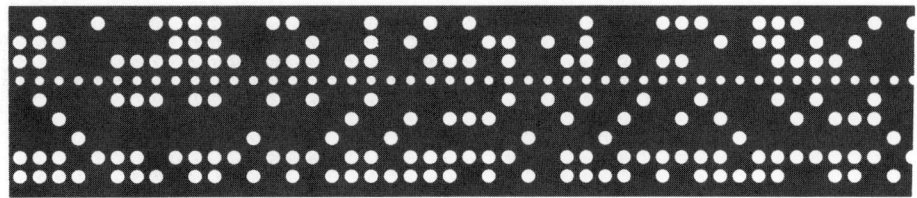

Magnetic Tapes and Disks

Paper tapes are easily damaged and torn by misuse. Therefore, a more durable material, the magnetic tape, was developed. Constructed of one-inch plastic strips, a thin magnetized metallic coating is applied over the plastic base. The tapes, on which vast quantities of data may be stored, are very similar to the tapes used in tape recorders. In fact, data are recorded on magnetic computer tapes in much the same way. Magnetic tapes may be used repeatedly and, with care, will last indefinitely. Also the data on the tape may be erased and new data may be recorded on the same tape.

The principle of magnetically storing data on a tape is similarly used in another device, the magnetic disk. In this case data are stored on flat, metallic surfaces that are similar to stereo records.

There are obvious differences between storing data on tape and on a disk. Generally, more data can be stored on tape. Also the cost of a magnetic taping device is considerably less than that of a disk storage unit. The data, however, must be stored sequentially on tape: record 1 before record 2, and so forth. They must also be read from a tape in the same sequence. Disk storage, on the other hand, permits the data to be retrieved randomly, which is one of the principal reasons for using a disk storage unit.

Terminal Devices

Initially one of the drawbacks related to the use of the computer was that extensive technical training was necessary. Since this training was not readily available, the use of computers was not widespread. Today the computer may be used by virtually anyone with a minimum of instruction.

The peripheral device largely responsible for making the computer simple to operate is the computer terminal. Data can be transmitted by striking keys as if on a typewriter. The use of telephone lines has made it possible to transmit data over long distances and to tie in several computers. The addition of the cathode ray tube provides an easy visual reference. As characters are punched on the keyboard, they appear on the screen of the picture tube.

The computer terminal can be used very effectively in a retail environment. Suppose, for example, that the terminal in a store is tied directly to a computer with access to all customer charge accounts. Then every time a charge sale is made, the sales person can check the validity and status of the customer's charge account by simply punching the account number into

IBM 7300 disk storage unit
SOURCE: Courtesy of International Business Machines Corporation

the terminal and waiting for the computer's reply. In this way charge account transactions can be greatly expedited and undesirable credit sales virtually eliminated.

J. L. Hudson in Detroit, for example, found that the number of their charge customers had risen 15 percent since 1971. Therefore, they installed a system of 1,300 computerized credit terminals so that all credit purchases over $1.00 could be checked. Fifteen mini-computers were used and it would take only ten seconds for each credit check. The computers would also handle authorizations of personal checks to pay for purchases.

COMPUTERIZED RETAIL SYSTEM

The computer can thus rapidly perform any number of manipulative tasks. It should be stressed again, however, that if erroneous or bad data are supplied to a computer, the results will be equally erroneous; hence arose the adage of computer analysts, "The garbage in equals the garbage out" (GIGO).

The use of computers can save a company untold thousands of dollars. We have already mentioned how the use of terminal devices could reduce

RCA terminal device
SOURCE: RCA Corporation, Cherry Hill, New Jersey

fraudulent charge sales in a retail store. It is now time to examine how a complete computerized retail system can provide a solution to all of a retailer's record-keeping needs.

Point-of-Sale Registers

An important source of data in a retail system is the actual sales transaction itself. It is at the cash register, which can double as a terminal, that data originate. It is of utmost importance, therefore, that the data thus collected by sales people be absolutely free of error.

As sales data are recorded, they can be transmitted to the computer for temporary storage. Subsequently, the data can be used in many different ways, as we will see shortly.

Using Sales Data

Just before a sale is completed, the sales person asks the customer, "Is this cash or charge?" A cash sale presents little difficulty, since it is easily entered into the register terminal and added to the total of other cash sales completed on that day. When the store closes, a figure for the total cash sales for the day is easily available. If the customer elects to charge the sale, the account can be validated through the terminal as described before. Charge sales can also be put into daily totals. They are also directly applied to the customers' charge accounts, which are immediately updated. Should a customer exceed his or her credit limit, the computer would issue the required correspondence.

The sale of an item of merchandise immediately affects the store's inventory. Therefore stores often require that both the stock-keeping unit (SKU) and the quantity bought be entered at the time of sale. The stock-keeping unit refers to either a single item of merchandise or a group of items for which separate sales and stock records are kept. The computer can thus use the data received to update the status of that item's inventory position.

Figure 15.5 shows a weekly computer run of sales and inventory data for a group of women's coats. With such a report the buyer can easily determine by style number how many coats were sold during the week and how many have been sold since they first arrived in stock. The on-hand and on-order figures for the downtown store and each of the eight branches are also shown.

If the item is a staple and part of the store's basic stock structure, the computer can be programmed to take note whenever the inventory dips below a predetermined level and automatically issue a purchase order for replenishment of stock.

Information on customer returns, credits, and payments can also be transmitted to the computer system by means of a terminal device. For example, a clerk in the credit office handling customer payments can enter the data on a customer (name, account number, payment code, amount of payment, and so forth) into the terminal. These data will then be posted against the customer's account. At the end of the month when accounts are closed, the computer will issue monthly customer statements including all new charges, credits, returns, and payments. Daily totals of payments received, credits given, and merchandise return can also be easily obtained.

The Data Base

All of the data pertaining to every sales transaction can be stored and made available later for statistical studies. This vast accumulation of data is referred to as a data base, which is simply a library of data. Since the data can be used at any time, the computer may be programmed to perform any number of sophisticated analyses. The results of these analyses can be made available in easily readable printed formats.

All such reports can be prepared very readily by means of the computer system's high-speed printing capability, the line printer. Most of the data output from computer systems come out of the high-speed printer. The inventory control report shown in Figure 15.5 is just one example of a computer print-out. The following are some other reports of special interest to the retailer that can be directly issued by computers:

1. Monthly customer statements
2. Purchase orders
3. Sales forecasts and analyses
4. Internal management reports
5. Customer surveys
6. Payroll reports
7. Employee turnover
8. Market research studies

Figure 15.5 *INVENTORY CONTROL REPORT*

DEPT 312 VENDOR 8 DUMAS RUN AS OF 12-30-72 MR G BLUESTONE PAGE 7

CLASS	STYLE NO.	STYLE DESCRIPTION: CODES / STYLE NAME	COST	CURR. RETAIL / FIRST RETAIL	COLOR CODE	CONSOLIDATED DATA: RETURN UNITS	DAYS LAST RCPT / LIFE	SALES WEEK	SALES LIFE	INVENTORY ON HAND	INVENTORY ON ORDER	TRIGGER DATE	LAST ACTION / DATE	STORE DATA (WEEK AND LIFE SALES — CURRENT ON HAND): DT	WR	TC	WW	KM	OX	BM	LV	LX
12	3112	CONTEMPORARY CAMEL				17	28	12	155	24	13		RECPT	-1		3	1	1		1	4	3
		1 204	33.00	65.00	0589		119						12-02	42		21	15	17		9	34	17
														5		4	7	-2		1	1	8
17	3114					2	70	3	43	7			TRANF				1	1			1	
		1 704	26.75	65.00	9		70						11-18	10		8	8	3		4	10	
														-1		1	2	3		1	1	
12	3809	COACHMAN DB				8	70	7	61	25			TRANF	1		1	4				1	
		1 204	30.00	65.00	0789		119						10-21	15		9	10	10		4	9	4
																3	3	1		7	5	6
16	3817	CREPE				3	7	24	68	48	4		RECPT	5		7	3	1		2	4	2
		1 604	26.75	60.00	689		35						12-23	11		15	10	5		7	9	11
														8		4	7	12		6	6	5
17	3844	LIGHTNING TWEED DB				6	91	1	56	4	1		TRANF			1						
		1 704	26.75	60.00	068		93						11-04	15		2	10	9		4	10	6
														1							1	2
18	6000	CAMEL HAIR DB NOTCHED COLLAR				11	100	4	153	4			RETRN	1								3
		1 808	35.25	70.00	89		189						12-04	32		28	13	15	1	9	29	26
														1		1		1	1	-2	2	
10	6166	CAMEL HAIR WRAP					42			3	3		ORDER									
		1 000	32.75	65.00	C		42						12-02									
														3								
18	6166	WRAP PC CAMELS HAIR				25	100	5	152	14			TRANF			2					2	1
		1 805	37.75	65.00	068		189						12-21	23		19	22	13	6	28	19	22
														3		2		2	1		4	2
18	6607	CASHMERE BUTTON 3				70	56	22	488	80			TRANF	4		2	4	3		3	5	1
		1 804	36.75	70.00	03579		324						12-21	88		67	56	40		35	156	46
														14		9	9	8	1	8	21	10
18	6721	CAMELS HAIR 1 PKT SB				9	189	2	71	-2			TRANF								2	
		1 804	35.25	70.00	8		189						11-04	12		12	5	8		5	19	10
																					-2	
18	6826	100% CASHMERE					329		19	2			RETRN									
		1 804	36.75	70.00	3		329						10-02	15				*			3	1
														2								
18	6864	CASH				21	100	6	157	23			TRANF	5		1						
		1 804	36.75	70.00	03789		189						12-21	37		29	18	19		12	25	17
														13		3			2	1	1	3
12	7000	FLEECE DB BACK BELT				2	119	1	35	25			TRANF								1	
		1 204	26.75	65.00	0		119						11-25	9		7	3	7		*	8	1
														1		7	7	1			3	6
12	7101	SB TIE BELT				7	56	2	53	16			TRANF	1				1				
		1 204	26.75	60.00	5		58						11-04	17		8	7	8			9	4
														9		1	2	2				2

Although the major function of a computerized retail system is to provide control over all sales and related activities, the system is not limited solely to that function. During the hours that the store is closed, the computer is free to perform other services considered essential to the efficient operation of a business. For example, weekly payrolls can be processed and weekly sales forecast. Figure 15.6 shows how data flow through a computerized retail system. Note that the entire process begins with data collected at the original point of sale.

The NCR 280 Retail System

It is evident that the computer is capable of providing supporting services to a vast retail system as well as processing all the related administrative paperwork generated by the store. The extent of a computer's capability to process data is highly dependent upon the capacity of the computer to store data. Particular importance must be placed on the size of the central processing unit (CPU).

When a store selects one of several computer systems, it must be sure that the system meets all of the store's requirements. Three factors are of central importance: (a) the data processing needs of the company, (b) the financial resources available to the company, and (c) the computer technology currently available.

The National Cash Register 280 retail system shown in Figure 15.7 is specifically designed for the retail business. The first operation of the system is the production of merchandise tags and labels.

These tags and labels must contain a variety of data pertaining to the respective items of merchandise to which they are attached. The tags may contain verbal descriptions of the data as well as their equivalent in specially prepared code. Note that each tag shows a department number, an SKU number, the size, and a retail price. Other information may be listed as well, for example, classification, vendor number, color, and style number. These special tags are manufactured at considerably less cost than conventional tags and labels.

When a sale is made, the item is physically brought to a register equipped with a tag-reading device referred to as a *wand tag reader*. To record the data on the label, the sales person simply passes the tag reader over the coded portion of the tag. The coded data will be fully and automatically read and transmitted to the register. Self-checking, electronic features built into the wand tag reader insure the completeness and accuracy of the retail data recorded. In this way the store management can effectively monitor all aspects of the merchandising cycle from the actual purchase to inventory control.

After the data have been fed into the register or retail terminal, they are transmitted to an intermediary storage device known as the *retail terminal support system*, as shown in the NCR 280 retail system. This terminal support system acts as a transfer point between the retail terminal and the computer system. The support terminal permits access to any of the central

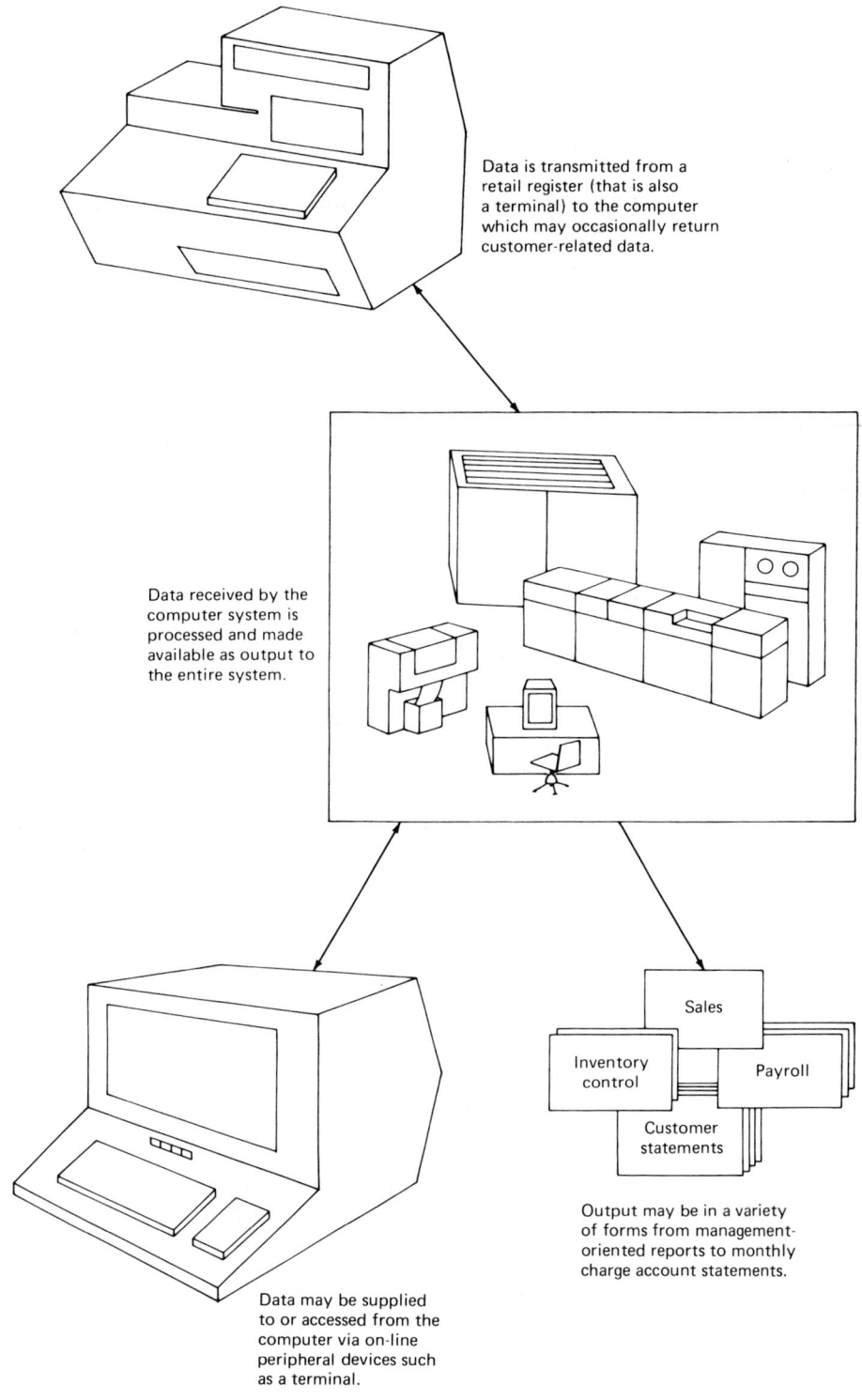

Figure 15.6
COMPUTERIZED RETAIL SYSTEM

Figure 15.7 NCR 280 RETAIL SYSTEM

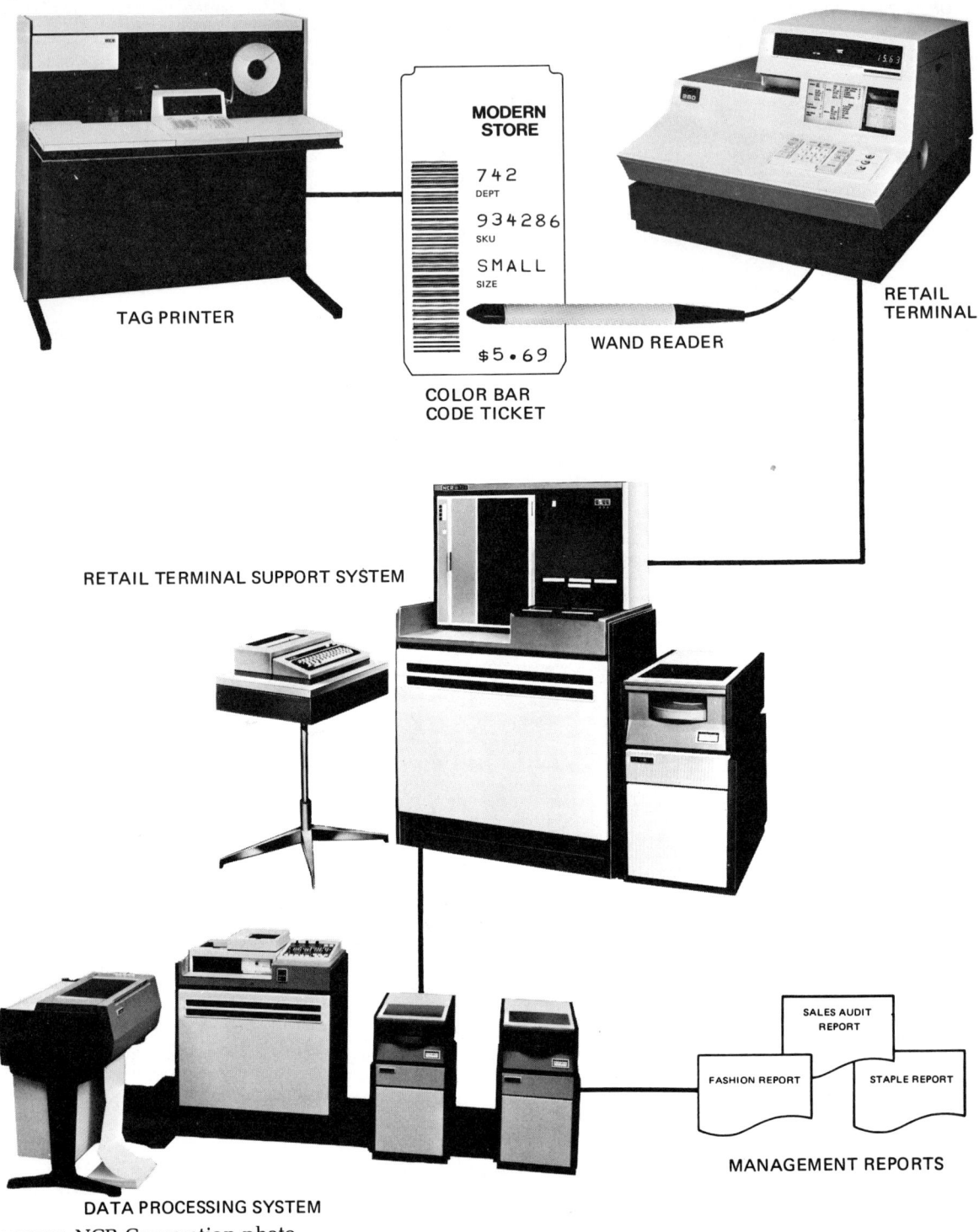

SOURCE: NCR Corporation photo

Wand Tag Reader
SOURCE: NCR Corporation photo

data files kept in the main computer system. Data retrieved from any file must pass through the support system on its way to the requesting terminal. For example, if a sales person requests the status of a customer's charge account via a retail terminal, the computer's response will pass through the support terminal.

The main computer configuration (the data processing system as illustrated by the NCR 280 retail system) is the heart of the retail system. The computer controls the transfer of all data in the retail system and the processing of any stored data. It also prepares all the reports that are requested by management.

Thus the NCR 280 retail system is designed to provide store management with an effective means of controlling and recording all of the transactions that occur within a retail organization.

TOMORROW'S COMPUTER TECHNOLOGY

The computer promises to make more startling changes in the ways retailers conduct their business in the future. On the horizon are revolutionary concepts that stores may soon take for granted. Three of these ideas, which will save the retailer considerable time and money and enable the store to serve the consumer more efficiently, are worth special mention.

The Computerized Supermarket Checkout Counter

Supermarket shoppers will soon be treated to the ease and convenience of the automated checkout counter. In April of 1973 the supermarket industry adopted a new standard code of vertical bars, standing for ten-digit numbers. Accordingly, the outside package of each product will be identifiable by its code. The clerk at the checkout counter will guide each purchase over an optical scanner, which will read the code for product identity, manufacturer, and size. The information that the scanner picks up will be transmitted to a computer programmed to associate the proper price to each item, and the correct price will then be rung up on the cash register. The clerk will be free to bag the groceries with one hand while guiding the items through the scanner with the other. The customer will receive an itemized receipt giving a description of each item purchased together with its price. A price verifier will be available at each checkout counter in case the customer wishes to check the price of an individual item. When such a system has finally been completed, the individual price stamps will disappear from merchandise packages, to be replaced by unit pricing on the shelf beneath the item. It is expected that half of all grocery products will be labeled with the new bar code by the end of 1974. In the near future it is likely that the new checkout process will expand well beyond the 2,000 stores that already have installations.

Coded Payment Card

A coded system for the sale and delivery of merchandise was invented recently by Luther G. Simjian of Greenwich, Connecticut. It is designed to reduce pilferage by both customers and sales people. With this system, merchandise frequently stolen is displayed only in protected showcases. When a customer finds something he wants to buy, he goes to a payment station and receives a coded card for the item. When he leaves the store, he turns the card (or cards) in at the dispensing station. The cards are fed through a mechanism that releases the item to the buyer when payment is made. The system is especially effective for reducing shoplifting of small, valuable articles that can be tucked easily into a pocket or bag.

Computer Trainers

Montgomery Ward in Chicago began sometime ago to make use of computers in the training of new buyers. The trainees are asked to solve buying problems. The computer will help them research the situation, but the trainees must make the final buying decisions. Then the computer will render judgment on whether the decisions were correct, and if not, what mistakes were made and how they can be corrected. The system has a viewing screen in a large computer terminal connected by telephone lines to a high-speed computer at the University of Illinois. It costs about $1.00 an hour, after the initial equipment purchases, to train a person with this computer. However, the university, which developed and owns the system, hopes that costs will fall even further within the next few years. It is expected that 4,000 such terminals will be in use in the near future to train persons for all sorts of jobs. In the meantime, Montgomery Ward has found the computer trainer to be a big time and money saver. The system will eventually replace the three-inch-thick training manual that is issued to each of the company's 10,000 department managers and that must be updated as often as twice a year.

CHAPTER SUMMARY	The electronic computer is capable of performing clerical and analytical tasks in a fraction of the time that the same tasks would take human beings. For huge companies and institutions deluged with paper work, the computer is a godsend. For smaller companies, too, the computer can be of valuable assistance on account of its speed, accuracy, and efficiency.

Although the computer is recognized as one of the technological marvels of our time, it is only as effective as the human being who supplies it with data. Therein lies the crucial difference between human beings and machines. Human beings can create, but the computer is incapable of creation. So if erroneous information is fed into the computer, the results will also be erroneous.

A computer cycle involves input, processing, output, and storage. Input is the placing of data into the computer system. The data are either processed for immediate output or stored for future processing. The storage capacity of the computer is one of its most remarkable qualities. Stored data can be indestructible and retrieved as often as is necessary. Output may be presented in any desired format. If written reports are needed, the computer's high-speed line printers can quickly produce them.

Computer systems are exceedingly expensive to install and operate. Although their use has been simplified to some degree, computer programmers and technicians need training and experience. Continued improvements and new discoveries are constantly making older systems obsolete. For these reasons, many companies prefer to subscribe to the services of one of the many commercial computer centers in the country. It is also possible to share computer time on an hourly basis by hooking onto a large computer at another location.

Selecting the right computer system for a retail organization is a major decision. The point-of-sale equipment that has been introduced has created a whole new performance standard for retail systems. The NCR 280 is an example of a system specifically designed for retail use. Using the point-of-sale approach, data are first fed into the system at the time of sale by passing a wand reader over a coded merchandise tag. The coded data are then automatically transmitted to the cash register. The system can also be used to check a customer's credit, and with the point-of-sale data keep track of the store's inventory and write new purchase orders when necessary. It can further be used to speed billing procedures as well as issue weekly payrolls and other company reports.

The appearance of newer and even more exciting computer devices is certain to have a lasting impact on retailing. For example, many supermarket checkout counters will soon be completely automated. Stores may try to use computers to reduce shoplifting. Merchandising executives may be trained with the help of computers instead of by traditional methods. These are just a few of the retailing innovations made possible by the computer, and it is safe to say the potentials of the computer are just beginning to be realized.

QUESTIONS FOR REVIEW

1. Describe the basic computer cycle and the nature of each basic element.
2. What are the three most important characteristics of the electronic computer?
3. Name at least two types of paper media and explain how they might be used.
4. Explain the difference between magnetic tapes and disks, and cite some advantages and disadvantages of each.
5. What does GIGO stand for? What does it have to do with computers?
6. What does MICR stand for? Give an illustration of how the process is used in everyday life.
7. What does SKU stand for?
8. State briefly the difference between random-access processing and the sequential processing of data.
9. Why is the point of sale so important when discussing a computerized retail system?
10. Why is the data base sometimes thought of as a library of data?

DISCUSSION QUESTION

The fully automated supermarket checkout counter is just around the corner. Are there any reasons why the consumer might not favor its adoption?

CASE PROBLEM

SOW NOW, REAP LATER

Janet Jones, buyer of women's coats for Gold's department store, has just received a call from Gene Baker, newly appointed supervisor of the store's data-processing department. According to Baker, the store is planning to purchase a new computerized retail system. In view of Jones' many years of buying experience in the ready-to-wear field, Baker wants her to act as a liaison between all ready-to-wear departments and the data-processing department.

For the past several years, the store has been using punch-card data processing in the unit control department. Price tickets are punched with sales information and later sorted and fed into tabulators that take the total of the stock-keeping units sold and print a report. If special management reports are required, the work is farmed out to a computer center in the city.

The credit department billing is also handled by the computer center. Because of steady business expansion, Gold's feels the time is ripe to install a complete electronic retail system of its own even though the initial investment will be very heavy.

Baker is planning to meet with his liaison representatives the following Thursday. He asks Ms. Jones to come to the meeting prepared to give her views and recommendations on the following:

a. The information needed on a machine-readable tag to be attached to every item of ready-to-wear.
b. A list of the data and types of written reports that ready-to-wear buyers would find useful.
c. The factors that should be considered before the store purchases a new computer system.

1. If you were Janet Jones, what would you tell Mr. Baker at the meeting?
2. Is it wise for Gold's to buy a new computer system instead of subscribing to a time-sharing service or making use of a data-processing center? Give reasons for and against each alternative.

GLOSSARY OF MERCHANDISING TERMS

Accessories. Items worn with women's apparel; includes jewelry, gloves, hosiery, neckwear, handbags, shoes, millinery, handkerchiefs, and ribbons.

Angel. A person who provides capital to a business, entertainment offering, or project with the expectation of making a profit but without assuming a management role.

Assistant Buyer. The person who takes charge of the department's merchandising operation during the buyer's absence. Duties normally include being responsible for the basic stock books, supervising the physical counts, writing orders, preparing markdowns, assisting with promotional plans including the writing of advertising copy, supervising the sales staff, and checking and pricing merchandise in the receiving room.

Assortment Plan. Sometimes referred to as a model stock, it is the required depth of stock by price, color, material, size, and classification to satisfy expected customer demand.

Automatic Reorder. Setting up a reorder cycle whereby basic merchandise is ordered as soon as the stock reaches a predetermined minimum level.

Basic Stock. An assortment of merchandise that receives a continuous heavy customer demand.

Book Inventory. A record of how much merchandise should be on hand at a given time based on what has been received and what has been sold. Book inventories can be calculated at any time using the perpetual inventory system and may be shown in terms of dollar value or in units of merchandise.

Boutique. A French word meaning "little shop." The merchandising operation is characterized by unique and carefully selected items, open displays, imaginative decor, informal atmosphere, and a sales staff encouraged to provide individual attention.

Bread and Butter Assortments. Basic merchandise that the store should always have on hand. It is important for a store to provide a continuity of product lines so that customers are assured they will find what they want in basic items.

Buyer's Clerical. The person responsible for the flow of paper work in a buyer's office. Duties may include unit control, posting of inventories, typing, and letter writing.

Classification. A group of merchandise of a given type or use, regardless of style, size, color, or price. Examples would be pile-lined coats, cocktail dresses, or men's dress shirts.

Closeout. A merchandise assortment offered by a vendor at a special price because styles, colors, and sizes are not balanced, aging or obsolescence has taken place, or the merchandise represents surplus stocks.

Commitment. An order for merchandise that the buyer has obligated the store to accept.

Cooperative Advertising. An arrangement whereby a manufacturer helps to pay for advertising costs incurred by a store.

Couturier. A French word meaning "designer." Many couturiers maintain their own dressmaking establishments, often in Paris.

Delicatessen Buying. Sampling many lines of merchandise without providing sufficient depth to satisfy customer demand.

Department Manager. A supervisor whose job is to oversee departmental selling activities in branch stores. A department manager seldom receives any open-to-buy, but must try to sell what the buyer has sent to the store.

Domestics. The category of merchandise that includes sheets, pillow cases, towels, and wash cloths.

Exclusive Agency (Retail Franchise). A store's right to carry a manufacturer's line exclusively within a paticular trading area.

Eyeball Control. A means of controlling stock by examining visually to see how much stock is on hand. Marks may be made on shelves, containers, or bins to indicate depletion points.

Fad. A style that becomes popular quickly and then disappears.

Fashion. A style with appeal for a large number of people at any given time.

Fifth Season. A midwinter selling season noted for cruise wear, apparel clearances, and white sales.

Flagship Store. The parent store of a chain. Usually located in a downtown area, it serves as the chain's buying headquarters and is often outsold by branch units.

Flying Squad. A group of salespeople who are flexible enough to be assigned to different departments of the store depending on where they are most needed.

Fringe Sizes. Sometimes called end sizes, these are the extremes on any size scale that are seldom ordered in depth.

Hand-to-Mouth Buying. Frequent placement of small orders to fulfill short-term needs. Commitments for large future orders are avoided.

Haute Couture. A French word meaning "fine sewing." It refers to the most prestigious dressmaking houses in Paris.

Head of Stock. A person responsible for the arrangement and identification of department stock both on the selling floor and in the stockroom.

Heart Sizes. The middle sizes of a size scale which sell well and are stocked in depth.

Housekeeping. The presentation and maintenance of stock in a neat, clean, and attractive manner so that it looks fresh and salable. Housekeeping is important in stock rooms as well as on selling floors.

Job Lot. A merchandise grouping, such as a close-out, which is sold by the vendor at a reduced price. The lot must be accepted "as is," and it often includes some unwanted sizes, styles, and colors.

Keystone Markup. A method of applying a markup whereby the cost price is doubled to arrive at the selling price.

Key Vendor. A manufacturer that a store can depend on for prompt deliveries, salable styles, fair prices, and outstanding promotional merchandise.

Knock-Off. A style that is a copy of a higher-priced original design. Two New York stores, Alexander's and Ohrbachs, are famous for their reproductions of couture originals.

Loss Leader. An item sold at, near, or below cost to attract customers into the store.

Model Stock. The minimum amount of merchandise in a classification according to price, size, color, and material that is required to satisfy expected customer demand during the slowest selling period.

National Retail Merchants Association (NRMA). A national trade association formed to promote the interests of department, chain, and specialty stores. Its administrative headquarters is located in New York City.

Never-out Merchandise. Merchandise that the store should always have in stock because the items receive a continuing high consumer demand; similar to basic merchandise.

Notions Department. The department that stocks small, sundry, and useful items such as thread, needles, thumb tacks, and pot holders.

Open Order. An order sent to a resident buyer when merchandise is needed in a hurry. The buyer gives the resident buyer authority to choose the best available resource and to negotiate the most advantageous deal.

Open Stock. Patterns of china, glassware, and silverware carried in bulk and for a long period of time for customer convenience and satisfaction.

Perpetual Inventory. A day-by-day analysis of how much stock is on hand. Daily sales and markdowns are deducted from the book inventory, while purchases received and returns to stock are added on.

Point-of-Sale. The location in the store where the sale is actually consummated. The cash register is frequently considered the point-of-sale.

Prêt-á-Porter. The term signifying the French ready-to-wear industry. Prêt-á-porter is made with machines, whereas couture clothes are made by hand.

Private Brand. A term used to identify merchandise made exclusively for stores belonging to the same resident buying office.

Runner. Sometimes referred to as a "hot number," it is an item that sells quickly for a period of time and is reordered frequently.

Season Letter. A code found on a price ticket to indicate when merchandise arrived in the store. Season letters enable stores to identify aging merchandise.

Staple Merchandise. An item that is in continuous heavy demand. It should be distinguished from basic stock in that basic stock is an assortment, i.e., basic stock includes staple items.

Style. The lines and characteristics of an article that make it different from other articles of the same kind.

Suggestion Selling. A selling technique used to build up the total sale by persuading the customer to buy additional items often related to the original purchase.

Trading Up. The introduction of better-quality, higher-priced merchandise to store assortments to improve the store's image and profits. The term is also used when a salesperson shows a higher quality or priced item than the customer originally requested in an attempt to make the sale bigger.

Twig Store. A small branch store carrying only a few specialized lines of merchandise.

Vendor. The manufacturer, wholesaler, importer, or exporter from whom merchandise is purchased.

Vendor Analysis. A study made of past sales to determine which manufacturer's styles sold best and were the most profitable and which sold poorly and at a loss.

APPENDIX I

Aliquot Parts

FRACTION	PERCENT	FRACTION	PERCENT
1/2	.50	1/9	.11 1/9
1/3	.33 1/3	2/9	.22 2/9
2/3	.66 2/3	4/9	.44 4/9
1/4	.25	5/9	.55 5/9
3/4	.75	7/9	.77 7/9
1/5	.20	8/9	.88 8/9
2/5	.40	1/10	.10
3/5	.60	1/11	.09 1/11
4/5	.80	2/11	.18 2/11
1/6	.16 2/3	3/11	.27 3/11
5/6	.83 1/3	4/11	.36 4/11
1/7	.14 2/7	5/11	.45 5/11
2/7	.28 4/7	6/11	.54 6/11
3/7	.42 6/7	7/11	.63 7/11
4/7	.57 1/7	8/11	.72 8/11
5/7	.71 3/7	9/11	.81 9/11
6/7	.85 5/7	10/11	.90 10/11
1/8	.12 1/2	1/12	.08 1/3
3/8	.37 1/2	5/12	.41 2/3
5/8	.62 1/2	7/12	.58 1/3
7/8	.87 1/2	11/12	.91 2/3

APPENDIX II

Markup Conversion Table

MARKUP ON COST	MARKUP ON RETAIL
11.1%	10%
25	20
42.9	30
53.9	35
66.7	40
81.8	45
100	50
122.2	55
150	60
185.7	65
233.3	70
300	75
400	80
900	90
Infinity	100

APPENDIX III

Mathematical Formulas for Merchandisers

Markup $	= $ Retail − $ Cost	
Markup % of retail	= $\dfrac{\$ \text{Retail} - \$ \text{Cost}}{\$ \text{Retail}}$	= $\dfrac{\$ \text{Markup}}{\$ \text{Cost}}$
Markup % of cost	= $\dfrac{\$ \text{Retail} - \$ \text{Cost}}{\$ \text{Cost}}$	= $\dfrac{\$ \text{Markup}}{\$ \text{Cost}}$
Initial markup $	= $ Original retail − $ Cost	
Initial markup %	= $\dfrac{\text{Expense \%} + \text{Operating profit \%} + \text{Reduction \%} - \text{Cash discounts earned \%} + \text{Alternations \%}}{\text{Net sales \%} + \text{Reductions \%}}$	
Maintained markup $	= $ Net sales − $ Cost	
Maintained markup %	= Initial markup % − Reduction % × (100% − Initial markup %)	
Gross margin $	= $ Maintained markup + $ Cash discounts earned − $ Alteration expense	
Gross margin %	= Maintained markup % + Cash discount % − Alteration expense %	
Stock turn at retail	= $\dfrac{\text{Net Sales}}{\text{Average retail stock}}$	
Stock turn at cost	= $\dfrac{\text{Cost of goods sold}}{\text{Average cost stock}}$	
Stock turn in units	= $\dfrac{\text{Unit sales}}{\text{Average unit stock}}$	
Capital turn	= $\dfrac{\text{Net sales}}{\text{Average stock at cost}}$	
Return on investment	= $\dfrac{\$ \text{Profit}}{\text{Average inventory at cost}}$	
Average sale	= $\dfrac{\text{Dollar sales}}{\text{Transactions}}$	
Number of transactions	= $\dfrac{\text{Dollar sales}}{\text{Average sales}}$	
Basic stock	= Average stock − Average monthly sales	
B.O.M. stock (Basic stock method)	= Basic stock + Planned sales for month	

B.O.M. (Percentage variation method)	=	Average stock $\times 1/2 \left(1 + \dfrac{\text{Sales for month}}{\text{Average monthly sales}}\right)$
Planned stock (Week's supply method)	=	Average stock in week's supply × Planned weekly sales
B.O.M. stock (Stock-sales ratio method)	=	B.O.M. stock-sales ratio × Planned sales for month
Planned purchases	=	Planned E.O.M. stock + Planned sales + Planned reductions − Planned B.O.M. stock
Dollar open-to-buy	=	Merchandise needed − Merchandise available or $ Planned purchase − $ Merchandise on order
Minimum stock	=	Reserve + (Delivery period × Weekly rate of sales)
Maximum stock	=	Minimum stock + (Reorder period × Weekly rate of sales)
Unit open-to-buy	=	Maximum stock − (Stock on hand + Stock on order) or Unit planned purchases − Units on order

BIBLIOGRAPHY

Buyer's Manual, rev. ed. National Retail Merchants Association, New York, 1965.

Corbman, Bernard P., and Murray Kreiger. *Mathematics of Retail Merchandising*, 2nd edition. Ronald Press, New York, 1972.

Crown, Paul. *Retail Merchandising*. Oceania Publications, Dobbs Ferry, N.Y., 1966.

Davidson, William R., and Alton F. Doody. *Retailing Management*, 3rd edition. Ronald Press, New York, 1966.

Gillespie, Karen R., and Joseph C. Hecht. *Retail Business Management*. McGraw-Hill, New York, 1970.

Jarnow, Jeannette A., and Beatrice Judelle. *Inside the Fashion Business*, 2nd edition. Wiley, New York, 1974.

Jones, Fred M. *Retail Management*. Irwin, Homewood, Ill., 1967.

Kneider, Albert P. *Mathematics of Merchandising*. Prentice-Hall, Englewood Cliffs, N.J., 1974.

Phillips, Charles F., and Delbert J. Duncan. *Marketing, Principles and Methods*, 6th edition. Irwin, Homewood, Ill., 1968.

Stanton, William J. *Fundamentals of Marketing*, 3rd edition. McGraw-Hill, New York, 1971.

Wingate, John W., and Joseph S. Friedlander. *The Management of Retail Buying*. Prentice-Hall, Englewood Cliffs, N.J., 1963.

Wingate, John W., Elmer O. Schaller, and F. Leonard Miller. *Retail Merchandise Management*. Prentice-Hall, Englewood Cliffs, N.J., 1972.

Wingate, John W., Elmer O. Schaller, and Irving Goldenthal. *Problems in Retail Merchandising*, 5th edition. Prentice-Hall, Englewood Cliffs, N.J., 1961.

INDEX

Alexander's, New York, 240
Alteration expenses, 81 - 82
Anticipation, 265 - 266
Associated Merchandising Corporation, New York, 10
Atkins, Frederick, New York, 10
Automatic markdown policy, 95

Beat Yesterday book, 169, 170 - 171 (fig.)
Bergdorf Goodman, New York, 241
Blanket orders, 60, 262
Blass, Bill, 95, 232
Bloomingdale's, Manhasset, New York, 172
Bonwit Teller, New York, 95
Branch stores
    importance of, 172 - 173
    organization for, 6, 7 - 8 (fig.)
    sales planning for, 176, 177 (fig.)
    stock planning for, 193 - 195
Bread and butter merchandise, 192, 217
Buyers
    duties of, 11 - 12
    order, 271 - 272, 273 (fig.), 274
    qualifications of, 12 - 14, 259
    resident 10, 243
    wheels, 48 - 49 (fig.)
Buying errors, 92-93

Capital turnover
    definition of, 157
    finding, 157 - 158
Cardin, Pierre, 231
Carload freight rates, 268
Central processing units
    bytes, 283
    main storage, 282
    in retail systems, 292
Chanel, Coco, 231, 238
Close-outs, 133
Coatvertising Weekly, 243
Coded payment card, 296
Colors, basic and high fashion, 247

Commissionaires, 239
Comparison shopping, 5, 130
Competing stores, 130 - 131, 172
Computer, 281 - 297
    characteristics, 281 - 282
    cycle, 282 - 283 (fig.)
    magnetic tapes and disks, 287
    paper tapes, 286
    peripheral devices, 283
    systems, 282 - 283, 288 - 295
        NCR 280 retail, 292 - 295, 294 (fig.)
        UNIVAC 90/30, 282 (fig.)
    technology for tomorrow, 295 - 297
    terminals, 287 - 288
    time-sharing, 284
    trainers, 296 - 297
Consignment buying and selling
    advantages and disadvantages to buyer, 270
    definition of, 270
Consumer, *see also* Customer
    changes in taste, 172
    demand, 194
    panels, 246
    surveys, 242
Controllable expenses, 32
Controllable margin, 32
Controllable profit, 17
Controller, 166, 190
Cost of goods sold, 28
Customer
    bread and butter, 234
    demand, 3, 98 - 99, 131
    discount, 98
    habit, 132
    returns and allowances, 119
    taste, 194

Daily News Record, 243
Data, 289 - 290
    base, 290
    handling, 283 - 284
        input and output of, 283

Dating, 260 - 261, 263 - 265
   end-of-month, 264
   extra, 264
   post, 265
   receipt of goods (ROG), 264
   regular, 263 - 264
Delivery period, 218
Demand
   consumer, 194
   customer, 3, 98 - 99, 131
   elasticity of, 131
Demographics, of trading area, 194
Dior, Christian, 231 - 232, 238
   labels, 238
   "new look," 231
Direct expenses
   classification of, 32
   definition of, 32
Discounts
   cash, 81, 261, 263 - 267
   to employees and customers, 75 - 76, 98
   quantity, 156, 262
      cumulative, 262
      noncumulative, 262
   seasonal, 263
   trade, 261
Dollar markup, 84
Dollar open-to-buy, 212 - 216
Dual cards, 285-286 (fig.)

Economic conditions, 132, 172
Elasticity of demand, 131
Electronic computer, *see* Computer
EOM (end-of-month) sales, 93, 150, 176
Esquire, 243
Estimated physical inventory, 120
Executive, compensation of, 14, 17 - 18, 14 - 17 (figs.)
Expenses
   classification of, 31 - 33, 31 (fig.)
   increase of, by rapid turnover, 156
   nature of, 30 - 31
   reduction of, by rapid turnover, 155

Fads, 3, 234
Fair trade, *see* Resale price maintenance
Fashion
   bureau, 5
   buying, 241 - 254
      nature of, 241 - 243
      plans for, 252, 253 - 254 (figs.)
   coordinator, 5
   counts, 242
   cycle, 235 (fig.)
   definition of, 3
   designers, 231
      changing role of, 231 - 232
   merchandise, 192, 217, 235, 241, 244 - 254
      elements of, 246 - 248
      policy, 241
      where to buy, 235 - 240
   publications, 242
   understanding, 231
FIFO method of inventory valuation, 93, 115 - 116
"fifth season," 3
Filene's, Boston, 95
Fishyback, 269
Fixed expenses, 32
F.O.B. (free-on-board)
   factory, 117, 240, 268
   store, 117, 268
   store, charges reversed, 268
Foreign merchandise, 237 - 240
FOR reports, 43
Freight
   consolidator, 270
   costs, 117, 268
   forwarder, 268
Fringe benefits, employee, 75 - 76
Fringe stocks, 154, 247

Galanos, James, 232
Gentlemen's Quarterly, 243
Gimbels, New York, 10, 131
Givenchy, Hubert, 95, 231, 238
Glamour, 243
Goods
   outstanding, 212
   in transit, 212
Great Atlantic and Pacific Tea Co. (A&P), 174
Gross margin, 25, 81 - 83
   as a percentage on net sales, 86 - 87
Gross profit, 25
Gross sales, 119

Harper's Bazaar, 243
Haute couture, 231
Heart stocks, 154, 247
High shades, 247
Hollerith, Dr. Herman, 284
Hudson, J. L., Detroit, 288

ILGWU, 236
Independent Retailers Syndicate, New York, 10
Indirect expenses
   classification of, 32
   definition of, 32

Initial markup, 75 - 77
  percentage, 84 - 85
Inventory
  book, 76, 109 - 110, 116 - 122
  periodic, 250
  perpetual, 109, 248, 250
  physical, 76, 109 - 110, 116 - 122
    reasons for taking, 109
  valuation, methods of, 110 - 116
    cost-or-market-whichever is lower, 112
    first-in, first out, 115 - 116
    last in, first-out, 115 - 116
    original-cost, 111 - 112
    retail, 112 - 113 (fig.)

Job lots, 62, 65, 94, 202

Key vendors, 99, 101, 248
Kirby Block, New York, 10

Landed cost, 240, 241 (fig.)
Leader pricing, 58
LIFO method of inventory valuation, 115 - 116
Line organization, 4 - 5
Loading invoices, 81, 266 - 267
Lord & Taylor, New York, 173, 241
Loss leaders, 4, 58, 131

Macy's, New York, 10, 131
Mademoiselle, 243
Magnin, I., 241
Maintained markup, 77 - 80
  percentage, 85 - 87
Management 4, 6, 9 - 10. *See also* Executive
Margin, controllable, 32
Markdown cancellations, 97
Markdown Manual, 94
Markdown percentages
  as percentage off original retail, 102
  as percentage of sales, 103
Markdown request, 96-98 (fig.)
Markdowns
  causes of, 92 - 94
  control of, 98 - 102
  definition of, 75, 92
Market centers
  American, 11, 235 - 236
  foreign, 237 - 239
Market trips, 239
Markups
  additional, 97, 117
  average, 57 - 69
    one cost and three or more retails, 65 - 66
    one cost and two retails, 62 - 64
    three or more costs and one retail, 68 - 69

    two costs and one retail, 67 - 68
  based on cost, 46 - 48
  based on retail, 42 - 46
  cumulative, 41, 49 - 51, 113
  formula for, 41
  individual, 41,
  keystone, 51 - 52
  nature of, 41
May Department Stores, 10, 239
Mazur, Paul M., 4
Merchandise
  availability, 192
  bread and butter, 192, 217
  classifications, 245 - 246, 251, 272
  foreign, 237 - 240
    advantages of, 239 - 240
    disadvantages of, 240
  managers, 4, 6, 9 - 10
    duties of, 6, 9 - 10
    qualifications of, 10
  mart, 11
  priorities, 192 - 193
  seasonal, 3
  staple, 2, 192, 195, 217, 220, 244
Merchandising
  calendar, 175
  definition of, 2
  division, 4 - 5 (figs.)
  five rights of, 2 - 4, 30, 98
MICR, 286
MOR reports, 42 - 43

National Retail Merchants Association, 31, 42, 76, 94, 156
Neiman-Marcus, Dallas, 10, 95, 173, 241
Net profit, 25
Net sales, 119
"Never-out" merchandise, 3, 192

Ohrbach's, New York, 240
One-price policy, 259
Open-to buy
  definition of, 9, 211 - 212
  generation of, 94
  ways to increase, 220 - 223
Operating expenses, 25
  change in, 28
Optical scanner, 286
Organization for merchandising
  branch stores, 5 - 6, 7 - 8 (figs.)
  divisional structure, 4 - 5, 5 - 6 (figs.)
  four/functional plan, 4
Other income, 25, 81n
Overages, 120

Packard, Vance, 234
Penney, J. C., 173

Piggyback, 269
Pilferage control, 77
Point-of-sale registers, 289
Prêt-á-porter, 238
Pretesting, 246
Preticketing, 270
Price
  change in, 27
  endings, 133, 136
  lines, 136 - 143, 154, 248
    analysis of, 138 - 143
    intervals between, 137
  lining, 138 - 143
    advantages of, 137 - 138
    disadvantages of, 138
  list, 261
  negotiation, 259 - 260
  net, 261
  quoted cost, 260
  zones, 135 - 136
Profit
  calculator, 48 - 49 (fig.)
  controllable, 17
  cushion, 81
  leader, 58
  mix, 25 - 30
  nature of, 24 - 25, 130
  variables, 27 - 30
Profit and loss statement, 122 - 123 (fig.)
Promotional merchandise, 193
Promotional plans, 176
Pucci, Emilio, 95
Punch cards, 284 - 285 (fig.)
Purchase
  planning, 209, 211
    formula for, 209
  returns and allowances, 117
Purchasing agents, 239

Quant, Mary, 238

Rapid stock turn, 154 - 156
  advantages of, 154 - 155
  disadvantages of, 155 - 156
Reorder period, 218
Reporting agencies, 243, 245 - 246 (figs.)
Resale price maintenance, 132 - 133
Reserve requisition control, 250
Resident buying offices
  foreign, 239
  types of, 10
Retail
  computerized system, 288 - 295
  deductions, 119
  method of inventory, 43, 112 - 123

  reductions, 75
  terminal support system, 292
Return on investment, 155, 160
Revision of retail downward, 97, 117
Robinson-Patman Act, 262
Runners, 101, 242

Safety factor (reserve stock), 218
St. Laurent, Yves, 231, 238
Saks Fifth Avenue, New York, 95
Sales
  analysis, 101
  data, 289 - 290
  forecasting, 166 - 184
    for branch stores, 176, 177 (fig.)
    when prices are stable, 176 - 182
    with fluctuating prices, 182 - 184
  trends, 169, 192
  volume, 25, 27, 131
    change in, 27
  with a return privilege, 270 - 271
Sales and merchandise plan, 166-167, 169, 190, 209, 211; 168, 191, 210 (figs.)
Sales-per-square-foot, 174
Sampling, 242 - 243
Sears, Roebuck, 136
Season letters (codes), 109, 113
Selling errors, 92 - 93
Seventh Avenue, 235, 238
Shortages, 76, 120
Simjian, Luther G., 296
Size charts, 247
SKU, *see* Stockkeeping unit
Space allocation, 174
Specialty Stores Association, New York, 10
Staff organization, 4 - 5
Stock control
  cards, 248 - 251, 249 (fig.)
  of fashion merchandise, 248 - 251
  importance of, 99
  of staple merchandise, 220 (fig.)
Stockkeeping unit, 290
Stock planning
  basic stock method of, 195, 197 - 199
  for branch stores, 193 - 195
  factors to consider, 192 - 193
  importance of, 190
  percentage-variation method of, 199 - 201
  shortcomings of methods used, 202
  stock-sales ratio method of, 202
  week's supply method of, 202
Stocks
  average, 148 - 151
  basic, 195, 220, 242, 290
  maximum, 218
  minimum, 218

model, 219 - 220, 221 (fig.), 251
  reserve (safety factor), 218
Stock-sales ratio
  calculation of, 159
  in stock planning, 193, 202
Stock turnover
  average, 152 - 154
  calculation of, 148 - 154
    at cost, 148 - 149
    at retail, 148 - 149
    in units, 148 - 149
  definition of, 3, 148
  goals, 156, 157 (fig.)
  ratio, 151 - 152
  in stock planning, 193
Stores
  branch, 5 - 6, 172 - 173, 176, 193 - 195
  change in policy, 173 - 174
  flagship, 176, 194 - 195
  twig, 172
  types of, 131
Stub card, 285 - 286
Style, 231
Styleouts, 242
Supermarket computerized checkout counter, 296

"Tobe Reports," 244 - 245 (figs.)
Total merchandise handled, 117
Trade mart, 11
"Trading up," 173
Transfers, of merchandise, 117
Trigere, Pauline, 232
Trunk shows, 242

Unfair-Trade-Practices Acts, 133
Unit open-to-buy, 216 - 219, 252

Valentino, 232
Variable and semivariable expenses, 32
Vendors
  aids, 270 - 271
  brand loyalty, 248
  help in determining consumer demand, 242
  need to negotiate with, 259
Visual control, 251
Vogue, 243

Wand tag reader, 292
Want slips, 98 - 99, 100 (fig.)
Ward, Montgomery, Chicago, 296
Women's Wear Daily, 3, 231, 243